About the Authors

Neil Howe and William Strauss, the authors of *Generations, 13th Gen,* and *The Fourth Turning,* write and lecture frequently on generational issues. They host active discussions with readers (at www.millennialsrising.com and www.fourthturning.com) and run a strategic planning consulting firm (LifeCourse Associates).

Strauss is the cofounder and director of the Capitol Steps, a political cabaret. An alumnus of Harvard Law and Kennedy Schools, he was a policy director for the U.S. Congress and coauthored two books on the Vietnam draft (including *Chance and Circumstance*) before shifting his focus to the performing arts. He has recently written two musicals on teen themes (*MaKiddo* and *StopScandal.Com*) and has founded the Cappies, America's largest theater awards program for high school students.

Howe is a senior advisor to the Concord Coalition and senior policy advisor to the Blackstone Group. With graduate degrees from Yale in history and economics, he was a journalist, magazine editor, and foundation policy executive while playing a growing role in the national debate over entitlement reform. He coauthored *On Borrowing Time,* about the impact of aging on fiscal policy, and coedits the Concord Coalition's *Facing Facts* newsletter.

Both Howe and Strauss live with their families in Fairfax County, Virginia.

MILLENNIALS RISING

the next great generation

by Neil Howe & William Strauss

Cartoons by R. J. Matson

Vintage Books

A Division of Random House, Inc.

New York

A VINTAGE ORIGINAL, SEPTEMBER 2000

Copyright © 2000 by Neil Howe and William Strauss

All rights reserved under International and Pan-American
Copyright Conventions. Published in the United States by Vintage Books,
a division of Random House, Inc., New York, and simultaneously in
Canada by Random House of Canada Limited, Toronto.

Vintage and colophon are registered trademarks of Random House, Inc.

Library of Congress Cataloging-in-Publication Data
Howe, Neil.
      Millennials rising : the next great generation / by Neil Howe and William
Strauss ; cartoons by R. J. Matson.
         p.   cm.
      Includes bibliographical references.
      ISBN 0-375-70719-0
      1. Youth—United States.   I. Strauss, William.   II. Title.

HQ796 .H74 2000
305.235'0973—dc21
                                        00-034949

Book design by Suvi Asch

www.vintagebooks.com

Printed in the United States of America

10 9 8 7 6 5

»» to our parents and our children

contents

PART ONE

where they come from

CHAPTER ONE

The Next Great Generation

The Next Great Generation
The Next Great Generation

Hold your head high and reach the top
Let the world see what you have got!
　　　　—*S CLUB 7, "Bring It All Back"*

"We're the Millennial Generation," asserts 15-year-old Tyler Hudgens of McLean, Virginia. "We're special, one of a kind. It's our turn, our time to shine."

"Kids Today," answers the "buzz" page in *Newsweek*. "They're just no good. No hardships + no cause = boredom, anger, and idiocy."

Who's right—Tyler Hudgens, or *Newsweek*?

Until very recently, the public has been accustomed to nonstop media chatter about bad kids—from mass murderers, hate criminals, and binge drinkers to test failers, test cheaters, drug users, and just all-around spoiled brats. To believe the news, you'd suppose our schools are full of kids who can't read in the classroom, shoot one another in the hallways, spend their loose change on tongue rings, and couldn't care less who runs the country. According to a national survey, barely one adult in three thinks that today's kids, once grown, will make the world a better place.

As for Miss Hudgens, where could she look to find allies? She won't find

Meet the Millennials, and rejoice.
　　　　—*Anna Quindlen,* Newsweek

Our generation isn't all about sex, drugs, and violence. It's about technology, discovery, and coming together as a nation.
　　　　—*Mikah Giffin, 17,* cjonline.com

Millennial Generation May Be the Best News Yet —*www.discovery.org*

them among hard-line culture warriors, whose agenda for moral renewal feeds on the supposed depravities of youth, nor among those on the other side, whose plans for expansive government depend upon youth's supposed pathologies. She won't find them in business, which has learned how to target the hard youth edge so well that it would rather avoid the risk of trying anything new. Only among Tyler's teenage peers will she find an unwavering optimism to match her own. Even there, one can imagine a well-trained note of irony: *We're special? Oh. And on whose planet?*

Yet the central message of this book is that *Newsweek* is wrong, and Hudgens is right.

A new generation is rising.

Meet the Millennials, born in or after 1982—the "Babies on Board" of the early Reagan years, the "Have You Hugged Your Child Today?" sixth graders of the early Clinton years, the teens of Columbine, and, this year, the much-touted high school Class of 2000, now invading the nation's campuses.

As a group, Millennials are unlike any other youth generation in living memory. They are more numerous, more affluent, better educated, and more ethnically diverse. More important, they are beginning to manifest a wide array of positive social habits that older Americans no longer associate with youth, including a new focus on teamwork, achievement, modesty, and good conduct. Only a few years from now, this can-do youth revolution will overwhelm the cynics and pessimists. Over the next decade, the Millennial Generation will entirely recast the image of youth from downbeat and alienated to upbeat and engaged—with potentially seismic consequences for America.

Look closely at the dramatic changes now unfolding in the attitudes and behaviors of today's youth, the 18-and-unders of the year 2000. The evidence is overwhelming—and just starting to attract notice. In the spring of 2000, newsweekly magazines with "good news" youth stories marked a possible turning of the media tide.

That's not all. When you fit these changes into the broader rhythms of American history, you can get a good idea of what kind of adult generation the Millennials are likely to become. You can foresee their future hopes and fears, strengths and weaknesses, as they rise to adulthood and, in time, to power. You can understand how today's kids are on track to become a powerhouse generation, full of technology planners, community shapers, institution builders, and world leaders, perhaps destined to dominate the twenty-first century like today's fading and ennobled G.I. Generation dominated the twentieth. Indeed, Millennials have a solid chance to become America's next great generation, as celebrated for their collective deeds a hundred years from now as the generation of John Kennedy, Ronald Reagan, Joe DiMaggio, and Jimmy Stewart is celebrated today.

By that time, no one will recall the *Newsweek*-style cynical barbs that greeted Tyler Hudgens as she, along with millions of other young people, began setting a new tone for America. And by that time, perhaps Miss Hudgens's sunny opinion of her generation will be widely shared, reinforced by the enduring memories of heroic achievements.

Is this possible? Yes. Is it certain? No.

While the outlook for this generation is largely positive, dangers abound, given its enormous potential power. Millennials do pose a threat to the future of this nation and the world. But if danger arrives, it won't come from the direction today's adults worry about—in the form of a selfish, alienated rabble of disaffected Ultra-Gen-X hyperslackers. Imagine, instead, an unstoppable mass hurtling down the track in the opposite direction, a cadre of young people so cohesive and so directional that, if their aspirations are thwarted, they might overwhelm the political defenses of their elders and mobilize around a risky, even destructive national agenda.

For decades, Americans have been wishing for a youth generation that would quit talking and start doing. Now that older generations—yes, Gen X, you too—are starting to produce kids like this, a new question arises: OK, Boomers and Gen Xers, now that you've got them, can you handle them?

Over the coming decade, the Oh-Ohs, this rising generation will introduce itself to the nation and push the nation into a new era. Once this new youth persona begins to focus on convention, community, and

Good-bye to body-piercing, green hair, grunge music and the deliberately uncouth look. Hello to kids who look up to their parents and think bowling is fun.

—Dyan Machan, Forbes

The older generation seems amazed every time we break the mold assigned to us.

—Elizabeth Romberg, 18

I just do not understand '90s children.

—Boomer mother, after her 16-year-old daughter had her and her husband arrested for growing marijuana in the basement

civic renewal, America will be on the brink of becoming someplace very new, very "millennial" in the fullest sense of the word. That's when the "end of history" stops, and the beginning of a new history, their *Millennial* history, starts.

The Preferred Name: "Millennials"

"Several thousand people sent suggestions to abcnews.com. Some thought that gen.com would be a good idea. Others said Generation Y, Generation Whatever. Gen-D was one. The Boomlets. The Prozac Generation. When everyone got talking about it online, the second-largest number thought there should be no label at all, and the greatest interest was in the Millennium Generation, or the Millennials."

—Peter Jennings, ABC World News Tonight, 12/19/97

TOP TEN SUGGESTED NAMES (abc.com poll)

1.	Millennials	6.	Generation.com
2.	"Don't Label Us"	7.	Generation 2000
3.	Generation Y (or Why?)	8.	Echo Boom
4.	Generation Tech	9.	Boomer Babies
5.	Generation Next	10.	Generation XX

Not X, Not Y—Call Them Millennials

If most Americans aren't very hopeful about today's rising generation, it's because so many of them figure that history generally moves in straight lines. They assume the next batch of youths will follow blindly along all the life-cycle trends initiated (thirty and forty years ago) by Boomers and confirmed (ten and twenty years ago) by Gen Xers. These trends point to more selfishness in personal manner, more splintering in public purpose, more profanity in culture and daily discourse, more risk-taking with sex and drugs, more apathy about politics, and more crime, violence, and social decay.

Some pundits—marketers, especially—dub these kids "Generation Y," as though they were a mere Generation X^2, *South Park* idiots beyond redemption, the ultimate price for America's post-'60s narcissism. Others, giving them names such as Generation Dot Com, depict them as an exaggerated extension of America's current mood of self-oriented commercialism.

How utterly depressing. And how utterly wrong.

Yes, there's a revolution under way among today's kids—a *good news revolution*. This generation is going to rebel by behaving not worse, but *better*. Their life mission will not be to tear down old institutions that don't work, but to build up new ones that do. Look closely at youth indicators, and you'll see that *Millennial attitudes and behaviors represent a sharp break from Generation X, and are running exactly counter to trends launched by the Boomers*. Across the board, Millennial kids are challenging a long list of common assumptions about what "postmodern" young people are supposed to become.

Are Millennials another "lost" generation?

No. The better word is "found." Born in an era when Americans began expressing more positive attitudes about children, the Millennials are products of a dramatic birth-rate reversal. During the Gen-X child era, planned parenting almost always meant contraceptives or abortions; during the Millennial childhood, it more often means visits to the fertility clinic. In 1998, the number of U.S. children surged past its previous Boomer-era peak, and over the next decade, college frosh enrollment is due to grow by roughly 300,000 per year.

Are they pessimists?

No. They're optimists. Surveys show that—compared to Xer teens a decade ago—today's teens are more upbeat about the world in which they're growing up. Nine in ten describe themselves as "happy," "confident," and "positive." A rapidly decreasing share worry about violence, sex, or drugs—and a rapidly increasing share say that growing up is easier for them than it was for their

Millennials will definitely not want to be known as Gen Y. Generation A plus, though—that might be a different story. —**Jay Taubman**

They're the Millennial Generation . . . growing up at a time of unprecedented prosperity—and unprecedented pressures.—Newsweek

parents. Teen suicide rates are now falling for the first time in decades.

Are they self-absorbed?

No. They're cooperative team players. From school uniforms to team learning to community service, Millennials are gravitating toward group activity. According to a recent Roper survey, more teenagers blamed "selfishness" than anything else when asked, "What is the major cause of problems in this country?" Unlike Gen Xers, they believe in their own collective power. By a huge ten-to-one majority, they believe it's their generation—and not their parents'—that will do the most to help the environment over the next twenty-five years.

Are they distrustful?

No. They accept authority. Most teens say they identify with their parents' values, and over nine in ten say they "trust" and "feel close to" their parents. The proportion who report conflict with their parents is declining. Half say they trust government to do what's right all or most of the time—twice the share of older people. Half believe that lack of parental discipline is a major social problem, and large majorities favor tougher rules against misbehavior in the classroom and society at large.

Are they rule breakers?

No. They're rule followers. Today's kids are disproving the experts who once predicted a tidal wave of juvenile crime during the late 1990s. Over the last five years, the rates of homicide, violent crime, abortion, and pregnancy among teens have all plummeted at the fastest rates ever recorded. A teen is now less likely to be a victim of a serious violent crime than at any time since Lyndon Johnson was president. Even including the Columbine massacre, there were only half as many violent deaths at schools nationwide in 1998–99 (twenty-five) as there were in the early 1990s (over fifty per year).

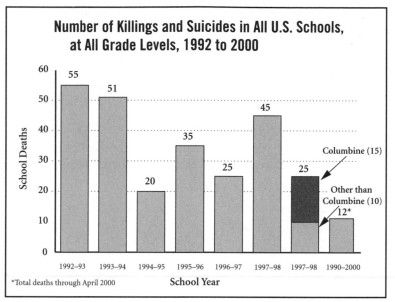

Number of Killings and Suicides in All U.S. Schools, at All Grade Levels, 1992 to 2000

School Deaths (y-axis) vs School Year (x-axis)

- 1992–93: 55
- 1993–94: 51
- 1994–95: 20
- 1995–96: 35
- 1996–97: 25
- 1997–98: 45
- 1997–98: 25 — Columbine (15), Other than Columbine (10)
- 1990–2000: 12*

*Total deaths through April 2000

Source: National School Safety Center (2000)

Are they neglected?

No. They're the most watched over generation in memory. Each year, adults subject the typical kid's day to ever more structure and supervision, making it a nonstop round of parents, relatives, teachers, coaches, baby-sitters, counselors, chaperones, minivans, surveillance cams, and curfews. Over the last decade, time spent on homework and housework is up, while time spent on weekday TV watching is down. From 1981 to 1997, according to researchers at the University of Michigan, "free" or "unsupervised" time in the typical preteen's day shrank by 37 percent.

Are they stupid?

No. They're smarter than most people think. During the 1990s, aptitude test scores have risen within every racial and ethnic group, especially in elementary schools. Eight in ten teenagers say it's "cool to be smart," while a record share of teenagers are taking AP tests, say they "look forward to school," and plan to attend college. In recent international math and science exams, U.S. fourth graders scored at or near the top—and, given the amount of homework they do and the new standards they must meet, they look like they could stay at the top as they grow older.

Have they given up on progress?

No. Today's kids believe in the future and see themselves as its cutting edge. They show a fascination for, and mastery of, new technologies—which explains why math and science scores are rising faster than verbal scores. Teens rank "scientists" and "young people" as the two groups that will cause "most changes for the better in the future." Nearly three in four 8- to 12-year-olds use computers, outdistancing older teens and adults alike.

Why is the image of Generation Y—alias Gen X^2—so off the mark? For the simple reason that the predictive assumption is wrong. Whatever the era they are living in, Americans habitually assume that the future will be a straight-line extension of the recent past. But that *never* occurs, either with societies or with generations.

Remember the 1960s? When the decade started, the experts who looked at Baby Boomers assumed they would come of age even more pliable and conformist than the gray-flanneled "Silent Generation" just before them. That didn't happen. And remember the 1980s? When that decade began, the experts who looked at post-Boomers (then called "baby busters") assumed they would come of age more idealistic and "postmaterialistic" than Boomers. That didn't happen either. Another twenty years have passed, and it's time for another surprise. The "Gen-Y" name implies that the future of today's kids can be aptly described as an extension of Gen X. *That won't happen either.*

Today's kids realize that their generation doesn't fit the dominant Gen-Y stereotype—far from it. According to our Class of 2000 Survey, high school seniors widely believe (by more than two to one) that Generation X has a negative reputation and overwhelmingly reject the name Generation Y. They are repelled by a label that puts them in the shadow of Gen Xers. "No one wants to be Generation Y," admits 17-year-old Shansel Nagia. "It's just a supplement or copy of X." Or, as others have buzzed on-line, it's a "step down" from X. "What an insult!" spewed one teen on hotmail.com.

Birth Year Markers and Famous Young People

BY BIRTH YEAR

1974 Leonardo DiCaprio, Alanis Morissette, Jedediah Purdy
1975 Lauryn Hill, Wendy Shalit, Tiger Woods, Livan Hernandez
1976 Alicia Silverstone, Peyton Manning, Jevon Kearse
1977 James Van Der Beek, Fiona Apple, Sarah Michelle Gellar
1978 College Class of 2000, Kobe Bryant, Steve Francis
1979 Brandy, Jennifer Love Hewitt, Aaliyah Haughton
1980 Chelsea Clinton, Macaulay Culkin, Christina Aguilera
1981 Britney Spears, Serena Williams, Rachael Leigh Cook,
     Anna Kournikova, Jonny Lang

GEN-X

MILLENNIALS

1982 High School Class of 2000, LeAnn Rimes, Tara Lipinski,
     Anna Paquin, Thora Birch, Kirsten Dunst,
     Kieran Culkin, LeeLee Sobieski
1983 Taylor Hanson, Mila Kunis
1984 Amelia Atwater-Rhodes, Jena Malone, Mandy Moore
1985 Zac Hanson, Frankie Muniz, Brendan Baker
1986 Eighth-Grade Class of 2000, Amanda Byncs,
     Mary Kate Olsen, Ashley Olsen, Jessica McClure,
     Megan Kanka, Baby M
1988 Sixth-Grade Class of 2000, Haley Joel Osment
1989 Jake Lloyd
1990 Jonathan Lipnicki, Myles Jeffrey
1991 Third-Grade Class of 2000, JonBenet Ramsey
1993 Elián González
1994 Kindergarten Class of 2000
1997 McCaughey septuplets
1998 Chukwu octuplets

I am continually gaining the sense with my peers, who were also born in 1981 or even 1980, that we are the lost years . . . in transition between the two generations. —Lin Jia, 18

Being part of the Class of 2000 only carries with it a lot of responsibility. In reality we're just another graduating class, but everyone sees us as a new beginning, a chance for a brand-new start. —Janet Chang, 16

I like to think of my generation, the Class of 2000, and neighboring years around it, as the Millennial Generation. We're the kids who are going to change things.

—Shansel Nagia, 17

Another name that has been used since the '80s—"Echo Boomers"—fares no better in the kids' minds, for a similar reason. As 18-year-old Lesley Milner explains, "Instead of giving us our own name, someone—probably someone who doesn't know much about us—just said, 'Hmm, well, this is Generation X, so why don't we call the next one Generation Y?' Or 'Well, they're the children of Boomers, so we can just call them Echo Boom.' Neither of these two names says anything unique about our generation. They say who we follow, but nothing at all about who we are. That's why those names are upsetting, and why nobody I know wants to use them."

By a margin of over four to one, the teens in our survey preferred "Millennial" over "Y." A recent ABC poll likewise found "Millennials" to be today's teens' name of choice. "I am 14, and my generation is called the Millennials," posted David on webtv.net, "so get your facts straight. . . ."

Today's teens want a name that is a founding word, a word that respects their newness, a word that resets the clock of secular history around their own timetable. The name "Millennial" acknowledges their technological superiority without defining them too explicitly in those terms. It's a name that hints at what their rising generation could grow up to become—not a lame variation on old Boomer/Xer themes, but a new force of history, a generational colossus far more consequential than most of today's parents and teachers (and, indeed, most kids) dare imagine.

"I like to think of my generation, the Class of 2000, as the Millennial Generation," says Nagia. "We're the kids who are going to change things."

A Fresh Look

When you liberate yourself from straight lines—and take a fresh look at how today's kids are defying expectations—many of the trends you may have had trouble understanding start making sense. You can see why the heroic theme of *Titanic* struck such a chord among teenagers, or why bubblegum rock is big and swing music is making a comeback. Or why the '90s trends in kid-vid—from Barney to Power Rangers to Poké-mon—have been so relentlessly team-oriented. Or why, when kids gather in public places, they so often appear in uniform and move in organized and supervised groups. Or why polls showed schoolkids to be the harshest critics of Bill Clinton's personal behavior.

Once you appreciate how Millennials have been regarded as special since birth and have been more obsessed-over at every age than Xers, recent adult trends come into sharper focus. Falling divorce and abortion rates begin to make sense. You can understand why harms against children (from familial child abuse and school gunfire to bloody video games and huge federal deficits) are far less tolerable today than a decade ago. You can clue in to what Dick Morris told Bill Clinton, who thereafter recast nearly every political issue of the 1990s into what newsweeklies call "kinderpolitics," as in: If it's good for children, do it— and if it isn't, don't.

During the past decade, in sharp contrast to America's indifference to kids during the Gen-X childhood era, child issues have risen to the top of the nation's political agenda. Youth advocacy groups have multiplied. An entire social-marketing industry has risen up to persuade kids to behave better. Social programs for kids remain the one area of government that attracts interest and zeal. Books and magazines for kids, songs for kids, movies for kids, TV and radio programming for kids, web sites for kids— *anything and everything for kids*—have been the hottest media growth markets of the '90s. Riding that growth are the commercial messages that target them, often as a group, with jingle-names ranging from Team Cheerios and Nickelodeon Nation to Barbie's Generation Girl and Kellogg's Generation K. Even the national media now engages in wall-to-wall child absorption. In the same late-November week of 1999, all three of the major newsweeklies featured cover stories about kids, each focusing on a different issue unrelated to the week's news. *Newsweek* zeroed in on dyslexia. *Time* fretted over Pokémon. And *U.S. News* warned against youth cheating.

Hardly a week passes in which the public does not hear some urgent pronouncement about how the nation must produce a better generation of children. Kids have to be not merely better, but new and improved according to a specific formula: not more creative, more spirited, more liberty-loving, or more skeptical—but better behaved, more achieving, more upbeat, and more civic-spirited. It is not unreasonable to expect these Millennials, like the kids of other eras for whom "better" had

I'm impressed, so far, with the Millennials. They seem to be alert to problems around them, but determined to keep their innocence.

—*Chuck Lipsig*

There is idealism rather than cynicism; a sense of community instead of individualism.

—**Dallas Morning News**

I take catalog orders from a lot of teenagers, and I cannot believe how many of them address me as "ma'am"! The local high school kids call myself and my husband "sir" or ma'am," and my kids' friends, without exception, address us as "Mr. and Mrs. So-and-So" rather than by our first names, even though I have told them I prefer to be addressed by my first name. This was unheard of ten or twenty years ago. Well, this "sir" and "ma'am" thing takes a little getting used to, but I think on some level I actually like it.

—*Susan Brombacher*

another definition, to grow up embodying much of what their elders overtly expect of them.

While no one can doubt that America has grown kid-fixated, some might question whether this is due to any big change in generational attitudes. The Generation-Y school, oriented mainly toward commerce, points to two alternative explanations: *money* (the fact that today's kids are more affluent) and *demography* (the fact that today's kids are more numerous).

Yes, a lot more cash is being spent *on* them, as anyone who has recently visited a typical kid's bedroom can attest. But it's doubtful whether the money spent *by* teens and younger kids *on their own* has risen any faster than the economy. The generosity of parental "allowances" and the number of paid hours worked by teens have actually declined over the last decade. What's happening instead is that kids are buying more things jointly with parents and influencing more parental buying decisions. Explaining that takes you right back to the question of shifting generational perceptions.

And yes, Millennials are numerous. Swelled by a resurgent fertility rate and by the large families of a record immigration surge, they are indeed a giant of a generation, 76 million strong at the end of 2000. Millennials

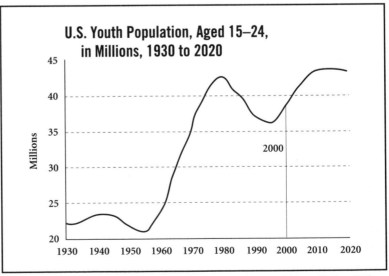

Future years taken from official middle series projections. Source: U.S. Bureau of the Census (2000)

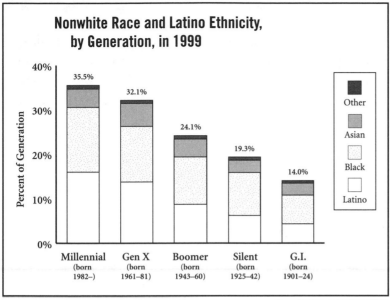

Nonwhite Race and Latino Ethnicity, by Generation, in 1999

Percent of Generation

Legend:
- Other (dark gray)
- Asian (medium gray)
- Black (light dots)
- Latino (white)

Generation	Value
Millennial (born 1982–)	35.5%
Gen X (born 1961–81)	32.1%
Boomer (born 1943–60)	24.1%
Silent (born 1925–42)	19.3%
G.I. (born 1901–24)	14.0%

Source: U. S. Bureau of the Census (2000)

already outnumber Boomers. By 2002 (which, for now, we assume to be their final birth year), they'll outnumber Xers as well. Add in subsequent immigration, and Millennials are well on their way to becoming America's first 100-million-person generation. Yet despite this rising trend, the current number of Millennial teens is still recovering from the Generation-X "birth dearth." As a share of the U.S. population, kids have merely held steady during the 1990s. An absolute head count shows that America had more youth spenders aged 15 to 24 in the early 1980s (over 40 million) than there will be again until the year 2004. Yet back in those days of Gen-X youths, hardly any politicians and not nearly as many marketers paid much attention to their age brackets.

Demographically, this is America's most racially and ethnically diverse, and least-Caucasian, generation. In 1999, nonwhites and Latinos accounted for nearly 36 percent of the 18-or-under population, a share half-again higher than for the Boomer age brackets, and nearly *three times* higher than for today's seniors. One Millennial in five has at least one immigrant parent, and one in ten has at least one noncitizen parent. Potentially the largest second-generation immigrant group in U.S. his-

Young people these days want to mix it up and continually blur the (racial) boundaries. —Matt Kelly, founder of Mavin *magazine*

It's great! Nobody is plain white, or plain black, or plain anything. Eventually I'm hoping every place will be like this. —Liz Short, 16, at a Wellesley College mixed-race symposium

tory, Millennials embody the irreversible browning of American civilization. Thanks to the internet, satellite news, porous national borders, and the end of the Cold War, they are also becoming the world's first generation to grow up thinking of itself as global.

Ethnicity raises another issue: whether a generational dynamic that works for a generation's nonethnic white majority can also apply to its large nonwhite minority. Yes, it can. Nonwhite Millennials are not only major contributors to their generation's fresh persona, but are in some ways *the most important* contributors.

Which kids are most likely to be wearing school uniforms? *Nonwhites.* Whose schools are moving fastest to impose uniform curricula, back-to-basics drilling, and achievement standards? *Nonwhites.* Whose neighborhoods are producing the swiftest decline in street murder, child poverty, teen pregnancy, and school violence? *Nonwhites.* Which kids are more likely to live with a two-parent family today than they were a decade ago? *Nonwhites*—in particular, African-American city children, who are now the focus of a community renaissance extending through Harlem and Watts to Oakland and Chicago's South Side. Black America has long been an outsized cultural contributor to generational currents, from civil rights (Silent Generation) to black power (Boomers) to hip-hop (Gen Xers). That contribution is continuing, albeit in new forms, with today's uniformed urban schoolchildren.

Latino kids, just now surpassing black kids in number, have added a new ethnic dimension to American youth. To date, most of their pop icons have keyed a distinctly Millennial genre of high-spirited fun, carnival rhythms, upbeat lyrics, and bright colors. With parents even more attached to "family values" (and fearful of their decline) than the white adult majority, the rapidly growing Latino and Asian youth populations are setting a distinctly Millennial tone in their schools and neighborhoods. For the most part, that tone is assertive, positive, team-playing, and friendly, whether in Seattle, Boston, Miami, San Diego, or a myriad of other cities and towns within those four cornerposts of American society.

Reversing History's Delta

Despite these positive trends, a question remains: When one compares today's young people with earlier generations in living memory, isn't it true that—for a great many—their condition remains perilous and their behavior disconcerting?

Of course. America has millions of kids who take drugs or have risky sex or lie or cheat or swear or are transfixed by the worst of the pop culture. Millions more live impoverished lives, with addicted or missing parents, facing life with little comfort and less hope. Thousands commit (and are victimized by) violent crimes. In a vast nation teeming with ethnic, economic, cultural, and lifestyle crosscurrents that today seem to pull more apart than together, one can easily identify any number of youth problems that remain worse than what many Americans, especially those over age 50, can recall of their own growing-up years.

Yet to talk about a generation is to talk not about its bits and pieces, but about its social and cultural center of gravity. For any new generation, like for any young and thriving and mortal organism, its *direction of change* can be more important than its current *location.* It is a generation's direction that best reveals its collective self-image and sense of destiny.

Here the Millennials are indeed special, since they are demonstrably reversing a wide array of negative youth trends, from crime to profanity to sex to test scores, that have prevailed in America for nearly half a century. In other words, Millennials are reversing the long-term direction of change—the delta of history. Today's kids are doing this so dramatically that, as a group, they are behaving better than their parents did as kids—and better than many of their parents (or leaders) behave even now, as adults. And

The drop in illegitimate births . . . is one of the most heartening American cultural developments in years.

—The American Enterprise

It's not just teen pregnancies that are down. So are teen sexual activity and approval of it. **—John Leo, U.S. News & World Report**

The New Purity: In Teen Circles, Virginity Is Cool

—headline, The Times of London

they are doing it against a demoralizing riptide of negative examples from many of the same adults who lecture them so fiercely. In the words of 17-year-old Josh Lee, in a letter to the *Chicago Sun-Times,* "the biggest problem [we have] is the example adults show kids today."

Are today's kids more spoiled and unethical than adults would like? In some ways, yes. Then again, *Millennials see national leaders and pop-culture celebrities as being vastly more spoiled and unethical than their own generation.*

In an era when a president can quibble on TV over what "the meaning of *is* is," thousands of schoolkids are each day summarily suspended—no appeal, no discussion—for "zero tolerance" offenses far less serious than his. Or consider the issue of cheating. In circa-2000 America, you can look everywhere from politics to business to sports and you'll find adult cheaters being excused, even celebrated, so long as they can prove themselves winners. Other adults, in charge of schools, often don't enforce anticheating rules (to the dismay of many students) and emphasize collaborative learning, practice testing, and web research in ways that make it unclear just what it now means to "cheat" at school. Yet think tanks and columnists unleash broadsides against a supposed "epidemic" of youth cheating.

Are today's schoolkids failing to meet adult-imposed standards of academic achievement? In some ways, yes. Then again, *Millennials are the first generation since World War II to be confronted with higher academic standards than the last generation—and to show early signs of meeting those standards.*

Who can recall the last time in America that young kids preferred ads and shows that portrayed people their own age as smart, studious, and articulate—the way they are starting to do now? Few Xers or Boomers are aware that today's grade-school kids are scoring higher, on average, than they did at like age—especially in math and science, and especially girls. Few are aware that a much higher share of today's kids are taking advanced placement tests and enrolling in colleges. Aside from their parents, practically no one knows that today's grade-school kids do far more homework and take far more tests than today's adults typically faced at that age. The further down the K–12 ladder you go, the more ambitious is the standard being set for Millennials on appearance, conduct, and achievement—a leading indicator, perhaps, of high-octane academic achievers by the time today's first graders reach high school.

Are today's kids more vulgar, sexually active, and violent than adults would like? In some ways, yes. But *Millennials are less vulgar, less sexually active, less violent than the youth culture adults have created for them.* They are the only teen generation in recent memory for whom this is so. Unlike young Boomers around 1960 or young Xers around 1980, Millennials are being pulled by the license of the adult culture far more than they are in any sense pushing it.

Nearly everyone knows that today's youth culture is filled with images and words most adults find offensive. But here's what hardly anyone knows: Most kids find them offensive too. In a 1998 survey of high-achieving high school students, 36 percent said they were "very" or "extremely" offended by sexual activity in the media—and another 26 percent said they were "moderately" offended. This is true for all ethnic groups. In an outlandish aspect of today's culture-war charades, many adults are shocked when they hear 15-year-olds spew back a few artifacts of a pop culture that includes *South Park* dialogue, Duke Nukem sound effects, and Limp Bizkit lyrics. Yet few adults express any particular shock at the 30-year-olds who write it, the 50-year-olds who produce it, or the 70-year-olds whose portfolios profit by it.

Events That Made the Biggest Impression on the High School Class of 2000

1. Columbine
2. War in Kosovo
3. Oklahoma City bombing
4. Princess Di's death
5. Clinton impeachment trial
6. O. J. Simpson trial
7. Rodney King riots
8. Lewinsky scandal
9. Fall of Berlin Wall
10. McGwire–Sosa homer derby

—*Class of 2000 Survey (1999)*

The products of today's media establishment are wildly inaccurate as indicators of Millennial sensibilities. As always, the commodified "youth

Don't tell us how bad we are. Look at yourself. —*Jessica Rawls, 14*

Y2Kids are civic minded, morally grounded, and more selfless than Baby Boomers.

—**Rockford Register Star**

culture" is entirely the creation of *nonyouth*—here, mainly Gen Xers and Boomers.

Imagine growing up, as a kid, in a world in which older people produce a trashy lineup for you, tailor it to your vernacular, market it in your media, and then condemn you for participating in it, even when all you're doing is casually checking it out. That's what it's like to be a teenager today. The only lasting significance the teen movies of the late '90s—from *Scream* to *Cruel Intentions*—will have for Millennials is to mark their point of life-cycle departure. As such, they may ultimately be recalled with a fair amount of embarrassed incredulity—much as Boomers wince when recalling how they flocked to see the *Beach Blanket Bingo*–style movies of the late 1950s.

"Our children are becoming a blur," remarked Bill Bradley—and, amid all the motion of youth, older generations have a real difficulty separating youth action from market reaction, or sorting out what's fresh and Millennial from what's merely the shadow of X. Thus far, the elder impression of this generation remains a tangle of contradictory evidence, without guideposts or translations for the visitor.

Take a tour through this Millennial "blur" and separate the negatives from the positives.

In our daily lives, yes, they're kids growing up in houses that contain 50 percent more things (measured by the pound) than houses did twenty years ago. Girls in teched-up bedrooms, with TV facing pillow. Boys with Nintendo-64 players. Tykes in day-care centers with guards and fences. Teens with beepers on beach week. Young drug runners in public-housing stairwells. Ten-year-olds who can recite Comedy Central jokes but not the names of presidents. Inner-city kindergarteners raised by thirtysomething grandmothers. Spoiled kids in mansions, selfish as the Rugrats' Angelica. Kids with cars, beepers, and cell phones, going from party to party, beyond the control of their parents. Boys for whom Homer Simpson is a father figure. Girls spending afternoons dabbling in cybersex . . .

. . . but they're also the Little Leaguers who treat umpires with more respect than their parents do. Test-tube babies. Babies aboard minivans with childseats, special mirrors, and radar that beeps when something's behind them. Pledgees for True Love Waits. Malcolm in the Middle *and* Brutally

Normal. *Kids with red-white-and-blue face paint and multicolored braces. Volunteers at the library, clocking in the community service needed to graduate. Middle schoolers designing web sites for their parents' businesses. Toddlers whose parents hire home-safety consultants to seal, cover, or remove every conceivable hazard. Young bicycle riders who wear helmets even though their moms and dads don't. High school grads having fun with parents at alcohol-free graduation parties. Tykes writing sweet letters to incarcerated dads. Teens who ask Mom why anyone would want to go slumming, burn a bra, or hitchhike with strangers.*

In schools, they're kids who get expelled for casually threatening to kill teachers. Owners of sporty new SUVs in high school parking lots. Vandals who spray paint or break windows. Lines of teens hustling out of high schools in mass-shooter drills. Boys with Motorola Flex Pagers hanging from belts. Bop talkers spreading the word *like* like a weed. First-graders with guns. Casual cheaters. Teens who swear at teachers. Girls in designer-label cliques. Kids in summer school because they flunked a new state test. Teens who come to school sleepy after staying up late watching videos. Overweight sophomores who switch out of PE and into AP classes. Jocks and goths trading insults in the halls. Boys who hate school and fantasize about blowing up classrooms. Kids who are drugged to make them behave.

. . . but they're also 15-year-olds walking to school with backpacks bulging with books. Calculus students swelling AP enrollments. Grade school kids studying phonics and reciting "Character Counts" placards. Kids buying presents for one another at The Learning Company. Posh high schoolers who tell reporters that virginity is cool again. Kids in SAT-prep summer camps. Cast and crew of amazing student musicals. Organizers of after-school prayer clubs. South Bronx middle schoolers who go to class from 7:30 to 5:00 every day, and half-day Saturdays. Eighth graders taking GT admissions tests that get harder every year. Urban kids in bright uniforms. Home schoolers net surfing with stay-at-home parents. Mud-soaked football linemen too modest to shower in front of other guys. Students teaching their teachers about computers. Second-generation Latino kids drilling their parents in civics.

In the economy, they're the kids who've never known a year in which America doesn't get richer. Girls with Hard Candy nail colors and ankle-

We like to let people in on a little secret. These kids are less likely to take drugs, less likely to assault somebody else, less likely to get pregnant and more likely to believe in God.

*—Vincent Schiraldi,
Justice Policy Institute*

Most teenagers are making good choices—focusing on their futures and saying no to anything that would jeopardize their dreams.

*—Donna Shalala,
Secretary, U.S. Department of
Health and Human Services*

breaking platform shoes. Free spenders in Niketown. Boys playing with toys that feature severed heads. Girls perusing boys' butts in Abercrombie & Fitch catalogues. Kids eating cafeteria lunches within sight of candy ads. Preteens at the multiplex, tittering at jokes about poop and story lines about masturbation. Girls who rush home to watch Jerry Springer, boys to watch WWF wrestling. Kids speculating on Beanie Babies. Fans of Snoop Doggy Dogg and Marilyn Manson. Suburban boys boomboxing gangsta rap and glaring at any adult who shows disapproval. Four-year-olds market-testing holiday toys. Girls spending hours putting on the glow. Prom teens in stretch limousines. Kids whose parents buy them cars before they get licenses . . .

. . . *but they're also the fans of Backstreet Boys, 'N Sync, bubblegum pop, ska and swing, Brandy and Cleopatra. Kids who avoid R-rated movies because they know they'll get carded. Fans of Harry Potter, Power Rangers, Sabrina, and PowerPuff Girls. Dabblers in marbles and yo-yos. Teens surfing web sites that teach them how to invest for the long term. Kids who've traded gangsta pants for khakis, skateboards for bikes. Preteens downloading MP3 tunes, making custom CDs, and sharing them with their friends. Grandkids going to Europe with Grandpas. Kids shopping for values at Old Navy. Readers of* Teen Newsweek, Time for Kids, *and* The New York Times Upfront. *Daughter going on Mom's business trip. Browsers at store windows with "Safe Place" stickers. Throngs of suburban tots who safely romp at "discovery zones" while parents watch and smile.*

In the news, they're girls sporting biceps tattoos and nose beads on magazine covers. Young witnesses at a hearing of a National Commission on Youth Violence. Columbine. Teen murderers shooting up a school while classmates fall, hide, run, cry in their parents' arms. TV docudramas featuring boys and guns, gangs, and drugs. Polly Klaas. Megan Kanka. JonBenet Ramsey. Teen murderers on a magazine cover, life story inside, with pictures of their crimes. Fourteen-year-olds passing around high-tar cigarettes imported from India. Child immigrants suffocating in sealed trucks. Sweatshops and child abusers. Teen murderers getting indicted, with blurry videos of their crimes available for $25, over a rock music sound track. Girls getting cosmetic surgery. A 16-year-old strafing smaller children at the National Zoo. Boys in a PBS documentary about hook-up parties. Middle schoolers in oral sex rings. Teen murderers getting sentenced, more scenes of their crimes, details at eleven . . .

ADULTHOOD IN CRISIS
NATIONAL YOUTH COMMISSION
ON SEX, VIOLENCE & MORAL TURPITUDE!

CLINTON | LEWINSKY | GINGRICH | MADONNA | SIMPSON

"WHO DID YOU *THINK* WAS WATCHING ?!?"

. . . but they're also the Columbine students who risked their lives staying with their dying teacher. Ten-year-old fans of 14-year-old classical singer Charlotte Church. Downward lines on charts about youth crime, teen pregnancies, and suicides. Kids of deadbeat dads who are having to pay up. Elementary school kids volunteering for political campaigns and voting in mock elections. The little girl in Section T, cheering the U.S. Women's World Cup team. High school girls summering at Camp CEO. Teens on a Florida "Truth Train" campaigning against cigarettes. A second-generation Asian winning the National Spelling Bee. Colorado middle schoolers organizing against child slavery in Sudan. Teens who refrain from chastising older generations when middle-aged mass murderers shoot up churches, offices, and day-trading outlets. Teenagers banding together in "Free the Children" to battle child exploitation in Asia.

The Millennial Generation is full of lots of kids doing lots of things. Some of it's bad, more is good, most of it new, all of it fresh to these kids, because it's all they've ever known. Taken as a whole, this is their starting point in life.

So, on balance, who *are* these kids, and what can one say about their generation? Sure, they're brash and bold, given to unseemly bursts of temper and cockiness and ambition, as though the world is being handed

A four-year-old boy was telling me how, at day care, they played "Mary Had a Little Lamb" on the "tampooder." Millennials are not only the first generation to have computers in day care, but the first to be exposed to them before they can pronounce the word! —**Ben Weiss**

I am making my dad's business's home page. He knows zippola about HTML. —**BURN, 14**

This is the first time in the history of the human race that a generation of kids has overtaken their parents in the use of new technology.

—**Peter Eio, Lego Systems**

The Kids Are All Right!
—**headline, P.C. magazine**

to them and all they have to do is grab it. Then again, they're doing a fine (and largely unreported) job coping confidently and high-spiritedly with a demoralizing youth culture not of their own making. Nearly all of today's teen negatives are residues of trends launched by Boomers and apexed by Gen Xers. Conversely, nearly all of today's teen positives are new trends, unique to Millennials, with much of the initiative coming from them.

Overcoming Pessimism

"The scariest thing about kids today," warns *San Francisco Examiner* columnist David Sarasohn, "is how adults feel about them." There are, to be sure, many reasons why adults speak ill of kids—and why so much that is positive about today's young Millennials remains half hidden behind clouds of elder doubt and suspicion.

One reason is timeless. Every generation derives comfort from its collective memories, that special grab bag of habits, tunes, images, gadgets, and words it calls its own. The older it grows, the more it sees in the rising generation a living reminder that such memories are mortal and must ultimately be paved over by those who don't share them. Never pleasant, such reminders are a natural breeding ground for tensions between young and old.

Today's adults cannot help feeling loss when they meet kids who have no memory of the Cold War or the civil rights movement or the long hot summers, of Vietnam or Watergate, of Bobby or Martin, of sports stars who earned less than presidents, of gas lines and unemployment lines, of stadiums named after heroes. Kids' faces go blank when you tell them to roll down the car window, turn the channel, press the carriage return, or quit sounding like a broken record. These kids never saw Muhammad Ali fight or Willie Mays play, and they think Kareem Abdul-Jabbar is a football player. To them, Kansas, Chicago, Alabama, and America are places, not rock groups—and if you say the words "Iron Curtain," they might think you're talking about a wrestler. Even the music, film, and fashion of the '80s doesn't speak much to them. Gen Xers, like Boomers, are learning that the kiss-off line "you're history" must someday apply to everybody.

When youth affluence or technology is at issue, adults don't just get grouchy, they *moralize*—in a jeremiad about laziness and decadence that dates back centuries. Americans heard it back in the time of six-shooters and telegraphs and streetcars, and again after the invention of automobiles and radios and air-conditioning and TV sets. Today, they hear it still—in complaints about kids who can't imagine a pizza that's not delivered, a phone that doesn't fit in a pocket, a movie that can't be owned, a toy that can't be programmed, or a summer camp with no menus. The loudest complaints come from Boomers, many of whom take a lifelong pride in vaunting values over technology and worry about the future of youths with such an appetite (and gift) for gadgets.

Yet the biggest obstacle now blocking a better adult appreciation of Millennials is one that today's adult generations did *not* face in their own youth. It is the obstacle that derives from straight-line thinking, from a near-universal adult consensus that, since the last two generations have defined a negative youth trend, the next American generation must necessarily follow in that path.

Today's older generations are full of people with institutional stakes in maintaining this perspective. Groups on one side of the political spectrum harvest public support by complaining about what People for the American Way calls "old-fashioned bigotry . . . among democracy's next generation," while groups on the other side do likewise by decrying what William Bennett calls a teen wave of "amoral superpredators" descending on America. Public agencies win funding by identifying "child crises," just as the media win market share by serving up more "boyz" and "girlz" fare they think young audiences want. "If it bleeds, it leads" goes the TV news slogan, and what bleeds on the air is usually under twenty years old. Corporate retailers think they're maximizing profit by following the prevailing wind—a wind they still think blows in a direction described by a *Washington Post* business reporter as "edgy, in-your-face, Generation Y 'tude.'"

Parents and grandparents who live with today's kids usually know better. But in an era of splintering households and lengthening lifespans, a rising share of American adults have scant daily contact with kids and are slow to absorb new information about them. Currently, only 34 percent of all U.S. households have children, an all-time low, down from 45 percent in 1970. This trend is accentuated by the growth of newly hyped definitions of "fulfilling" adult lifestyles that exclude children.

She is a glorified 1950s high school cheerleader with an undertone of perverse 1990s sexuality. Britney is simultaneously wholesome and ripely sensual. She's Lolita on aerobics.

—*Camille Paglia,*
on Britney Spears

She's not just a superkid. She's obedient, too. —*Jon Pareles,*
on Britney Spears

Many parents of today's kids look negatively upon the young generation because they separate the good they see happening in their own families, neighborhoods, and schools from the bad they imagine happening everywhere else. A recent *Los Angeles Times* poll revealed roughly half of all Californians giving themselves an "A" as parents (one in five an "A-plus"), while roughly four in five gave statewide parents, as a group, grades of "D" or "F." What author David Whitman called America's "optimism gap" appears in other adult surveys on youth, indicating that most parents regard Generation Y as a riotous crew who inhabit their cable TV studios and newspaper style sections, but who rarely visit their own homes in person.

The result is a national youth discussion mired in cognitive dissonance, with too few adults seeing what should be plainly visible. Editorials bemoan the "murder epidemic" in high schools, while failing to advise readers that their children are far less likely to be murdered in a school than to be hit by lightning or run over by a freight train—and failing to report that the real lasting impact of Columbine is less youth fear than adult fear, as measured by all the students being put in uniforms or passed through metal detectors. Public officials regularly claim (or hysterically imply) that youth arrests, child abuse, child poverty, classroom cheating, teen sex, TV watching, after-school jobs, or youth suicides are all up, while test scores, school days, homework, college ambitions, teen happiness, and attachment to parents are all down. To date, hardly anybody has confronted them with the plain fact that *all of those statements are false*—in many cases, dramatically so. Knowing the truth would require nothing more than a quick look at an officially published number or, at most, a phone call to an expert who really understands the topic, but few of today's opinion leaders take the trouble.

Even when summarizing their own survey data, many of today's youth researchers are tempted to give their findings a negative spin. "Kids These Days '99," a much-cited report from the Public Agenda Foundation, leads with the adverse finding that "only a handful of adults say it's typical to come across children who are friendly and helpful toward their neighbors." As evidence, the authors assert that a mere 18 percent of adults say that it's "very common" to come across friendly and helpful kids. What they leave buried inside the report is the fact that an additional 52 percent of adults say it's "somewhat common" to come across such kids. The Josephson Institute of Ethics, in its recent 1998 "report card" on youth, sternly highlights that 59 percent of teens aged 14 and 15 admit they cheated at least once on a test. Left unmentioned is another more interesting number: 73 percent of the kids report that they had *refused* to cheat even though they saw others cheating.

When adults speak harshly about what kids do, they usually insist they're not really *blaming* the kids, merely trying to pressure parents, teachers, and public officials to do their jobs better. Thus, even the most positive official news typically comes draped in somber language. In 1997, Health and Human Services Secretary Donna Shalala began what should have been a totally good-news release by saying, "We welcome the news that the long-term increase in teenage sexual activity may finally have stopped." Then, instead of commending kids for this improved behavior, she recited a long list of areas where kids and parents and government were still failing. If history always moved in straight lines, this sort of benign exaggeration might be excusable, or at least harmless. If kids truly are on the edge of incorrigibility, then nothing short of shock therapy would be conscionable—since even with that, the kids are likely to go from bad to worse anyway.

But history does *not* move in straight lines, and Millennials are *not* going in the same direction as the line from Boomers to Gen Xers. With Millennials on the rise, the direction of American youth is rapidly changing. And as it changes, the prevailing torrent of pessimism about kids carries the risk of real damage, to their generation and the nation.

It harms by betraying the trust adults ask of youths, and by failing to inspire, join, or endorse their highest aspirations. This would mean, at best, the loss of a wonderful opportunity.

It harms by stifling the spirit and assertiveness of young boys, who thus far have lagged behind girls as Millennial trendsetters.

It harms by diverting adults from their higher duty: providing exemplars, electing leaders with moral authority, and bolstering the integrity, realism, and farsightedness of today's adult regime.

And it harms by underestimating the unusual collective power Millennials will soon be capable of exercising, a kind of youth power that most of today's older generations have never witnessed. This will be less

There is good reason to believe that society has begun a process of "remoralizing" itself and walking back from the cultural abyss it faced.

—*Francis Fukuyama,* **author of** **The Great Disruption**

the familiar youth power to *stop* institutions than a newfound power to *energize* them. If downbeat elders cannot harness this potential energy to a constructive mission of sufficient scope, even a minor economic or political setback could transform it into a dangerous juggernaut.

Millennials have the capacity to become America's next great generation. But this capacity does not ensure any particular outcome. Nor does it suggest that Millennials don't have potential weaknesses. They do. As Millennials fully come of age, older people are likely to begin complaining about young people who are more bland, less creative, and more dependent on peer support than other recent youth generations. As time passes, critics of this generation will dwell less on the trenchcoated outcasts than on the power cliques that don't tolerate deviation from the group norm. This problem could undermine their greatness.

Millennials resemble a fully charged rocket—or, to use Ortega y Gasset's classic definition of a generation, "a species of biological missile hurled into space at a given instant, with a certain velocity and direction." So long as Millennials can wheel themselves onto the right launchpad and point themselves in the right direction, they can deliver excellent results. They represent an opportunity that, once fully understood and appreciated, must be acted on by people of all ages.

Past, Present, and Future

What is any generation, really? When you ask people around any given age who they are, they often given an answer divided into three parts: Their past, their present, and their future. Each tense helps illuminate the whole picture. You can't understand who Boomers or Gen Xers are or were if you have no idea where they came from or hope to go. The same is true for Millennials—except for them, the past is a smaller fraction of their lives. That's why this book is arranged as it is.

The rest of this opening section, "Where They Come From," explains what it means to be a generation—and, more to the point, what it means to be *this* generation with *this* location in history and *these* generational neighbors. New generations always defy straight lines, but that doesn't mean they arrive at random. There are good reasons why Millennials are growing up to embody a *sharp break* from Gen-X youth trends and a *direct reversal* of Boomer youth trends.

In the "Who They Are" middle section, we explore their world, moving from one social arena to the next—from demography, politics, and family to conduct, culture, commerce, and more. Along the way, we challenge the negative stereotypes that older generations still widely apply to young people. For older readers—those whose first-person youth experiences are best captured by *Summer of '42, American Graffiti,* or even *The Breakfast Club*—we tell you things you probably don't know about today's kids, while showing you how and why their location in history is different from your own. For Millennial readers, we try to put important facts about you and your friends in a life-cycle perspective.

The final section, "Where They're Going," extends the Millennial story into the future. What can be said about a collective lifespan that will extend past the year 2100? Quite a bit, actually, when you apply what is known about today's kids against their foreseeable timetable of marriage, family, career, and politics. To answer the most difficult question—what impact Millennials could have on America's future—we introduce the concept of the "hero" generation. By the time Millennials reach old age, deep into the twenty-first century, their accomplishments and reputation could compare with those of other children who began life similarly, including today's much-heralded G.I. "greatest generation." Yet we also offer words of warning about how history could be gearing up to deal Millennials some fateful surprises.

Throughout, we'll tell you some stories, fill you with facts, and show you some cartoons from R. J. Matson along with a chorus of sidebar voices from Millennials and adults active in the world of youth. We supplement this with our own Class of 2000 Survey, which we conducted among 660 northern Virginia high school students, and our Fairfax Teacher's Survey, in which we polled 200 elementary, middle, and high school teachers.

To readers of all ages and generations, we say welcome—and please read on.

This is a generation that must be reckoned with. They are going to overtake the country.

—David Spangler, director of market research, Levi's

from Babies on Board to Power Teens

from Babies on Board to Power Teens
from Babies on Board to Power Teens

There's a new horizon
And the promise of a favorable wind
— *LEANN RIMES, "One Way Ticket"*

In 1981, gossip columnists let loose some chatter about a new rash of celebrity pregnancies, culminating in a 1982 *Time* cover story about a floodtide of thirtysomething Boomers choosing at long last to become moms and dads. Bright yellow "Baby on Board" signs began popping up in car windows, coast to coast, especially in brand-new models of child-friendly minivans. By the Christmas of 1983, adult America fell in love with Cabbage Patch Kids—a precious new doll, harvested pure from nature, so wrinkly and cuddly cute that millions of Boomers wanted to take one home to love. Many had spent the prior two decades avoiding childbirth. Now they were "into" the deeper meaning of creating families.

The era of the wanted child had begun.

In September 1982, a tragic crime involving cyanide-tainted Tylenol triggered an October wave of parental panic over trick-or-treating. Halloween suddenly found itself encased in hotlines, advisories, statutes, and public outrage—a fate that would soon befall many other once-innocent

Everything for the children. All adults seem to care about is the children.
— *Lori Leibovich, salon.com*

Zit-geist
— *Variety, on America's late-'90s obsession with teenagers*

This is not about teenage marketing. It's about the coming of age of a generation. — *J. Walker Smith, Yankelovich Partners*

For a benchmark question, separating Millennials from Gen Xers, let me propose: "Were you ever afraid of World War III?" —Tobias Burmeister

We are foolish to expect students to be any more knowledgeable about Vietnam than they are about the New Deal or the Second World War. It's all history to them. If you didn't live through it, it doesn't matter if it was five years ago or five centuries ago. It's an expectation by grown-ups that their kids will share the same passions they did. —Michael Zuckerman, Professor of History, University of Pennsylvania

Things I will never forget: the Oklahoma City bombing, the death of Princess Diana, and the Columbine school massacre. . . . I'll never forget where I was when these events occurred.

—Janine Storm Van Leeuwen, 17

child pastimes, from bike riding to BB guns. A few months later came word of a sweeping national hysteria over the sexual abuse of toddlers, leading to dozens of front-page adult convictions after what many observers agreed were Salem-like trials. A flurry of books (with dark titles such as *The Disappearance of Childhood, Children Without Childhood, Our Endangered Children*) assailed the anything-goes parental treatment of children since the mid-1960s. The family and school and neighborhood wagons were circling.

The era of the protected child had begun.

In 1984, Hollywood figured nothing could go wrong with *Children of the Corn* and *Firestarter,* the two latest installments in a child-horror film genre that had packed theaters ever since *Rosemary's Baby* and *The Exorcist.* Both films totally bombed, as parents began flocking to a new kind of movie about adorable babies and wonderful kids.

That same year, newspaper editorials reverberated with the findings of the federal "Nation at Risk" report on education, which blasted grade-school students as "a rising tide of mediocrity" and implored America's teachers and adults to do better by America's next batch of kids. According to many indicators, they started doing just that. The early 1980s is when the national rates for many behaviors damaging to children—divorce, abortion, violent crime, alcohol consumption, and drug abuse—reached their postwar high-water mark. That was also when the well-being of children began to dominate the national debate over most family issues— from welfare and latchkey households to drug abuse and pornography.

The era of the worthy child had begun.

Wanted. Protected. Worthy. Thus did the heralded Class of 2000 arrive in America's nurseries and cribs. Soon a much longer glossary of (mainly) positive adjectives would describe them. From conception to graduation, this 1982 cohort has marked a watershed in adult attitudes toward, treatment of, and expectations for children. Over that eighteen-year span, whatever age bracket those 1982-born children have inhabited has been the target of intense hope, worry, and wonder from parents, pollsters, pundits, and politicians.

Not since the Progressive era, near the dawn of the twentieth century, has America greeted the arrival of a new generation with such a dramatic rise in adult attention to the needs of children.

Like every generation, the Millennials can be defined by their self-image, by their beliefs and behaviors, and by their location in history. All these attributes are in turn shaped by older Americans who themselves belong to prior generations. An ancient circle is at work: Generations are created young by history, and later go on to create history in their turn.

Seeing where Millennials are situated in this generational rhythm is the first step to understanding where they come from, where they stand today, and where they're going.

Follow the Breaking Wave

Virtually from birth, the leading edge of every new generation is accompanied by a rapid and unexpected shift in how children are perceived. Such shifts, in fact, are partly what cause new generations to arise.

The arrival of Generation X in the early '60s coincided with an era of decline in the U.S. fertility rate and a society-wide aversion to children. And so it remained for the next twenty years: Small kids were seldom the focus of positive media attention, adults complained loudly to pollsters about how kids impeded their self-discovery, and kids found themselves excluded from a vaunted new definition of the "adult lifestyle." Kids came attached to new adjectives, like unwanted, at-risk, throwaway, homeless, latchkey. Parents found comfort in experts who reassured them that little Gen Xers thrived best when left to their own wits, to grow up tough and self-reliant, like the Gary Coleman or Tatum O'Neal child proto-adults then popular in the media.

Come the early '80s, with Jane Pauley's twins and Bruce Willis's Lamaze class, that perception came to an abrupt end. For the Millennial Generation, the ascendant Boomer cultural elite rewrote the rules. Starting as babies, kids were now to be desperately desired, to be in need of endless love and sacrifice and care—and to be regarded by parents as the highest form of self-discovery. By the late '80s, Hollywood and fashion celebrities began turning baby-making into a fad and flaunting their pregnancies, a trend that culminated with a nude and very expectant Demi Moore on the August 1991 cover of *Vanity Fair*. Meanwhile, commercial facilities—from airlines to motels to restaurants—began getting out toys and high chairs and rewelcoming toddlers.

I said, "The kids would go crazy for this," and the kids couldn't have cared less. . . . They were like, "Who is this guy?"
—*Heather Keegan, Digital Research, describing a preschool test of a Kermit the Frog toy*

These new arrivals found a stunningly receptive public. In 1987, the whole nation nervously followed the fate of three little girls in distress: "Everybody's Baby," Jessica McClure, trapped in an abandoned well in Lubbock, Texas; 2-year-old Tabatha Foster, whose five organ transplants were made possible by celebrity donations; and 4-year-old Cecilia Chichan, the sole survivor rescued from a plane crash in Detroit. Remarkably, the Pew Research Center for the People and the Press ranks the saga of Jessica McClure as the fifth most closely followed news story in America over the past fifteen years, ranking just ahead of the Columbine massacre, which occurred when Jessica was a high school freshman.

By the early '90s, elementary school kids entered the spotlight. During the Gulf War Super Bowl of 1991, kids marched onto the field at halftime amid abundant news stories (unseen during the Vietnam War) about the children of dads serving abroad. By 1996, Dole and Clinton dueled for the presidency in a race that featured much debate about the middle school children of "soccer moms" and the special problems of early teens. By the end of the decade, the public focused on high schools more than at any time since the late '50s, the Sputnik era, when the first Boomers reached that age.

At every turn, the entertainment media picked up the beat. By the mid-'80s, movies about hardened, nasty, or demonic kids were replaced by *Raising Arizona, Baby Boom, She's Having a Baby, Look Who's Talking,* and *Three Men and a Baby* (which soon matured into *Three Men and a Little Lady*)—all starring huggable protagonists who inspire adults to grow up a bit themselves. A few years later, these magical children became the little Jonahs who provided a touchstone to *Sleepless in Seattle* parents—or, in films such as *The Piano* and *Angels in the Outfield,* played angels whose very presence was an epiphany. "Was there ever a bad child in the world—a spiteful, stubborn, domineering sapper of his parents' spirit?" asked a *Time* reviewer by the mid-'90s. "There is rarely one in a Hollywood movie."

Between 1986 and 1991, the number of periodicals offered to young children doubled (to eighty-one titles), and between 1991 and 1994, the sale of children's music doubled—directly anticipating the explosion of teen magazines and music later in the '90s. Having laid off cartoonists during the prior, X-rated decade, the Walt Disney Company began rehir-

U.S. Rates of Divorce and Abortion, 1976 to 1996

Rate per 1,000 Women*

Abortions   Divorces

*Women aged 15–44 for abortions; married women over age 15 for divorce.

Source: U.S. National Center for Health Statistics (2000); abortion numbers
are derived from data tabulated by the Alan Guttmacher Institute (1999)

ing them in the 1980s to produce such child epics as *The Little Mermaid* and *The Lion King.* Competitors vied with *An American Tail, Oliver and Company,* and *The Land Before Time,* each of which depicted children as smart and noble. TV sitcoms picked up the trend, and the new pop-culture families (like Bart Simpson's) acquired younger children who were better behaved than their older siblings. It was a trend that would continue in later teen movies—exactly the reverse of the old Boomer-era *Leave It to Beaver* formula, in which the older kids were more duty-bound.

As adults changed their perception of kids, so too did they change their behavior toward kids—starting with a new desire to bear and raise them. Accompanied by a quadrupling in the number of infertility-related doctor visits from 1986 to 1988, a rising birthrate boosted a demographic "echo boomlet" already under way. Early on, adults resolved to do better at shielding small children from harm. Worried parents became avid consumers for a thriving childproofing industry (which snapped up new patents for everything from stove-knob covers to safety mirrors) and triggered a fierce popular crusade for programs and policies that looked after their kids. No new adult-imposed goal seemed too ambitious for the Class of 2000, christened in kindergarten as early as 1987, who were to be

I understand how it happened; the moralistic tendencies of my generation combined with the '80s anxiety about the deteriorating and unsafe child's world led us to impose a regimen on our children that we would never have tolerated ourselves, creating a mind-set utterly foreign to our own. It's a weird thing if you think about it. —**Brian Rush**

Indeed, the longer you look at "our kids," the more you can trace back the problems and any possible solutions to the baby-boomers themselves.

—*Lexington,* **The Economist**

free from drugs and tobacco and abuse and drunk drivers. And no new Megan's Law or Joan's Law or Amber's Law was too draconian for those who threatened little kids with "stranger danger" nightmares.

Entering the '90s, two ascendant words—*family values*—began capturing the gist of Millennial nurture. Beginning around 1990, this Boomer "cocooning" produced a tripling in the popularity of "staying home with family," with two parents in three now saying they would accept a pay cut in return for more family time. It also produced stricter parental rules about child behavior. "The '60s Generation, Once High on Drugs, Warns Its Children," headlined *The Wall Street Journal* in 1990. "Do As I Say, Not As I Did," echoed *The New York Times* about Boomer parents who (polls confirmed) did not want their own children to have the same freedom with drugs, alcohol, and sex that they had once enjoyed. Well-educated Boomer moms saw themselves less as victims and more as deputies of what Hillary Clinton later called "the village," the new rule-enforcing community of child-first adults. Family-focused Boomer dads saw themselves less as pals and more as standard setters— not in the old *Father Knows Best* genre, but in a new Promise Keepers or Million Man Marcher style.

As Millennials replaced Gen Xers in the puberty age bracket, the adult message in practically every medium became more prescriptive and less equivocal. In tot-TV, *Barney and Friends* (with its happy teamwork and stress on what all kids share in common) stole the limelight from *Sesame Street* (with its more nuanced story lines and stress on what makes each kid different). On bookshelves, William Bennett–style books with crisply teachable "virtues" crowded out the Judy Blume–style vignettes about feelings and healing. In public-school sex-ed, abstinence training eclipsed comprehensive safe-sex training. Even Barbie's band changed to suit the new parental demands: Out were the Rockers, in were the cleaned-up Sensations.

America's growing fixation on children inevitably influenced politics. In the early '80s, public figures began using a new term—"antichild"—to attack policies such as federal borrowing or social service cuts deemed uniquely hurtful to the young. In 1985, the Grace Commission sponsored TV public service ads linking the national debt with a crying baby. A KIDS-PAC lobby was formed, the United Way launched a giant new children's agenda, and in the 1988 and 1992 presidential elections, nearly every big issue—whether crime or welfare, technology or gun control, health care or budget policy—was recast in terms of "soccer-mom" kinderpolitics. For Democrats and Republicans alike, America's kids were becoming not just a political trump card, but something akin to public property.

Along the way, America's most vexing social problems invited leaders to start drawing a triage line between the two generations then cohabiting the preadult age brackets: older Gen-X teens, who were beyond hope, and younger Millennial children, who were redeemable. "I'm sorry to say it," federal judge Vincent Femia observed in 1989, "but we've lost a generation of youth to the war on drugs. We have to start with the younger group, concentrate on the kindergartners." The "only way" to stop the cycle of poverty, dependency, and crime, said Ohio governor George Voinovich, "is to pick one generation of children, draw a line in the sand, and say 'This is where it stops.'" When George Bush spoke of a "weed and seed" urban agenda in the wake of the Rodney King riots, he was clearly distinguishing between Xers and Millennials. Sometimes the line was literally engraved into law. When Congress expanded Medicaid to all poor children in 1990, benefits were phased in by restricting eligibility to kids born in 1983 and after. No Gen-X kid, no matter how poor, was covered.

Nowhere was this generational dividing line more noticeable than in school reform. In the early '80s, while educators complained of demoralized teachers and apathetic students, new parents obsessed feverishly over their preschool "trophy children." The sale of Gesell Test materials,

It's almost like Boomers woke up one day to discover, "We've won the Cold War, but how are we doing with the next generation? Oh-oh."

—Rita Sutton

It is so true that for the Boomers, overprotection is about control whereas for young Xer parents, it is about reality. —Joe Bexton

Bicycle helmet usage rose from 18 percent in 1991 to 50 percent in 1998. In that latter year, 69 percent of children under 16 wore helmets, versus 38 percent of adult bike riders.

—www.kidsource.com

When my parents were young, they had to do more for themselves. They had to ride their bikes or walk. We get rides every place.

—Stephanie Beckman, 13

The Boomer Generation tries way too hard to overprotect us.

—Bobby Rhatigan, 17

used for determining a child's kindergarten readiness, jumped 67 percent between 1984 and 1987. By the late '80s, what school-reformer Chester Finn called "a seismic shock" began gripping the adult mood toward education, with sharply increasing support for more homework, longer school days, more tests, and standardized curricula. Teacher pay reversed its '70s-era losses, and elementary school PTAs and competing PTOs (Parent-Teacher Organizations) began flourishing with new membership, money, and purpose.

During the Bush presidency, the nation's leaders made numerous promises to transform the nation's public schools in time, again, for the Class of 2000. As leading-edge Millennials passed through elementary school, new educational buzzwords appeared: collaborative learning, back to basics, zero tolerance, school accountability, and (especially) standards of learning. And just behind the leading edge marched a swelling legion of kids bearing a new badge of generational identity that, in youth, would have been anathema to Boomers and incomprehensible to Gen Xers: the brightly colored school uniform.

In the year 1997, the American public first discovered this generation—when its leading edge was only fifteen years old. The stage was set during the previous fall's presidential campaign, when both parties talked more than ever about whatever kids were reading or driving or drinking or smoking. Bill Clinton's child focus grew so overt, quipped Ellen Goodman, that it literally defined his speaking schedule: "If this is Thursday, it must be Curfews. If this is Friday, it must be School Uniforms. V-Chips on Monday, Smoking on Tuesday." As the public's mood about the nation and economy began to revive, the demand for everything at the darker edge of the Gen-X youth culture began to sag. CD sales plunged for the most heavily hyped alternative and grunge-rock groups. Viewers tired of heroin-chic fashion ads and plotless Gen-X film ideas. Critics stopped laughing at *Beavis and Butt-Head.*

Meanwhile, a new teen culture began to emerge. Two films became surprise hits among younger teens—one (*Scream*) a witty antigoth slasher movie, the other (*Titanic*) a big story of public catastrophe and private valor. With the debut of groups like the Spice Girls, Backstreet Boys, and Hanson, a whole new teenybop music sound appeared—happier, brighter, more innocent. "They like brands with heritage. Contrived, hard-edged fashion is dead. Attitude is over," announced MTV president

Judy McGrath in 1997 when asked about these kids. "They like what's nice and fun in fashion and sports. They like the Baby Gap ads; they're simple and sweet."

Throughout that breakthrough year, the news media chose to announce (under various labels) the arrival of a "new generation" in America—and *CBS Evening News* and *USA Today* started focusing on the "High School Class of 2000" as a running news story. Media companies underwrote a stunning multiplication of teen magazines, teen news inserts, teen web sites, teen marketing campaigns, and teen-targeted movies and TV shows, a trend that continues to this day. Youth opinion polls proliferated to the point where, nearly every week, America was alerted to some new fact about teenage life.

Two years later came a grimmer rite of passage: the 1999 suicide-massacre of fourteen students and one teacher at Columbine High School in Littleton, Colorado, the worst of a series of public-school mass gunfire tragedies (in Arkansas, Kentucky, Oregon, and Mississippi) involving kids born just before and after the first Millennial cohorts.

In the wake of these shootings, Millennial kids candidly acknowledged the role played by the growing peer pressure of their generation—a tendency, less evident among Gen Xers, to ostracize outsiders and compel conformity. The adult reaction was frenzy and fear utterly disproportionate to the actual risks faced by teenagers, whose world, statistically, is much safer than it was three, two, or (especially) one decade earlier. In high schools across America, the months after Columbine were marked by false alarms, SWAT drills, stern speeches, and strict new codes for dress and behavior that students have accepted with little dissent. The actual numbers didn't matter. Both teens and adults were apt to vastly overestimate violent deaths in U.S. schools. (When asked, high school students typically supposed the toll was in the tens of thousands annually.) What mattered was that kids killing kids was no longer tolerable—unlike in the late Xer child era, when more than twice as many kids killed one another to far less public complaint.

Columbine is a critical event in the lives of Millennials and, hence, is likely to remain an important generational marker separating those who were in grade school at the time from those who were about to graduate or beyond. In our survey of the Class of 2000, these Millennial kids declared the Columbine shooting, together with its aftermath, to be the

Millennials, unlike my generation, are getting tremendous reinforcement, tremendous media attention.

—*Ruth Donlin*

Youth culture [is] a subject about which this newspaper has been somewhat out of touch. Editors have been pushing reporters to come up with more stories about young people.

—*E. R. Shipp, ombudsman,*
The Washington Post *(1999)*

We decided children's priorities should be the bottom line of our news policy. —*Max Keeping,*
Canadian Broadcasting *(1999)*

number-one event of their youth that they expect to remember all their lives.

Never before in living memory has a generation been so celebrated, from conception to birth to preschool through elementary, middle, and high school. And the celebration could be just beginning.

How History Shapes Generations

The subject of generations has recently been shrouded in well-earned public skepticism. Throughout the last decade, Americans have heard constant talk about generations—and have watched countless generationally targeted ads, TV shows, and movies. Most generational "experts" are, in fact, youth marketeers. But there is far more to generations than the consumer habits of people in different age brackets.

A generation can be defined as a society-wide peer group, born over a period roughly the same length as the passage from youth to adulthood (in today's America, around twenty or twenty-one years), who collectively possess a common persona. The length need not always be the same. A generation can be a bit longer or shorter, depending on its coming-of-age experience and the vagaries of history. Of the nine American generations born over the past two centuries, none has been less than seventeen years or longer than twenty-four years in length.

Millennials are the latest link in a long generational chain. They are the eighteenth New World generation, the fourteenth to know the American nation and flag, the fifth (and last) to be born in the twentieth century. Six generations of Americans have members still alive today.

Their birth-year boundaries are significant. Demographers who insist on locating Boomers according to the fertility "boom" of 1946 to 1964, and then Gen Xers according to the fertility "bust" of 1965 to 1976, are not defining generations in any useful historical sense. Birth numbers are only one factor (and not always a critical factor) in locating a generation. When drawn correctly, generational birth years should indicate the boundaries for each generational persona.

What is a generational persona? It is a distinctly human, and variable, creation embodying attitudes about family life, gender roles, institutions, politics, religion, culture, lifestyle, and the future. A generation can think, feel, or do anything a person might think, feel, or do. It can be safe or reck-

Generation	Birth Years	Famous Man	Famous Woman
Lost	1883–1900	Harry Truman	Mae West
G.I.	1901–1924	Ronald Reagan	Ann Landers
Silent	1925–1942	Martin Luther King, Jr.	Sandra Day O'Connor
Boom	1943–1960	George W. Bush	Hillary Clinton
X	1961–1981	Michael Jordan	Courtney Love
Millennial	1982–2002	Zac Hanson	Tara Lipinski

less, individualist or collegial, spiritual or secular. Like any social category (race, class, religion, or nationality), a generation can allow plenty of individual exceptions and be fuzzy at the edges. But unlike most other categories, it possesses its own personal biography. It can feel nostalgia for a unique past, express urgency about a future of limited duration, and comprehend its own mortality. As a generation arrives, advances, and recedes, this core persona invariably reveals itself. Not every member will share it, of course, but every member will have to deal with it, willingly or not, over a lifetime. As Martin Heidegger observed, "The fateful act of living in and with one's generation completes the drama of human existence."

To identify the persona of a generation, look for three attributes: *perceived membership* in a common generation; *common beliefs and behaviors;* and a *common location in history.*

Perceived membership. Generational self-perception begins to dawn during adolescence and typically takes full shape during and immediately after collegiate, military, marriage, or initial work experience.

Ordinarily, a generation's earlier-born cohorts acquire this self-perception at a somewhat older age than later-born cohorts, since they must first be motivated to shed an identity (of the prior generation) that no longer fits. Thanks to the media and advertising obsession with today's teens, however, this delay has shrunk drastically. Firstborn Millennials are showing a clearer sense of generational membership, earlier in their life cycle, than any other youths in American history, including Boomers and Gen Xers. Around 1960, if anyone had asked Boomers whether they were part of a "new generation," the answer would have

We live in the South Park *culture, where disrespect of everyone and everything is the norm.*

—Warren Thompson, school psychologist

An unflinching look at the humiliating horrors of being a teenager and still a virgin.

—ad copy, American Pie

This is the ocean in which our children swim. This is the sound of our culture.   —Peggy Noonan, **The Wall Street Journal**

Mommy, what does "horny" mean?

—Marvin Brannon, 11, after hearing an Austin Powers doll talk

been "huh?" In the late '70s, the media paid almost no attention to Gen Xers who, come their early-'90s discovery, often denied that there was such a thing as Gen X. But when you ask that question of today's Millennials, you get a crisp, culturally informed answer—usually a "yes."

By degrees, the media have begun to register this self-perception. Until first-wave Millennials reached their teens, the only words typically attached to them were the early-'80s cachets "Baby Boomlet" and "Echo Boom," which merely referred to their growing size by birth cohort. The only exceptions were the "Millennial Generation" label (first used by your authors in 1987) and the "Generation Y" label (coined by *Advertising Age* in 1993). Neither term gained much traction until the discovery year of 1997, when these and many other labels—including Digital or Net Gen, Generation 2000, Generation Next, Y2Kids, and Generation "Why"—sprang into print. All of a sudden, marketers, educators, criminologists, politicians, and journalists were straining to say that something, somehow, was different about this new crop of kids.

The volume of generations-talk in the media might prompt some skeptics to wonder whether young people of all ages aren't now conditioned to think of themselves as "a new generation." That has not happened. In our Class of 2000 Survey, Millennials were emphatic about their new identity. Over twice as many students born in 1982 said they "felt part of something coming after" Generation X as said they "felt part of" Generation X. Yet just one year earlier, another college poll of the 1979 and 1980 birth cohorts found a solid majority *denying* that they felt part of any "new generation."

Curiously, the rising media crescendo over Millennials followed the early-'90s media hype over Generation X by only about six or seven years. Does this mean, as some have suggested, that generations are getting shorter in today's America? No. The average length of a generation, keeping time with the phases of the human lifespan, is still around twenty or twenty-one years. Thus, if the first Gen-X birth year can be located in the early 1960s, it is only natural to find the first birth year of the next generation in the early 1980s—and to look for the last year of that (Millennial) generation sometime in the early Oh-Ohs.

In part, the rapid media transition from X to Millennial reflects an early confusion about locating the birth-year dividing line. Many of the original (1993) "Generation Y" stories referred to teenagers born between 1974 and 1980, cohorts which today are regarded as the late wave of Gen X. This explains both why these kids were discussed so soon after Gen X (later on, they would be regarded as *part* of Gen X) and why descriptions of "Generation Y" still often sound so much like descriptions of "Generation X" (originally, they *overlapped*).

Also, the speedy transition from X to Millennial highlights the very unequal attention these two generations have received. From childhood through early adulthood, Xers were mostly ignored as a group. Gen X attracted notice relatively late—and didn't receive its name until 1991, when its leading-edge members (including *Generation X* author Douglas Coupland) were already reaching age 30. As children, first-wave Millennials were the focus of an adult attention that child Xers never experienced—and as teens are attracting public scrutiny at a much earlier age.

Common beliefs and behaviors. In today's data-rich infosphere, people's attitudes (toward family, career, risk, romance, politics, and religion), together with their behavioral tendencies (in job choice, test scores, health, risk, crime, sex, and drugs), can be tracked by birth cohort. These indicators reveal a clear break between those born in and after 1982 and those born before. They also point to an entirely new generational persona—as different from Gen X as Xers themselves are different from Boomers.

This Millennial persona has seven distinguishing traits. Into the Oh-Oh decade, America can expect to see more evidence that Millennials are:

>> *Special.* From precious-baby movies of the early '80s to the effusive rhetoric surrounding the high school Class of 2000, older generations have inculcated in Millennials the sense that they are, collectively, vital to the nation and to their parents' sense of purpose.

>> *Sheltered.* Starting with the early-'80s child-abuse frenzy, continuing through the explosion of kid safety rules and devices, and now climaxing with a post-Columbine lockdown of public schools, Millennials are the focus of the most sweeping youth safety movement in American history.

The fact that so many Gen-X parents are in jail is and will play havoc on their children. . . . Overall, my guess is that few gang members will truly want to see their children follow in their footsteps. —**Grace Mary Perez**

SEBASTIAN: *I mean, we're destroying an innocent girl. You do realize that?*
KATHRYN: *That never bothered you before.* —**Cruel Intentions**

>> *Confident.* With high levels of trust and optimism—and a newly felt connection to parents and future—Millennial teens are beginning to equate good news for themselves with good news for their country. They often boast about their generation's power and potential.

>> *Team-oriented.* From Barney and soccer to school uniforms and a new classroom emphasis on group learning, Millennials are developing strong team instincts and tight peer bonds.

>> *Achieving.* With accountability and higher school standards rising to the very top of America's political agenda, Millennials are on track to become the best-educated and best-behaved adults in the nation's history.

>> *Pressured.* Pushed to study hard, avoid personal risks, and take full advantage of the collective opportunities adults are offering them, Millennials feel a "trophy kid" pressure to excel.

>> *Conventional.* Taking pride in their improving behavior and more comfortable with their parents' values than any other generation in living memory, Millennials support convention—the idea that social rules can help.

All these traits represent a sharp break from the traits that are associated with Generation X. Special? Collectively, Gen-X kids felt more like castaways, avoided by adults more interested at that time in rediscovering themselves. *Sheltered?* Hardly. During the Gen-X childhood, youth dangers from divorce to crime to sexually transmitted disease rose rapidly to little public concern. *Confident, team-oriented, or achieving?* No on all counts. Gen-X teens were more inclined to trust the individual, and to apologize for (or deny the very existence of) their own generation. *Pressured?* That word can't describe latchkey kids who were told to set their own standards and avoid burdening distracted adults. *Conventional?* The Gen-X childhood would better be described as "experimental," featuring a splintered and alienated youth culture in which social rules seemed pointless.

To date, these Millennial traits have been measured and tracked mostly for the eldest edge of this generation, since that's where most of the data are. As happened with Boomers born between 1943 and 1947 and Gen Xers born between 1961 and 1965, the first five Millennial cohorts (babies born between 1982 and 1986) are the trendsetters.

These oldest Millennials will, in time, tell only part of the story. This first Millennial wave, now just filling high schools and entering college, is riding the recent surge of new adult concerns about, protections for, and demands upon young people in whatever age bracket they've occupied. To the extent they are celebrated, it is mixed with adult criticism for residual Gen-Xish attitudes and behaviors. Later-born Millennials—starting with today's preteens and middle schoolers—will follow this corrective adult presence at every age. As they arrive, the older Millennial persona will be taken for granted. The new challenge, for later-born kids and their parents and teachers, will be to exceed that standard with yet further improvements in attitudes and behaviors.

Compared with Your Students 10–15 Years Ago, Are Your Elementary School Students Today. . .

	YES	NO
More racially diverse	77%	3%
More affluent	66%	10%
Healthier	35%	15%

—Asked of elementary school teachers
in Fairfax County (VA), in Teachers' Survey (1999)

Thus, *Millennials will be a generation of trends,* in which all of their traits will grow more obvious with each passing birth cohort. And most of these trends will represent *a direct reversal from the trends associated with Boomers.* From the late '40s to the late '60s, American adults deliberately relaxed their style of child-rearing. They put more emphasis on individualism and inner creativity and less on teamwork and external convention. Today's Boomers are the recognizable product of this child-rearing style. As kids, they showed, from first birth-year cohorts to last, a progressive worsening in scholastic achievement (the seventeen-year SAT

I sort of feel bittersweet about all this attention and praise that the Millennials are getting. If we Gen Xers probably share one common memory, it's how the adults in the world just forgot about us in terms of education, structure, values, and family support. And it does seem ironic and cruel that now the new kids are getting all the attention because suddenly the adults woke up and realized that we Gen Xers didn't turn out right. It's like our elders conveniently forget that they were supposed to be there for us too.

—Deanna Beppu

I distinctly remember being perfectly aware, on a conscious level, of the change in attitude toward children that happened around the early '80s, at the time it was occurring. I wondered if anyone else was, as well. And if anyone else was kinda pissed.

—Laura, Gen Xer

[W]hen I was born (1966) children were looked at as a hindrance, something to hold you back, a drag. When Millennials were born, children were a yuppie accessory, a Must-Have. Anyway, the '70s were a terrible time to grow up. . . . Thank your lucky stars and make the most of the advantage you have. —Amanda, "Official Member of Generation X"

slide was nearly all on the Boomer clock) and in most measures of behavior—crime, violent crime, suicide, self-inflicted accidents, sex, alcohol, and illicit drug use. The Millennial trends are running the other way.

Boomers started out as the objects of loosening child standards in an era of conformist adults. Millennials are starting out as the objects of tightening child standards in an era of nonconformist adults. By the time the last Millennials (in all likelihood, those born right around now) come of age, they could become the smartest youths in American history, and the cleanest-cut young adults in living memory.

We cannot predict the exact timetable for this improvement, nor even claim that it all has started (or will start) exactly with the 1982 birth cohort. The 1982 cohort is decisive because it marks a threshold of self-consciousness: These are the kids who feel part of something new. But a close look at attitudes and behavior sometimes points toward a slightly earlier or later cohort. The last five Gen-X cohorts (born 1977–81), for example, have contributed to the recent fall in the rates of youth crime and teen pregnancy—and have pioneered such Millennial trends as greater economic optimism, higher educational ambitions, and less risky career goals. In this sense, the "Generation Y" label may indeed serve a purpose—to refer to these last-wave Xers who have anticipated some of the changes that would mark the generation coming next.

Some other key trends, however, won't be fully showcased either by these "Gen-Y" Xers or by first-wave Millennials. Rather, they await the arrival of the Millennials' second wave (born 1987–91). Educational achievement is a key example. Test scores, though improving gradually for first wavers, are likely to ramp up steeply once these heavy-homeworked, super-tested, zero-toleranced kids start hitting their high school years.

Common location in history. At any given age, every rising generation defines itself against a backdrop of contemporary trends and events. Being a school-age child during the '90s—with its culture wars, new technologies, rising affluence, and civic apathy—was a vastly different experience from being in midlife during the '90s, or being a child in some earlier decade. For Millennials, the Dow Jones only goes up, people only get wealthier, and America only fights effortless wars. For them, technology rules, markets are global, government is impotent, and the gap between rich and poor is always widening. For them, no one who isn't getting direct mail from AARP has ever cared much about voting or unions or company loyalty or what goes on in Congress.

The experiences that Millennials have *not* personally known also define them. On the one hand, they've never known what it was like to grow up without miracle vaccines, eat foods without vitamin additives, entertain themselves without electronic games of immense complexity, write a term paper without internet and word processor, be barred from schools because of race or from sports because of gender, or duck and cover in nuclear war drills at school. They've never known recessions, student riots, political assassinations, red scares, or foreign crises that directly threatened the lives of their families.

So, too, have they never known pro athletes who didn't regularly shop their skill and celebrity to the highest bidder, or a sexual landscape that wasn't dotted with lawyers and deadly diseases, or a school curriculum that wasn't an ideological battleground, or a film era that wasn't vulgar and hyperviolent, or parents for whom military service was a widely shared experience, or political leaders who weren't the butt of endless jokes about corporate bribery, selling national secrets, attack ads, on-the-job sex, and spin control.

One way to define a generation's location in history is to think of a turning point in the national memory that its earliest birth cohorts just missed. Boomers, for example, are the generation whose eldest members (born in 1943) have no memory of VJ Day. Gen Xers are the generation whose eldest members (born in 1961) have no memory of John Kennedy's assassination. Millennials are the generation whose eldest members (born in 1982) have no memory of sitting in school watching the *Challenger* shuttle explode.

Starting with Boomers, the historical location of each generation's childhood can be summarized as follows. Boomers arrived during the "American High" (roughly, 1945 to 1964). Following the Great Depression and World War II, this era has defined the Boomers as a *postcrisis generation.* As Boomers were entering young adulthood, Gen Xers arrived during the "Consciousness Revolution" (roughly, 1965 to 1984). The special burdens of growing up in this era have defined Xers as an *awakening-era generation.* As Xers have entered young adulthood and Boomers have entered midlife, Millennials have arrived during the most

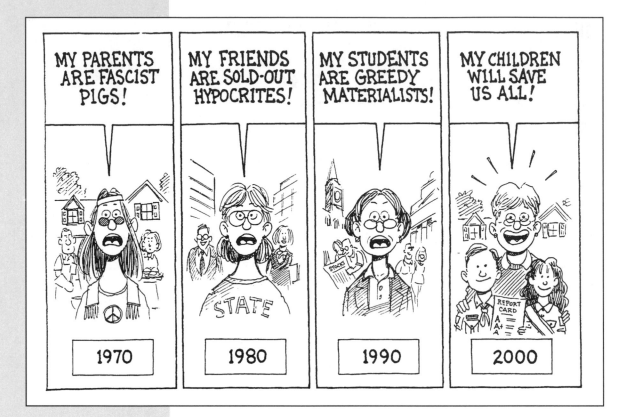

recent era, which we'll call "Culture Wars & Roaring Nineties" (roughly, 1985 to the present). This era is shaping Millennials as a *postawakening generation*.

In history, therefore, Millennials represent a sharp break from Generation X. Gen Xers can recall growing up during one of the most passionate eras of social and cultural upheaval in American history, with often painful consequences for political, economic, family, and educational institutions—and a harrowing if temporary derogation of the needs of children. All this has left a deep impression on most of today's young adults. But Millennials can recall none of it.

History also reveals Millennials as inhabiting an era of numerous trend reversals from the Boomer child years. Boomers can recall growing up with a homogenizing popular culture and wide gender-role gap in an era when community came first and family stability was strong (though starting to weaken). Millennials are growing up with a fragmenting pop

MILLENNIAL CHILDHOOD LOCATION IN HISTORY

	Boomer Childhood c. 1945–65	Xer Childhood c. 1965–85	Millennial Childhood c. 1985–today
HISTORY & EVENTS			
Era	American High	Consciousness Revolution	Culture Wars & Roaring Nineties
Presidents	Truman to Kennedy	LBJ to Carter	Reagan to Clinton
Confrontations Abroad	Korea to Cuba	Vietnam to Iran	Iraq to Kosovo
Economy	Affluent Society	Stagflation	Long Boom
Popular Phrases	Cold War Ask Not . . . Pax Americana I Have A Dream	Great Society Hell No! Limits to Growth Malaise	Morning Again Kinder, Gentler Family Values Culture Wars
TECHNOLOGY			
Electronic Products	broadcast TV 78s and LPs 8mm film vacuum tubes mainframes	cable TV cassettes and CDs VCRs transistors calculators	interactive TV streaming and MP3s DVDs microchips personal computers
Consumer Products	made in U.S.A sedans and stationwagons electric ranges room fans	imports Beetles and hatchbacks microwaves A/C units	global production minivans and SUVs delivered food climate control
Public Infrastructure	test satellites B-52s interstate highways	moon launches ICBMs telcom satellites	space shuttles stealth and smart bombs the internet

SOCIETY & CULTURE	Boomer Childhood c. 1945–65	Xer Childhood c. 1965–85	Millennial Childhood c. 1985–today
Child Nurture	relaxing	underprotective	tightening
Family Stability	high, starting to fall	falling	low, starting to rise
Family Policy Priority	needs of community	needs of adults	needs of children
School Emphasis	excellence	liberation	standards
Crime and Drugs	low, starting to rise	rising	high, starting to fall
Popular Culture	homogenizing	confrontational	fragmenting
Gender-Role Gap	wide	narrowing	narrow
Racial Goal	integration	assertion	diversity
Immigration	low	rising	high
Income Equality	rising	peaking	falling
Fiscal Tilt	to working-age adults	to retirees	to kids
Public Generosity to Poor	rising	peaking	falling

culture and narrow gender-role gap in an era when individuals come first and family stability is weak (though starting to strengthen). As a postcrisis generation, Boomers arrived just when conforming, uniting, and turning outward seemed the logical priority. As a postawakening generation, Millennials began to arrive just when diversifying, atomizing, and turning inward seemed preferable. Such reversals reflect a fundamental difference in the two generations' location in history.

How Boomers have responded to their own location is a story that is mostly written, a story replete with the most curious ironies and paradoxes. How Millennials will respond to theirs is a drama waiting to unfold, sure to reveal its own about-faces with the passage of years.

How Generations Shape History

Like all generations-in-the-making, the Millennials are being shaped by the history that surrounds them. And what in turn shapes that history? The aging of older generations.

To understand how this happens, let's lay out what we call America's present-day "generational constellation" and take another look at America's six living generations. The middle four of these—G.I., Silent, Boom, and Gen X—are the generations who have a direct formative influence on the world of today's youth. As we focus on the Millennial connection to these older peer groups, keep in mind the bygone history that once shaped them:

GENERATION	CURRENT AGE	ENTERING CHILDHOOD	ENTERING YOUNG ADULTHOOD
Lost	100 & over	Third Great Awakening	World War I & Prohibition
G.I.	76 to 99	World War I & Prohibition	New Deal & World War II
Silent	58 to 75	New Deal & World War II	American High
Boom	40 to 57	American High	Consciousness Revolution
X	19 to 39	Consciousness Revolution	Culture Wars & Roaring '90s
Millennial	0 to 18	Culture Wars & Roaring '90s	

Let's now take a look at what each of these four generations is doing with or for today's kids—and what today's kids see in each of them.

Having been proclaimed by Tom Brokaw as America's "greatest generation," the G.I. Generation is passing away gradually to fond memories. Many of those memories call to mind a generation of mythic heroism and civic grandeur—of the Americans who pulled the nation out of the Great Depression, conquered half the globe as wartime soldiers, unleashed nuclear power, founded suburbia, took mankind to the moon, and laid the cornerstones for a "Great Society" that their more self-absorbed offspring were unable or unwilling to complete.

The G.I.s' most important link to the Millennials is in the void they

What Boomers say is right for their kids will be enforced, with zero toleration for protest. Just as Boomers were "right" when exercising their freedom 30 years ago, so too are they now "right" when denying their children the same self-expression.

—*Rich Tauchar*

It's very important to us [Boomers] that our children grow up to be similarly independent thinkers, as long as they reach the same conclusions we do. —*Ivy Main*

Our parents grew up in the '60s and lived a life of rebellion. They challenged authority at every chance. Now our generation is filled with rules. —*Ian Bauer, 16*

The Boomer-constructed world of condoms and contraceptive services made sex reasonably safe, but it also made boring the culture of scoring. Will kids, always contrarian, now find another way to confound their parents? —*Jim Pinkerton, Newsday*

It's almost as if the Boomers are using us to erase the many mistakes they did while in their high school years. And also possibly erasing the mistakes of their Xer kids.   —Oscar Soto, 16

Can we for two seconds ignore the fact that you are severely unhinged and discuss my need for a night of teenage normalcy?   —Bianca, to her father, in 10 Things I Hate About You

leave behind. With the departure of what Robert Putnam calls "America's long civic generation," no other adult peer group possesses anything close to their upbeat, high-achieving, team-playing, and civic-minded reputation. Sensing this role unfilled, today's adults have stressed the teaching of these (G.I.) values to Millennial children—who themselves are gravitating toward the G.I. archetype as the only available script for correcting or complementing the Boomer persona. You don't rebel against Boomers by being *über*-Xers. You rebel by being G.I. redux, a youthful update of the generation against which the Boomers themselves rebelled, so famously, in the 1960s and '70s.

Throughout their life cycle, from Prohibition to the G.I. Bill to Medicare, the well-being of the G.I. Generation was always a high public priority for older and younger voters. In this role as well, the departure of G.I. senior citizens has created a void that '90s-era politicians have filled, pointedly, with Millennial junior citizens.

According to our Class of 2000 Survey, nearly all of today's high school seniors think of the "G.I." or "World War II" generation as a synonym for "grandparent"—though for many Millennials, G.I.s are in fact their *great*-grandparents. More important, these students associate the word "hero" more with people in their eighties (that is, with G.I.s) than with people in any other age bracket. By a lopsided five-to-one margin, they believe that this elder generation has a "mainly positive" reputation—a much greater "positive" margain than they give to any younger generation.

The Silent Generation, now straddling retirement, provides the real bulk of the Millennials' grandparents. This is the generation that was born just too late to be heroes during World War II and just too early to be youthful free spirits during the Consciousness Revolution. As heavily protected children, the Silent grew up watching older people make great sacrifices on their behalf. Reaching maturity in an era of "lonely crowd" conformism, they avoided risking their spotless reputations (hence their names) while making early and unconditional commitments to family and career. Much later, in a "midlife crisis" rebellion against these youthful promises, the Silent triggered the divorce boom and invented the hands-off child-raising style of the '70s that Gen-X kids recall as their own. No-fault divorce, schools without walls, gradeless report cards, new realism in child media, and more open attitudes about sex, drugs, and lifestyle diversity—all this prevailed while the Silent were assuming the helm of America's institutional life.

Given their life-cycle perspective, the Silent are less enthusiastic than Boomers and Gen Xers about trying to push Millennials in the direction of more protection and structure. Yet the humility and sensitivity of many in this generation, combined with their lingering guilt about family and civic duties left unperformed, has led them to take a very "involved" role in the lives of their grandchildren. Rather than emulate the G.I.s and separate into elders-only Sun Cities, the Silent are more likely to retire to swinging mixed-age town homes teeming with youthful fun. Quite unlike G.I.s, the Silent want to participate, to listen, to be (and be seen as) hip—as volunteer teachers' aides, as museum docents, as organizers of "grandtravel" trips and purchasers from grandchildren gift catalogues. Extended families are again in vogue, as Silent grandparents either move in with their grown-up Boomer or Gen-X kids or step in to take custody of Millennial kids who have been abandoned by (or stripped by government from) their natural parents.

As the wealthiest and earliest retiring generation of elders in American history, the Silent have provided younger Millennial kids with fun, indulgence, and subversive mischief in the face of more serious-minded (and workaholic) Boomer and Gen-X parents. Think of them as a generation of Bill Cosbys and Golden Girls. Gen Xers had an altogether different experience. Their typical grandparents are G.I.s, and when Xers were kids these two generations never developed a close relationship—a circumstance that inspired several amusing anecdotes in Douglas Coupland's seminal *Generation X*.

According to our Class of 2000 Survey, the Silent supply the younger tier of grandparents for today's high school seniors—but very few (only 5 percent) of their parents. Those Silents who complain that their Korean War and Civil Rights experiences have never gotten the recognition they deserve won't find much solace in our survey. Most teens (like most older people) are pretty hazy about what comes between G.I.s and Boomers and have trouble ascribing many clear personality traits to the sixties age bracket. The few traits they *can* ascribe are telling. Though less heroic than the G.I.s, the sixties age bracket received the lowest score of all generations for "selfishness" and "complaining"—an advantage over G.I.s that may be due to the late-in-life G.I. reputation for senior citizen lobbying.

On the one hand, you are bragging about your alcohol abuse and sexual exploitation of women. But on the other hand, you're saying that behavior would not be good enough for your kids.

—*Minnesota State Senator Jane Ranum, criticizing (Boomer) Governor Jesse Ventura's autobiography*

By appealing to the needs of Generation X parents, Clinton was able to eclipse their doubts about his character and show himself to be a president who made it easier for them to raise children who would turn out to be better adults than he was.

—*Dick Morris*

Show our children, by the power of our own example, how to resolve conflicts peacefully.

—*President Clinton, commenting on Columbine while NATO was bombing Yugoslavia*

I think the baby boomer parent ought to say, "I've learned from mistakes I may or may not have made, and I'd like to share some wisdom with you."

—*George W. Bush*

The Boom Generation occupies the most consequential adult role in Millennial lives. Boomers have taken the lead in most of the family and school trends—from greater protection to zero tolerance to higher standards—that mark the shift from X to Millennial nurture. First-wave Millennials are especially likely to have Boomer parents. Of our Class of 2000 seniors, 93 percent have Boomer moms and 90 percent have Boomer dads. Late-wave Millennials are more likely to have Gen-X parents.

Every generation, including Millennials, possesses biological parents spread over the prior two generations. By the time the Millennials are all born and counted, they are likely to have at least as many Gen Xer parents as Boomer parents. Throughout American history, however, the rearing of each new generation has always been dominated by the elder of two parental generations. G.I.s like Walt Disney and Doctor Spock set the tone for Boomer kids during the 1950s (though the Silent were then raising plenty of late-wave Boomers). Silent like Norman Lear and Jim Henson set the tone for Gen-X kids during the 1970s (though Boomers were then raising plenty of late-wave Xers). Likewise, Boomers like Steven Spielberg and Laura Schlessinger are setting the tone for today's kids (though Xers are now raising plenty of late-wave Millennials). Gen X will in turn set the tone for the batch of kids coming along after the Millennials—and Millennials for the batch after that.

During the Consciousness Revolution, Boomers came of age forging a lifelong reputation for narcissism, judgmentalism, and cultural dominance. When they ascended to the leadership of America's institutions, their moralistic "values" focus began to define the Millennials' childhood environment. Like all midlife generations, Boomers are seeking to create kids who complement rather than mirror their own parental persona. This requires parents and teachers to focus more on standards and teamwork (Boomer weaknesses) than on inner vision and creativity (Boomer strengths). "By intuition or design," writes Michael Sandel, "Clinton has discovered a solution: Don't impose moral restraints on adults; impose them on children."

Even when Millennial teens go along with this adult agenda, which is most of the time, they see through its double standard very clearly. And they see it not just in Bill Clinton, but in the entire "cultural elite" of his generation. To the Millennial eye, Boomers are forever demanding more of other generations (now the young) than they demand of themselves—and are forever pointing to the quality of their attitudes and ideals to excuse the shortcomings of their own behavior.

Not surprisingly, when you ask Millennials for descriptions of Boomers, two words (other than "parent") top the list: "strict" and "hypocritical." Ask for more adjectives, and you'll hear "intolerant," "self-loving," "argumentative," and the like. By a slight margin, according to our Class of 2000 Survey, Boomers get the smallest Millennial vote for "most admired." Overwhelmingly, however, Millennials consider their Boomer teachers to be the smartest, the most demanding, the hardest grading, the most focused on students' future career needs—and the most likely to talk about politics.

In its relationship with Millennials, Generation X can be divided into two halves. One half, mainly late-wave Xers now in their twenties, include most of the childless participants and performers of today's youth culture. Whatever positive qualities older Americans may ascribe to this Gen-X culture—and these are few—nearly all of them (together with many Xers) would agree that a steady diet of *Friends, Fight Club,* Nine Inch Nails, *South Park,* Woodstock '99, Tupac, Duke Nukem, Korn, and *Married with Children* is not healthy for children. Beyond pop culture, in the realm of sports or business, the impact of such undisputed titans as

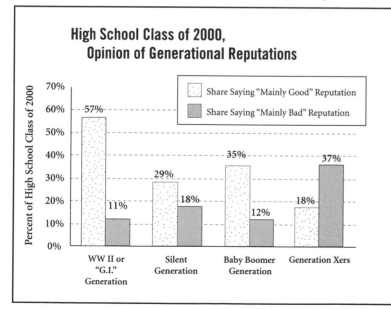

High School Class of 2000, Opinion of Generational Reputations

Source: High School Class of 2000 Survey (2000)

Gen X dressed in ripped jeans and dark, sullen, earthy tones, while the Echo Boom chooses neat styles and bright colors.

—Jonathan Last, on teenagers at a new California mega-mall

A few months ago, I had a debate with a group of Gen Xers a few years older than me about how much control individuals have over their own lives. I stated (and several of my Millennial peers agreed) that how successful people are is ultimately a product of their own effort. The Gen Xers laughed at me and told me how the world might "screw you over."

—Michael Eliason, 17

The last thing I want is for us to be known as a bunch of losers like Gen X.

—Amy Glaser, 17

Michael Jordan or Michael Dell is tarnished by Gen X's broader reputation for impatience, risk, and rootless ambition. Fairly or not, most of America regards the media and celebrity image of this generation as a negative example of what Millennials should not only avoid, but be shielded from by adults in every possible way.

Yet there is another, more numerous, praiseworthy, and consequential side of Gen X: the young-adult householders mostly in their thirties who, married or not, are parenting and raising most of today's late-wave Millennials. Through the 1990s, these Xers have transformed the attitudes of young parents toward their kids in an intensely protective direction. Where the typical Boomer parents discovered "family values" as a conscious and deliberate lifestyle choice, pragmatic Gen-X parents are drawn in a similar direction more by natural instinct—reinforced, often, by unpleasant memories of their own latchkey childhoods.

According to *Time* magazine, "Gen Xer" has come to mean "Gen Nester," as young parents invent new expedients (home schooling, telecommuting, trading extra pay for extra time, moving close to parents) to separate their children from whatever seems threatening and unreliable. For many Gen Xers, starting and maintaining a stable family can be a unique source of pride—the pride you get for achieving something that your own parents did not.

Our Class of 2000 Survey confirms that few of today's high school seniors (only 6 percent) have Gen X parents—while nearly two-thirds agree that "older brother or sister" best describes their impression of a Gen Xer. Their comments thus reflect the mixture of disdain and affection one might expect from a younger sibling.

On the negative side, these graduating seniors agree by a large margin that Gen X has the worst reputation of all living generations. This helps explain why most teenagers recoil from the X (or Y) label. Millennials also view their next-elders by four as the most selfish and complaining generation, and the least heroic. Ask for one-word descriptors, and you hear a harsh critique, with terms like *slacker, alienated,* and *punkish.* On the positive side, when Millennials compare Xer and Boomer teachers, they overwhelmingly say that the Xers are more fun to be around. Seventy-three percent of Millennials say that Xers are the most "easygoing," while only 6 percent say the same about Boomers—who are deemed to be the *least* easygoing of all generations.

These four older generations comprise the adults—in their various age roles, from great-grandparent to older sibling—who are setting the stage on which youth is about to enter. Together, they are shaping the Millennial Generation directly, through personal contact and influence on the kids' world, and indirectly, by creating an adult world that youth is evaluating with fresh eyes.

It is this adult world, with its attendant trends—rising prosperity, declining divorce, expanding technology, celebrity politics, spreading gap between rich and poor, resplendent individualism, humanitarian globalism, cultural decadence, and culture-wars crusading—that has defined the Millennial child era, and that will in time define the Millennial life-cycle trajectory. Deep into the next century, today's kids will, as grownups, recall the mood of their childhood years with some mixture of pride, embarrassment, and nostalgia in stories they tell to their own children and grandchildren.

Contrast this to the generational constellation Gen-X kids encountered during the Consciousness Revolution. During that era, America's new elders were the politically powerful and "entitled" G.I.s—who wanted to separate themselves from a burgeoning youth culture they considered alien and hateful. Entering midlife were flexible, compassionate, divorce-prone Silents, presiding over marriages and institutions they no longer fully trusted. The new young adults were the Boomers who, whether hippies or not, stood at America's cultural center, defining "cool" for all age brackets. Meanwhile, child Gen Xers were at best expected to emulate the era's call for self-discovery—or, at worst, treated as avoidable hindrances to personal fulfillment.

Likewise, contrast the Millennials' generational constellation with what Boomer kids encountered during the American High. During that era, America's new elders were the self-reliant, impoverished, and politically powerless Lost Generation, whose members kept their distance from politics while taking great satisfaction in the rising affluence of young postwar families. Entering midlife were the G.I.s, building their "power elite" reputation as can-do builders at a time when Americans were better known for what they built than what they thought. The new young adults were the Silent, merging uneventfully into their suburban duties while raising only isolated voices of careful dissent or subversive humor. Meanwhile, child Boomers were being reared with a new indul-

Big Bird is passé. . . . It's too fast; the world it presents is too unsettling. . . . After all, the first generation to grow up on Sesame Street has now come of age—and look how they turned out: alienated, cynical, completely devoid of any kind of attention span.

—Adam Cadre

GENERATIONAL CONSTELLATIONS SINCE WORLD WAR II

Phase of Life	Boomer Childhood Era: c. 1945–65	Xer Childhood Era: c. 1965–85	Millennial Childhood Era: c. 1985–today
Entering Elderhood	Tough *Lost*	Entitled *G.I.s*	Empathic *Silent*
Entering Midlife	Powerful *G.I.s*	Experimental *Silent*	Judgmental *Boomers*
Entering Young Adulthood	Conformist *Silent*	Narcissistic *Boomers*	Pragmatic *Xers*
Entering Childhood	Indulged *Boomers*	Overlooked *Xers*	Protected *Millennials*

gence by adults who worried about America's cultural sterility and groupthink—and were inclined to heed Dr. Spock's suggestion that "we need idealistic children."

Each of these constellations tells a special story, creates a special mood, and thereby sets in motion a very distinctive rising generation of youth.

This life-cycle dynamic has been changing throughout American history, and it will continue to change in the decades ahead. Into the Oh-Ohs and beyond, the generations will change as they move up the age ladder—and so will the phase-of-life behaviors. This is why one can say, with confidence, that Millennials are a new generation whose persona will, in due course, likewise reveal itself as new.

But what we can expect Millennials to be like? Exactly *how* will they be unlike Boomers or Xers?

To answer these questions, we need to ask: How will Millennials rebel against the elder-built world? One often hears it said that every generation rebels. In a manner of speaking, that is true. But it is far from true that every new batch of young people rebels as Boomers and Xers have come to know the word. The G.I. Generation didn't. And the Millennials won't, either.

CHAPTER THREE

the coming millennial revolution

the coming millennial revolution
the coming millennial revolution

How we are is gonna change
We'll make this world a better place
　　　　　—CLEOPATRA, "Life Ain't Easy"

"What were you doing in '62?" asked a famous ad for *American Graffiti.* That was, in Boomer parlance, "the year before," the last tranquil year before John Kennedy's assassination, which signaled the beginning of the "real sixties." Exactly what *were* Boomer teenagers doing back then? Much of the time, they were flocking to surfer movies, where they watched Annette Funicello and Frankie Avalon jiggle and giggle by day, hug and smooch by night, and give every indication that they were about to merge seamlessly into a date-and-mate world of tract houses, corporate jobs, and stay-at-home moms.

These images said absolutely nothing about what Boomers would be, and do, over the next decade. And that's a striking fact. When most Boomers look back at their life cycle from today's vantage point, they call to mind their collective story as an organic and continuous biography. (And what a heavy trip it's been, man!) Ask today's 50-year-olds about their younger years, and they'll likely insist that the Consciousness

Many people I know of in my generation have a strange thought— that we seem to be different from older people in a weird way. I don't know what it is, precisely, but I think it is not necessarily a bad thing.
　　　　　—Chris Loyd, 17

The generation gap seems to be closing. 　　*—Melina Beck,*
The Wall Street Journal

I wish we could be regular kids.
—Buffy, in **Buffy the Vampire Slayer**

Revolution was a necessary reaction to what they first experienced as children and teens. But looking forward from those days satirized in Pleasantville, when the future conjured up the friendly sterility of Epcot Center, nobody made that same logical jump forward, projecting that, *of course*, the current teenagers would someday reject it all.

Why do so few people, even so few experts, know how to anticipate generational change? It's because, whatever the era they inhabit, they invariably assume that the future will be a linear extension of the recent past—and that somehow the next youth generation will lose the capacity to reinterpret the world and forge its own fresh path. That never happens, either with societies or with generations.

Always a Surprise

Each time, it seems, Americans get taken by surprise when a new generation arrives. Let's reflect on how this happened on each of the last three occasions.

Back around 1940, with a world war stirring, Americans were counting on young adults to be strong, loyal, even heroic. When General George Marshall declared the nation's troops to be "the best damn kids in the world," he was implicitly setting a high standard for those who came next. Through the immediate postwar years, the presumed path of youth was toward the doing of big deeds—joining all-powerful armies or history-bending class struggles. The late '40s invasion of returning G.I.s onto college campuses perpetuated the image of youth as world conquerors. No one foresaw *Fortune* magazine's chiding of the first mostly nonveteran college class (of '49) as passive, compliant, "taking no chances."

Two decades later, around 1960, most experts assumed that the onrushing bulge of children known as the "baby boom" would grow up even more pliable and conformist than that era's gray-flanneled young adults, just then starting to chafe under the name "Silent." College presidents were predicting a new crop of serious technocrats—and the youth culture was still crammed with ditzy doo-wop, folksy hootenanny, and Pat Boone's sanitized rock'n'roll. The big-name social scientists—from Margaret Mead to Erik Erikson—saw no hint of the youth revolution about to explode.

Then, around 1980, youth experts began commenting on the emergence of a post-Boom "baby bust" generation. What would they be like? More idealistic, more progressive, and more rebellious (according to the consensus), extending what *American Demographics* termed "an ongoing trend away from material aspirations toward nonmaterialistic goals." That seemed like an easy verdict at a time when Elton John and Diane Keaton were among the biggest-hyped youth icons—but it would be rudely overturned when the scrappy, pragmatic, and free-agent Gen-X persona began emerging a few years later.

Since then, another two decades have passed—and now marketing consultants are hawking an image of new youth as "Generation Y"—just like Gen X, except more accelerated, more diverse, more cynical, and more edgy. It's not going to happen. Brace for another big surprise.

Which "Bill" might you pick as godfather for your child?

Bill Cosby	76%
Bill Murray	11%
Bill Gates	10%
Bill Clinton	1%

—*"Mom and Pop Culture Survey,"* Child *(April 1999)*

How All Generations Rebel

Clearly, generations do not ultimately turn out as they first appear, as teens, to adults or even to themselves. Outwardly, what the Silent were around 1940, what Boomers were around 1960, and what Xers were around 1980 were reflections of cultural images and a social mood created by their elders. If you go back through American history, you'll see a similar pattern, albeit in times when the popular culture was propagated through simpler technologies.

This realization points to an important question. If it is true (as Alexis de Tocqueville once wrote) that "in America, each generation is a new people," is there any pattern or dynamic that determines *how* each generation will be new? Or, to ask it another way, are there general rules that

The best way to rebel is for me to dress formally all the time, be honest, respect my elders, love my country and drive a used Toyota, instead of the prerequisite SUV or suitable car for the under-35 bracket.

—Chris Loyd, 17

They were like, "You want to go where? What is on your mind?"

—Tanika Griffith, 16, describing her parents' reaction to her decision to enroll in a military high school

"I FEEL SORRY FOR KIDS TODAY. THEY'VE GOT NOTHING TO REBEL AGAINST!"

The Millennial generation really seems to be diverging from the Xers, and from the other generations. As a Millennial myself, I can see this clearly. —*Robert Reed, 17*

Sometimes I think everyone aged 20 to 40 sounds like a cast member on Friends. —*Chris Loyd, 17*

Unlike the grunge point of view of Generation X, there is more optimism in this group.

—*Judy McGrath, MTV president*

I think we're more preppy. They liked that grungy stuff. It was, like, cool for them not to take a shower.

—*Alexandra Fondren, 13*

explain how any given generation (such as Millennials) can be expected to come of age "rebelling" against an elder-built world?

Yes. These three basic principles apply to any rising generation in non-traditional societies (like America) that allow young people some freedom to redirect society according to their own inclinations. Each generation:

>> solves a problem facing the ***prior youth generation,*** whose style has become dysfunctional in the new era;

>> corrects for the behavioral excess it perceives in the ***current midlife generation;*** and

>> fills the social role being vacated by the ***departing elder generation.***

Let's look at how these rules can be applied to today's three older generations.

The *Silent* rebelled by solving a problem facing G.I.s by the McCarthy era—the reflexive habit G.I.s had developed (since 1932) of mobilizing endlessly to direct their society toward the right collective future. Rather than be punished by another grand whipsaw of history, the Silent learned to take the new order for granted, keep their heads down, fit in, and develop expertise "within the system."

Meanwhile, the Silent corrected the excesses of the tough and laconic generation that had shaped them in childhood (Harry Truman's Lost Generation, born 1883–1900). In keeping with today's Korean War *M*A*S*H* stereotype, these young men and women did indeed turn toward refinement and sensitivity, and a less hard-boiled, more therapeutic view of the world.

In so doing, the Silent stepped into the social role vacated by the passing of the Progressive Generation, born from 1843 to 1859, the likes of Clarence Darrow (who died in 1938), Louis Brandeis (1941), and John Dewey (1952). Once the children of the Civil War, the Progressives had aged, as elders, into the most compassionate, cautious, and rights-fixated generation of the New Deal and World War II.

Older generations first noticed the Silent, as kids, at the height of the war, in news stories about Sinatra-worshiping bobby-soxers at teen canteens. The media began defining a new youth culture around 1950, when

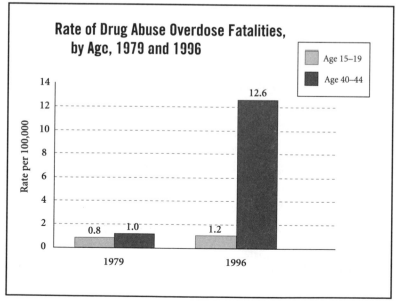

Rate of Drug Abuse Overdose Fatalities, by Age, 1979 and 1996

Rate per 100,000

Age 15–19
Age 40–44

1979: 0.8, 1.0
1996: 1.2, 12.6

Source: U.S. National Center for Health Statistics (1999)

[A] group of 4th and 5th graders in Aurora, Colorado . . . decided to collect money to buy back slaves in the Sudan. One of the children said, "What are we going to do about this?" Unimaginable 15 years ago. Boomers would have gotten high and contemplated it. Xers would have written angst-filled songs about it. The Millennials, only 10 years old, are doing something about it. When asked why the "leaders" aren't doing anything, a child replied, "If they can't . . . we will." —Robert Hoffman

My Boomer eighth-grade social-studies teacher once told our class that we must be dismayed by the fact that our parents have gone so far and that there is little left for us to do. The class was outraged. One student told him that his generation did nothing to improve the world, and that it was going to be our responsibility to fix it.

—Michael Eliason, 17

KID: *Mom, I'm class president.*
MOM: *I knew that.*
KID: *Oh yeah? Name one of my reforms, just one.*   —Doonesbury

older veterans finally vacated their college campuses. The Silent began creating newly personal and sophisticated music (like small-group jazz), jokes (like in *Mad* magazine), and points of view (such as William F. Buckley's) that challenged the gung-ho secularism of older G.I.s. They broke out as a generation over the next five years, with vintage rock'n'roll, several wry youth publications, obsessive yearnings about sex amid widespread teen virginity, movies about angst-ridden "juvenile delinquents" (*The Blackboard Jungle, Rebel Without a Cause*), and the emergence of the "beat generation" with its poetry readings and coffeehouse culture. By 1960, when a Princeton professor was fired for writing *The Unsilent Generation,* the subject had become tired.

Boomers rebelled by solving the obvious problem facing the next-elder Silents, their too-complete capitulation to the prevailing conformity. Boomers threw bricks instead of polysyllabic warnings. They screamed "Hell no, we won't go," trashed campuses and inner cities, radicalized both the left and right in politics, and took pleasure in flouting convention.

Boomer youths assailed what they firmly believed were horrible G.I. excesses—too much optimism, rationalism, and group-mindedness—and corrected them by turning toward rage, spiritualism, and self. Did they regard G.I.s as a "greatest generation" deserving of vast monuments? Hardly. Back then, Boomers were more likely to condemn G.I.s as America's *worst* generation, to throw pig's blood at their institutional walls.

At the time, Boomers filled the social role vacated by a passing generation that had enjoyed a lifelong reputation for spiritual wisdom and indomitable self-esteem. This was the Missionary Generation, born from 1860 to 1882, the likes of Albert Einstein (died 1955), W. E. B. Du Bois (1963), Robert Frost (1963), and Douglas MacArthur (1964).

Boomer kids were discovered in the years between Sputnik and Kennedy, with a surge of zany new toys (hula hoops), dances (the twist), and spunky child characters (Dennis the Menace). They took possession of the youth culture in the mid-1960s, with the Beatles' first U.S. tour, Berkeley's Free Speech movement, and a series of inner-city riots. Before they had assumed any particular name, Boomers became the focus of impassioned national attention in the late '60s, with the Summer of Love, the Chicago riots, Woodstock, Kent State, the George Wallace campaign, anti-Vietnam agitation, angry new currents in rock'n'roll, and much talk of a "generation gap" between college-age (Boomer) kids and their middle-aged (G.I.) parents. In time, the youth frenzy ebbed. Generations, especially any talk about the rising one, became a tired subject by 1973—after giving 18-year-olds the right to vote failed to make any perceptible difference in national politics.

Gen Xers rebelled by solving the problem facing young-adult Boomers, whose loud crusades no longer made sense in an era of individualism when the "Establishment" no longer seemed very powerful or controlling. Doing what Boomers then wouldn't or couldn't, Xers learned young to become free agents, to rely only on one's small circle, and to pursue the tangibles of life.

They corrected the hypersensitive excesses of the Silent Generation, then entering midlife, by turning toward a sharp-eyed pragmatism. Where the trusting Silent had once bonded young to institutions whose complexity they mastered, cynical Xers took pride in self-reliance and in rejecting complexity in favor of the bottom line—or sound bite.

In so doing, Gen Xers filled the social role vacated by the passing of the Lost Generation born from 1883 to 1900, the likes of Dorothy Parker (died 1967), Harry Truman (1972), Norman Rockwell (1978), and Henry Miller (1980). In the 1988 movie *18 Again!*, 92-year-old George Burns and 22-year-old Charlie Schlatter provide a revealing glimpse at the emotional affinity connecting these old and new "lost" generations.

Though not then permanently named or in any other way celebrated, Gen Xers were discovered right around 1980, a year in which colleges noticed a smoother and less argumentative type of freshman, the number and quality of military recruits soared, and young hockey fans startled the media by chanting "USA! USA!" at the winter Olympics. In the mid-'80s, Xers took over the youth culture with the spread of new innovations in popular music (rap, new wave, MTV), a spate of dark-themed youth movies by older directors (*The Breakfast Club*, *St. Elmo's Fire*), a new sitcom presence (Michael J. Fox in *Family Ties*), and a new on-campus interest in investment banking and other moneymaking jobs—especially anything entrepreneurial or involving cutting-edge technology. Gen Xers broke out around 1990, with grunge, mainstream rap, a flurry of books and films by and for themselves, and Douglas Coupland's novel *Generation X*. By 1996, when politicians turned their entire focus to the Millennials, the Gen-X subject felt so tired that Coupland felt obliged to report "Generation X is over."

My 12-year-old came down to breakfast, stole the sports page from under my eggs and said, "So, Pops, who you dissin' this week?" I gave him my hurt-and-stunned look. He stuffed a half box of Frosted Flakes in his mouth and said, "Yurnghh alghays rippinngh smmmbundy."

—*Rick Reilly,* **Sports Illustrated**

Because the nation is so focused on what is wrong, it becomes impossible to see what is right.

—*Sarah Fulton, 17*

Our generation, my friends at least, are tired of hearing the negative aspects of society and are disgusted by the lack of moral values our leaders have and want that to change.

—*Katharine Emerson, 17*

Nature has a certain order. The ants pick the food, the ants eat the food, and the grasshoppers leave!

—*Princess Atta,*
in A Bug's Life

The Coming Millennial Revolution

Will Millennials rebel? Of course. To predict the timing and nature of their rebellion, let's apply these same rules that worked so consistently for these three earlier generations.

As the new youth generation, Millennials will reveal themselves as the answer to the central problem facing Xers, the prior youth generation. They will show what can be done about over-the-top free agency, social splintering, cultural exhaustion, and civic decay in an era when Americans are increasingly yearning for community. The Millennial solution will be to set high standards, get organized, team up, and do civic deeds.

Millennials will also correct for what today's teens perceive are the excesses of middle-aged Boomers—the narcissism, impatience, iconoclasm, and constant focus on talk (usually argument) over action. Millennials can do this, over time, by turning toward community, patience, trust, and a new focus on action over talk. *That's* the path by which today's kids can rebel against aging ex-rebels. Instead of growing up to be "Generation Y" or "Echo Boomers," Millennials will grow up to be *de*-X'd *anti*-Boomers.

Wait Until Married to Have Sex?

Very important: **53%**

Somewhat important: **23%**

Not important: **22%**

—*Survey of 12- to 14-year-olds,* Time *(July 5, 1999)*

In so doing, today's kids will fill the very consequential social role now being vacated by the departing G.I.s, the likes of Lucille Ball (died 1989), Jimmy Stewart (1997), Joe DiMaggio (1999), Ronald Reagan, and millions of World War II soldiers and Rosie-the-Riveters—the role of civic achievers, institution builders, team players, *heroes.* "I am the doer, he's the talker," remarked 73-year-old Bob Dole in one of his 1996 debates with Bill Clinton—words to make a person wonder when Americans will

"BUT DAAAD, I DON'T WANT TO GROW UP TO BE SMUG LIKE YOU"

again see a generation fill in for the "doer" in its national conversations. The answer: when Millennials grow a bit older.

Per the experience of earlier generations, the coming of age of the Millennial Generation is likely to take place in the midst of a profound shift in America's social mood, a shift that will match and reflect the new generation's persona. For Millennials, this shift will focus on the needs of the community more than the individual, so it is likely to induce large-scale institutional change. Thus, the word *rebellion* is not entirely appropriate. The word *revolution* might better catch the spirit of what lies ahead.

On what timetable can the coming Millennial revolution be expected? Once again, the pattern for earlier generations offers some pretty good clues:

>> *The public discovery of a new generation* typically occurs fifteen to twenty years after its first birth year. For Boomers, this happened in the late '50s. For Gen Xers, the late '70s. For

I think of the old classic movies, and then today I see movies like The Water Boy, Austin Powers, *and* There's Something About Mary, *and I think they are outrageous.*
—Andrea Greenwich, 17

60 Minutes *showed an 8-year-old genius named Greg who's about to graduate from high school, and who turns off the TV or leaves a movie if and when he hears the third curse word.* —**Lis Libengood**

Are we cynical? No, why should we be? —**Lorena Cortese, 17**

As a group, today's teens are infused with an optimism not seen among kids in decades. (It doesn't hurt to have grown up in a time of relative peace and the longest economic expansion in U.S. history).
—**Newsweek**

Millennials, the schedule should be the late '90s—and, in fact, the first discovery year for Millennials was 1997.

>> *The new generation's full possession of the youth culture* occurs twenty to twenty-five years after its first birth year. For Boomers, this happened in the mid-'60s. For Gen Xers, the mid-'80s. For Millennials, it should happen around the middle Oh-Ohs.

>> *The new generation's complete breakout,* when it attracts maximum social attention, occurs twenty-five to thirty years after its first birth year. For Boomers, this happened in the late '60s. For Gen Xers, the early '90s. For Millennials, it should happen around 2010.

>> *The ebbing of public interest,* when the generation's identity becomes a tired subject, occurs thirty to thirty-five years after its first birth year. For Boomers, this happened in the mid-'70s. For Gen Xers, the mid-'90s. For Millennials, it should happen in the Oh-Teens.

Clearly, Millennials have a long way to go before their generational revolution will fully make its mark. Do not be misled by the barrage of teen-oriented generational marketing that arrived in the late '90s. Even if the discovery (and naming) of Millennials is occurring with greater media fanfare than was true for any earlier generation in American history—including Boomers—there's no reason to believe that the timetable will vary from the historical norm.

But if Millennials can be expected to mature at ordinary speed, that doesn't mean they will be a generation of ordinary significance. Using history as a guide, we believe the emerging Millennial persona will mature over time into a peer group destined to play a pivotal role in the future of the American nation—and, perhaps, the world. Deep into the next century, if these historical patterns are predictive, the Millennial life cycle will acquire, with the benefit of hindsight, a sense of logical continuity—as was true with the Silents, Boomers, and Gen Xers, in their own turn.

This future is the focus of Part Three. Here, let's simply mention one example of how this sense of life-cycle continuity may emerge: uniform clothing.

Back in the late '80s, many Boomers in charge of kids began to look with genuine favor on school uniforms—an idea that would have been condemned as fascist twenty years earlier. In a number of cities, uniforms were first introduced in 1988 for the first graders of that cutting-edge Class of 2000. At first, these uniforms seemed perhaps nothing more than a momentary gesture. Yet, by the late '90s, school uniforms became a defining symbol of a much larger effort to clean up child behavior—first in elementary schools, next in middle schools, finally in high schools. From Gap ads to soccer fields, meanwhile, standard-issue clothing was broadcasting a clear message about the non-X-ness of America's new kids.

Will the Millennial uniform trend stop there? Don't count on it. Around the time leading-edge Millennials graduate from college—especially if this coincides with economic (or other) trouble—no one should be surprised to hear serious proposals for a national service corps. Americans of all ages will be so familiar with seeing this generation regularized, to positive effect, that compulsory uniformed service could feel fitting and right even to aging Boomers who once spent long years dodging the draft.

Further down the road, one can picture this rising generation in young-adult "general issue" clothing reminiscent of the G.I.s into whose role they are stepping—clothing that may come to symbolize large-scale deeds. Move ahead still further, and one can imagine how the Millennials' uniforms may come to represent, to their own kids and grandkids, a collective grandeur far beyond anything else in the living memory of that era. If so, aging Millennials may come to define, in the minds of their juniors, a huge directional turn in world history dating back to this generation's first arrival at the tranquil end of the twentieth century. Should this come to pass, future historians may look back on today's school (and soccer) uniforms as harbingers of monumental deeds that came later—much as America's first Boy and Girl Scout uniforms pointed toward the later exploits of the young generation (of G.I.s) who wore them.

Back in the late 1980s, those brightly colored outfits on 6-year-olds seemed no more consequential for kids at that time than William Gaines's *Mad* magazine or Bill Haley's "Rock Around the Clock" did back in the early 1950s. Time taught us otherwise for Boomers. So, too, could time teach us otherwise for Millennials.

The history of this nation's generational rhythms suggests that it's not just possible, but probable, that Millennials will emerge as anti-Boomers. Consider how . . .

Though I am not old enough to vote, I am writing this on behalf of my generation. . . . The American people have chosen to become selfish, and my generation—your children—are growing up seeing the highest authority in America, a man who cannot control himself. . . . And if we cannot trust the man our parents elect, can we trust our parents?

—Christopher, 16,
in a letter to the Arkansas Gazette

Boomers are hypocrites.

—Bobby Rhatigan, 17

My sister's friend was walking home last week when she came to an intersection where a Millennial crossing guard was helping a fellow schoolchild. My sister's friend headed off across the street without bothering to use the crossing guard. The Millennial kid shouted out, "Use the crossing guard, you flower-shirted freak!" Clearly this generation is bringing more with it than many of us technically wanted.

—Matthew Elmslie

I want you to stop trying to control my life just because you can't control yours.   —Kat, to her father,
in 10 Things I Hate About You

Boomers followed a generation that was criticized in youth for being too placid and conformist. Millennials are following a generation criticized for being too kinetic and splintery.

Boomers grew up when institutions felt too strong, individuals too weak. Millennials are growing up when institutions feel too weak, individuals too strong.

Boomers were kids when rationalism ruled and spiritualism lay dormant. Millennials are kids when spiritualism rules and rationalism lies dormant.

Boomers looked up to a midlife generation of "power elites" whose lives were motivated by an agenda—big deeds to be done. Millennials look up to a midlife generation of "cultural elites" whose lives are motivated by a message—big ideas to be expressed.

Boomers recall a time when "uptight" middle-aged folk were pleased to meet kids who could let go a little. Millennials know a time when "cool" middle-aged folk are pleased to meet kids who can control themselves.

In a durable society, the rebellion of every new youth generation serves an invaluable function: curbing the excesses and complementing the strengths of older generations—who may not be getting the kids they expect, but who usually get the kids they need. No generation can fairly be described as better, or worse, than any other. They simply have different locations in history, and thus different needs, desires, fears, obsessions, blind spots, opportunities for greatness, and tendencies toward tragedy. Each generation does what it must, within the context of the history and generational constellation into which it is born.

Millennials are no exception. They will surely find their own path to rebellion, do what history requires, blossom into a young-adult generation extremely unlike Boomers or Xers, and move on. Those who follow them, including their own children, will repeat this process—correcting the Millennials' own excesses.

Let's hold further talk of the future for later. In the next part of this book, we address the more immediate questions: Who are Millennials, *now?* How are they being raised and schooled? What are they thinking and doing? What are they watching, hearing, and buying? Why? And what new patterns do they reveal?

The answers to these questions may not be what you think.

PART TWO

who they are

CHAPTER FOUR

The Baby Boomlet *(demography)*

The Baby Boomlet (demography)
The Baby Boomlet (demography)

I was born to make you happy . . .
I'd give you my world.
      —*BRITNEY SPEARS, "Born to Make You Happy"*

The early 1980s, those years of pain and panic to many heartland manufacturers, brought sweet relief to any firm whose product was swallowed, worn, or nibbled on by America's very youngest consumers.

The reason? Annual U.S. births were back up to a steady 3.6 million for the first time since LBJ was president. In the mid-1970s, when births had fallen almost all the way to 3.0 million, Gerber Products had desperately experimented with a new line of adult food, which bombed. Now the company was rescued by a tide of new babies—bearing good news not just to the premier baby-food producer, but also to any other company that made cribs, strollers, rockers, safety seats, PJs, dolls, safety gadgets, and toddler books and videos.

The two ways that a society provides for its future are its level of physical capital accumulation and the number and the quality of its kids.

                    —*Frank Levy,*
              University of Maryland

Children Are From Heaven
          —*book title (1999), John Gray,*
          author of Men Are from Mars,
          Women Are from Venus

Typical Fears of Parents for a Child's Health

Late 1940s: Polio, diphtheria, whooping cough, meningitis

Late 1990s: Meningitis, ear infections, colds, brain tumors, cancer

—The Oregonian *(October 29, 1997)*

Not only did America have more of these babies, but their parents were inclined to spend more on them. Thanks to two incomes, a new breed of "yuppie" parents often had more disposable cash than the parents of the '70s. Affluent, early-retiring grandparents were in a new mood to dote. Among families that were less well off, a new kids-come-first attitude was likewise settling in. And communities nationwide were taking a new interest in trying to provide each child with some minimal standard of material welfare. Helping this cause, a rising share of these babies were firstborns, a special focus of family attention. Firstborns ate 11 percent more baby food, exulted Gerber planners, because they didn't have older siblings urging them to eat "grown up" food so early.

Most experts anticipated that this birth surge would be minor and short lived, but it turned out to be neither. Throughout the 1980s, the annual nursery tallies kept on climbing—until by 1990, in many regions, hospitals looked with alarm at overcrowded delivery rooms and fee-for-service pediatricians became hard to book. Meanwhile, in classic "pig-in-a-python" fashion, the larger number of the early-'80s babies began filling and overfilling America's elementary schools in the late '80s, middle schools in the mid-1990s, and high schools in the late '90s. Teacher shortages, classroom shortages, gym and rec-room and summer camp shortages—all of these became the early '90s staple of the education press, just as hype about teen spending became the late '90s staple of the business press.

Owing to these demographic trends, and the stories about them, the best-known single fact about the Millennial Generation is that it is large. In total number, including all immigrants, Millennials may ultimately exceed 100 million members—nearly a third more than the Boomers. Even in native births per year (expected to average almost exactly 3.9 million), Millennials will tower over Gen Xers, Boomers, and every earlier

generation in America. In 1982, nearly a decade before anyone discussed the Millennials as a social generation, journalists were regularly using phrases like "Baby Boomlet" and "Echo Boom" to describe their larger numbers.

In one important respect, these terms were (and still are) misleading. They implied that the large number of Millennials is mainly a matter of arithmetic—as though a "baby boomlet" mechanically had to follow a "baby boom." This is not the case. What gave rise to the large number of Millennials was, mostly, the passionate desire of their parents *to bear and raise more of them.*

The large numbers that quantify this generation are therefore an extension of the early-'80s shift in adult attitudes toward children that began to shape the Millennials as a generational persona. The same is true for the parental preparations that preceded their births, the names they received, the special care showered upon them as babies, and the

Boomers, whose self-absorption has long been ridiculed, have finally managed to get over themselves. They have found a new object of their affection. They don't need self-love any more. They've got Mini-Me.

—**David Plotz,** *slate.com*

I don't get it. Doesn't she know that I would do anything for her? I mean, I love her. She is the reason that I was born. —**Adele,** *describing her teenage daughter,* **Anywhere But Here**

extraordinary improvements in health that have so far followed them through their life cycle.

Simply put, adult Americans fell in love with babies again in the 1980s, a decade in which people committed themselves to having, caring for, and celebrating children—for reasons peculiar to how Boomers and Gen Xers then felt about themselves as America entered a postawakening era.

Thus have Millennial kids become the largest, healthiest, and most cared-for child generation in American history.

Behind the Rising Numbers

After reaching a postwar nadir around the time of Watergate, annual U.S. births ticked upward in 1975 and kept rising through the rest of the decade. There was no mystery about this rise. Demographers had long predicted it. They knew all along that the post–World War II "baby boom," which began in 1946 and peaked in the late 1950s, would inevitably enter its main childbearing age bracket, at which time it would generate a "baby echo"—an extra number of births. By most Boom-era estimates, the echo would start in the mid-1970s and run out of gas by the mid-'80s. Births would thereafter start falling again.

Unchanged fertility means unchanged at every age from 1975 levels. Source: National Center for Health Statistics (2000)

But once the national birth rate leveled off at about 3.6 million between 1980 and 1983, it did something demographers did not expect: The rate didn't start to drift down. Instead, the birth rate rose again, to 3.8 million in 1987, 4.0 million in 1989, and 4.2 million in 1990. By the late 1990s, the annual number of births had stabilized at around 3.9 million—*roughly 20 percent higher than if the fertility of women at each age had remained at mid-'70s rates.* This fertility boost provided a quantitative exclamation point to the mood shift that was producing all those new infant seats in all those new minivans with all those new "Baby on Board" signs. Quite without anyone planning it, the "Me Decade" '70s ran smack into the "family values" '80s, an era of resplendent natalism.

During the 1980s, older Boomer women (past age 30) were mostly responsible for this fertility boost. This started with first-wave Boomers in the early '80s and moved on to later-born cohorts as the decade progressed. By 1990, first-wave Xers in their late twenties were also joining the shift—plus a (temporary) surge in teen births. Since 1975, the only age groups *not* to have experienced a lasting upward fertility shift have been women in their teens and early twenties.

All this transpired, in part, because one generation opted to retime its births over its life cycle. Boomers, having refused to become young parents in the 1970s, chose to become older parents in the 1980s—while Gen-X moms reverted back to the earlier birth-age norm. So one way to think of the Baby Boomlet is to compare it with the original Baby Boom—which occurred because homecoming G.I.s had their babies late while young Silent parents tried to get a head start in the newly stable era by having them early. Substitute Boomers for G.I.s, Gen Xers for the Silent, the Consciousness Revolution for the Great Depression and World War II, and you can see how Millennials fit in the nation's demographics. Whereas an economic and military crisis had caused the G.I.s to delay having their (Boomer) babies, a cultural upheaval caused the Boomers to delay having their (Millennial) babies.

Some experts argue that baby booms and busts, because they often just reflect the parental timing of births, aren't a good indicator of how adults truly feel about having more children. However, this argument assumes that people see the future as clearly as they see the past. Until a fertility rebound happens, no one knows how likely it is, since not even the delaying parents can foresee that a more baby-friendly era is yet to come.

You'd think that every baby toy was made to increase IQ points. . . . Cloth cars, for example, are good for "opening up your child's eyes to the meaning of size relationships." Translation: They come in small, medium, and large.

—**U.S. News & World Report**

Debra Mills, a neuroscientist at the University of San Diego who consulted on the development of "Brilliant Beginnings," a $40 book-and-CD kit for parents interested in "nurturing the genius in your child," acknowledged there are no studies linking brain growth to specific infant activities. Nevertheless, she said, the kit is a useful guide to the enriching experiences a baby needs.

—**The Washington Post**

Words like "smart" and "genius" show up a lot in toy names [because] Mom and Pop have to be persuaded that buying them will improve the kid's chances for MIT.

—*Robert La Franco,* **Forbes**

Parents with a coldly utilitarian focus on the infant cerebellum—parents pestering their toddlers with Japanese-language flash cards—are at least paying attention. —*George Will*

Women in the early 1940s could not count on the '50s mood change, just as women in the early 1970s could not count on the '80s mood change—which is why both baby rebounds came as such surprises.

There is good evidence, moreover, that Gen Xers are aiming to have more babies than Boomers entirely apart from the issue of timing. Women born in the early '60s are the first cohorts on record to tell Census surveyers that they intend to have more babies *over their lifetime* than earlier-born women. Other polls have consistently indicated that Gen Xers, from youth onward, have placed more importance on family formation as a future goal than Boomers did at like age. Back in 1974, at the height of the Boomer youth era, only 55 percent of college freshmen declared that "raising a family" was an "essential or very important" life goal. In 1998, near the end of the Gen-X youth era, the share of college freshmen who felt that way reached 78 percent, an all-time high.

A special bond connects older Boomer and younger Xer parents with the children they have raised since the early 1980s. This bond did *not* develop gradually as these kids passed from birth through childhood. No, it was there from the beginning, starting with the act of conception and the birth of millions of babies. Had parents not chosen to defy the behavioral trends of the prior era, this bond—and, no doubt, many of these babies—would have never existed.

America's New Love Affair with Babies

During the era of Gen-X babies, adults went to great efforts *not* to produce children, resulting in a vast new demand for contraceptive technologies and for sterilization and abortion clinics. During the Millennial baby era, by contrast, adults have gone to great efforts to produce them. This has made fertility technology one of today's hottest medical frontiers. Sterilization rates, which rose sharply in the 1960s and '70s, plateaued in the middle '80s and have since fallen. The national abortion rate, which ramped up during the Gen-X baby era, hit a peak in 1980 and has since declined (through 1996) by 22 percent. Meanwhile, the share of all births declared to be "unwanted" by their mothers has also declined—with an especially sharp drop in unwantedness by black mothers.

The "wantedness" of these Millennials is further illustrated by the huge rise in births by women well into midlife, for whom having a baby poses added health risks and financial burdens. From 1981 to 1997, the fertility rate of women aged 45 to 49 rose by an astounding 88 percent. In that latter year, the Census Bureau began to report births (114 in 1997) by women in their fifties. The rising number of older mothers, plus the spreading use of fertility drugs to encourage pregnancies, has led to a predictable explosion in the number of multiple births. From 1980 to 1997, while the number of singleton babies rose by 6 percent (itself a significant rise), the number of twins rose by 52 percent and the number of triplets by 404 percent. With growing frequency, Americans hear about "super-moms" giving birth to as many as seven Millennials at a time—like Iowa's Bobbi McCaughey (whose celebrity was buoyed by her postbirthing book, *Seven from Heaven*) and Texas's Janet Chukwu, seven of whose "Chukwu octuplets" survived.

For those who couldn't have a normal pregnancy, science had new answers. The first U.S. infant conceived *in vitro*, Elizabeth Carr, was born in Norfolk in December 1981. All later *in vitro* babies have been Millennials. In 1986, only one clinic offered this service. By 1997, 227 did. Every year, Millennial-making technologies have advanced. In 1983, the first surrogate mom donated an egg. By 1997, five thousand fertile woman had donated eggs, a jump of 50 percent over the previous year—in one case, turning a 63-year-old into an expectant mother. Egg prices, once as low as $3,000, soared as high as $50,000 for an ovarian purchase from an attractive, high-IQ student from a prestigious university.

> **Old Advice:** "Put him outside in the sun."
>
> **New Thinking:** "Protect your baby from harmful rays."
>
> —*"When Mom Knows Best,"* Child *(May, 1999)*

This late-in-life quest for pregnancies has been propelled by a near-doubling of the rate of childlessness among 40- to 44-year-olds, from 10 percent (of Silent women) in 1980 to 19 percent (of Boomer women) in 1998. The highest childless rates are among women who are employed, affluent, white, and *not* living in the Sunbelt. In part, this rise reflects a growing number of older women who have decided that they are happier childless, a decision many Silent women felt less free to make. Yet it also

The percentage of births to first-time mothers in their 40s has doubled since 1950, but is still only 1 percent.
—*Census Bureau*

Imagine being 48 years old and having quadruplets. —*John Kiely, professor of pediatrics*

points to a growing number of Boomer women who postponed child-bearing in their younger years before finding out, too late, that the option had closed—often because either they or their partners were no longer fertile. Although Gen-X women are likely to pull this childness rate down in the years ahead, it will probably remain high by historical standards.

Midlife childlessness, combined with a newfound love of children, has produced a rapidly rising demand for adoptable babies in the face of a rapidly declining domestic supply. Back in the late 1960s, two of every three unmarried mothers gave up their babies to adoption agencies. Today, now that the social stigma facing unmarried moms has waned, only one in twenty unmarried moms lets her baby go. The waiting list for U.S.-born Caucasian infants has grown to at least five years, from the time a couple is accepted by a domestic agency. This has prompted a boom in costly private agencies and, especially, overseas adoptions—which have quadrupled through the Millennial child era. In the early '80s, most children came from South Korea, Central America, and South America. Today, the biggest donor countries are, in order, China (girls only), Russia, South Korea, Guatemala, and Romania. The cost per child is now $15,000 to $30,000, plus travel. Some of these children have disabilities, and no children are loved more.

Percent of College Freshman Having . . .

	1973	1998
Mother with college degree or higher	20%	41%
Father with college degree or higher	32%	44%

—The American Freshman, *UCLA (1997–98)*

A number of further demographic changes are working to the advantage of these new Millennial arrivals:

Older parents. Since the middle of Gen X, the average age of mothers at birth has climbed from its twentieth-century low point (age 24.4 in 1974) to its all-time U.S. high (age 27.0 in 1997, and rising). Older parentage has long been associated with better child behavior and higher achievement.

Smaller families. Despite their rising number per birth cohort, the Millennials are spread over more families—meaning that they are growing up, on average, in the smallest families ever. From first-wave Gen Xers to first-wave Millennials, the median number of siblings related to each child has fallen from two to one (meaning that over half of all kids today have one or no sibling). Smaller families mean more parental time and resources per child.

More firstborns. Arriving after a birth dearth, a historically high share of this generation—roughly 40 percent—are firstborns. By the time their parents stop having children, about 10 percent will find themselves to be singleton or "only" children. According to those who study birth order, firstborn and only children are associated with higher achievement, identification with parental authority, aversion to risk, and (some say) social conservatism.

More parental education. Without question, today's kids have the best-educated parents ever. One Millennial in four has at least one parent with a four-year college degree or higher. Kids born in the late '90s are the first in American history whose mothers are better educated (by a small margin) than their fathers.

Slowing down of family breakup. The ongoing rise in single-parent families remains a major challenge for the Millennials. But this growth has slowed down since the Gen-X child era, and the legions of single parents now include fewer divorced moms and more never-married moms—a trend that is creating a very different family environment.

What's in a Millennial Name?

The names given to people as babies don't reflect their own hopes and dreams, but rather the hopes and dreams of their parents and the era in which they are born. As such, those names remain forever fixed in their grown-up minds as a testament to the mood of their childhood era. "Go, Amanda! Nice shot, Justin!" will forever ring in Millennials' ears as memories of their childhood '90s, much as "Dick and Jane" books have for Boomer memories of the '50s.

We went through Dallas–Fort Worth airport customs last week. They had three bathrooms. Three? There was one entrance for men, one for women, and one for "family" restrooms for adults and small children.

—*Jon Paugh*

Nowadays, you can go to a middle-school choir concert, peruse a program with two hundred names, and not see two first names spelled the same way. The diversity of these names partly reflects global immigration, but also the Boomer and Gen X penchant to bestow unique and crafted names on their offspring. Back in 1951, the top ten boys' and girls' names accounted for 25 percent of all names. In 1999, those lists together accounted for just 12 percent.

Names have become harder to pronounce and spell. Where nearly all the top names for Boomer males have only one syllable (Bob, Bill, John, Dave) and for Boomer females only two syllables (Mary, Susan, Karen, Linda), always with standard spellings, the names Boomers prefer for their own kids are polysyllabic, complex, and often hard to spell. Not since 1991 has any one-syllable boy's name made the top ten. Gen Xers have amplified this trend—especially African-American single moms, many of whom have given their babies totally original phonic names (as in a family of three daughters named Mica, Mooca, and Moca). One can imagine adult Millennials, tiring of the need to spell out their names (a problem their parents seldom faced), returning to simpler names for their own children.

Where G.I.-given Boomer names reflected a yearning for a world that was modern, simple, democratic, and friendly, Boomer-given Millennial names reflect a yearning for a world that is traditional, pious, mysterious, romantic, even mystical. Many of these new names are taken from the Old Testament, "American Girl" stories based on musty Victorian diaries, Celtic lore, and other archaic sources. Parents seldom shorten them into easy nicknames: Matthew and Joshua become Matt and Josh less often than they would have in earlier generations. Gen-X parents are continuing this pattern with a new set of gender-concealing names such as Ashley, Tyler, Taylor, and Madison.

Madison, now the third most popular name for girls, is perhaps the most curious new choice. Apparently, it became popular not because of any interest in the fourth U.S. president, but because the *Splash* mermaid, played by Daryl Hannah, chose her name by reading a Manhattan street sign. (The name Hannah is close behind, at number six.) The twentieth century's most enduring names are Sarah for girls—that's the only top-50 girl's name that was at all popular sixty years ago—and Michael for boys, which has ranked number one without interruption from 1964 through 1998. In recent years, that may reflect the popularity of Michael Jordan, whose last name has also been on the rise for both boy and girl babies. Meanwhile, several of the discarded names and nicknames once common among G.I. and Silent Generation men have found a new venue, as names Boomers and Gen Xers give their male dogs. *Here, Fred! Down, Skip! Sit, Butch!*

Second-Generation Immigrants

In California, what are the two most popular baby names these days? José and Maria. That, in turn, mirrors one of the most important demographic realities affecting today's kids. A very large share of them are the offspring of a steeply rising immigration wave that has been sweeping America since the mid-'60s—making them the generation with the largest share of "second-generation" immigrants in eighty years.

Clearly, one important precondition for the rising immigrant inflow was America's societywide embrace of more tolerant attitudes toward minority groups during the Consciousness Revolution era, combined with declining public support for the institutions entrusted with policing the nation's borders. Much of this boom has been from regions abroad that have not contributed significantly to American immigration before. By 1990, half of the inflow came from Latin America (one-third from Mexico alone), another one-fourth from Asia, and only 15 percent from Europe. Between 1970 and 1990, the number of Americans born in Latin America rose from 1.8 to 8.4 million. Meanwhile, the number born in Asia rose from 800,000 to 5.0 million.

To date, only 2.4 million Millennials, or 3.5 percent of the entire generation, are themselves immigrants. But some 14 million Millennials are the *children* of immigrants, mostly Gen Xers. That number has grown by half since 1990—and now accounts for an astounding 20 percent of this entire generation, up from around 6 to 8 percent for Boomers. More Millennials can be expected to immigrate to the United States in future decades, of course, but in all likelihood Generation X will remain the largest *first*-generation immigrant cohort group of its time (known for preserving their native cultures), with Millennials making a mark more

The United States of the 21st Century will be undeniably ours. Again. It's Manifest Destiny. . . . We are not only numerous, we are also growing at a rate seven times that of the general population.

—*Christy Haubegger, publisher,* Latina *magazine*

Her lips are devil red And her skin's the color of mocha

—*Ricky Martin,* "Livin' La Vida Loca"

as *second*-generation immigrants (who tend to be more assimilationist). Not since the early years of the twentieth century, back in the G.I. child era, can you find such a large percentage of U.S. kids with first-generation immigrant parents.

By the standard measures of American life, the Millennial children of immigrant parents face daunting challenges. A third of them live below the poverty line. A third of them have no health insurance. Three in five immigrant children (and two in five second-generation-immigrant children) live in overcrowded housing. Yet balancing such hardships are, typically, parental memories of much darker and less hopeful times in native countries plus close families that know how to thrive despite material hardships. Despite their poverty and lack of health-care access, for example, the babies of immigrant mothers actually have a lower mortality rate than those of native-born mothers—due to healthier diets, less drug abuse, stronger marriages, fewer bouts of emotional depression, and more reliable support from relatives.

Child Immunization Rate *(full series):*

1992: **55%**
1996: **75%**

—*Donna Shalala, Secretary of Health and Human Services (April 10, 1999)*

True to the tradition of second-generation immigrants, Millennial children of foreign-born Gen Xers can enjoy certain advantages that native-born kids may lack. Their families tend to be stable, with breadwinners dedicated to the work ethic. They often reveal very high achievement aspirations, get arrested less, and score higher on school tests than third- or fourth-generation immigrants within their same ethnic group. Their health tends to be better than that of native-born kids. The biggest fear of many immigrant parents is not poverty, but watching their children become drawn to the American youth culture, which from an immigrant's perspective can appear destructive of religion and family. Even so, many immigrant workers who initially intended to return to their native country have ended up staying here once they realized the new possibilities in life their Millennial children are likely to enjoy.

As a group, Millennials appear to fit the usual pattern of second-generation immigrants. Many of them want to trade the language and culture of their parents' nationalities for the common elements of their new home. Roughly half of these second-generation immigrant kids—one-tenth of the entire Millennial Generation—do not speak English at home, but a study by the Russell Sage Foundation concluded that these kids are showing "rapid linguistic assimilation" across all ethnicities and socioeconomic levels.

Because Latino immigrants have been so numerous, and because their fertility rates are high (about double the native-born American average of two kids per mother), the new immigration wave has significantly enhanced the Millennial birth boom, especially in the '90s. This can be tracked by looking at the geographic distribution of the baby boomlet. Through the mid-'80s, annual births rose in all but four states, and by more than 10 percent in 22 states. But once rising immigration (mostly to the Sunbelt) began to overlap with internal migration by young families (also mostly to the Sunbelt), the boomlet became geographically lopsided. From the mid-'80s through the late '90s, California, Texas, and Florida accounted for roughly two-thirds of the total birth surge. Add Arizona, New York, and Illinois, and you have the geographic nexus of Millennial brownness.

These states are becoming quite familiar with a new Millennial family demographic: the "mixed status" family, anchored in the United States by a child citizen. Roughly half of all children of immigrants (that is, 10 percent of all Millennials) are living in families in which at least one parent is not a U.S. citizen. In New York, 15 percent of Millennials live in such families; in California, 30 percent; in Los Angeles, 47 percent. Through the '90s, several laws were changed to the advantage of "mixed-status" child citizens, entitling them to a vast array of cash payments and government services (including health care), which are usually denied to their undocumented parents.

Thanks to this recent immigration surge, Millennials have become, by far, the most racially and ethnically diverse generation in U.S. history. Nearly 35 percent of Millennials are nonwhite or Latino, versus only 14 percent of G.I.s. Not much of this change comes from African-

The fact that [Russian children] had arrived in this country without English was much less important than the fact that they came from educated, middle-class backgrounds and had been taught early study habits that made them good at school.

—*Sylwia Kapucinski,*
The New York Times Magazine

Let us say someone earning $2,000 per year in Guatemala in 1980 immigrates to the U.S. If this person ends up in a U.S. job that pays $10,000 per year, he would certainly be richer. However, since $10,000 is in the poverty rate for the U.S., the number would show up in U.S. statistics as both an increase in the poverty rate and earnings inequality.

—*Robert Nelson,*
Forbes

Americans, who gain little from immigration and whose fertility rate has fallen in recent decades. This "browning of America" is partly Asian but mostly Latino. Among Millennials, Latinos of all backgrounds are the largest minority group (16 percent), followed by blacks (14 percent)—making this the first U.S. generation in history in which blacks are no longer the largest of all racial and ethnic minorities. In four states (Hawaii, California, New Mexico, and Texas) and the District of Columbia, white Millennials are in the minority. And in Los Angeles County, Latino Millennials are a numerical majority. "The civil rights slogan of African Americans was 'We Shall Overcome,'" notes Christy Haubegger, 30-year-old founder of *Latina,* a bilingual magazine for young women. "Ours is going to be 'We Shall Overwhelm.'"

Regardless of their skin color, and regardless of the diverse national origin of their parents, Millennials share the common bonds of being more wanted, protected, and cared for than the Gen Xers who preceded them. Nowhere is this better illustrated than in the great concern that parents and governments have shown toward their health.

The Rising Well-Being of Babies

The story of Millennial health starts from conception. No generation has been tended with such care through pregnancy. Starting in the mid-1980s, when prenatal classes began to be featured on TV sitcoms, the share of expectant mothers who went through Lamaze training (or its equivalent) rose sharply—from one in four in 1987 to one in two by 1992. Today's expectant mothers treat their *in utero* Millennials with unprecedented fuss. They take prenatal vitamins. They worry about their diet and exercise. They even worry about their worrying—and train themselves to avoid stress. Since 1990, the number of pregnant women who smoke cigarettes has fallen from 18 percent to 13 percent. Prenatal alcohol use has similarly declined.

The share of women who use intensive prenatal care has doubled, even if much of this rise has occurred among the well-educated, affluent women whose babies are less at risk. But baby health does not always reflect socioeconomic standing. Of all racial and ethnic groups, the healthiest babies belong to Southeast Asian immigrant mothers. The newborns of unmarried black mothers continue to encounter an unusually high number of risk factors, which has recently become the focus of new government attention. In the late '90s, a federal "Healthy Start" program began targeting communities with high infant mortality rates and sponsored the first-ever prenatal hot line.

When the moment comes to welcome the newborn Millennial, a mother today is able to select from among an ever-widening array of options, from the high-tech choice of induced births, now nearly one of every five, to such low-tech choices as midwifery, home birth, even new-age birthing tanks. Often, Boomer and Gen-X parents choose some blended birthing process, a uniquely '90s blend of high-tech and mother nature extremely unlike the way the parents themselves were pulled by forceps into the world a few decades ago. If for any reason a newborn is truly unwanted, civic leaders or church groups no longer urge policies that put the baby at risk in order to shame or punish the mother. Many communities are setting up "safe haven" programs where distraught parents can safely deposit their babies, no questions asked, rather than abandon them to die.

Death Rate per 10,000 U.S. Births:		
	1946	1996
For mothers:	16	1
For infants:	338	72

—*U.S. National Center for Health Statistics (1999)*

This has helped further reduce infant death. Throughout the twentieth century, U.S. infant mortality has steadily declined by about 3 percent per year—or by nearly 50 percent from the first to last cohort of every twenty-year generation. In this respect, the Millennial record since 1982—3 percent per year improvement—is merely average by historical standards.

Yet there's a story behind this number. In previous decades, much of the improvement in infant mortality was due to dramatic high-tech advances like incubators and infant surgeries, which prevent death immediately after birth. By the time Millennials came along, new easy fixes were getting harder to locate, despite huge new sums spent on elaborate care

We used to blame childhood accidents on fate or God's will or "stuff happens." Now we believe the adult is responsible for the child's safety. Accidents are really preventable injuries. —Heather Paul, *National Safe Kids' Campaign*

(like the "surfactants" now used to protect the lungs of preemies). In 1970, a two-pound had only a 5-percent chance of living. By the mid-1980s, 90 percent of the two-pounders were surviving, at an average cost of $100,000. Through the Millennial birth years, the survival rate for tiny babies has remained at that high level, but has not advanced much further.

Where America has seen stunning improvement during the Millennial baby era has been in the prevention of infant death *after* thirty days, when parental love and care can be far more important than surgeons or high-tech intensive care units. Health experts marvel over the stunning parental compliance to warnings in the early '90s about Sudden Infant Death Syndrome (urging parents not to let their infants sleep facedown). From 1992 to 1997, the rate of SIDS deaths dropped by half. Overall, for all persons between the ages of 30 days and 5 years, the U.S. child-mortality rate fell faster in the 1990s than in any earlier decade since World War II.

Mixed in with this good news is a not-so-good trend toward more preterm deliveries and "low" and "very low" birth-weight babies. This is a deceptive trend, though, because in past decades many of these babies would not have survived—either because medicine could not have saved them or because parents and doctors would not have bothered. Now it can and they do. The broadest measure of a newborn's health is the Apgar score, by which pediatricians routinely measure how loudly babies cry, respond to touch, and so forth. The share of American babies receiving a "healthy" Apgar score rose from 59 percent in 1985 to 67 percent in 1995, much of it thanks to healthier pregnancies.

The Rising Well-Being of Kids and Teens

The recent adult crusade against all the causes of youthful illness and death has benefited older kids, too. Through the Millennial child era, the mortality rate has declined significantly for every youth age bracket, with an especially sharp 15 percent decline in the teenage death rate during the 1990s. Compare this with a 20 percent *rise* in the teenage death rate during the 1960s, back when young Boomers were driving fast around Dead Man's Curve and getting high in Itchycoo Park.

Accidents are always a major cause of death for kids—and for Millennials, accidents of all kinds are down. All the infant car seats, bicycle helmets, poison hotline stickers, kidproof pill caps, and the myriad other child safety devices have made a real difference. Entire companies, and local consulting trades, have grown up around the new demand for more baby-safe households. Federal recalls of child products (swallowable toys, collapsing cribs, and baby walkers that tumble down stairs) have become frequent and well publicized.

Environment poisoning is way down, as kids have become central to the nation's progress against pollution. If the air and running water in most regions has been getting cleaner, it's thanks in part to adults responding to ads featuring kids. Newsweeklies still run fretful stories about children and lead poisoning, yet fewer than 5 percent of today's Millennial toddlers have lead levels in their blood above 10 micrograms per decaliter—a threshold exceeded by 90 percent of Gen-X toddlers in the late 1970s. Public authorities are moving with vigor against industrial and medical uses of mercury. The U.S. Environmental Protection Agency has been setting pesticide exposure limits with explicit regard to child health. Pediatricians are now handed a new "green book" on child envi-

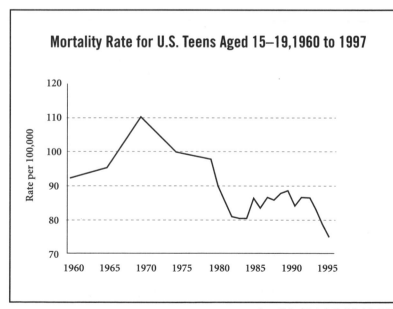

Mortality Rate for U.S. Teens Aged 15–19, 1960 to 1997

Rate per 100,000

Source: National Center for Health Statistics (2000)

Even kids' bodies have changed: Whereas Gen X celebrated the thin, frail torpor of heroin chic, nearly all the kids at The Block still have a healthy smidgen of baby fat.

—Jonathan Last, describing a new mega-mall near Los Angeles

Teenage boys consume an average of three soft drinks a day, triple the amount from 20 years ago.

—abcnews.go.com

Before long, Generation X may be replaced by Generation XL.

—Laura Beil, on rising rates of child obesity

ronmental risks to accompany their traditional "red book" on infectious diseases.

Vaccinations are up. After an early-'90s scare, with the brief return of old scourges such as mumps and whooping cough, full-series immunizations have risen into the 80–90 percent range, due largely to the refusal of public schools to admit kids who lack proof of them. Millennials are routinely protected against diseases (including measles, mumps, chicken pox, rubella, and hepatitis B) against which their parents were never immunized. The level of teen AIDS (nearly all involving HIV acquired at birth) peaked in 1993 and is slowly declining. Pregnant women are now routinely tested for AIDS, and those who test positive are treated with drugs that significantly reduce the risk to their fetuses.

Despite the one in seven children who lack health insurance, routine medical care is better for Millennials than for any earlier child generation. Physician visits are up. Heart disease, anemia, epilepsy, and blindness are all down. Teeth are whiter, straighter, healthier. Physicians now test ears of newborns, so immediate treatment can begin for those with any hearing impairment. Eyes are sharper, with ophthalmologists advising parents to put sunglasses on their 3-year-olds. Skin is softer, thanks to

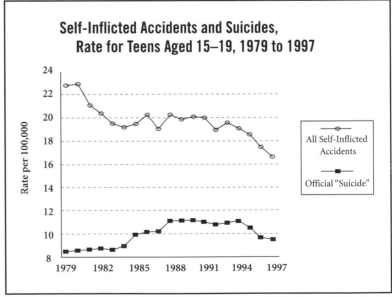

Source: U.S. National Center for Health Statistics (1999)

super UV-block sunscreens and doctors who warn parents about the life-long ill effects of child sunburns. Sick days lost by eighth and tenth graders have declined through the Millennial school era. Stature continues to climb, although at a slower pace than for Xers—indicating that Millennials may be reaching the natural limit. And contrary to popular impression, the average age of sexual maturity for girls—today about 12.5—has shown no downward trend. It remains the same for Millennial girls as for Boomer girls in 1960.

Kids' emotional health appears to be improving. Controversy rages over whether this is linked to the more aggressive use of medication to treat kids diagnosed with mental or emotional problems. But the trend itself is unmistakable. Until recently, many health experts had practically given up hoping for any turnaround in the teen suicide rate, which had been steadily rising since the late 1950s—that is, through the adolescences of Boomers and Gen Xers. But in the mid-1990s, just as the first Millennials reached their teens, this rate turned a corner and began heading down, for both sexes and for blacks and whites alike. Because suicide is often not a clear-cut cause of death, pathologists often like to compare any change in the suicide rate with trends involving apparent accidents over which the victim has some control (shootings, falls, drownings, and so on). With the Millennials, these accidents are decreasing too, suggesting that the suicide decline is no statistical accident.

Where Millennials do face a number of new health and safety risks, many are widely regarded as the unintended side effect of something adults are trying to do for their benefit.

>> Kids have been prescribed so many antibiotics, to treat everything from earaches to pinkeye, that they are now threatened by new bacteria that acquire resistance to those drugs.

>> Mental retardation and some other serious chronic conditions are slowly rising, perhaps due to the rising share of older moms having babies and the rising share of very premature or very low-birthweight babies who now survive.

>> Passenger-side auto airbags have killed several dozen children.

Ritalin, Ritalin, seizure drugs, Ritalin. . . ." So goes the rhythm of noontime as [an East Boston school nurse] trots her tray of brown plastic vials and paper water cups from class to class, dispensing pills into outstretched young palms.

—The New York Times

Generation X and Boomers took pot, cocaine, and LSD. Millennials take Prozac and Ritalin. The difference: Other generations took drugs so they could be messed up. Kids today take drugs so they can be normal.

—"Voices of a New Generation," geocities.com

Just as a pair of glasses help the nearsighted person focus and see the world more clearly, so can medication help the person with ADD see the world more clearly.

—Edward Hallowell and John Ratey, Driven to Distraction

>> Heavy school backpacks, stuffed with books, are causing some back injuries and drawing complaints from kids and pediatricians.

>> Joint injuries are plaguing girl athletes, whose participation in competitive contact sports has been encouraged by parents and schools. Arthritis looms as a problem for their young adulthood.

>> Repetitive stress injuries of the arms and wrists now afflict some teenagers who spend long hours keypunching on computers.

Three child afflictions have grown dramatically over the Millennial child era:

Asthma. From 1980 to 1994, the reported rate for asthma among children under age 4 has risen by 160 percent; and among children

"DID YOU FORGET TO GIVE HIM HIS RITALIN TODAY?"

aged 5 to 14 by 75 percent. Office visits and prescriptions for asthma have skyrocketed, and many school clinics are now outfitted with cots and inhalers. Adult asthma has also increased, but by not nearly as much.

Obesity. When health experts choose a fixed ratio of height to weight that defines 5 percent of children in 1960 as "obese," they find that by 1994 the incidence of obesity had risen to 12 to 14 percent for grade school kids—roughly a 250 percent increase since the days of Boomer children. Broader measures of "overweight" show similar increases. Many of these kids also have elevated cholesterol, high blood pressure, type-2 diabetes, and other heart-disease risk factors that are associated with excessive weight. As with asthma, adult obesity has also increased—but again, by not nearly as much.

High School Students Taking a Daily Gym Class

1991:	42 percent
1997:	27 percent

—Newsweek *(August 2, 1999)*

Attention Deficit Disorder (ADD). An estimated 3 to 5 percent of school-age kids—one or two students per classroom—are now diagnosed with ADD (or its "hyperactive" variant, ADHD). Experts think the ADD/ADHD affliction rates have risen sharply over the past two decades, but no one knows how much, since the diagnosis is based on subjective factors. Ritalin (alias methylphenidate, a mild stimulant related to cocaine) has shown some success in treating these disorders. Since 1990, Ritalin prescriptions have risen eightfold, and some 3 million Millennial kids—roughly 80 percent of them boys—are believed to take the drug regularly. In the late '90s, doctors began prescribing stimulant therapy for ADHD at younger ages—at age 5 or 6 rather than at age 7 or 8. "As we hurry kids along and put more expectations on them, they're going to display more symptoms of ADHD and I think there's a tendency to start treating them younger," says Mark A. Stein of the Children's National Medical Center in Washington, D.C.

There is no ironclad explanation for the rising incidence of any of

Social conformity and mental health are becoming the same terms. The person with a different perspective is seen as a candidate for medication.

*—**Father who refused teacher suggestions that his 7-year-old daughter be medicated for ADHD***

Many of these [ADD] cases probably wouldn't even come about in a classroom that was thoughtfully designed for typical boys' temperaments . . . one in which the teacher understood that so much of boys' outward agitation and rowdiness is often just masked emotional pain.

*—**William Pollack,** Real Boys*

these three child afflictions. Yet one common Millennial thread ties them together: All have been directly and credibly linked to the more structured, regimented, and indoor lifestyle of today's children and teens—a lifestyle that results in less free play at recess, less unsupervised exercise, and less unorganized outdoor activity.

The link is easiest to recognize for obesity, since a more controlled lifestyle that lowers the metabolic rate is likely to be followed by weight gain. The link for ADHD has been hypothesized by many doctors—and can be intuited by any parent who has noticed how serene many unmedicated kids (boys, especially) can become after a long day of vigorous activity. As for asthma, weight gain has long been known to trigger symptoms. Beyond weight, experts are focusing on two other possible triggers. The first is too much youth contact with indoor pollutants—perhaps created by today's sealed, energy-efficient homes. The other is *too little* contact with germs which, combined with comprehensive immunizations and frequent use of antibiotics, does not allow the young person's immune system to mature normally.

Today's preferred response to any threat to children nowadays—prophylaxis, enclosure, rules, inactivity, and composure (chemically induced, if necessary)—may on balance be helpful to kids, but with the side effect of exacerbating these high-profile maladies.

One circumstance is shared by every Millennial affliction. Once discovered, a child problem soon becomes a public priority. To guard against drug overprescription, the U.S. Food and Drug Administration recently set child-dose limits for every drug. To deal with asthma, the federal government recently established children's health centers at eight universities. Automakers now must give airbags "off" switches. Even backpack solutions are being studied. Across the board, all levels of government are becoming more activist and effectual in protecting Millennial children.

On health and safety issues, Millennials have emerged as generational *public property* to an extent far beyond any other living generation at like age, with the significant exception of the G.I.s. Today's 80- and 90-year-olds spent a lifetime watching their major needs—from child-era nutrition to Depression-era jobs to postwar housing to old-age health—become nationalized, largely at the expense of other generations. The same agenda-setting public preoccupation that riveted on the G.I. (elder) age brackets in the 1960s and '70s has clamped on to Millennial (child) brackets in the 1980s and '90s.

New Millennial health and safety priorities seldom produce much partisan wrangling—mainly because every time the debate first stirs, those who wish to short-shrift children invariably end up losing. Culture-wars arguments persist, but for Millennials, both sides' agendas join in a cocoon of protection. One side defines child needs as a civic issue requiring bigger public services, while the other side defines them as a moral issue requiring firmer rules to motivate better private behavior. To which most Americans say: *You're both right.* So, through the '90s, both pro-child agendas, liberal and conservative, were put in place. Through the Millennial-child era, government has offered carrots to kids and sticks to parents, again and again—exactly what government so plainly did *not* do during the Gen Xer child years.

Through the '80s and '90s, as American parents bore and raised these special children, they hoped that other Americans—from neighbors to leaders—would give top priority to the physical well being of these kids. These neighbors and leaders have not let them down. The result is the largest, healthiest, most cared-for youth generation in living memory.

Parenthood having become the new religion of the aging yuppie class, for a new parent to acknowledge unhappiness or dissatisfaction of any kind is blasphemy.

—**Michael Kimmelman,**
The New York Times Magazine

kinderpolitics (political economy)

kinderpolitics (political economy)
kinderpolitics (political economy)

*Sometimes when I'm sad, I sit and watch
the power station.*

—*TAMMY, in* Election

n anti-child spirit is loose in the land," Sylvia Ann Hewlett wrote in *When the Bough Breaks,* published (in 1991) just as the oldest Millennials were turning nine. "True, some children continue to be raised in supportive communities by thoughtful, attentive parents, but the larger fact is that the whole drift of our society, our government policies, and our private adult choices is toward blighting our youngsters and stunting their potential."

Even when she wrote it, Hewlett's message was becoming so widely believed that it served less to *inform* readers about a problem they didn't know than to motivate them to *do* something about it.

Americans understood that they were living in a newly individualistic era, and they liked the openness, affluence, and lifestyle freedom it seemed to bring into their lives. Yet poll after poll showed that they also worried about America's weakening sense of national cohesion and looked with special alarm at how unmet community needs were endangering the lives

Save the Next Generation!
—*editorial,* Los Angeles Times, *after
the 1991 Rodney King riots*

*This child does not need drug
education. That child needs
protection, that child needs order, and
that child needs love.*

—*William Bennett,
on a crack-house child (1990)*

It takes a village to raise a child.
—*Hillary Clinton*

of their children. Already in the '80s, they were mobilizing public leaders (especially at the local level) to pay more attention to small children. By the mid-'90s, as first-wave Millennials grew older and as Hewlett's message became mainstream, one major newsweekly invented a new word—*kinderpolitics*—to describe the growing voter determination to translate America's fears about kids into aggressive public policies that would protect their health, stop their crime, improve their learning, filter their media, and perhaps, over time, shape them into positive examples of civic virtue.

The Millennials' first perception of the public world and the adults who run it has thus been dominated by two basic elements: first, by a confident individualism, which kids see reflected both in rising personal optimism and in a booming free-market economy; and second, by a disturbing social fragmentation, which kids see reflected in the vast distance now separating persons and families—by income, race, language, and lifestyle. Meanwhile, adult efforts to resolve this challenge by retooling America's political economy toward youth have issued in a third perceptual element: The Millennials' dawning awareness that they have been earmarked to supply the sense of community their parents cannot.

What the Millennials have noticed, upon first glimpse of the adult world in the '90s, has been entirely unlike Boomers' first glimpse in the '50s. Boomers also grew up in an era of rising affluence—but that affluence was widely regarded as institutionally planned in an era of growing income equality, a strengthening middle class, and serious worries about too much conformism. Boomer kids were not supposed to furnish answers to civic institutions in disarray; instead, they were supposed to raise questions for civic institutions that had grown monumental.

These Millennial impressions bear even less resemblance to those of child Gen Xers in the '70s. Back then, the individual was at war with the establishment. Polls showed Americans hugely discontented with their personal lives and with the various unwanted burdens placed upon them by family and society. The economy churned, sputtered, stagflated, and disappointed just about everyone. Young Xers got the message: They weren't here to furnish questions or answers, but simply to stay out of the way and focus on the immediate and practical.

The era of the Millennial child dawned when individualism had tri-

umphed and when the new economy was releasing a hundred million income-earning free agents, prompting Apple ads to declare on nationwide TV that "1984 Won't Be Like *1984*"—an Orwellian prediction Millennials never knew about until well after it was repudiated. Suddenly America witnessed the emergence of a brash new breed of 30- to 40ish Boomer—the workaholic, market-oriented, antitax, antibig, high-tech, PC-toting, Dockers-jeaned, Reagan-voting "yuppie" of 1984—and, often, a new dad or mom too. Fifteen years later, one can point to that year, and that Boomer, as heralding a turbocharged economic upswing and a fantastic social unraveling that defines, thus far, the alpha and the omega of the American experience to this rising generation.

Parents of poor kids are better educated and working more than at any time in the last twenty years.

—*Caitlin Johnson, connectforkids.org*

If we were a nation of white suburban kids, we'd still have the second highest rate [of child poverty] among western industrialized nations.

—*J. Lawrence Aber, National Center for Children and Poverty*

Millennials and the Long Boom

On August 12, 1982, around the time the very oldest Millennials were still crawling on carpets, the national economy was swamped in a bad recession and downwind of a decade of stormy bear markets. That day, the Dow Jones Industrial Average closed at 776.92—lower (in real dollars) than it had closed on any day since 1953. Anyone who hasn't been living underwater knows what's happened since then. Over the next fifteen years, the Dow rose to well over 10,000—a ninefold improvement, even after adjusting for inflation and even ignoring the still-faster rise of high-tech companies on the NASDAQ.

So did fate decree that the entire Millennial childhood should coincide, thus far almost perfectly, with the most monumental financial boom in American history. Whether or not they deserve it, anyone has to admit that, as a generation, they are lucky.

Millennials have never, on the whole, witnessed economic trouble. During the Gen-X child era, from 1965 to 1984, the U.S. economy experienced an average of ten weeks of recession per year. During the Millennial child era, since 1985, it has experienced an average of two weeks of recession per year. And those two weeks were all due to a single Gulf War downturn that was so quick and mild that Millennials may fairly be described as the first generation ever to reach age 18 without even a single recollection of an economy-wide bust.

During the Xer child era, the overall trend in the unemployment and inflation rate disappointed the nation by rising. Kids grew up hearing about national leaders getting cashiered for the failure of their economic policies. During the Millennial child era, the overall trend in the unemployment and inflation rate has delighted the nation by falling—to levels unseen since the early 1960s. Kids now grow up hearing about voters who want to deify the Fed chairman.

A major force behind the Long Boom has been a gradual rise in the personal satisfaction adults derive from their work—in part, perhaps, because they now feel freer about when, how, and where they work. This has fueled a dramatic rise in dual family incomes and longer average workweeks—especially among women. Seven of every ten mothers with children under age 18 are now in the labor force, up from six in ten in 1985 and four in ten in 1970. This trend has been augmented by the surge in women's education, giving Millennials kids the best-educated moms in U.S. history. Kids today can watch their (and their friends') moms ascend to positions of influence and power that would have been unimaginable to most previous generations. When Boomers were children, working wives rarely outearned husbands. When the first Millennials were born, one in six did. Today, nearly one in four does.

By 1997, the share of children with no resident parent in the labor force declined to the lowest figure ever recorded (9 percent). For single-mother families, many spurred by a new welfare law, this share fell to 28 percent from 39 percent in 1985. Back in the early '80s, Americans looked with pity at the grindstone workweek of the typical Japanese worker. In 1999, the International Labor Organization reported that Americans now lead the world—including Japan—in hours worked per capita.

Unlike young Gen Xers, young Millennials see workaholism as a pervasive condition of the adult world. On the positive side, this has delivered a bushel of dollars to their doorsteps. During the Xer child era, productivity and family wages went from robust growth (through

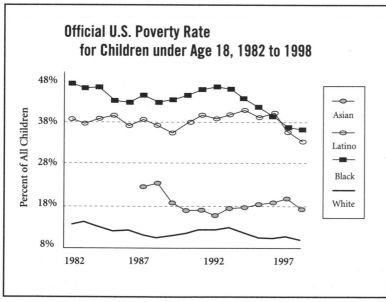

Official U.S. Poverty Rate for Children under Age 18, 1982 to 1998

Source: U.S. Bureau of the Census (1999)

Nixon) to no growth (through Carter). During the Millennial era, that pattern was exactly reversed. The American economy has steadily sped up—from no growth or fitful growth in the '80s to a long and breathtaking acceleration in the '90s. From 1981 until 1994, the median income of families with children showed little gain. Since then, average family incomes have surged by about 10 percent, reaching $45,000 overall and $54,000 for married couples.

Meanwhile, America witnessed a surprising turnaround in the share of kids experiencing real destitution. The poverty rate for children rose through much of the Xer childhood era, peaked in the early '80s just when the first Millennials arrived, and has been trending downward ever since. The total decline—from 22 percent in 1983 to 18 percent in 1998—is not large, but becomes a lot more impressive when you look separately at each racial or ethnic group. Since 1983, the poverty rate for non-Latino white kids has fallen from 14 to 10 percent; for black kids, from 47 to 36 percent; and for Latino kids from 40 to 34 percent. White and Latino kids are now at their lowest poverty rate since the late '70s—and, since 1996, black kids have been at their lowest poverty rate ever.

That's just the official poverty rate, which measures only pretax cash income. When you apply the Census Bureau's newer measure of "total-income" poverty, which accounts for taxes and in-kind income like food stamps and Medicaid, the decline is even more impressive. For African-American families with children, this poverty rate has been cut in half since 1983. The trend both confirms and helps explain the economic and civic revival seen in many black urban communities through the '90s.

Of course, not everything about the "new" economy is rosy for the Millennials. Many kids fervently wish their parents weren't so stressed out by work. Despite all the hype about higher productivity, the fact remains that the lion's share of family income growth in the late '90s was directly paid for by longer hours. Many kids also feel firsthand their parents' anxiety about the faster pace of competitive change. They sense the fears about downsizing and outsourcing, along with the allure of moving ahead (or the dread of falling behind) in an era of raging economic mobility.

Whatever the reason—whether to assuage their anxieties or fulfill their callings or to buy a million-dollar home with an indoor gym—

Boomer and Xer parents put on a tremendous display of the work ethic for their Millennial children. And like all parental displays, it will likely be interpreted by Millennials as both a gift and a warning. The old adage "behind every hurried child is a hurried parent" applies in full to these kids of the soaring Dow.

Millennials and Social Fragmentation

Any generation that comes of age wanting to tear down, smash, and break up the "establishment" probably grew up at a time when society's political and economic institutions were powerful enough to feel intimidating and unifying enough to feel dictatorial.

That's how many Boomers recollect the giant new edifices of their childhood—Marshall Plan and NATO, Social Security and AFL-CIO, Interstates and Apollo missions, Selective Service and CIA, loyalty oaths and schools painted in army-surplus green, the "new industrial state" and the "military-industrial complex." These and more reflected a vision of America forged during the New Deal and World II, just before the Boomers came along. Adults trusted institutions and built them in a giant square geometry that in turn seemed to impose its squarishness back on the adults. That was a time when most Americans believed that together as a nation they were more than the sum of their parts.

Come the 1990s, the public world from a child's perspective had entirely changed shape. America was no longer run by midlife world-war veterans; instead, it was run by midlife values-war veterans. During the Boomer childhood, confidence in the efficacy of government rose over the duration of their childhood, culminating in the "Great Society" Congress of 1964–65. During the Millennial childhood, politics has become increasingly irrelevant. "The era of big government is over," proclaimed a Democratic president in a year of legislative "train wrecks" and "national health" fiascos—at the midpoint of one of the least consequential decades in American political history.

If today's adults don't care as much about big unifying national things, what do they care about? The politics of meaning. Personal rootedness. Inner values. Spiritual energy. Empathic gestures. Not top-down, but bottom-up. Not centralized A-frame organizations, but M-frame

The village mentality run wild. . . . Big Brother's intervention as we have never seen it before. . . . Americans have never experienced such an intrusion in their family lives.

—Henry Hyde, describing an Alabama program that provides fifty social worker visits per year to "at risk" families

networks. Not commands, but requests. Not shame, but guilt. Not the economics of poverty, but the culture of discontent. Not us, but me. Circa 2000, most Americans believe that as a nation they are *less* than the sum of their parts.

Gen Xers recall, as kids, the upheaval that gripped America when the establishment was toppled. They witnessed the triumph of individualism over community and of markets over government. But by the time Millennials came along, the new values regime was fully in place. They have no more recollection of Woodstock, Watergate, or Jimmy Carter than Boomers do of the New Deal, Pearl Harbor, or Franklin Roosevelt.

Given the Millennials' location in history, the theme of lockstep institutional repression, a theme that so disturbed young Boomers, finds little resonance in the new youth mind-set. The public trend that *is* making a deeper impression on today's youth is quite the opposite—*the ongoing fragmentation of American life.*

Here's what Millennials see, in the adult world:

They see lifestyle fragmentation. They cannot recall an era of two political parties, three TV networks, and four major sports leagues—an era in which the "average" person's beliefs or lifestyle might usefully be described. For them, politicians are squabblers; media audiences are segmented into an infinitude of special-interest magazines, cable stations, and web sites; and pro sports are less about teams than stars. As for opinions and fashions, the only ones worth noticing belong to self-authenticating "niche groups," each focusing zealously on a sex, race, religion, ideology, occupation, or hobby—and occasionally (as with the Branch Davidians, Heaven's Gate, or the Michigan Militia) breaking out in maniacal midlife fury.

They see geographic fragmentation. In the middle '80s, what Joel Garreau calls "Edge Cities" began springing up around new work and shopping areas. By the late '90s, these exurbs became their own source of unzoned sprawl and strip-mall ugliness. Fights often brewed between younger parents who wanted sidewalks (often Gen Xers who worried about the safety of their small kids) and older parents who preferred the unkempt gravel look (often Boomers whose kids were grown up or had cars).

They see racial and ethnic fragmentation. In 1984, Jesse Jackson launched the Rainbow Coalition, declaring America to be "a quilt of many patches, many pieces, many colors, various textures." Today, after endless national debates over ethnic pride, hate crimes, nullification juries, affirmative action, and balanced textbooks, multiculturalism has entirely displaced assimilation as a national goal.

Millennials are noticing less mixing in the schools, because that's exactly what's happening: The decades-long trend toward integration in public schools has begun to reverse. The Harvard Civil Rights Project now reports that the share of black students attending majority-white public schools reached its all-time apogee (of 44 percent) in 1988, the same year the first Millennials entered first grade. By 1996, it had fallen back to 35 percent, where it had been in the early 1970s. The decline has occurred in virtually every region—and for Latinos as well as African Americans. Some of it is due to self-selecting geographic mobility. But with cities across the country phasing out their desegregation plans—most recently, Buffalo, Nashville, Mobile, Minneapolis, and Seattle—much of it is due to declining enthusiasm for school integration. With the passing of the G.I. Generation, the idea of bringing the country together racially has lost much of its appeal.

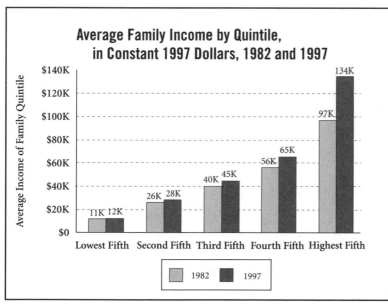

Source: U.S. Bureau of the Census (2000)

In the 1980s, there was a sense that adult need for self-actualization trumped children's needs. Now, I think the cultural value of parental altruism, of sacrificing for kids, may be returning.

—T. Berry Brazelton (1991)

I think there is something profound going on, a backlash to the thinking in the '70s and '80s that families could evolve away from basic values and exist without those foundations. It doesn't work.

—Linda and Richard Eyre, Teaching Your Children Values (1991)

Most important, Millennials see income fragmentation. When the first of them were born, only a few of their parents had yet noticed this trend. In 1984, with Mario Cuomo's "Two Societies" speech and Charles Murray's book *Losing Ground,* the public at large first became acquainted with the growing gap between rich and poor. By century's end, after rising sharply in the (Reagan) mid-'80s and again in the (Clinton) mid-'90s, the gap had grown dramatically.

While the share of children living in absolute poverty has declined, the gap between those living in struggling families and those living in prospering families has widened. Since 1982, the average real income of the lower two-fifths of all families climbed by only 8 percent (to $20,000 in 1997), but the average for the top one-fifth climbed by 38 percent (to $134,000) and for the top one-twentieth by 70 percent (to $235,000). For all families with children, the income ratio between the poorest and richest has nearly doubled over the last twenty years. So where Boomers discovered the "yuppie" on the edge of midlife, and Gen Xers stepped into the *90210* world coming of age, Millennials have opened their eyes as children to see this trend already in place.

In their education, the growing share of Millennials in private or "home" schools no longer know what a randomly chosen fellow citizen looks like. Those going to public school can often see up close what Jonathan Kozol calls the "savage inequalities" between rich and poor school districts—sometimes due to heavily organized parental spending designed to end-run judicially imposed state equalization formulas. In Chicago, Jesse Jackson's Rainbow-PUSH Coalition persuaded two classrooms to trade places for a day. The inner-city kids, from a school that annually spends $5,000 per student, visited a plush suburban school that had three new gymnasiums, two Olympic-size pools, and elegantly appointed chemistry and computer labs, thereby learning what $15,000 per student can buy.

In their neighborhoods, many Millennials number among the 9 million people living in what Mary Gail Snyder calls "Fortress America"—gated luxury neighborhoods full of enormous houses purchased by dual-income parents who might not have time to enjoy them, let alone clean them. Gated residents don't have to worry about unwelcome passersby, including schoolchildren from less affluent families. Silver Oak

Elementary School near San Jose, California, has two entrances where parents can drop off their kids: one in the front for the general public, the other for kids in the exclusive gated Silver Creek Country Club community that sits right behind the school, with its 1,500 $2-million homes, all surrounded by a stylish green fence and guarded gates.

Should New Parents Take a Mandatory Parenting Class?

Blacks: **72%**

Latinos: **67%**

Asians: **56%**

Whites: **47%**

—*percent saying yes in survey,* Los Angeles Times *(June 13, 1999)*

Autos are another income classifier, distinguishing some older kids who have pricey new ones from classmates whose families don't make that much all year. Among younger kids, lines are drawn between those whose moms crowd into elementary schools with their truck-sized SUVs and those who still arrive via the slow yellow bus.

What about toys? Parents are resigning themselves to a hard fact of life: There is no collector Beanie Baby so expensive or Pokémon hardware so obscure that some parents won't want to buy it and some kids won't want to flaunt it.

Or the vacations. Gone are the funky old summers at Camp Granada. Many packagers now offer weeks with private chefs preparing gourmet foods, Humvee racing in the Mojave Desert, major leaguers teaching how to throw a curve ball, theme parks that let kids swim with dolphins for $179 a day, or Sail Caribbean cruises on fifty-foot yachts for kids wanting to study marine biology.

Yes, there are a whole lot of really rich kids these days. And there are still plenty of poor ones. The gap between the two groups is glaring. What's behind it?

The first place to look is the changing American economy. The rise of knowledge-intensive innovation and the quickening of immigration and global trade has widened the market-determined spread between high

After a 19-month string of school shootings, an invisible undercurrent in the workplace—parents' anxiety about their teenagers—has exploded into high visibility. A collective impulse to embrace adolescents and find new ways to keep them safe swept like a seiche this week through offices and factories. —**Sue Shellenbarger, The Wall Street Journal** *After Columbine*

and low wages. Over the Millennial childhood, workers with high educational credentials have received a growing wage premium. At the low end, immigrants are swamping the supply of unskilled labor.

Then consider family structure, which unquestionably trumps the economic impact of race alone. Among all families with children, black families get only 52 percent as much income as white families. But among two-parent families, black kids are raised with 84 percent as much income. These days, in other words, what matters most is whether a family has one or two parents. In *both* black and white families, single parents earn only about 30 percent of what two-parent families make. The Millennial black-white disparity is mostly due to the lower share of black kids growing up in two-parent families (two in five) than white kids (three in four).

For Latino families, recent immigration also plays a major role and explains why they have roughly the same average income as black families though they are much more likely to be intact. Many Latino Millennials are growing up in the poorest two-parent families in America, a circumstance more easily borne by parents (who recall their family origins) than by their children (whom parents try to shield from demoralizing comparisons with their native-born peers).

Family structure not only works to push down the bottom of the income distribution, but to pull up the top. The reason: married women in the workforce. Even when Mom is living with Dad, she's still pulling in big extra bucks. Over the Millennial child era, moreover, her rising educational credentials have enhanced her earning power. That's not all. If she's a high earner, she's increasingly likely to have stayed married—and (say some social scientists) to have married a high-earning dad in the first place. In 1998, among married-couple families, the median income for those in which the wife worked full-time was $68,000, versus $42,000 when the wife didn't work at all. That's a big gap, and it's been growing. Since 1981, the former figure has risen by 9 percent in real dollars, while the latter figure has declined by 7 percent.

The growing American diversity in family wealth has also added to the wedge between rich and poor kids. The fantastic rise in the Dow has widened the gap between families who had the assets or incomes to buy into the market early (especially Boomers) and those who didn't (especially Xers). Intergenerational dependency within the family is also more unequal than ever. Some Millennials have rich grandparents who cushion their families with huge gifts and bequests, while others have needy ones who require time and money from busy parents.

When you apply all these economic forces together, you can see that the "tale of two Millennial cities" is largely a contrast between two sets of kids: those with two-income Boomer parents—with highly educated soccer moms, bursting stock portfolios, and gift-giving grandparents— and those with one-income Gen-X parents, many of them never-married black moms or recent Latino immigrants.

One intriguing generational aspect of the Millennial child era has been first the tolerance, then the defense, and eventually the exuberant celebration of a new "overclass" of midlife Boomers who long ago once accused their own G.I. parents of materialism. Looking back, the G.I.s' boxy cars (often condemned by Boomer radicals as "obscenely big") were no match for the SUVs owned by millions of Boomers today, and G.I. materialism pales against Boomer-owned houses that contain 50 percent more stuff (in tonnage) than their parents' houses did. In retrospect, young Boomers did not reveal a dislike for affluence per se—but rather for the conformist and security-enhancing purposes to which they saw it put during their childhood.

This has made many Boomers oddly indifferent to the growing national prosperity of the '90s as well as to the lopsidedness of its distribution. To them, money is about individualism and values expression— not about the collective security, well-being, or cohesion of the society at large.

At the same time, many Boomers are plenty worried about how the absence of community may endanger their kids. They don't like to see a generation growing up without any sense of belonging to a larger social whole, with the larger sense of purpose that entails. Boomers don't want their own children to follow in the path of Gen X, whom they regard as a civic lost cause. At the same time, many Xer parents regret their own participation in the institution-bashing cynicism they feel originated with Boomers. And however fretful they may be about their own kids, many parents in both generations are indignant about what's happening to *other people's* kids. By degrees, the entire adult community is coming to

From statehouses to corporate boardrooms to Congress, a movement is building for greater spending on programs targeted for poor young children—but often at the expense of reduced welfare assistance for their parents and other poor adults.

—David Broder and Paul Tyler, **The Washington Post** *(1991)*

What this country needs is a G.I. Bill for Kids. —U.S. Education Secretary Lamar Alexander (1992)

Children's issues moved ahead of such prominent issues as Medicare and Social Security in the public's ranking of issue priorities, suggesting the possible emergence of a new "third rail" of American politics.

—Coalition for America's Children (1997)

understand that there is only one way to resolve the contradiction between their own preferences and the needs of their kids. They have agreed that the rising generation—not themselves—must develop a closer connection to the national community and to the institutions embodying it.

Millennials and Kinderpolitics

"My name is Joan, and *I am my kid's mom*," announces the typical caller to Laura Schlessinger's top-rated national radio show. By such new habits of expression, parents are transforming their Millennial kids into the defining focal point for a new concept of public space, a new sense of community, a new civic purpose.

Far more than during the Gen-X child era, today's adults define themselves in terms of their children. In many neighborhoods, Boomer and Gen-X parents have little to do with one another until they interact through their kids ("Oh, you're Jordan's dad. You must be Kaitlyn's mom")—after which they develop long-term friendships. This child-derived social infrastructure was much weaker, and less needed, among the Boomers' own G.I. parents, who maintained a strong peer community apart from their kids. Back then, G.I.s kept their doors unlocked for one another, but later learned to lock them against one another's kids. Boomers learned early to lock their doors (and install security systems) against their like-aged neighbors—but have lately begun to unlock them for their neighbors' kids.

One way parents have also begun to unlock doors to one another's children is through government. While adults have become iconoclastic, free-agent individuals, diminishing any sense of community among themselves, at times joyously so, they have demanded that a stronger community life be wrapped around their kids. Lately, two parallel governments have been at work. One—the part that affects nearly every domestic issue *not* involving children—has reached a state of chronic paralysis and deadlock. The other—the part that affects children—keeps pushing its agenda through the Congress, across the president's desk, into the lawbooks, and out to the hinterlands with piles of federal cash.

Through the Gen-X childhood era, federal deficits rose from small to vast. Through the Millennial era, the deficits have fallen back to zero and then below zero. Leaders refrain from touching the uncommitted surpluses (for fear kids might need it), while Boomer and Xer parents routinely remind one another that Social Security will ultimately get the axe (to save kids from getting hit by new taxes). Before Millennials arrived, the typical debate over welfare reform focused on saving money and punishing bad parents. The debate preceding the sweeping Welfare Reform Act of 1996 was, by contrast, all about saving children and helping good parents. The 1990s became the first decade since the 1920s in which federal spending on kids rose faster than spending on working-age adults or elders. Through the first half of the 1990s, real federal spending per child jumped by 37 percent, more than twice the rate for the elderly. The growth in welfare and food stamps slowed, but all the other child initiatives (expanded Head Start, KidCare, and the like) more than made up the difference. When superimposed on the spreading income gap

There is no constitutional or unconstitutional when it comes to our children. —*Maureen Kanka, whose 7-year-old daughter Megan was killed by a sex offender living across the street*

If you dare to prey on our children, the law will follow you wherever you go—state to state, town to town.

—*President Clinton, signing Megan's Law*

Hey you. Anything happens to my daughter, I've got a .45 and a shovel. I doubt anyone would miss you.

—*Mel, to his daughter's date, in* Clueless

Laws Named After Victimized Millennials:

Megan's Law—Megan Kanka, 7

Joan's Law—Joan D'Alessandro, 9

Amber's Law—Amber Hagerman, 9

Jimmy Ryce Law—Jimmy Ryce, 9

between families, expansions in the eligibility of poor kids to government benefits have led to a vast number of child beneficiaries. By the late 1990s, it was estimated that in fully one-third of all pregnancies and child births, at least part of the medical cost was paid for by federal-state Medicaid programs.

At the ballot box, meanwhile, kids' issues have ascended above all other voter priorities. One reason state and local leaders have risen in esteem relative to national leaders is their greater contact with children's issues, especially education and adolescent crime. At every level of government, election campaigns have bristled with proposals for child-oriented laws and spending programs—curfews, after-school programs, V-chips, day-care subsidies, parental leave, aggressive antiabuse campaigns, fierce antialcohol and antidrug initiatives, tougher penalties for crimes committed by or upon children, and a vast array of plans for "fixing" public schools. Back in the Gen-X child era, politicians seldom thought about fiscal "family values," or proposed new big-ticket child-health initiatives, or demanded tougher laws against child victimizers, or demanded greater regulation of child safety. Now, in the Millennial child era, they do.

Most of these Millennial programs and dollars can be placed under one rubric: *safety.* And safety has two objectives: protection against *physical* (outer-world) dangers and *moral* (inner-world) dangers. These days, practically every federal agency is working on at least one of them:

>> The Consumer Product Safety Commission is focusing on the protection of babies and children—from everything from cribs to vinyl miniblinds—with such pervasive zeal that some are calling it the "Child" Product Safety Commission.

>> The Department of Labor has boosted the enforcement of child labor laws, especially in immigrant sweatshops. It also oversees the Family and Medical Leave Act of 1993, which allows millions of Americans to take up to twelve weeks of unpaid leave, without losing their jobs, to care for a newborn or adopted child. Lately, the Labor Secretary has proposed going further and allowing states to use Unemployment Insurance funds to support parental leave.

>> The National Transportation Safety Board is exploring whether to require child seats to be available in trucks, buses, and planes.

>> The National Highway Transportation Safety Administration has regulated dashboard air bags and is now inquiring into side-impact air bags, to make sure they don't hurt kids.

>> The Environmental Protection Agency has made children a new priority in the regulation of pesticides, such as chlorpyrifos, that have side effects harmful to children.

>> The Treasury Department's Bureau of Alcohol, Tobacco, and Firearms has a national demonstration project, Mosaic 2000, through which twenty-five schools will try to use personality tests to identify children who might commit violent acts.

>> The Department of Justice has agents lurking on the web, cracking down on child-porn collectors and abusers. In 1998, federal agents conducted the biggest internet porn sting in history, with the arrest of sixty alleged members of the Wonderland Club in the United States and thirteen other countries.

>> The Federal Trade Commission has issued its first Internet regulations—expressly targeting the web abuse of kids' privacy.

>> The Office of Personnel Management has established an Interagency Family Friendly Workplace Working Group so that all parts of the federal workforce can share best-practice policy regarding Millennial kids.

Of course, what the federal government does to help children doesn't matter nearly as much as what states and cities do with police and social workers. Through the 1990s, local authorities were busy on all fronts. In the weeks following Columbine, state legislatures passed a flurry of statutes regulating teenage behavior—barring them from playing video

I'm kinda glad that there are people like the police who probe juveniles who are out late at night roaming the streets. We have no right whatsoever to be out past the established curfew.
—*Chris Thomas, 16*

I think curfews can prevent crime because, if the kids stay out after dark, there are more chances of being murdered or raped. —*Amber, 12*

I am a middle-aged liberal who has been on the left-wing side of every social issue for the past three-and-a-half decades. So why am I supporting the teen curfew? —*Elizabeth Siegel,*
The Washington Post

poker, state lotteries, operating boats without a license, or getting married without a judge's permission, and more.

Which Security Measures Do You Favor?

metal detectors in schools:	**86%**
regulating violent video games and TV shows:	**69%**
restricting violence in movies and on CDs:	**59%**

—*survey of adults and teens, in* USA Weekend *(July 4, 1999)*

Curfews have emerged as a major urban teen-protection tool. Since 1993, when the U.S. Supreme Court upheld a Dallas curfew law, American mayors have rushed to follow suit. Nearly three hundred cities now have youth curfew laws, which typically restrict teens to their homes from 10 or 11 P.M. to sunrise. Curfew enforcement is often strict but seldom severe. It allows enforcement discretion. And it is popular with most urban officials. According to a recent survey by the U.S. Conference of Mayors, 90 percent of urban officials consider curfews a useful gang-fighting tool, and more than 80 percent feel they make streets safer. The biggest impact of curfew laws has been in identifying troubled kids and delivering them to social service agencies to deal with their real problems. Lately, shopping malls have enforced their own private curfews, banning unescorted teens at night and sometimes even on weekends.

New crimes have been defined. States have been especially busy criminalizing behavior that might harm Millennials, empowering police to apply a greatly expanded list of petty and felony offenses. Back in the 1980s, judges began locking up drug-addicted pregnant women to keep them from harming their fetuses. That launched a new trend of get-tough-on-parents laws. In Oregon, it's now a felony for parents to hit spouses in front of kids.

Workplaces and stores have become child-friendlier. Now that Boomer CEOs are taking over businesses, child-friendly workplaces are the new fad—something they seldom were during the Gen Xer child era, when Silent CEOs were in charge. Companies have more in-house day care, sometimes even in-house schools. Parents have to apologize less for taking time off due to a family emergency. For travelers, shoppers, and diners, child seats await in restaurants, child videos on planes and cruise ships, play areas in malls, changing tables in restrooms (sometimes a third "family" bathroom in addition to "men" and "women"), reserved parking for pregnant women or moms with small children, and huge indoor playgrounds (Planet Play, Chuck E Cheese).

Motor vehicles, always a child safety issue, have now become a bigger one. Back in the late '70s, when Gen Xers were kids, only three car riders in ten wore seat belts, no cars had air bags, and "regulatory reform" meant getting rid of safety standards. By the late '90s, with Millennials, seven riders in ten were belted, air bags were standard equipment, and safety crusaders clearly had the upper hand. After proposing a nationwide network for correctly installing small-child safety seats, federal regulators prodded industry to improve safety seats for the "forgotten children" ages 5 to 15. School buses have also emerged as a concern, with 35 deaths and roughly 10,000 injuries per year, mostly from lack of seat belts—which NHTSA favors installing at $2,000 per bus. Thanks to regulations, many school buses will also soon be equipped with fancy new mirrors, safety arms that stop oncoming traffic, and sensor alarms aimed at drivers' blind spots.

Motor vehicles are also dangerous to teens who drive. More teens own cars than ever before, often purchased entirely at their parents' expense. Even those who don't own cars are often in them, either with friends or (increasingly) in taxis that take groups of kids to shopping malls or other common locations. Although auto accidents and deaths are trending downward, the improvement isn't coming fast enough for many public officials who advocate stricter, more paternal rules for teen drivers. In twenty-three states, "graduated licenses" are limiting teens' nighttime driving, restricting their number of passengers, and requiring parents to attend initiation classes.

Bicycling has changed, marking a big contrast between the freer Boomer childhood and the more protected Millennial childhood. Back then, bicycles were simpler, no one wore helmets, and kids biked a lot—to school, on errands, in races, just for fun. Times have changed. From 1975 to 1995, in the 5- to 15-year-old age bracket, there has been a 60 percent decline in bicycling. Urban sprawl is partly to blame, along with

The national labs are charged with issues of national security. I'm a parent. I think school safety is national security. —**Mary Green, Sandia National Laboratory, whose engineers are developing new school safety technology**

I never thought at any point in my career I would recommend electronic cameras in schools. —**Paul Vance, school superintendent**

greater access of car transport, parental fears of accidents and kidnappings, and simply a lack of free time. But when they do bike, they have much finer equipment—and wear helmets.

Air travel is now a child issue. "Stranded?" asks a *U.S. News* headline. "Going home alone is daunting for kids." Back in the Gen-X child era, unaccompanied minors were on their own. Now airlines carefully usher kids between connecting flights. Southwest Airlines requires parents to wait at the gate until their kid's plane actually takes off. Even so, as 7 million kids travel alone each year, often to visit noncustodial parents in distant cities, airlines are reporting a rising number of hysterical calls from parents with stranded kids. For a price, Delta and TWA offer parents the new option of sending a kid home with an airline employee to spend the night.

Schools, especially since Columbine, have been the object of some truly extraordinary police measures. Houston schools have assembled a 177-member police department that is armed, trained in assault tactics, equipped with bulletproof vests and bomb-sniffing dogs, and supported by twenty-four-hour emergency dispatchers. Disrupting class can bring a criminal citation, and refusing to pay school-imposed fines can mean jail time. In Rustin, Louisiana, school officials require students and faculty to wear ID badges with photo, name, and Social Security number. Principals in Loudoun County, Virginia, have asked for a law that would ban wooden staffs from being used as swords in Shakespeare plays. Elsewhere, schools have bolted lockers shut, installed security cameras, and either banned backpacks or required them to be made of transparent material. Some districts are suspending, expelling, even jailing kids for jotting diary notes about guns, writing Halloween assignments about murder, or even jokingly pointing their fingers and saying "bang."

Lunch hour has become a time of concern to Boomer administrators who may recall how, back when they were teenagers, they demanded and won the right to leave school to get a fast-food burger and fries (then seen as a treat) at some local youth hangout. Now hangouts are deemed bad, and the old closed-campus rules are coming back. "The idea was to keep things simple, with everyone in the building all day, without the potential for distraction," said Michael Walsh, a Maryland school spokesman defending a new lunch-only-at-school policy. "The idea was to have there be one less car trip, one less kid coming back late to class or not at all, one less opportunity to go off and drink or smoke."

Before and after school are seen as even riskier times. "It's 4:00 P.M. Do You Know Where Your Children Are?" screamed a 1998 *Newsweek* headline. In the Millennial-child era, more parents know *exactly* where their kids are, every minute of the day. With so many working parents, kids must sometimes be dropped off long before school starts, or linger around the neighborhood until whenever a parent's workday is over. To address this problem, many communities have crafted new "out of school" programs, either at the schools themselves or at nearby teen centers.

When the Rodney King riots hit Los Angeles back in the Gen-X teen years, not one local high school offered anything after school except sports. Today, most of them do. Colin Powell has called upon American communities to give children "safe places" where they can go after school—a YMCA, a Boys and Girls Club, a church rec room. Clinton's "midnight basketball" program was ridiculed by Republicans when he suggested it in 1993, but Republican-led Congresses have kept funding such programs, giving $20 million per year to the Boys and Girls Clubs of America. By 1998, said *Newsweek,* "Among cops, social service types and policymakers, there's a new awareness that structured activity during out-of-school hours is absolutely critical." Milwaukee has pioneered adult-supervised "Safe Night" teen parties with four simple rules: no drugs, no alcohol, no weapons, and no arguments.

Sexual harassment is a newly defined problem at school, dating back to the mid-'90s episode when a North Carolina first grader was suspended for kissing a girl classmate. Many schools now ban handholding, the passing of romantic notes, and chasing members of the opposite sex during recess. Litigious parents have become a problem here, but in 1999, the Supreme Court raised the bar by letting child plaintiffs sue only those schools that knowingly tolerate abusive behavior.

The internet is giving parents both dreams and nightmares. Six of ten parents say children without web access are at a disadvantage. But eight in ten worry about the sites their children may visit, and two-thirds of parents with school-aged kids and home internet access say they do not allow their kids on line when they are not present. Meanwhile, FBI, Postal Service, and Customs Bureau agents routinely cruise the web, posing as

Children's privacy became a hot-button issue [in 1998] after a FTC study found that 89% of Web sites aimed at kids collect personal data from them, but only 23% of those sites asked children to seek parental consent. —**The Wall Street Journal**

This guy who I was talking to seemed really sweet, so I gave him my info. A couple of days later . . . he began talking about how he was going to "get me" and described what he was going to do to me (basically all kinds of disgusting things). I felt so vulnerable. He knew where I lived! . . . Finally, I told AOL administration what was going on. They handled it, and I never heard from the gross guy again.

—*Carolyn, 15*

All the adults in the media ever seem to talk about is instructions on how to make a nuclear bomb, pornography, and hackers, etc. They don't see the side we see. They don't understand what the internet is. —*Lauren, 16*

We're indoors. We're padded. Parents can feel their child is safe.

—*Dick Guggenheimer, Discovery Zone*

children, tripping up child-porn collectors and would-be abusers. With Millennials in mind, the U.S. Congress has passed two very restrictive internet-censoring bills. The more sweeping first measure (the 1996 Communications Decency Act) was voided by the Supreme Court, and the second (the 1998 Child Online Protection Act) has been nixed by lower courts and awaits high court review. Though fighting these bills, internet companies are encouraging parents to use screening programs such as CyberSitter, Web Chaperone, and X-Stop to control what their kids can see on-line. One-third of all parents of web-linked kids now use these services. Cyber Patrol compiled such a thorough list of 100,000 screened-out sites that porn fans tried (but failed) to buy the links. Congress is debating measures to require schools and libraries to put filters on their computers—triggering a mini–culture war over the choice of screening software. Parents can now choose between screens that block gay sites and ones that block anti-gay sites.

The pop culture is, of course, the number-one priority of those eager to protect Millennial morals. New technologies abound, from V-chips to small black boxes, affixable to the family TV, that read closed-caption texts and mute out any offensive language. (There are two settings: "tolerant" and "strict.") Music CDs, video games, and even many prime-time TV sitcoms now carry parental advisories.

Proportion of Parents Claiming to Have "Strict" Rules on Child TV Watching

1976: **49%**
1994: **62%**

—Roper poll of parents,
in The New York Times (October 11, 1995)

Columbine sparked new adult efforts—from both sides of the culture wars—to restrict teen access to the edgier elements of the culture other adults continue to make for them. The WB network pulled a season finale of *Buffy the Vampire Slayer* (which depicted violence at a graduation ceremony), and President Clinton persuaded theater owners to require photo IDs for kids who try to enter R-rated films. Meanwhile, Laura Schlessinger waged an all-out talk-show war on the American Library Association's "Go Ask Alice for Teens" web site and its ultra-explicit answers to teens' questions about sex. Though the ACLU makes headlines by objecting, its strategy shows all the signs of a fighting retreat.

Raising Boomers, Raising Millennials

Around the kitchen table and on radio talk shows, Millennials hear their Boomer parents reminisce about the freedom and innocence of their childhood years—supposedly the perfect incubator for raising imaginative children who grow up to become creative adults. Millennials also hear their parents fret about the pressures and temptations and horrifying dangers that force them to structure their kids' lives more than their own parents ever did for them.

These kitchen-table musings have a basis in truth. Ironically, during the American High, it was the very conformism that G.I. parents imposed on their own behavior that enabled Boomers to grow up in a "permissive" world of loosening rules. And it was the strong ethic of community and institutional trust that G.I.s promoted—for example, the ethic that assumed neighbors would watch out for each other's kids—that allowed young Boomers to romp without rules or worry. Then came the Consciousness Revolution, when Americans of all ages began to attack institutional obligations as oppressive. The new era would work for kids, many hoped, by giving them so many rights that adults wouldn't have to bother as much about duties.

Two decades later, having seen enough of that, Boomer parents began to reverse course. They sensed that the needs of kids looked different from the vantage of midlife. And they were right—from the vantage of *their* midlife. The main reason Boomers could enjoy so much freedom as kids is because their own parents, wrapped up in their civic obligations, had denied themselves freedom. And the only reason their Millennial kids must be buckled, watched, fussed over, and fenced in by wall-to-wall rules and chaperones is precisely because adults today hold their own freedoms in such huge regard.

This era, and these parents, appear to be leading Millennials in an entirely opposite life-cycle direction from the paths their Boomer parents have pursued. Along the way, the focus of government and the identification with community is passing from the generation of yesteryear's adults to the generation of today's youths—from "senior citizens" to "junior citizens"—while skipping the generations in between.

Ground zero of the culture wars *(family)*

Ground zero of the culture wars *(family)*

God has been so good,
blessing me with family who've done all they could
        —BACKSTREET BOYS, "The Perfect Fan"

Nothing so troubles most Americans about today's kids as the condition of the American family. Boomers, especially, have let loose such a pessimistic torrent about the weakness and disarray of family life that it leaves little room for comment, much less dissent.

Beneath all the lurid adjectives, the logic of Boomer pessimism is simple. The first premise is that most families today—in their work roles, gender roles, source of authority, daily schedule, you name it—are very different from the typical family in which Boomers were raised. The second (more debatable) premise is that Boomers, who were the direct result of the earlier type of family, have matured into adults who pretty much represent the apogee of human progress. The Boomer conclusion: Today's families are producing kids that could put an end to civilization as we know it.

In broad outline, this is a line of thinking shared by both sides of the culture wars, with conservatives complaining about the weakening of

The great experiment: Today's parents are raising children in ways that little resemble their own youth.

—**headline,** Time

Determined to correct what we judge to have been the mistake of our own parents, we have chosen to make our commitment to our kids absolute, our involvement in their lives total.

—**James Carman,**
Wilson Quarterly

I just wish I had fewer choices.

—*Gen Xer mom,*
The Washington Post

family values and parental character, and liberals lamenting the harms done by an unresponsive government and the untrammeled marketplace.

This logic is seldom tested against what is known about how hard most parents are trying to make families work, or whether kids think their families do in fact work. Nor is it tested against the recent yet abundant evidence that today's kids are doing better—and are actually reversing many of the unwelcome behavioral trends Boomers set in their youth. What it reflects, instead, are a number of impressions Boomers formed before today's kids ever came along: regrets about what they may have done (or overdone) to family life during the '60s and '70s; dismay at the Xer offspring of those decades; and, above all, the realization that they are incapable of building the family their parents built, and thus of creating another generation like themselves.

Boomers are surely right about not creating replicas of themselves. But they are surely wrong about their family pessimism.

Yes, there was a time—twenty or thirty years ago—when Americans staged an angry and passionate debate over the worth, and *even the survival,* of the American family. But guess what? The debate's over. And the family not only survived—it *thrives,* even if in somewhat altered forms. Given the universal distrust now felt for nearly all other institutions (from churches to governments), one could even claim that the family is a more exclusively venerated and popular focus of national life today than it has ever been before in American history.

Of All the People You Know or Know About, Who Do You Look Up to the Most?

My parents:	**79%**
Athletes:	**13%**

—survey of 12- to 14-year-olds, Time *(July 5, 1999)*

The Millennial-Era Family

During the Gen-X child era, the American family endured countless new movements and trends—feminism, sexual freedom, a divorce epidemic, fewer G-rated movies, child-raising handbooks telling parents to "consider yourself" ahead of a child's needs, gay rights, Chappaquiddick, film nudity, a Zero Population Growth ethic, *Kramer vs. Kramer,* and *Roe v. Wade.* A prominent academic in 1969 proclaimed in the *Washington Post* that the family needed "a decent burial." The White House Conference on Families, convened by Jimmy Carter in 1979 to celebrate a new "diversity" of family life, resulted in raucous and bitter arguments—and the drawing of the culture-war battle lines that are still with us.

Contrast all this with the Millennial child era, dating back to the middle '80s, an era in which every political figure has had to swear by family values to have the slightest chance of public approval. Today, many suburban "minivan cities" have no social focal point other than Gymboree and Baby Depot—eliciting lampoons in Gen-X magazines, like the recent one in *GQ* ("Kids Are Us") skewering America's newfound "religion of child-centeredness." In her recent book *The Baby Boon: How Family-Friendly*

[Today's] fathers are spending a half-hour more each workday, and one hour more each day off, caring for and doing things with their children than in 1977. **—Sue Shellenbarger, The Wall Street Journal**

Seventy percent of men in their twenties and seventy-one percent of men in their thirties said they would be willing to give up some of their pay in exchange for more time with their families. Only twenty-six percent of men over 65 said they would trade pay for more family time.

—Radcliffe Public Policy Center

I always look up in the stands and my dad will be there in his suit and tie. I once overheard my uncle say that my dad missed two big meetings to drive to another town to watch me in a game that I didn't even play half of. He never told me. **—Lisa, 17**

America Cheats the Childless, Elinor Burkett claims that adults without families often feel treated as free riders and second-class citizens.

On one side, Bill Clinton's electoral successes hinged on his "New Democratic" re-embrace of the family, energized by the activism of middle-aged Boomers. Among them was his wife, Hillary, who had earlier written treatises on children's rights (for Gen Xers), but who later (for Millennials) crafted an *It Takes A Village*–style communitarian ethic full of civic duties. On the conservative side, another set of middle-aged Boomers—Bill Bennett, Gary Bauer, George W. Bush, among others—have championed a *Book of Virtues*–style character ethic full of personal duties. One side summons mostly public action and the other mostly private action, but there is near unanimity that "the children," alias Millennials, have to come first. Liberal feminists are now emphatically pro-mom, and conservative Christians (and Muslims) just as emphatically pro-dad. Today, not even antinatal environmentalists—who now run ads like "Negative Population Growth loves babies"—dare say a bad word about kids. Modern families may be diverse, but their priorities are surely not.

As Cornel West and Sylvia Ann Hewlett have written, "our 'blackness' and our 'femaleness' pale in the light of an even more fundamental identifier: that of being a parent. After all, we share the bedrock stuff: We are crazy about our kids." Back in the 1970s, best-selling Ivy League authors weren't writing that about Gen Xers.

Among the creators of popular culture, the pro-child shift has been just as staggering. If he could remake *Close Encounters of the Third Kind,* says Steven Spielberg (now a parent), he wouldn't have the father abandon his family to join the aliens. Bart Simpson's cocreator Matt Groening (now a parent) has apologized for the antifamily tone of the early episodes. (Where Bart used to roam free, now he's on Ritalin.) In late-'90s Hollywood, even the most vulgar and violent movies commonly have a story line, characters, and a closing scene that is pro-family and pro-child. Two of the most popular WB weekly dramas, *7th Heaven* and *Safe Harbor,* show parents and kids who struggle each week to keep their families close and together. Not so long ago, movies and sitcoms reflected a hands-off parenting style. Now it's nearly always hands-on.

Back in the Boomer-child era, parental-advice manuals assumed families were strict, and gently urged more indulgences. In the Gen-X era, manuals assumed families were changing, and usually urged parents to embrace that change. In the Millennial era, the advice manuals assume families are indulgent and gravely urge more strictness.

Percentage of 3- to 5-Year-Olds Who Have a Story Read to Them at Least Three Times a Week

	1991	1996
White kids:	40%	59%
Black kids:	34%	47%
Latino kids:	38%	47%

—*National Household Education Surveys (1991, 1996)*

Where Dr. Spock reassured and soothed moms who were steeped in the structured, rule-bound lore of the Great Depression (associated with behaviorists such as John B. Watson), today's books scold and energize moms who are steeped in the unstructured, feel-good lore of the Consciousness Revolution. Where Dr. Spock gave conversational advice, inviting parents to trust their instinct, the new books are deeply programmed with step-by-step lists, what-not-to-do's, even exercises and quizzes. Where Dr. Spock wrote one book that was meant for everyone, today there's a baby book for every race, gender, sexual orientation, ideology, and religion.

Where the Gen-X-era books celebrated the mutual independence of parent and child, the Millennial books celebrate a symbiosis William and Martha Sears call "attachment parenting"—such as sleeping with toddlers and taking them to work. (The "detachment" parenting of the Xer child era, they say, is now "outmoded.") Where '70s-era books assessed parent-child relationships in terms of how they made everyone feel, today's books assess them in terms of how children are being shaped as future adults. Revealingly, most of the '70s child-raising books were dedicated to friends, lovers, and spouses of the writers, while the '90s books are mostly dedicated to kids.

Many of the new Millennial-nurture books have a decidedly Boomer edge—with a "save the world" undertone of child upbringing, a frequent summons to culture wars battle stations, an emphasis on the parent's own "self-inventory," a holistic view of health and intelligence, and the

Help your children become the sort of self-confident, sensitive, considerate, cooperative, and caring children who enjoy being able to help each other, who get more satisfaction out of knowing that they have done something to contribute to the family and to their brother or sister than they do from one-upping them.

—*Peter Goldenthal,* **author of Beyond Sibling Rivalry**

The teen-agers reported generally respectful, honest and firmly structured relations with their parents. . . . Nearly 90 percent said they had rules on when to be home at night. —**New York Times/CBS poll**

Any parent who allows a child under age 17 to be out past curfew has abdicated his or her role as a parent.

—*Elizabeth Siegel,* **D.C. Action for Kids**

Unsupervised, spontaneous play has become a thing of the past.

—*Caroline Wellberg*

use of emotional closeness as a disciplinary tool. Yet some are beginning to reveal a new Gen-X survivalism: Keep everything simple, follow basic rules, and—above all—make sure the baby always feels *safe* and *watched*.

To be sure, today's families face plenty of dire challenges. As most experts point out, the one-size-fits-all, married-for-life, mom-at-home Ozzie and Harriet family no longer dominates as an example of how today's family works—which is equivalent to saying America isn't heading back to the '50s and today's Millennials aren't reliving the childhood of their Boomer parents. Instead, experts point to two troubling indicators of what's threatening today's family, and with it today's kids: the rising share of kids not living with two parents, and the rising share of kids with two working parents who don't have time for them.

These are serious problems. More Millennials are growing up with single parents than was true of Gen Xers, and single parenthood (all other things being equal) is associated with double or triple the risk that kids will get arrested, do drugs, fail at school, or commit suicide. Likewise, more Millennials are growing up with two working parents, and more are relegated, for more hours of the day, to the supervision of third parties. Yet while these trends justify parental worry and public concern, they are by no means the last word on family strength. They require some qualification and perspective.

To begin with, look for the "delta" of family change, trends occurring while children are growing up, not trends occurring before they arrive. When you focus on this delta, you'll notice that, through the Boomer childhood era, the basic stability of the family was accompanied by early signs of splintering. During the Xer childhood, these changes accelerated. And for Millennials, they have all decelerated—and, in some cases, have begun to reverse.

Back in the early '80s, the common theme of surveys of the state of the American family (by Harris, Yankelovich, and others) was how rapidly and drastically the family was changing. Come the early '90s, the common theme became how such change had slowed. In the mid-'80s, the U.S. Census Bureau projected that five of every ten marriages would someday end in divorce—but then, in 1992, the Census backtracked, reducing that forecast to four in ten. The 1990s were a "stabilization period" for the family, announced Census analyst Ken Bryson in 1993. "We're at a place where the whole thing has flattened out."

That flattening includes both of the family trends that most worry Americans. From 1965 to 1985, the share of all kids not living with two parents doubled, from 13 to 26 percent. Since then, it has risen to 32 percent, with almost no rise at all after 1995. (For black kids, this single-parent share has actually *fallen* over the '90s, which is a huge reversal from its earlier trend.) Ditto for working mothers. From 1965 to 1985, the employed share of all mothers with children under age 18 rose from 35 to 62 percent. Since then, it has risen to about 72 percent (50 percent full-time). And again, as with single parenthood, it has risen little since 1995—despite the recent red-hot economy.

But there's a bigger story here than just numbers and deltas. Beneath the quantitative shifts lie profound qualitative shifts in family life that are shaping a different kind of child.

Single Parents, Then and Now

Consider the different kinds of single-parent homes that have been most common in Boomer, Gen-X, and Millennial child eras. In the 1940s and '50s, a single-parent child usually got that way because of the death (perhaps in war) of a mother or father—a fate that was five times more likely

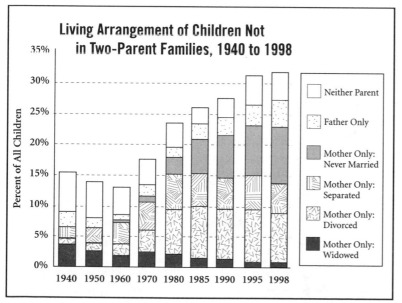

Living Arrangement of Children Not in Two-Parent Families, 1940 to 1998

Legend:
- Neither Parent
- Father Only
- Mother Only: Never Married
- Mother Only: Separated
- Mother Only: Divorced
- Mother Only: Widowed

Source: U.S. Bureau of the Census (2000)

The family unit is on the decline, but the desire for family satisfaction is on the rise. —*J. Walker Smith,*
Yankelovich Partners

Among children aged 9 to 17, 82 percent think a one-parent home is as much of a family as a two-parent home. —*Nickelodeon/Yankelovich*
Youth Monitor survey

My dad works at home sometimes, and it doesn't make any difference, or not much. He's physically there, but mentally he's isolated.

—*15-year-old boy,*
The Wall Street Journal

More than two-thirds agreed that "it is much better for the family" if the father works outside the home and the mother tends to the children. . . . The view was most pronounced among Latino parents, 83% of whom endorsed it.

—**Los Angeles Times** *poll*

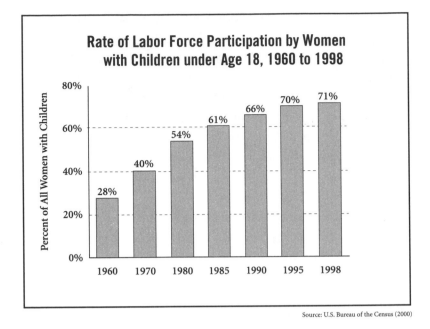

Rate of Labor Force Participation by Women with Children under Age 18, 1960 to 1998

Source: U.S. Bureau of the Census (2000)

then than it is now. Through the 1960s and '70s, the fastest-growing and newly dominant category of single-parent kids were those whose moms were divorced (but not remarried) or deserted (but still married). After rising from 5 to 13 percent of all kids by 1980, this combined category has since shown little growth: It plateaued in the early '90s at 14 percent, is now back below 13 percent, and has begun falling sharply for the younger kids of Gen-X moms. Since 1980, the entire growth in single parenthood has come from two entirely new categories: single fathers and, especially, *never-married* moms.

Among Children Who Live with a Single Mom, the Percentage Whose Mom Is . . .			
	1950	1980	1998
Widowed:	34%	11%	4%
Divorced:	22%	42%	34%
Never-Married:	2%	15%	40%

—U.S. Bureau of the Census (2000)

These single-parent genres represent very different family situations. Boomer kids being raised by widows considered their mothers' status, and their own, to be the result of larger global or natural forces beyond anyone's control. After a parent's death, other family members usually stepped in to help fill any void thereby created. Gen-X kids raised by divorced or deserted moms felt a betrayal and resentment at the rupture of a human promise wholly unlike what the kids of deceased parents ever knew. After divorce or desertion, kids often found themselves in a chaotic and suddenly impoverished world of patchwork child care. For Millennials, the divorced mom is a waning trend. The rising trends toward single dads and never-married mothers reflect, yet again, a new era.

The recent surge in single fathers, from 1.1 to 3.1 million since 1980, mostly reflects the growing desire of fathers to vie with moms for child custody. While the ruptures and resentments can still be very real, children now are made to feel more wanted. Even when Dad cannot be there,

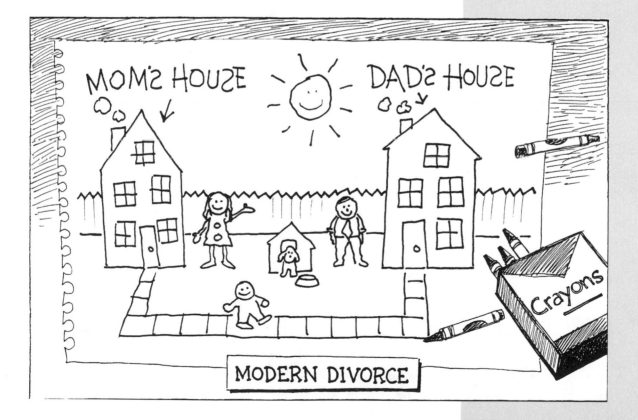

Millennials are more likely than Xers were to go to bed at night knowing that Dad *wants* to be there.

Today's 7 million Millennial children of never-married moms present an entirely novel situation, whose impact—especially to a child's eye—is not the same as divorce. In these families, there seldom hangs the shadow of life-shattering betrayal because no child-centered family ever existed in the first place. Many of these households have a real or putative father who is still present from time to time. An estimated 80 percent of the biological fathers are romantically involved with never-married mothers at the time of childbirth, and half of them have lived together. "You could still be called a daddy if the mother's not your wife," raps Ed O.G. and Da Bulldogs. Over time, these men tend to drift away. Yet whether they are present or not, life in a family with a never-married mom is all their kids have ever known, it's all many of their friends have ever known, and it's simply a fact of life in their child's world. It's not ideal, but it's not divorce either.

Yes, divorce is still breaking up plenty of families with children. But even here, there's a difference. A growing share of all divorces are non-contentious, mediated, and expressly arranged to be as child-friendly as possible. More separated moms and dads make an effort to live close by. In some cases, the children are even kept in the same house, and it's the mom and dad who come and go. "Although no one keeps statistics on the trend," reports *The Washington Post*, "divorce lawyers, judges, mediators, therapists and single-parent organizations all say they have noticed an increase in divorce plans tailored to children's needs."

Meanwhile, political leaders, academics, churches, the fatherhood movement, and women's and grandparents' groups are joining forces to reverse what Barbara Defoe Whitehead calls the "Divorce Culture." Louisiana and Arizona have adopted "covenant marriage" laws under which new spouses can voluntarily agree to more stringent conditions for divorce. The governors of Oklahoma and Arkansas have set statewide goals for achieving, by the year 2010, a one-third reduction in the divorce rate. Other states are encouraging premarital counseling for all newlyweds. The new trend has begun to make an impact on many Gen-X newlyweds, for whom a divorce-free life is most likely to seem a real achievement. Already, they are confounding the old social-science dictum that the children of divorce are much more likely to divorce themselves. It's no longer true for Gen Xers.

Filling in the Family Gaps

What's most important about the slower pace of family change during the Millennial child era is that it has allowed time for everyone to adjust and fill in the gaps. Both single parents and two-earner families are benefiting from new ways of protecting and supervising children that just weren't there yet for child Gen Xers.

Parents are making new work-life choices. Boomers and Gen Xers are arranging for flexible and part-time work hours, taking kids along on business trips (done with 32 million kids in 1998, versus just 9 million a decade earlier), "sequencing" back and forth between work and nonwork, and—especially—finding ways to earn their living at home. Paid work at private homes reached a low point in 1980. Thereafter, it began to ratchet upward even before the internet made telecommuting easier, and it has been climbing ever since. By 1997, 9 percent of all workers, including over 4 million home-based business owners, were doing paid work at home. Fully 30 percent of the U.S. workforce is now opting for what economists call "nontraditional" employment—including contract work, self-employment, and temp jobs—which are refashioning a modern equivalent to the old preindustrial "craft" household.

Other family members are offering kinship care, mirroring the '90s-era TV sitcoms that show relatives and siblings helping to take care of kids. The biggest new contributors are Silent Generation grandparents. According to a recent survey by the American Association of Retired Persons, four in ten grandparents see their grandchildren every week, and one in ten is raising or providing regular day care for at least one grandchild. Among nonwhite families, grandparents have become especially visible, often coming to the aid of their single-mother children—or being assigned the child by local authorities in cases of parental neglect or abuse. In 1997, 5.4 million kids lived with a grandparent. Of these, 3.9 million (half of them under age 6) lived in homes owned or rented by a grandparent, up 75 percent since 1970.

The shift from the era of Gen-X children and "Sun City" G.I. grandpar-

I take catalog orders from a lot of teenagers, and I cannot believe how many of them address me as "ma'am"! The local high school kids call myself and my husband "sir" or ma'am," and my kids' friends, without exception, address us as "Mr. and Mrs. So-and-So" rather than by our first names, even though I have told them I prefer to be addressed by my first name. This was unheard of ten or twenty years ago. Well, this "sir" and "ma'am" thing takes a little getting used to, but I think on some level I actually like it.

—Susan Brombacher

It's such a lonely thing. You can't really talk about it with your friends because they are all seeing their grandchildren and you can see it in their eyes. They are thinking, "You seem like such a nice person. What is it that you're doing that you can't see your grandchildren?"

—A grandmother who sued to obtain visitation rights to her grandson

We even offer a class for grandparents, explaining how parenting has changed. **—radio ad, Evergreen Maternity Center**

ents has been huge—in part because today's young (Xer) parents generally get along better with their (Silent) parents. In 1973, only 33 percent of young adults felt it was a good idea for older people to share a home with grown children. Fifty-six percent felt it was a bad idea. In 1994, those proportions reversed themselves—to 55 percent versus 28 percent, respectively. Twenty years ago, grandparents had no visitation rights with their Gen-X grandkids in case of parental divorce. The G.I.s tolerated this, but not the Silent: Thanks to new groups like the Grandparents Rights Organization and the National Coalition of Grandparents, every state has now established such a right. In the State of Washington, this right became so intrusive that the U.S. Supreme Court stepped in to curtail it somewhat.

Employers, schools, and government are helping out. Employers are becoming more flexible with hours, and many maintain on-site child care, lactation rooms, health clinics, even on-site schools. Schools are beginning classes year-round—and have structured activities that extend from early morning to evening. In 1988–89, "out-of-school time" programs were offered by 15 percent of public schools and 33 percent of private schools. By 1993–94, those numbers reached 30 percent and 50 percent, and they're still rising. Meanwhile, in addition to all of its protective activities, government is busily tracking down deadbeat dads through on-line searches—sometimes nabbing them when they visit new moms at the hospital.

Institutional child care has matured out of its chaotic Gen-X-era chrysalis. Back in the '70s, child care was often an unprofitable and disreputable activity, run by untrained people in dingy settings. Today, it's a credentialed, regulated, high-tech, brand-name business—and increasingly bifurcated by the income of the parental consumer. Major corporate players are merging and going high value, high margin, and high brand, with a pricey synergy among such tyke services as language tutoring, expensive toys, gyms, camps, and an edge on slots in private schools. While premium operators such as Crème de la Crème are opening new facilities in high-tech corridors, low-income parents must often scramble to find anything convenient and worthwhile.

Millennials are by far the most day-cared generation ever, but the proportions should be kept in perspective: Only 9 percent of children under age 4 are primarily cared for in institutional settings. Among kids of full-time working parents, 30 percent spend time in child-care centers and another 17 percent are cared for by nannies or sitters outside their own homes, a service industry with an average 1997 wage of $6.89 per hour. Many skeptics wonder what effect this will have on today's kids. Most of the studies (including one that has tracked over a thousand kids since 1991) offer mixed news. The good news is that kids in high-quality child care later fare better in school than those who remained with a stay-at-home mom. The bad news is that high-quality child care is often hard to come by, and kids with lesser-quality care later fare worse than if they had stayed home. Perhaps the most provocative finding is that the child-cared kids who fare best are those with *part-time* working moms.

Heavy doses of institutional care, across a fair swath of this generation, are shaping the early Millennial persona. Child experts generally agree that kids who spend a lot of early time in day care, particularly before age 3, can have difficulty bonding with parents. Karl Zinsmeister warns of the implications of the "rigidity" and "standardization" of this institutional upbringing, a "uniform emotional environment, with scant room for individual expression. . . . Grace saying, coat donning, one-at-a-time hand washing—these become exhausting rituals in depersonalization."

The bottom line is: Yes, the family is under enormous stress today, and parents feel enormous pressure not to let their kids down. Beneath the surface clamor of the culture wars, however, Boomers and Gen Xers are judging their own—and each other's—parental choices less by the outward look of family structure than by how well each parent is making his or her own family work.

Back in the Boomer and Gen-X child eras, parents (especially moms) often felt judged by what their family looked like—in the former case, the brunt was felt by working or divorced women; in the latter case, by moms who bucked the trend and stayed home. Today, the stay-at-home mom is back in vogue, the working or divorced mom fully accepted, and even the never-married mom is better treated and less castigated. A declining share of the public, and a very small share of Millennial teens, think a working or single mom can't be as effective as other moms. In short, a mom or dad is as a mom or dad does. As a result, more people in that parent's life—from employers to grandparents to brand-name child-care providers—are energized and mobilized to serve the best interests of the child.

You might argue that it's overkill and that babyproofing companies are in the business to frighten you and convince you that your entire home needs to be surrounded by bubble wrap, but I'm a paranoid kind of gal, and I'll buy whatever protection I can afford. —Vicki Iovine, *author of* The Girlfriends' Guide to Toddlers

At this so-called Better Baby Institute, the goal is to create physically and intelligently superb beings. They eat no sugar, and stay away from red meat. If they want a treat, they go to the health food store and buy a cereal bar. But they're sweetened with fruit juice, not sugar. They don't watch TV at all—only the very occasional nature video. . . . To me, this whole thing smacks of trying to create a "master race." —Brian Beecher

Parental Care in the Millennial Era

Listening to the critics of today's family state their case, you hear a few basic points repeated again and again. Today's families can't possibly be doing a good job, these critics assert, because kids are less supervised, get less parental time, heed fewer traditions, suffer more abuse, and are poorly disciplined. Don't believe it. Certain assertions about this generation get repeated so often that many people might think they're true—even when they're not.

>> Kids are getting more supervision.

Given all the lurid news stories about what kids do during after-school "danger hours," many people assume parents aren't looking after kids like they once did. On the contrary: Precisely because adults are so worried about "danger hours," today's kids may comprise the most supervised and scheduled child generation ever. For most, hardly an hour goes by in which they are not within sight of a parent, a teacher, a coach, a relative, or a child-care provider (with Mom and Dad occasionally peeking in via their internet "kiddiecam")—or, strapped into a minivan, in supervised transit between various adult-watched activities.

Parents and teachers of small kids don't need to be reminded of all this. For those who want numbers, the best available come from the University of Michigan's Institute for Social Research, which compared time diaries for (Gen-X) children aged 3 to 12 in 1981 with like-aged (Millennial) children in 1997. The results? Compared with Gen Xers, Millennial kids showed a stunning 37 percent decline in the amount of time (from 52 to 33 hours per week) spent in any "unstructured" activity—with the biggest declines in "free play" and "outdoor play."

Much worry has been expressed over the number of kids in self-care—that is, kids who spend some time home alone with no adult present. The best research indicates that this number has *not* grown over the last decade and is not alarmingly large. On a typical school day in 1997, less than 10 percent of all children in grades K through 5 spent any time alone at home; and of those who did, the average time alone was less than 50 minutes. Self-care is least likely among kids whose parents are middle-income, who do not have college degrees, and who are younger (that is, Gen X rather than Boomer). Interestingly, it makes little difference whether or not the mother is employed.

>> Kids are spending more time with their parents.

But surely everyone knows that kids and parents aren't spending as much time together, right? Wrong. According to the University of Maryland's "Use of Time Project," the weekly time spent by parents with and on their children fell sharply from 1965 to 1975—but then rebounded strongly over the next two decades. By 1995, the weekly hours were about the same as they were thirty years earlier. And since families were smaller, this actually meant more parental time per child. The Michigan time-diary study comes to a similar conclusion for changes in parental time from 1981 to 1997. Yet another report, from the Families and Work Institute, also concludes that parent-child time grew—by 9 percent between 1977 and 1997—largely due to all the extra time dads were spending with their kids.

Both the Maryland and Michigan projects confirm that single parents and dual-income parents spend somewhat less time on their kids than "traditional" parents. But because the child-time trend *within each family type* is steeply rising, the average for all families is also rising, albeit less steeply. How are parents doing this, given the huge increases in their work hours? The answer is simple: Moms and dads are finding more time for their kids by spending less time on housework, on their own personal leisure, and with each other. Fewer nights out and fewer made beds—but plenty of pizza with the kids. That's the story of today's typical Millennial family.

While half of all parents (56 percent of dads, 44 percent of moms) *think* their children would like them to spend more time together, only 15 percent of kids themselves say they want more dad time and just 10 percent more mom time. According to Ellen Galinsky, who interviewed hundreds of kids, what Millennials really want is for moms and dads to be less tired and stressed (30 percent) or to make more money (23 percent). Apparently, kids see lack of money as a cause of parental stress. Forty percent think their time with parents feels too rushed. Whereas three in five

Five years ago, the Phoenician was known more for its discreet, poolside cabanas. Now the Funician Club, as it's called, sees 2,500 children running across its groomed lawn every year.

—**The Wall Street Journal**

parents say they love their jobs, only two of five Millennials think their parents actually do.

Percentage of Women Who Would Quit Their Jobs If They Stopped Needing the Money

1970s:	about 30%
1989:	38%
1991:	56%

—The Wall Street Journal *(July 23, 1993)*

The time-money trade-off remains a sore spot for the Millennials' moms. Through the '70s and '80s, the proportion of mothers who said they would quit their jobs if they could afford to do so held steady at around 30 percent. Through the '90s, that percentage rose, and now a majority of working women say they would rather work less, if they didn't need the money to help their kids get a good start in life.

>> Families still do things together.

Time spent on traditional family activities has declined, but not much—and that gap is being filled by other kinds of together time. Where 91 percent of today's moms say they ate family meals when they grew up, 80 percent still do today. Similarly, 78 percent say their parents were usually at home when they returned from school; today, 61 percent say they are at home for their own kids. Counterbalancing this, the share of moms who attend their kids' school activities (like school plays or sporting events) has risen from 76 to 94 percent, reflecting today's stronger connection between the social lives of parents and kids. While no data exist on this, surely parents spend much more time moving kids from place to place than their own parents ever did with them.

>> Child abuse is on the decline.

The start of the Millennial child era in the early '80s marked a breathtaking jump in public fears about child abuse—with the share of Americans worried about it leaping (according to one study) from *one* in ten to *nine* in ten between 1976 and 1982. In this new era of hypersensitivity, people have been alarmed by government reports that child abuse is on the rise. In particular, the 1996 National Incidence Study (NIS) carried out by the National Center for Child Abuse and Neglect caused a great stir by reporting a huge jump of over 50 percent in the rates of most types of child abuse (violence and neglect as well as sexual abuse) between 1986 and 1993. Research by the National Child Abuse and Neglect Data System shows the problem getting sharply worse in the early '90s and then better in the late '90s. All these scenarios are troubling: Is the rate of child abuse really going up?

The answer is: Probably not. What the government numbers track is not the actual *incidence* rate, but the official *intervention* rate. And in the Millennial child era, experts suspect that rising interventions parallel a rising willingness by neighbors, teachers, nurses, and officers to report possible cases of abuse. As for the trend in actual incidence, the best personal survey data—compiled and analyzed by Murray Straus at the University of New Hampshire—point in the opposite direction: toward a dramatic *decline* of over 40 percent in the rate of parental violence against children from 1975 to 1992 (with even larger declines in violence against preteen kids). A similar reassessment is overtaking government reports about rising infant homicides and the like: They may be good (and welcome) indicators of rising official awareness, but not much more than that.

> **>> Parents are still disciplining their kids, albeit differently than before.**

A number of recent polls suggest that today's parents have forgotten how to say no to their children. Here, the picture is mixed. According to *Parents* magazine, 92 percent of today's parents feel confident about their ability to teach right from wrong, but only 52 percent consider themselves effective at using discipline to enforce what they teach.

When disciplining children, Boomers have problems their G.I. parents didn't. The Boomer ethic of parallel parenting leaves children a greater opening for playing one parent against the other, whereas G.I. parents followed the *Father Knows Best* rule of mandatory support from mom.

No child-rearing task saps your confidence like disciplining does, according to the results of the latest Parents poll. . . . But, despite your misgivings, you're trying harder and doing better than you realize—better, perhaps, than any preceding generation. —**Parents** *magazine*

HOW DO YOUR PARENTS PUNISH YOU?

> *Grounding: 37%*
> *Sent to room: 29%*
> *Yell, shout, or swear: 7%*
> *Spank, hit, or whip: 6%*
> *Loss of TV privileges: 4%*
> —**The Oregonian**

[Millennials] are the first group of kids savvy enough to know who to call in order to send social workers after their parents when the parents discipline the kids. —*Ray Waters*

The second problem is the Boomers' penchant for all-or-nothing rhetoric, which inclines them toward doomsday warnings more than consistent follow-through. The third problem is simple after-work exhaustion, perhaps mixed with a little guilt from parental absenteeism. Put all these together, and Boomers can be far bigger pushovers than their G.I. parents were. John Rosemond chides his female Boomer peers for being "the most unliberated women to ever inhabit this country" since they "work all day and then go home and wait on their kids."

Mothers with Children Younger than 6, Percent Employed

	1960	1998
any employment:	20%	61%
full-time:	NA	42%

—U.S. Bureau of the Census (2000)

But there's another side to this picture. Compared to G.I. parents at the same stage of life, Boomers take a much harder line in the principles and policies they advocate. They are more supportive, for example, of stricter sentencing for adolescent criminals, Zero Tolerance for school offenders, behavioral modification for hyperactive kids, and a vast new genre of defiantly antipermissive discipline theories from the likes of Dr. Dobson or Dr. Laura. And if Boomers don't excel in practical enforcement, this could simply mean they are pickier about choosing the battles that really matter. When you compare today's (Boomer and Gen-X) parents of Millennials with earlier (Silent and Boomer) parents of Gen Xers, today's batch is more lenient on lifestyle issues such as clothing, shopping, language, friends, and chores—but stricter on such bottom-line issues as drinking, drugs, driving, and hours.

Today's parents are less likely to issue G.I.-style orders than to exercise their will informally, through trust, constant involvement, and even an open admission of their need for help—which apparently is succeeding in getting Millennial kids to pitch in more with chores. When the boom must fall, today's parents prefer to employ isolation-style punishments (such as a "time out," silence at the table, or banishment to a child's room) that don't require a parent to pull rank but which do compel a child to change attitude as well as behavior. Boomers are less likely to spank or threaten or intimidate than their parents were. While 68 percent of Boomers say they were spanked as children (36 percent "hard enough to hurt" every week), 75 percent say they don't spank their own kids.

This perceived laxity has prompted culture-wars debates over what the *Babywise* authors Gary and Anne Marie Ezzo label "child-centered parenting." They advise "highchair manners" to avoid a "sinful disability called me-ism," and they defend spanking (only with the hand, never on the face, and never on the skin). Potty training has also emerged as a hot-button issue. In the Boomer child era, 92 percent of 18-month-old kids were toilet-trained. Today, at that age, only 4 percent are—and only 60 percent by 36 months. Conservatives see this as an example of parental weakness, to which T. Berry Brazelton (his work partly subsidized by Pampers) responds: "The tough love, far religious right people are reverting back to where we started in the 1920s."

Many of today's parents begrudgingly admit that they're struggling with discipline—much as they are with many of the other demanding duties of being a parent.

When asked how effectively they are doing their job, today's parents

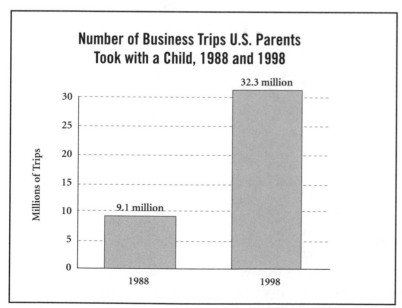

Number of Business Trips U.S. Parents Took with a Child, 1988 and 1998

Millions of Trips

1988: 9.1 million
1998: 32.3 million

Source: Travel Industry Association of America (1999)

offer mixed answers. Over half of all women say that today's mothers are "doing a worse job than their own mothers did twenty or thirty years ago." Only about one in ten say "a better job." When asked about fathers, people are more evenly split. Despite the large growth of mom-only families, Americans agree, by a 49 to 41 percent majority, that "fathers today generally play a greater role in raising their children than twenty or thirty years ago."

But when today's parents are asked about how hard they are trying, the hedging disappears. Fully 78 percent of today's parents feel they face a "much harder" challenge than their own (Silent or G.I.) parents, and only 4 percent a "much easier" task. Nine in ten adults—parents and nonparents alike—say it's "very" or "somewhat common" to find "parents who sacrifice and work hard so their kids can have a better life." Today's Millennial kids are quite willing to grade their parents more for their effort than for their self-assessed performance. Four in five kids give their moms an "A" for being with them when needed, and three of four give them an "A" for raising them with good values. (But only 29 percent give their moms an "A" for controlling their tempers.)

More than ever before in the history of polling, Americans have very positive feelings about the personal rewards of parenting and family life. Millennial kids mostly agree. The past two decades have shown a steady rise in the share of all teens who say they eventually want to get married and start a family, and of female teens who agree that being a mother "is one of the most rewarding experiences a woman can have." In 1975, a poll of high-achieving high school students found only a 43 percent minority saying they would raise their own children "the same way your parents raised you." By 1998, a 67 percent majority said they would.

So, on balance, *are* today's families truly weaker than before?

Families Past and Present

When people compare today's families with past families, they too often assume that what history requires of parents and children is unchanging. The truth is, history changes, what people do changes—and so, necessarily, the definition of strong or weak families must change.

Yes, an expert can point to plenty of data on family durability and say that families are "weaker" for today's Millennial kids than they were for Boomer kids. But this argument overlooks the underappreciated flip side of history, the countervailing "delta" of family change, which may be the most important single force causing generations to become so different from one another.

Precisely because the family was such a powerful institution back in the American High, parents didn't need to work at it so much—and took it for granted. Once World War II ended, family formation and parenthood weren't a choice, but a social *expectation*. To the mind-set of that era, everything was on autopilot: Dads earned money and stayed married, moms stayed home with the kids, and both were supported by powerful institutions that, most parents felt, would reinforce their best efforts. The inner emotional tension of this family conformism produced an indulgent-mom, distant-dad, hot-house nurture that sociologist Kenneth Keniston would later declare a cause of the youth fury during the Consciousness Revolution.

Millennials, by contrast, are the products of the opposite set of trends. Once the Consciousness Revolution ended, family formation and parenthood weren't a social expectation, but a choice, even a profound personal statement. To the current mind-set, nothing is on autopilot. Family lives are full of options. There are many kinds of dads and many kinds of moms, who must cope with weak or discredited public institutions that, they fear, could undermine their best efforts. The tension has produced a parental fixation on control, and a cooler style of nurture, that are together shaping a very different—and in many ways, *opposite*—kind of generation.

Where Boomers came of age inclined to weaken the authority of powerful institutions that had seemed too all-controlling of their parents (if liberating for themselves), Millennials could come of age inclined to retool and rebuild weak institutions that seemed to offer their own struggling parents too little help.

The families of the post–World War II decades were very effective, measured against the needs of that era. The new Boomer kids were raised to provide what parents then felt their society needed, based on the kind of family life it then had. The families of today's post–Consciousness Revolution era are also very effective, *measured against the needs of today.*

Although individual parents have little power to influence the culture of children's peer groups, larger numbers of parents acting together have a great deal of power.

—*Judith Rich Harris, author of* **The Nurture Assumption**

The family is an enclave, the last bastion of safety, and the children, standing at the center, perched upon pedestals, are being consciously, painstakingly raised to lead lives of quality, achievement, and excellence.

—*Neil Murray*

A good kid is a good dishwasher.

—*Kylie, 9, CA, greatkids.com*

Today's Millennials are being raised to provide what parents now feel their society needs, based on the kind of family life it now has.

There's good news for everybody here. Culture-wars liberals can rest reassured that family life hasn't moved back, and isn't moving back, to some new facsimile of the decade they like least, the 1950s. And, as a consequence, cultural-wars conservatives can rest reassured that the youth product from today's families will not grow up resembling the youth of the decade *they* like least, the 1960s.

Thanks largely to the family nurture they're receiving, today's Millennial kids, and America with them, appear to be headed someplace else entirely.

CHAPTER SEVEN

Raising Standards for Regular Kids (school)

He has a gift, and when you acknowledge that,
then maybe we'll have something to talk about.
—FRED, in Searching for Bobby Fischer

n the spring of 1995, fourth, eighth, and twelfth graders engaged in what is rapidly becoming a routine activity for American kids: They sat down with bubble-sheet answer forms, picked up number-two pencils, and took a multiple-choice test. To their relief, they were told that this was a global test, one that wouldn't affect their grades. What they *weren't* told was that results of this test would become the centerpiece of loud new demands for still more tests, higher testing standards, and curricula that teaches to those standards.

This particular test was known as the "Tims" (TIMSS), the Third International Mathematics and Science Study. The results were mixed. The twelfth graders (Gen Xers born in 1977) did very poorly, outperforming rivals from only two of twenty-one nations. *"Hey, we're number 19!"* jeered columnist John Leo. America's eighth graders (Gen Xers born in 1981) did somewhat better, ranking above the median in science but below it in math. The fourth graders (Millennials born in 1985) did

Scrutiny of the nation's high schools has never been greater.

—U.S. News & World Report

There's pressure to achieve in everything. It can make the brightest kid in the world feel inadequate.

—Marilyn Cook,
high school principal

Getting into college has become a tough competition because of the number of successful students in our generation. We're forced to work twice as hard just to receive the same recognition as others who used to be able to get by.

—Whitley Lassen, 17

extremely well, second only to Korea in science and well above the median in math.

By 1998, after these results had been analyzed and digested, a consensus emerged about what the Tims results supposedly proved—that U.S. schoolchildren started out well in elementary school but then lost ground in the higher grades. Summing up the expert consensus, John Jennings, director of the Center on Education Policy, asked, "What goes wrong as students progress through American schools from early elementary to middle school to high school?"

The Tims furor is a classic example of how people can overlook clear evidence of generational change. The test didn't track the *same* children from the fourth through the twelfth grades, as those quotes might imply. It evaluated *different cohorts* of children, whose scores provide powerful proof that later-born U.S. kids are doing better (vis-à-vis their global rivals) than those who came before. The kids born in 1985 do better at math and science, for their age, than those born in 1981 or 1977. In the year 2000, these three Tims cohorts are graduating from eighth grade, twelfth grade, and college. It's too bad no one is repeating this test, *with these same cohorts,* because if they did, isn't it just possible that the 1985-born Millennials would still hold their high global standing? And that 1989-born kids now in fourth grade would be doing even better?

The findings of our Teachers' Survey suggest that they would. Overwhelmingly, these teachers indicate that a positive trend is in the making: The further down the grade ladder you go, the better American students are doing, in comparison to kids in the same grade ten or more years ago. When asked whether today's elementary school kids are more or less knowledgeable and proficient at science than their predecessors in the 1980s, the teachers say "more" by nearly a five-to-one margin. For reading, it's four to one. For math, civics, history, writing, and foreign languages, it's two to one or better. In this same survey, teachers give less positive ratings to today's middle school kids, declaring them better than those of the 1980s in science and foreign languages, about the same in math, but not as good in reading or civics, and not nearly as good in writing and geography. They give even worse scores—in some subjects, truly dismal—to pre-Millennial high school seniors.

This was a survey of just two hundred teachers in one county, but it

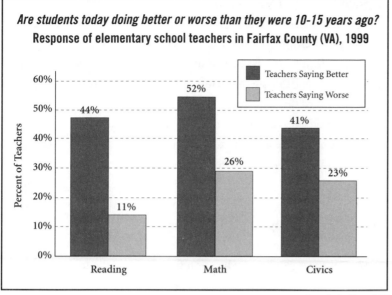

Are students today doing better or worse than they were 10-15 years ago?
Response of elementary school teachers in Fairfax County (VA), 1999

Source: Teachers' Survey (2000)

backed up the good news hidden in the Tims, news that the media and most education experts failed to see: *Millennials are becoming a generation of positive trends in educational achievement.*

The Wake-Up Call

The first Millennials were barely a year old when education reform hit its modern ground zero. In the 1983 "Nation at Risk" report, the U.S. Department of Education declared American schools (and, implicitly, their Gen-X students) to be "a rising tide of mediocrity that threatens our very future as a nation and people." The report was a national wake-up call. "It is possible that our entire public school system is nearing collapse," warned UCLA dean John Goodlad. Educational experts immediately set to work on studies that were published through the rest of the decade, invariably deriding Gen-X kids for being stupid at math, science, reading, writing, geography, history, *just about everything.*

Next came the calls for action. In 1989, the nation's leaders (among them the self-declared "Education President," George Bush) summoned the First National Education Summit. At that time, they set "Goals 2000,"

Perhaps the most irresponsible goal was the one calling for the nation to be first in math and science. We shouldn't want first place even if we could have it. Koreans and Japanese score high not only with curriculum we might emulate but also by subjecting children to intense cramming and competitive test pressure. . . . Perhaps we should aim for fifth, not first. Or perhaps we should seek absolute standards and ignore international ranking.

—*Richard Rothstein*

I'm 47, and I have 25-year-old teachers telling me what to do with my home life. —*David Kooyman*

It's like what used to happen to us at the college level has now been brought down to fifth grade. The whole feeling is much more pressure, pressure, pressure.

—*Sylvia Wertheimer, parent*

Homework makes me so depressed and stressed. —*Maxx,* Kids Talk

It breaks a mother's heart to see her child in tears because they have so much homework that supper was their only break in the evening.

—*letter to the editor,* Lincoln Journal Star

an ambitious list of eight major goals, one of which was to make the newly minted Class of 2000—alias the first Millennials, then in second grade—number one in the world in math and science by the time they graduated from high school. The summit established a National Education Goals panel to issue annual reports measuring national and state progress toward the eight goals.

By the mid-'90s, according to *U.S. News,* education in America was shifting from an "age of lament" to an "age of accountability"—an age in which candidates rush to endorse this or that school-reform plan, schools replace Social Security as the trump card of politics, and adults under age 50 consistently name education as the nation's highest priority, ahead of the economy and national defense.

In the new millennium, Americans can look back over dramatic changes in the direction of education from one decade to the next. During the 1950s, schools were pushed to become more democratic, to foster excellence and progress, and to address unmet *Blackboard Jungle* social

needs. The 1960s saw growing attention to student creativity, an erosion of school authority, and entirely new public missions (race, gender, poverty). The 1970s were a decade of experimentation, curricular diversity, rejection of standards, open classrooms, teachers as pals, and the elevation of student self-esteem as a major goal. The 1980s emerged as the decade of alarm, arguments over mistakes made, teacher morale problems, and growing parental discontent. Following this, the '90s became the decade of getting back to basics, teaching values, setting standards, and holding schools and students accountable.

At each turn, the meaning of education to those who teach has changed to a similar rhythm. The '60s had been the era of the young draft-deferred male; the '70s of *Welcome Back, Kotter* teachers trying to do something "relevant"; and the '80s of deep discontent and flagging collegiate interest in the field. The '90s have seen another change—and, again, it's a real turnaround. The share of teachers who say they'd be a teacher again, which had fallen from 84 percent (in 1966) to 42 percent (in 1981), has soared back up to 67 percent (in 1996). Teacher pay has recouped the large inflation-adjusted decline it had suffered in the '70s. The share of teachers with master's degrees has risen from one-sixth to over half. Teaching now carries a cachet that it hasn't had since the 1960s as a profession with "meaning"—enticing many Teach for America Gen Xers to test their mettle in the classroom, and many burned-out Boomer professionals to come back to school and do something "real" with their lives.

Parents, meanwhile, are getting more perfectionist and passionate about their kids' education. For the mom or dad of Millennials, no age is too young to begin preparing them for school. The simple baby flashcards of the mid-'80s were gradually upgraded, by the mid-'90s, to "lapware" programs, "Brainy Baby" videos, and hugely popular, pre- and post-natal "Mozart Effect" CDs (which the states of Georgia and Tennessee now send home with every newborn). No school activity is to be taken lightly. Seven in ten parents of elementary school students now say it is "extremely important" for them to get their kids to do their homework. Four in ten have spoken to their kids' teachers more than five times during the year and have volunteered to help their teachers more than once during the year. And, of course, no subject can be taught at school without Mom and Dad's curiosity, scrutiny, and oversight.

I was talking with a friend the other day who has a son in first grade. She was telling me that her son has two hours of homework every night. I was a bit shocked, I mean, first grade? I don't remember having any homework until what they then called Junior High. —Donna, a 35-year-old mother

When you have homework on a regular basis, you learn persistence, diligence, and delayed gratification. —Nanine Bempechat, Harvard School of Education

You begin to view homework as just another intrusion into everyone's overscheduled, late-late-20th-century lives. —Eugenie Allen

Our whole high-school experience has stopped being fun and carefree. . . . No matter how far you step off campus, you still have to think and work on school assignments. —Lorena, 16

I am weighed down a lot after school with an overstuffed backpack. It can damage your back, you know! There should be a law about the maximum weight a child can carry home. —Dana, 11

I don't think the homework is that bad, but the taking home of your whole locker annoys me to death! —Kate, 11

Scientific Observations by Fifth and Sixth Graders:

When people run around and around in circles,
we say they are crazy. When planets do it, we
say they are orbiting.

We say the cause of perfume disappearing is
evaporation. Evaporation gets blamed for a lot
of things people forget to put the top on.

The moon is a planet just like the earth, only it
is even deader.

—clem.mscd.edu

This all mirrors a larger national purpose than merely to teach kids: It's
the urge to shape them into a better and smarter generation than the Gen
Xers whose lagging achievement prompted the "Nation at Risk" report.

Through the '80s, the new Millennial-era school debate focused
mostly on achievement, but by the '90s, a deeper debate emerged, about
character. Academics became intertwined with other issues about the
proper morals-shaping (and culture-shaping) role for schools. Where
before, culture-wars liberals had sought more freedom and conservatives
more authority, liberals began seeking more authority and conservatives
more choice. One side wanted kids to grow up as environmentalists and
feminists, and not as homophobes or hate criminals. The other side
wanted them to believe in God and revere traditional values. Both sides
wanted schools to have the authority, and parents the freedom, to ensure
that kids are taught their desired agenda. And both sides feared that the
other side (Hollywood, the "Christian right") intended to interfere with
their own plans for their own kids—and for other kids.

School "Choice"

It's within this context that the word *choice* has become a new canard in
the education debate. From union-hating conservatives to bureaucracy-
hating liberals such as Jerry Brown, "freedom" of school choice has

become a clarion call. Yet what Boomer and Gen-X parents want isn't "freedom" for kids, like what they remember having in the '70s or '80s. No, what they covet is freedom for *themselves:* the freedom to move their kids to the schools they like best, and the freedom to restrict as they please the choices their own kids face on matters of values, behavior, appearance, and peer groups. Adults seek what education journalist Jay Mathews calls a "parent-sensitive environment"—which translates into *less* sensitivity to the child's own desires.

While private schools have long been available to parents dissatisfied with public schools, their growing importance—along with new options such as charter schooling and home schooling—is putting new pressure on public schools to change their ways.

For decades, until the end of the '80s, private schools had been gradually declining in their share of all students nationwide. Then, just as the first Millennials set out with their lunch boxes, the share started rising—and has continued to rise at all grade levels throughout the '90s. Nine in ten private schools have at least a nominal religious affiliation, and church schools have ridden this new wave of parental reform-mindedness. Back in 1960, Catholic elementary schools were educating 4.4 million Boomers. By 1990, they were enrolling only 1.9 million Gen Xers. Now they're back up to over 2 million Millennials, with their fastest growth in inner cities. Enrollment at "Bible" or "Christian" schools has meanwhile doubled.

Parochial schools lie at the center of the brewing debate over vouchers, through which public funds would be paid to help subsidize private school tuitions for low-income students. The idea is vigorously opposed by teachers' unions and most civil rights groups, but draws support from an odd alliance between what columnist Matt Miller has dubbed the "voucher right" (evangelicals) and "voucher left" (72 percent of blacks and 59 percent of all urbanites). Milwaukee began the first voucher program in 1990, but the movement has since stalled. By the end of 1999, public vouchers were reaching only about 10,000 kids in Milwaukee, Cleveland, and Florida, with only a smattering of other programs in the works.

The charter school movement has won less notice but has had a bigger impact on Millennials. By obtaining a charter, private entrepreneurs can use public funds to run magnet schools that can sidestep unions, bureaucrats, and state regulations. In 1992, there was only one charter school in

---

America's high schools [are] sorting machines, tagging and labeling young people as successful, run of the mill, or low achievers. **—Richard Riley, U.S. Secretary of Education**

I see a lot of parents who are chronically disappointed in their kids. . . . Many say they feel obligated to be disapproving or the kid will never make it in the world.

—William Stixrud, clinical neurologist

Our parents expect us to go to college. It was never such a big deal before. The Boomers would leave high school, and, if it didn't suit them to go and get a higher education, they would get a job for a while, and when they had the means or the intuition they would go back to school. This is an abnormality now. You would be considered a failure by your peers.

—Kirsten Johnson, 16

Living in the 1990s and being 17 is tough. We have to keep up with the pressures and expectations our parents and society put on us.

—Jenn Silvi, 17

GILES: *This is the SATs, Buffy. Not connect the dots. Please pay attention. A low score can seriously harm your chances of getting into college.*

BUFFY: *Gee, thanks. That takes the pressure right off.*

—Buffy the Vampire Slayer

the United States, but by decade's end, 1,684 charter schools in thirty-two states and the District of Columbia were enrolling 350,000 students (nearly 1 percent of school-age kids)—double the total enrollment gains of parochial schools.

But by far the biggest and most consequential instrument of parental "choice" has been home schooling, which has shown a 7 to 15 percent *annual* growth rate through the '90s. No one has an accurate head count, but the number of home schoolers has risen from maybe 100,000 in the early 1980s to nearly 1.5 million today (3 percent of school-age Millennials), more than the entire public-school student body of the state of New Jersey. The steep rise in home schooling preceded the internet, but is now getting an extra boost from parents who can now telecommute (and thereby teach) at home, and from on-line educational aids.

When charter- and home-schooled children are added to the tally, the total enrollment of students *not* in traditional public schools rose between 1990 and 1999, from 5.2 million to around 7.7 million kids, or by 48 percent. Meanwhile, the number in traditional public school settings rose by only 11 percent. At the margin, therefore, school "choice" has become a real motivator, moving America toward what teachers' union official Adam Urbanski calls "a system of schools instead of a school system."

**Number of States with Academic Standards
in Core Subjects:**

1996: **14**

1999: **49**

Traditional public schools remain the locus for 84 percent of Millennial schoolchildren, but they're feeling more parental heat. PTA memberships have reversed their long membership slide from the G.I.-parent/Boomer-child era of the early '60s (12.1 million) to the Silent-parent/Gen-X-child era of the early '80s (5.3 million), and are back up to 6.5 million today. This upswing is partly due to the usefulness of PTA fund-raising to get around state spending equalization formulas—enabling affluent parents to make sure their children have all the latest teaching tools. But the culture wars are asserting themselves here as well.

In Loudoun County, Virginia, a hotbed of home schooling, twenty PTAs have been challenged by sixteen conservative PTOs that challenge the status-quo orthodoxy on sex education, phonics, and other matters.

From the 1950s through the 1980s, American parents became gradually less intrusive in public schools. Now, they're becoming more so. And as they put pressure on public schools to provide more "choice" for parents, so too do they want less choice, ergo more *values,* for kids.

Values

When parents pull their children out of public schools, the usual reason is values. Parents want schooling to be something that shapes kids, an intellectual and moral process that reaches them deep within, much like a spiritual faith.

Consider *The Book of Virtues,* Bill Bennett's landmark Millennial corrective with the medicinal cover. His ten values—self-discipline, compas-

Our schools should not cultivate confusion. They must cultivate conscience.   —George W. Bush

We are witnessing the schools' rewakening to what was historically one of their most essential tasks, the formation of character among the children in their care.

—*Kevin Ryan and Karen Bohlin,* **Building Character in Schools**

I think teens are not getting in that much trouble anymore because they are more worried about their education and their future more than anything.   —*Jake, 14*

sion, responsibility, friendship, work, courage, perseverance, honesty, loyalty, and faith—are what many midlife Boomers, liberal and conservative, agree that children need to be taught on this lee side of the Consciousness Revolution. Such values seem desperately needed in an era of *South Park,* Dennis Rodman, and Monica Lewinsky. But they haven't always seemed so necessary. One reason Bennett's values are called "traditional" is because many of them were *not* as stressed by the modern postwar parents who had just conquered global fascism only to confront global communism—and who were not so eager to teach children to be obedient, loyal, team-playing followers of authority. Instead, G.I.s felt their Boomer children instead needed to develop independence, creativity, and if necessary the courage to defy lockstep authority.

Times have changed. Recall how the Boomer child era was a time of fading *in loco parentis,* of outmoded puritanism, of a fresh God-is-dead rationalism. Adults wanted to unleash kids' creativity, not suppress it. Then came the Gen-X era. While teachers tried to solve a myriad of social woes, they refused to take the lead. *Tell me your values,* adults told kids, *and we'll help you get there.* By the 1990s, schoolchild Millennials stepped into a moral relativism that now felt tired and outmoded in its turn. Pulled on every side by rapid economic change, cultural fragmentation, and ethnic influx, Americans wanted kids to acquire values that were clearer and less ambiguous—solid counterweights to the freewheeling behavior of adults.

Schools are as much a battleground as ever, but with an increasing consensus about what values adults think kids ought to develop. Politicians of all stripes (including George W. Bush and Al Gore) are eager to get "faith-based organizations" back into public education. Whenever you notice both sides of the culture wars focusing on the same message, it's usually landing hard on Millennials. Take teasing: *Veggie Tales* says it's anti-Christian, whereas *Sesame Street* says it breeds intolerance. Either way, the message is the same: *Don't!*

The culture wars still flare, especially around holiday time (Columbus Day, Halloween, or Christmas) and over sex ed, evolution, multicultural readings, and the teaching of history. But today's parents widely agree that kids—their own, other people's, and especially recent immigrants'— should be taught "absolutely essential" American ideals, ones adhered to by all the dominant faiths. "You don't need to believe in God to believe in trustworthiness," says Michael Josephson, founder of Character Counts!—one of many new "character education" curricula that schools are using to teach Millennials, particularly in the elementary grades.

"Good character, this thinking goes, is about good habits," writes Lisa Miller, and the new "character education" curricula have produced a variety of slogans and jingles to drill the point home. In the Character First! curriculum (a joint venture between public schools and a Christian organization), children recite a poem-pledge: "I will look at someone speaking / And I'll listen all I can / I will sit and stand up straight / Like a soldier on command." In another program, students are asked to make a daily pledge to comply with six "Character Pillars" (which kids call "caterpillars"): "Each day in our words and actions, we will persevere to exhibit respect, caring, fairness, trustworthiness, responsibility, and citizenship." Afterward, they recite the Pledge of Allegiance.

Proportion of Kindergartners Spending Full Days (Rather than Half-Days) in School:

1970: **12%**

1980: **29%**

1990: **42%**

—USA Today *(June 30, 1992)*

In "character education," kids are seldom taught to question adult standards. They are simply told what is expected, encouraged to suggest extra rules to better apply the standard (which often get pinned to the wall: "No pushing in front of drinking fountain"), and then rewarded (often in groups) for good behavior. When kids don't obey the standard, they are not invited to discuss and explore the reasons behind it. Instead, a punishment or treatment protocol deals with the issue in purely behavioral terms—from detention to expulsion, from an apology to classmates to a recommendation for medical attention. If they are diagnosed with Attention Deficit and Hyperactive Disorder (ADHD), they may be prescribed psychotropic drugs to help them sit still, learn, and not bother others—which most schools are fully prepared (with nurses) to dispense to kids on a strict schedule.

States are requiring more courses, and moving away from the anything-goes, shopping-mall high school that was in vogue thirty years ago..

—*Christopher Cross,*
Council for Basic Education

We recognized we had not challenged our students to the extent they need to be challenged. We're encouraging a much higher level of performance.

—*Nancy Grasmick,*
Superintendent of Schools,
State of Maryland

The team approach—teachers setting their own agendas for small clusters of students—has swept the Washington area, almost completely replacing the traditional junior high school.

—*Jay Matthews,*
The Washington Post

In many ways, the education accountability movement echoes the restructuring process American businesses went through in the late 1970s to address lagging productivity.

—**The New York Times**

Ironically, where young Boomers once turned to drugs to prompt impulses and think outside the box, today they turn to drugs to suppress their kids' impulses and keep their behavior inside the box. Rousseau the young dreamer, meet Rousseau the graying communitarian. Nowadays, Dennis the Menace would be on Ritalin, Charlie Brown on Prozac.

Not long ago, educators celebrated the differences between the values of different kids. No longer. The new stress is on the values Millennials have in common. If everybody is part of a team, then that, in turn, requires team skills.

Teamwork

In 1998, the Fairfax County, Virginia, School Board heard from a number of parents who were displeased that their kids did not have the same opportunities as those at Thomas Jefferson High School, a selective "gifted and talented" (GT) school that routinely produces America's largest number of National Merit Scholars. Speaking out on behalf of what educators call "regular kids," Lois Spotila said, "These are the kids who are going to comprise the mass of society, and we need to make sure they have the skills they need to be successful, productive members." The board promptly passed a resolution to provide every student with a "gifted quality education"—by reducing class sizes, subsidizing AP exams, establishing International Baccalaureate programs, and providing more demanding classes at all the county's high schools.

Until the early '90s, school systems often gave more attention to "special needs" programs for gifted or disabled kids than they did to the needs of nongifted, nondisabled kids. In most districts, special-education budgets rose three or four times faster than overall school budgets. From 1967 to 1996, special-ed spending alone rose from 4 to 19 percent of all school spending. While no one regrets the huge recent gains in the quality of GT and special-ed programs, parents of "regular kids" are starting to demand that their kids have better programs too.

The "regular kid" versus special need debate began in earnest after World War II, when educators realized that the war had been won in part through the brilliance of allied scientists. For that reason, the postwar draft deferred students, teachers, scientists, and PhD candidates. In 1959,

James Bryant Conant's influential report, *The American High School Today,* made the case for fast (college prep) and slow (vocational), as well as medium, tracks. Entering the Boomer child era, the regular kid still ruled. By the time Gen-X children came along, school systems were diversifying their tracks, methods, and curricula. Now, after several decades of stressing the "tails" of the academic bell curves, schools are again starting to focus on the "bell" itself.

While GT and special-ed programs remain strong, the new emphasis is toward mainstreaming the gifted or disabled—bringing kids together rather than splitting them apart. In California and Massachusetts, middle schools are doing away with tracking altogether. Especially in the younger grades, the new purpose of tracking is less to create heterogeneity than homogeneity (by weeding out rule breakers). Some high schools are eliminating the "valedictorian" designation and treating honor roll membership as a private matter (for parents, teachers, and colleges to know) but *not* a public matter (for the whole student body to know).

For Millennials, "collaborative learning" has become as popular as independent study was for Boomers or open classrooms for Gen Xers. Kids do projects, and are often graded, in groups. Parents who never

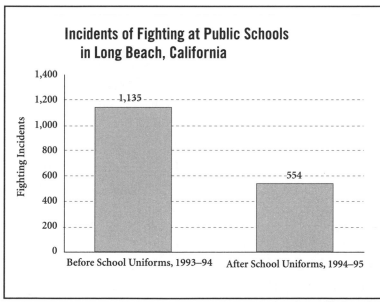

Incidents of Fighting at Public Schools in Long Beach, California

Fighting Incidents

- 1,400
- 1,200 — 1,135
- 1,000
- 800
- 600 — 554
- 400
- 200
- 0

Before School Uniforms, 1993–94   After School Uniforms, 1994–95

Source: *Los Angeles Times* (August 21, 1995)

I've seen immense changes. The children felt better about themselves. It gave them a sense of belonging.

—*Denise McCarthy, elementary school principal on uniforms*

Sometimes I really like getting all dressed up and looking nice. That's why I like uniforms.

—*Marvin Smith, 8*

Badges promote a sense of belonging. . . . Badges provide unity since every student is put on the same level and required to wear one. . . . Ready or not, badges are one of the keys on the road to becoming a more responsible adult.   —*Jessica Birt, 17*

If I have to wear it, I want it to say something about me.

—*Robyn Christy, 15, who painted a purple metallic trim around her school ID badge*

experienced this themselves sometimes get upset when their kid receives a bad grade from poor work done by his or her team—or from a student grader. "Hands-on math" is done in groups. The Junior Engineering Technical Society runs a contest that tests teams, not individuals. "Forget Einstein. Think Team!" reads a headline in *The Washington Post* about the new trend in high school science. Peer review is increasingly being extended to honor code enforcement, prom-night behavior (through the work of Students Against Destructive Decisions), and interscholastic competitions. In Virginia's Cappies program, students write critical reviews of one another's plays and musicals that are then published in local newspapers.

Nothing symbolizes Millennial teamwork more than their standardized appearance. Where Boomers broke dress codes back when their parents had a strong one, Millennials are conforming to new dress codes at a time when their parents have a weak one. Clothing that was tolerated during the Gen-X school era—baseball caps, halter tops, short skirts, baggy pants, jangling jewelry, and gang-message T-shirts—can now get a kid sent home. Kids grumble at this, but nonetheless are moving toward a depunked, degrunged Old Navy or Abercrombie & Fitch–style appearance.

And then there are the *real* uniforms. The school uniform movement began in the late 1980s, when first-wave Millennials put them on in Long Beach, California, and Washington, D.C. In the early '90s, uniforms became popular among inner-city elementary schoolkids. By the mid-'90s, they aged into middle schools—and began to break out into nonurban areas—and soon after reached high schools. By 1997, three-fourths of all Chicago schools required uniforms. By 1999, they were appearing at all grades, elementary through high school, in roughly half of New York City schools. In 2000, they became mandatory in Philadelphia schools. They're especially popular in inner cities. From 1990 to 1997, the share of all U.S. students in uniform has grown from virtually nothing to 10 percent, with another 15 percent in districts that are actively considering them. "The rest of the world goes casual. We go professional," says David Levin, founder of a charter school that requires every student to wear a school-insignia shirt of some kind.

New school-uniform policies are often hotly debated before they are implemented, but not afterward. That's because they're generally popular, even among Millennials, once the community gets used to them.

Time-pressed kids and parents find it simplifies the choices they have to make, and educators like the tone it sets. "You have to dress properly for a job," says Roanoke school official Ann Harmon, "and education is their job." When uniforms are introduced, principals report that discipline improves right away, and achievement improves over time.

Standards

"School is different now," says Chicago teacher Esme Raji Codell. "It's not like you can come in and teach that Columbus sailed in 1492 and two plus two equals four." It's not? To many visitors, that's exactly what *is* different about school these days. Enter a classroom today, and you might hear an entire class reciting facts and tables in unison. Why? Because these questions are starting to appear on "high stakes" tests that can spell the difference between success and failure for students, teachers, schools, even governors. Such is the power of the new "standards" movement in public schools.

Standards went out of fashion during the Boomer child years. When Gen-X kids started going to school, educators decided there was no single body of knowledge, so they didn't teach it. Just as the first Gen Xers were graduating, educators changed their minds and admitted that, yes, there was such a body of what E. D. Hirsch called "cultural literacy," and that Gen Xers didn't know it. Now, with Millennials, standards are coming back, with a roar.

The "standards" movement arose out of an original suggestion, stemming from a 1989 summit, that the federal government should establish guideposts for what was initially (and ill-fatedly) known as "outcomes-based education." This "OBE" plan became enmeshed in culture wars and devolution arguments, accused of political correctness and a power grab from states and school boards, and abandoned. Then the states took over, and essentially the same idea has moved swiftly forward with enormous public support.

One by one, states developed their own multiple-choice tests, like Texas's TAAS, Massachusetts's MCAS, and Virginia's SOL. After an experimental run or two, the tests are given bite. Usually, the first results are highly embarrassing for schools and students alike. Then, the second time, schools and students do better, and public officials bask in praise.

Does it matter to have educational standards?? Does it keep people's eye on the ball? Absolutely. This is what leadership is all about. We're not here to make people happy.

—Margaret LaMontagne, education aide to George W. Bush

The test changed the whole school around. . . . It's made everything worse. And when I said I wouldn't take it, they said the realty people were relying on our test results to sell houses. *—Alex Summerfield, 17, one of seven Danvers, MA, high school students suspended for refusing to take a state standards test*

Kids and schools know there are consequences looming on the horizon if they don't do well, and that gives this school season a different kind of edge. *—Robert Schwartz, Achieve, Inc.*

My father teased me. He said I might be a dropout if I don't pass. . . . I lied in bed wondering what was going to happen, if I was going to fail or pass. How many would I get wrong? How many would I get right?

—Meghan Collard, 9, on the New York state test for fourth graders

Texas Governor George W. Bush cited improved TAAS scores as a major credential for his run for the presidency.

"What is different now," says Jay Matthews, "is that the tests have become a public measuring and punishing stick." Once the tests fully take effect—which, for many states, remains a few years in the future—the consequences can be substantial. Principals and teachers can be paid bonuses or fired. Florida now gives every school a letter grade, "A" to "F," based on the state test results. Real-estate values can rise or fall. Students can be graduated or denied diplomas, promoted or forced to repeat grades, given awards or ordered to summer schools (now mandatory in New York City for anyone who scores below the fifteenth percentile), transferred to GT programs or demoted to special ed.

Every state but Iowa now has (or is implementing) standardized testing—and, in twenty-seven states, these tests are linked to everything from grade promotion and graduation to school funding. By degrees, standardized testing is becoming just about the only measure of academic quality that really counts in many school systems. With their students' promotions (not to mention their own jobs) on the line, teachers are teaching to the tests and reallocating class time to help students with test-taking skills.

Compared to 10–15 Years Ago, Does Your Middle School Curriculum Emphasize . . .

	More	Less
Teaching to tests	96%	0%
Group projects	75%	8%
Community service	63%	18%
Good citizenship	50%	29%
Tracking by ability	16%	63%

—asked of middle school teachers in Fairfax County (VA), in Teacher's Survey (1999)

Who benefits most from this? "Regular kids." With so much pressure on schools to pass the requisite number of students, the priority students are neither the gifted (who are sure to pass) nor the disabled (many of whom can be exempted), but the kids expected to score just above or below the passing mark. When the teaching focus moves back toward the facts and ideas that appear in textbooks, it holds every kid more accountable and tends to equalize the opportunity for kids in different socioeconomic strata. When preparing for a standardized test, the quality of family conversations, bookshelves, or museum trips matters less and the quantity of studying helps more—which puts the children of lawyers and of domestic workers on a more level field of competition. This is why principals of urban schools tend to be happier with these tests than their counterparts in the suburbs.

The state standards tests have enriched a standardized test industry, which now totals $200 million in annual sales. The tests have empowered a back-to-basics curricular industry with companies such as Direct Instruction, Core Knowledge, and Junior Great Books. Success for All, which began in Baltimore in 1987 and is now taught in 1,130 elementary schools, follows a very basic and fast-paced set of scripted lessons that the entire class recites orally. Critics call it "robo-teaching"—but it's getting results. Boomer teachers are often offended by its regimented, cookie-cutter style, while Xer teachers are less bothered by it. The tests have energized the teaching of phonics and arithmetic, and have rewarded behavioral teach-

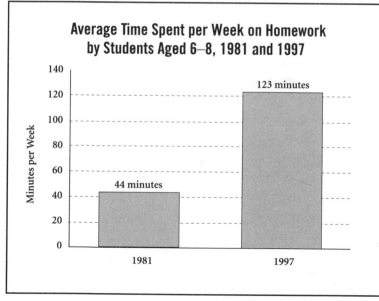

Average Time Spent per Week on Homework by Students Aged 6–8, 1981 and 1997

- 1981: 44 minutes
- 1997: 123 minutes

Source: Institute for Social Research, University of Michigan (1999)

www.cramcentral.com [is] a very different sort of educational product aimed at smart, college-bound high school students . . . that offers crash online courses on various topics for advanced-placement tests.

—The Wall Street Journal

Our chances of getting into a good college are dropping every day, as expectations soar, unrestrained. The pressure's on.   —Tyler Hudgens, 15

The Princeton Review got so many tutoring requests in the ritzy Hamptons this year that it had to rent a summer house to accommodate all the tutors.   —Time

Singapore math and the Japanese math curriculum known as Kumon . . . are the two Asian approaches that have made the most inroads in U.S. schools. The Kumon method, used as a supplemental curriculum, has spread to . . . more than 109,000 students in North America.   —The Washington Post

It's getting pretty grim out there. Colleges want to see that high-school students aren't sitting around watching Seinfeld reruns all summer.

—Time,
on pre-course tutoring

ing methods by which teachers guide students through small steps toward a successful test score—rather than through bigger steps that may or may not better prepare them for college.

Standards are becoming consequential because the adults running the schools, from teachers to governors, are being held accountable. With more charter schools available, and with parochial and home schooling more popular, poor scores can induce parents to "walk" with their kids. When enough of them do, this creates real problems for administrators and politicians. Accordingly, a trend has begun among school officials to promise to step down if they fail to improve scores. Aspiring teachers are feeling the standardized-test bite right at the source. Several states have toughened the national teacher-certifying Praxis test so that now only 50 percent pass the test, whereas 90 percent used to pass it.

This all appeals to market-oriented parents, Boomers and Gen X alike. That's how the rest of the world works nowadays, and they see no reason why schools should be different. However, test results differ from marketplace results in that the outcome can be more easily gamed. School administrators can selectively exclude certain kids from taking the test. Charges of administrators' cheating, even to the extent of erasing and fixing wrong answers, have already been leveled in some districts.

Millennials are feeling the heat in ways Boomers and Gen Xers could never imagine. Employers are asking to see high school transcripts, test scores, even attendance records. Social promotions are being discontinued. More homework is being assigned in the younger grades. Recesses are disappearing (or, with a heavy adult hand, are being reconfigured as "socialized recesses"). Class periods are lengthening. School years are being extended. Summers are newly serious, with teachers assigning vacation homework, kids packing off to academic camps, and summer schools bursting with mandatory attendees. More nervous students are turning to a rapidly expanding network of tutoring companies such as Sylvan, Score!, and the Japanese Kumon Math & Reading Centers, which alone has 1,400 centers in North America.

Senior year is developing an arms-race quality, as colleges tempt students to make ever-earlier decisions, while becoming ever more selective. By all accounts, the Class of 2000 faced the stiffest college-admission competition in history. The number of stellar student résumés keeps rising, but the number of elite colleges does not. In April 2000, Harvard mailed those dreaded thin (rejection) envelopes to a thousand high school valedictorians—many of whom, back in the Boomer era, would have been accepted.

Think About Students a Few Years Older Than You. When They Were Your Age, Did They Have More or Less . . .

	Less	More
Homework	64%	11%
Scheduled activities	58%	12%
Demanding teachers	46%	15%

—*Class of 2000 Survey (1999)*

Classes are becoming more of a connect-the-dots enterprise. *Cliff's Notes*, a badge of shame for Boomer teens, are more helpful than ever. Teachers are starting to return to more formulaic grading systems—x percent for each test, y percent for each homework assignment—to deter nasty arguments with students or (worse) their parents. Kids are fearful of grades and fearful of failing—because the stakes seem higher than before. ("I am afraid to go to school because of homework, not violence," emailed an anonymous teen on Kid Exchange.) Achieving kids feel the pressure too, as more high-quality students compete with one another (and with foreigners) for a fixed number of slots. Jenny Hung, a California high school senior who took all the honors courses she could, said that "going to bed at midnight was a luxury, one A.M. was normal, three A.M. meant time to panic, and four A.M. meant it was time to go to sleep defeated."

Surveys confirm that Millennials don't mind a more structured curriculum, more order, more stress on basics. They prefer those subjects in which they, and the world, can measure their objective progress. They insist they admire their "hard" teachers at least as much as their "cool" ones. They say they like math and science more than the humanities and arts and much more than history—perhaps because the latter subjects lack clear-cut answers or come loaded with excessive ideological freight, or are just taught dully (to the test).

Millennials reveal both a new seriousness and a new distance from

You will continue to see a more and more rote type of teaching and learning. Why? Because the Millennials do much better work when given worksheet-type work.

—Paul Beavers, teacher

We're not measuring creative writing. . . . Instead, we are assessing organized thoughts through writing on very specific topics. . . . These things can be scored by a computer.

—Frederic McHale, describing a new Educational Testing Service plan to grade writing samples by computer

If Bodkin Elementary School Principal Rocce Ferretti had any doubt that the rigid writing program he instituted to beef up his school's state exam scores was sinking in, that ended when he saw one parent's Mother's Day card. . . . "It was like, 'Dear Mom, you are the best mother in the world for the following reasons. . . .'" Then it backed up the claim with three examples and summed it up with a conclusion . . . in the form of an answer for Maryland School Performance Assessment Program exams. —**The Washington Post**

school. In this new era of teaching to standards, they don't go to school to express their inner selves. Polls show them liking school less, with each passing year, but accepting it more, as necessary for the future. If they don't give their schools the same high grades they give their parents, it's because—despite the new stress on standards and grades—they still don't find the curriculum interesting or challenging enough to really engage their energy. A recent Public Agenda survey found that 65 percent of high school students admitted they weren't trying very hard, and 75 percent said they'd try harder if pushed.

But plenty of them *are* being pushed, by parents. Says Alexandria, Virginia, high school teacher Patrick Welsh, "I've seen increasing expectations, anxiety, and downright disappointment from parents . . . who expect their seventeen- or eighteen-year-old kids to have attained some rarefied state of perfection. . . . At some parent conferences, I find myself defending bright, talented students whose mothers and fathers act as if they have a defective product on their hands." Not many of those parents take the time to see what's really going on in schools, now, in this new era of values, teams, tests, and standards.

Results

So, on the whole, how *are* Millennials doing?

Before the Millennial child era, there was no "National Report Card," because adults were less inclined to judge the nation in terms of how children were faring. Now, tellingly, such a report card exists, in what educators call the periodic reports of National Assessment of Educational Progress, also known as the "Nape" (NAEP).

Dating back to the early '70s, the Nape has measured the performance of 9-, 13-, and 17-year-olds in math, science, reading, and writing. The largest gains have been made in math and science, for ages 9 and 13. Millennial 9- and 13-year-olds are doing as well or better in math and science than any Gen Xers did at that age. Through 1996, meanwhile, 17-year-old Gen Xers had *not* shown the same degree of improvement.

Verbal skills show less-clear trends. Millennials have corrected a late-'80s decline in writing proficiency, and are now writing about as well as Gen Xers in the early '80s and a bit better than Boomers in the early '70s.

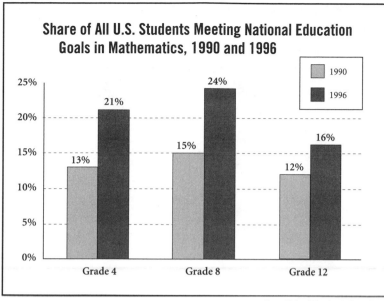

Share of All U.S. Students Meeting National Education Goals in Mathematics, 1990 and 1996

Legend: 1990, 1996

Grade 4: 13% (1990), 21% (1996)
Grade 8: 15% (1990), 24% (1996)
Grade 12: 12% (1990), 16% (1996)

Source: National Education Goals Panel (1998)

Reading scores show scant gains through the '90s, though the 1998 scores (which have not yet been analyzed for trends) suggest that today's 9- and 13-year-olds may be reading better than those of a few years ago.

The aggregate scores for Millennials as a whole, across all four Nape subject areas, reveal only slight progress. Remember, though, that this is a generation with steeply rising shares of minority students, many of them second-generation immigrants. When you disaggregate Nape scores by race and ethnicity, the positive trends come more clearly into focus. All ethnic groups (including Caucasians) are improving faster than the average for all groups. From 1973 to 1996, white students increased their Nape math scores by 3 scale points, blacks by 16, and Latinos by 18. In all four Nape-tested areas, the achievement gap between whites and minorities has narrowed significantly. State tests confirm this: In Texas, Latino achievement is soaring. In California, where Latinos aren't improving as much, black scores are rising.

The gender picture is cloudier. On the Nape tests, boys continue to score higher on math and science, girls on reading and writing. Other math and science tests show girls closing that gender gap, while other verbal tests confirm that boys still lag behind girls there. On the whole,

I just got off the phone with the mother of a 9-year-old who's a wreck because he can't remember his Shakespeare lines.

—*Dee Shepherd-Look, psychologist*

My friend came home the other day bawling. When I asked her what was wrong, she said that she was getting a B in physics. —*Katheryn Wright, 17*

It was one of the few things a high-school senior could depend on: Maintain a B-plus average and waltz into a major public university. Not any more. These days, even a perfect 4.0 grade-point average doesn't guarantee admission.

—**The Washington Post**

At NYU, the average SAT score for incoming freshmen rose from 1283 to 1335 between the high school classes of 1995 and 2000.

—**U.S. News & World Report**

Offices of admission today are functioning more like offices of rejection. —*Sue Biemeret, high school counselor*

Millennial boys tend to do better than girls in solo test taking, girls better than boys in grades, Advanced Placement classes, honor societies, and college admissions—that is, anything with a social dimension.

High School Seniors (per 1,000) Who Took AP Examinations		
	1984	1996
White	48	133
Latino	24	74
Black	8	32

—*U.S. National Center for*
Education Statistics (1998)

Meanwhile, the number of high-achieving high school students keeps rising. Compared to Gen Xers in the late '80s, today's Millennial seniors are nearly three times as likely to take calculus, twice as likely to take all three major sciences (biology, chemistry, physics), and are taking twice as many Advanced Placement tests. The number of high school graduates who attend college the next semester has risen from 50 percent among Boomers in 1975, to 60 percent among Gen Xers in 1990, to 65 percent in 1996. The high school graduation rate has remained fairly flat, with a late-'90s dip that reflects the recent trend against social promotions.

The relatively faster gains in math and science, relative to reading and writing, suggest that Millennials may develop a rational (left-brained) slant to their achievements. Adults may well be encouraging this shift. In recent years, many schools have reduced the time spent on art, music, electives, and unstructured recess to enable more time to be spent on the basic curricula. A price is being paid. "I wish I had a dime for every time I heard a teacher say, 'These kids this year aren't creative at all, nothing like the kids we had five or ten years ago,'" says Paul Beavers, a teacher at the J. T. Moore Middle School in Nashville.

Several of the state standards tests are now in their second or third phases, and scores are improving. In Virginia's D.C. suburbs, every single school scored better on the 1999 state exam than on the 1998 version. In Texas, 86 percent of third graders passed the state reading exam in 1999, up from 77 percent in 1994. California fourth graders showed a five-point improvement on state reading tests over those same five years. But, as *Washington Post* education reporter Linda Perlstein asks, "Are our children getting smarter? Or just better at tests?"—to which proponents of state standards might answer, *both*.

On balance, the Millennial trends reveal some improvement now and prospects for even further gains in the years ahead—a distinct turnaround from the Boomer and early Gen-X middle and high school eras, when nearly every trend pointed in a negative direction.

You'd never know that from the test results that get publicized from time to time, asserting that some shockingly small percentage of today's students can write a coherent paragraph, know historical dates, locate countries on a map, or understand their civic heritage. On a recent Nape history test, 60 percent of 17-year-olds scored "below basic"—but there were no trend lines comparing it to the past, so "below basic" was merely a label offering no basis for comparison. Perhaps Nape, Tims, and other tests will someday be administered to a random sampling of Gen Xers, Boomers, Silents, or G.I.s—with the results publicly reported. So far, none of the test makers have seen fit to do this.

"Adults concerned about the apparent ignorance of children should remember," says Gerald Bracey, "that when they were kids themselves, they probably didn't know nearly as much as they think they did." In Quail Glen Elementary School, near Sacramento, a fifth-grade class discussed the hit TV quiz show *Who Wants to Be a Millionaire*. The kids remarked that the contestants often gave incorrect answers to questions the fifth graders considered easy. "It's surprising that adults didn't get them," said student Elizabeth Clement.

Fixing the Future through Education

In every political handout these days, you read about the need to "prepare today's children for the twenty-first century." There's less talk about exactly *how* to do that, save for familiar verbiage about a high technology workforce in a global economy, as though the typical Millennial will be a software manager in a dot-com IPO.

In any era, schools teach a child generation to be parents, citizens, soldiers, leaders, artists, workers, consumers, and more. But the emphasis

> *We're setting higher expectations, and students are learning up to those expectations.* —Frank S. Hollerman, Deputy Secretary, U.S. Department of Education

> *I see more and more black students in my AP classes—middle-class kids as well as kids from poor backgrounds. Reinforced by a wave of African immigrants, these high-achievers are beginning to set the tone for other black kids in the school.*
>
> —Patrick Welsh, teacher

> *"Challenge me." Two powerful words that kids are saying to their teachers, their schools, their parents. . . . Seventy-five percent of kids say they'd study harder if their schools gave them tougher tests.* —Ad Council

> *A 14-year-old [Natalia Toro] who studied the elusive subatomic particles called neutrinos won the prestigious Intel Science Talent Search . . . the youngest winner in the history of the 58-year-old event.* —Associated Press

> *There's no magic. We just reintroduced something called studying.* —Blondean Davis, Chicago school official, on the turnaround in city schools

can and does change, from one era to the next, as educators try to equip children to address a perceived societal need.

>> *In the 1930s and '40s, schools prepared the Silent to be book-smart corporate careerists.*

>> *In the 1950s and '60s, schools prepared Boomers to be inner-driven, ideal-cultivating individualists.*

>> *In the 1970s and '80s, schools prepared Gen Xers to be street-smart free-agent entrepreneurs.*

>> *In the 1990s, schools prepared Millennials to be outer-driven, ideal-following team players.*

Thus has each recent generation, including Millennials, been schooled to fix a deficiency seen in the prior generation, in a manner which makes it the opposite (and corrective) of the second-older generation.

Millennials are quite unlike Boomers in how they feel about school, and how they're doing there. By most accounts, Boomers generally enjoyed school, but battled against the values it represented, and became worse behaved as the rules became more lenient. Millennials tell pollsters they dislike school, but they comply with the values it represents and become better-behaved as the rules become stricter. Where Boomers wanted less structure, Millennials want more. Boomers liked subjects that defied accountability. Millennials prefer subjects in which they, and others, can measure their progress.

And, especially, Boomers did progressively worse at school, from one birth year to the next, accounting for fifteen of the seventeen years of the famous SAT slide. In the Tims, the Nape, our Teachers' Survey, and other measures, Millennials show early signs of doing progressively better at school, from one birth year to the next.

Just as much as Boomers ever did, Millennial kids are inviting a change in American education that's as dramatic and far-reaching as all the changes back in the 1960s and '70s. This time, though, the changes are running in the opposite direction.

CHAPTER EIGHT

Jiggy with It *(pace of life)*

Jiggy with it (pace of life)
Jiggy with it (pace of life)

Just can't sit
Gotta get jiggy wit' it
> —WILL SMITH, "Gettin' Jiggy wit' It"

"You've never seen such enthusiasm and positiveness on the faces of these youngsters," exuded Colin Powell upon seeing a recent batch of high school ROTC trainees. "Some would say you're making little machines out of them. I don't care what we're making out of them. They're proud, and these kids are getting something that will hold them in good stead . . ."

"What's surprising," said Janice Cromer, the author of a recent youth survey, "is that the students are so 'normal.' They have a lot of regard for adults. The respect their teachers, for the most part. They get along with their parents." In 1999, a reporter from *The Times* of London visited a California high school and remarked about "America's new teen constituency, the suddenly sane."

Be Happy
> *—pennant in Tracy's bedroom,*
> *in* Election

Why can't our lives just be normal?
> *—Ann, to her mother,*
> Anywhere But Here

I don't have a lot of time to do just whatever.
> *—Molly, 11*

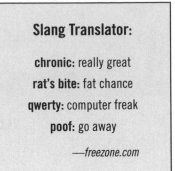

Slang Translator:

chronic: really great
rat's bite: fat chance
qwerty: computer freak
poof: go away

—freezone.com

What Powell, Cromer, time diaries, and opinion surveys are all finding in today's teens is a new, post-X mixture of optimism and activity. Millennials are busy kids. They're doers. Their attitudes, and use of time, reflect this.

The Millennial Time Machine

Over the last decade, as money problems have eased, Americans have become obsessed with time. Time is what most people lack, what they value, and what they're increasingly willing to use money to acquire. Naturally, when older people evaluate younger people, they inquire into how they use time. Of all the misleading reports about today's kids, nothing has drawn more adult anxiety than the suggestion that, every day, kids have an unprecedented quantity of free and unsupervised time. Time to watch WWF wrestling or Jerry Springer. Time to peruse on-line porn sites. Time to have sex, take drugs, or commit crimes. Time *alone*.

Wrong. In the Boomer-child '50s, kids knew there was more high-risk mischief afoot on those long afternoons than many stay-at-home moms ever suspected. (*Where did you go, dear? Out. And what did you do? Nothing.*) In the Millennial-child '90s, kids can often prove to their working moms that nothing's afoot by reciting their activity calendar. (*Look, Mom, even if I wanted to, I just don't have the time!*)

No less than the workaholic adults of their world, students from elementary school through high school feel they have too little free time, not too much. Long gone are the old Boomer days of kids coming home from school and being shooed outside "to play." Today, Millennials spend their

"YOU GET *FIVE* MINUTES BETWEEN SOCCER AND PIANO? WHAT DO YOU DO WITH ALL THAT FREE TIME ?!?"

afternoons getting shepherded from one adult-supervised activity to the next. They don't have as much time as their parents did, when young, to lie on the grass and stare at the clouds, to sit on the porch and watch the world go by, to climb into a treehouse and imagine castles and pirate ships, to gather some friends, a ball, and a bat, and put together a game of workups. "I don't have time to be a kid," 10-year-old Stephanie Mazza-maro told *Time* magazine.

Recall the typical Boomer-child sitcom, in which the older sibling seemed more serious and committed, the younger sibling more playful and free. These days, younger-sibling Millennials think their older brothers and sisters had it easy. In our Class of 2000 Survey, first-wave Millennial teens report by sizable margins that, compared to when their older siblings were their age, Millennials have *less* free time alone, more snoopy parents, more demanding teachers (by a two-to-two majority), and more homework and scheduled activities (by a three to one majority).

These days, kids have less time for what's merely fun. From 1991 to

There's a lot of pressure on school administrators to increase standardized test scores, but how productive are we when we don't make time for essential human functions like eating? It's not healthy. You don't need a CDC scientist to tell you that. —Howell Wechsler, Centers for Disease Control

You mostly stuff food in your mouth and go. —Ann Luu, 15, describing the high school "lunch crunch"

"NO, ✳ MEANS FASTBALL AND ✳ MEANS CURVE!"

1998, according to the Monitoring the Future survey, eighth and tenth graders showed sharp reductions in their share of those who engage "every day" or "at least once a week" in such customary teen activities as going to movies, cruising in cars and motorcycles, or walking around shopping malls. The share who say they never go to rock concerts rose from 60 to 72 percent for eighth graders, and from 51 to 63 percent for tenth graders. Since the mid-'80s, according to the National Association of Secondary School Principals, the share of grade school teens who listen to or watch sports games fell by one-sixth to one-fourth for every sport except ice hockey. The number of kids who regularly listen to or watch football fell from four in five to less than three in five.

Contrary to popular impression, the teen trend in most types of media use (including reading) is down. TV-watching peaked for teenage girls in the early '80s, for teenage boys in the early '90s—and has fallen gradually since. From 1991 to 1998, the share of kids who do *not* watch TV "almost every day" climbed from 16 to 25 percent among eighth graders, from 19 to 27 percent among tenth graders. This occurred even as more kids were getting TV sets for their own bedrooms—until 1998, when parents began removing those TVs. Nearly all surveys report that the share of kids who read newspapers daily, or listen to the radio for any reason, has fallen sharply. The time teenagers spend pleasure reading has also declined—but that's partly because they're reading more of what they are assigned to read. Escape reading remains very popular, with mysteries, fantasies, and horror thrillers (popular among girls) among the hottest items on teen bookshelves.

Which Would You Rather Play?

Video games: **26%**

Soccer: **74%**

—American Dialogue *Survey of 8- to 12-year-olds, TBWA/Chiat/Day (1996)*

One activity that is unmistakably rising among Millennial teens is computer use for all purposes other than game playing, which is declining. The proportion of children and teenagers who regularly use the internet, and who read or send email, has grown sharply in recent years. Middle schoolers now spend more time on this than high school students. Teenagers' use of beepers (which 18 percent now own) and cell phones (10 percent) has also increased, suggesting more time spent tracking down and communicating with friends and family.

For younger kids, the best numbers come from the University of Michigan's Institute for Social Research, which compared time diaries for (Gen-X) children aged 3 to 12 in 1981 with like-aged (Millennial) children in 1997. As mentioned earlier, the pressure-cooking bottom line is that Millennial kids showed a stunning 37 percent decline in the amount of "unstructured" free time, from 52 to 33 hours per week. Some of the biggest declines, by activity:

>> *Free play and unorganized outdoor sports, down by four hours and thirty minutes (4:30) per week.* This includes video and computer games. In total time loss, this is by far the most squeezed activity.

>> *TV watching, down by 2:00.* Since this includes videos and cable networks, the decline in broadcast-TV watching has been even more dramatic.

Like their parents, [children] seem pressed for time. The afternoons and weekends that many baby boomers spent "just hanging out" have now been taken over by chess clubs, soccer leagues, tennis lessons, and tae-kwon-do. —**Melinda Beck, The Wall Street Journal**

*I don't like sitting around
I don't like beating the ground*
—**The Moffatts, "Wild at Heart"**

Adults take a coffee break. They feel perfectly entitled to it. But children are expected to work all day.
—**Rosemarie Alley**

Maybe I'm spending too much of my time starting up clubs and putting on plays. —**Max, in Rushmore**

We're losing our kids to overscheduled hyperactivity. It's a question of balance. Dance and karate, these are all good things. Parents are not making appointments with drug dealers for their children. But we want parents to say, "Am I overdoing the providing of activity opportunities and underdoing the providing of family time?" —**William J. Doherty, a professor of family social science, University of Minnesota**

One mother recalls a recent play date where her son and the daughter of a friend spent the entire afternoon on the girl's computer—to her mother's consternation. "She actually begged them to watch TV instead," the boy's mother said. —**Ralph Gardner, Jr.**

>> *Eating and household conversation, down by 1:40.* Today's kids are rushing to eat, and conversations often occur on the fly (or while doing something else). Efficiency foods like Lunchables, Go-Gurt, and Juicy Juice are a staple for this generation.

>> *Church, down by 1:10.* Since family church attendance has been stable, this decline suggests that kids are doing fewer nonfamily religious activities—or are doing them in places other than churches (for example, in private homes or school facilities).

Those are the main small-child activities getting scrunched in the Millennial time compactor. Here's a rundown of the activities that are consuming more of their time:

>> *School, up by 8:20 hours per week.* This is the single most expanded child activity. More kids aged 4 and 5 (what for other generations were called "preschoolers") are now in school. More kindergartens offer all-day programs. More

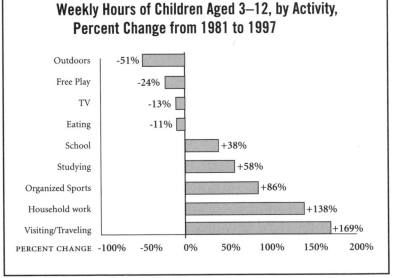

Weekly Hours of Children Aged 3–12, by Activity, Percent Change from 1981 to 1997

Activity	Percent Change
Outdoors	-51%
Free Play	-24%
TV	-13%
Eating	-11%
School	+38%
Studying	+58%
Organized Sports	+86%
Household work	+138%
Visiting/Traveling	+169%

PERCENT CHANGE -100% -50% 0% 50% 100% 150% 200%

Source: Institute for Social Research, University of Michigan (1999)

grade schools have early morning classes, after school programs, hobby groups, prayer clubs, "extra learning opportunity" programs, and summer school—which is now mandatory in many districts for kids who score low on certain tests and don't want to repeat a grade.

>> *Household chores, up by 3:30.* Many more chores are done by today's kids, either alone or (as with grocery shopping) together with a parent.

>> *Personal care (showering, hair care, dressing), up by 3:00.* The let-it-be "nature child" look of the Xer kid era is definitely passé.

>> *Travel or visiting, up by 2:30.* This includes visits to noncustodial parents, who sometimes live in distant cities, or time spent in transit between scheduled events.

>> *Organized sports, up by 2:00.*

>> *Studying or reading, up by 1:00.*

>> *Other passive leisure, up by 2:30.* This includes time on computers (not at games) and other activities (including structured events such as museums and local library programs).

Add this all up, and you can see that today's kids are busy, very busy, and not in ways most adults think. The expanding activities mainly relate to school, family (*doing* with family, not just being with family), and other kinds of supervised activities. Many parents fail to recognize this new time stress on kids. They think what their children want is more time with them—but what they really want is just more free time and less stress all around, for themselves and their parents.

Yes, Millennials are busy, and not necessarily in the familiar ways. But is this, in current parlance, "a life"? Recall the recurring themes of this generation described in Chapter 2, how they're *special, sheltered, confident,*

Don't think life is easy, because when you get older, it is hard work. I used to think life was easy. Now I have to do the dishes every day.

—*Nick Coleman, 9*

team-oriented, achieving, pressured, and *conventional.* From those perspectives, take a look at what Millennials think about the lives they're leading.

Millennials and Specialness

"Like Mom always says, I'm different, special," says Tracy Flick in the film *Election.* Britney Spears would agree: "I'm, like, God has totally blessed me," she says, with a cheery gratitude one seldom heard from teen stars of earlier decades. Where child Gen Xers had reason to feel like a throwaway generation whose problems older people ignored, Millennials have always felt themselves to be the focus of public attention.

They have ample reason to feel this way. Over the course of their brief lifespans, issues affecting children have risen from the middle or bottom of adult priorities to the very top of the list—especially education, drugs, youth violence, child health, and moral values. In 1996, a survey report by the Coalition for America's Children concluded that "the children's agenda has definitely moved . . . to a public agenda," which may explain why, "perhaps for the first time ever, children's issues were observed to play an important role in the election of a President." In 1998, over half of all adults said that "getting kids off to the right start" ought to be America's number-one national priority. Some youth issues that had a very high profile in the 1980s (such as child abuse) are declining now that the problem is considered under control—and now that first-wave Millennials are moving on to older age brackets. Others (like family and moral "decline") have become more prominent just as these first-wavers have entered their teens.

What's Bad About Being a Kid?

What Parents Mainly Say:
crime, youth violence, guns: **39%**

What Their Kids Mainly Say:
school, homework, getting bossed around: **32%**

—*Survey of 12- to 14-year-olds and their parents,*
Time *(July 5, 1999)*

As citizens and voters, adults are demanding a preferential treatment of today's kids in public life. When legislatures vote, or politicians debate, it's often on kids' issues. When agencies and businesses appoint commissions, task forces, focus groups, and surveys, it's often to find out more about kids' issues. Even national issues having nothing directly to do with children—from Social Security to ethnic cleansing to unemployment—are now routinely discussed in terms of their "child" impact. When President Clinton says, "No more nuclear missiles are pointing at our children," Millennials pick up the cue. Kids *always* notice who's noticing them.

All the attention foisted on the 1982 cohort's High School Class of 2000 has ruffled some feathers just a year or two older. "Long before my high-school Class of 1999 had even graduated," remarked Lin Jia, "the media began initiating stories on nightly newscasts with Peter Jennings, Dan Rather, or Tom Brokaw following the lives of students in the Class of 2000," causing her to feel "very resentful" to see her class "being swept into the waste-disposal of time to make room for the Class of 2000." But 17-year-old Tamara El-Khoury won't listen to any negativity. She feels "so lucky" to be part of such a heavily-publicized Millennium-marking class.

As Millennials absorb the adult message that they rank atop America's list of priorities, they naturally come to the conclusion that their problems are the nation's problems, that their future is the nation's future—and that, by extension, everyone in America is naturally inclined to help them solve their problems.

The list of what Millennial teens think are the nation's top problems largely overlaps with issues very close to their daily lives. Compared to their parents, they would place more emphasis on problems of school instruction, and less on problems of sex and drugs—but they still agree that they are the proper focus of public attention. Ask teens which national issues they would be most willing to volunteer time for, and their top choices are mostly child-focused—from child abuse and kidnapping to homelessness and teen suicide. A similar youth slant shows up in their perception of global problems.

Most Millennials are far more trusting than their parents about the capacity of large national institutions to do the right thing on their (and the nation's) behalf. When teens are asked who's going to improve the

Millennial proverbs (fourth graders):
If at first you don't succeed, get new batteries.
Strike while the bug is close.
Laugh and the world laughs with you. Cry, and someone yells, "Shut up!"

—www.warped.com

LANEY: *Do you know how many gallons of chemicals are dumped into the oceans each year?*
ZACH: *Don't you ever just kick back? I know the world has its problems, but would it hurt you to smile once in a while?* —She's All That

schools, clean up the environment, cut the crime rate, they answer, without irony, that it will be teachers, government, and police. They are also more willing than other recent generations to acknowledge the importance of their own personal choices and actions. When asked about violence in schools, for example, the vast majority insist it is purely the fault of students—not of the culture, guns, or anything else.

This specialness extends to Millennials' self-perceived role in history, in solving world problems that vex their elders. When asked which groups will be most likely to help America toward a better future, teens rank "young people" ahead of government. When asked whose generation can have the greatest impact on what the global environment will become twenty-five years from now, 86 percent of Millennial teens say theirs, and only 9 percent say their parents'. When asked the same question, their parents mostly agreed, 71 percent saying that kids will have the most impact. Adults see Millennials not only as special children, but also as a generation with a special power over the future.

Millennials and Sheltering

Throughout the '90s, Boomers and Gen Xers have tightened the security perimeters around Millennial kids. They've done so in every possible place (in homes, autos, web sites, schools), for every possible occasion (prom nights, grad parties, soccer tournaments), through every possible means (family meetings, PTA councils, legislative committees, courts of justice), against every imaginable danger (sharp objects, unhealthy food, predatory people).

This trend is nothing like what these older generations recall from their own youth eras, when adult protectiveness was being dismantled (for Boomers) or was far weaker (for Gen Xers). For Millennials, the edifice of parental care is like a castle that keeps getting new bricks added—V-chips last month, carding at movies this month, graduated licenses next month. The older kids recall the most freedom and open sky, while the younger ones look up at the growing walls unable to imagine what they might see in their absence.

Millennials perceive that adults, parents especially, are getting stricter with them. From 1983 to 1996, the share of 13- to 15-year-olds who complain of being treated "like a child" grew from 30 to 44 percent. Significantly, the rise for 16- and 17-year-olds was much smaller. Given Boomers' own history of youthful highjinks (or worse), this reinvention of parental strictness elicits from Millennials the common complaint of "hypocrisy." By more than two to one, the Class of 2000 believes that its own members are being held to a higher moral standard (regarding sex, drugs, and truth-telling) than their parents apply to their own behavior.

Even so, today's teens widely acknowledge that the rules they must follow are fair. They respect authority and widely support new measures to suppress disorder in the classroom or out on the street—what Public Agenda's Deborah Wadsworth calls a "plea for order, structure, and moral authority in their lives." According to a *USA Weekend* on-line teen poll, 87 percent believe there should be limits on where teens can go in the internet, 75 percent say authorities should be able to search lockers for drugs or guns without a student's permission, and 50 percent believe an evening curfew is OK.

Of All Male Seniors at McLean (VA) High School:

98% participate in after-school activity
60% bite their fingernails
13% have some piercing
10% have a tattoo

—survey by McLean AP Statistics Class (1999)

Younger kids are even more supportive of extra protection than older kids. A few months after Columbine, older teens wanted to increase rather than decrease school security by a two-to-one margin, while younger teens said the same by a four-to-one margin. When sweeping new rules such as for school uniforms or student identity cards are first proposed, the usual experience is that most teens are initially resistant, yet after those measures are put in place, they change their minds and become supportive. And by huge majorities, they favor harsh punishments (including expulsion) for those who misbehave.

True to the wishes of adult America, Millennials *are* protected, *feel* protected, and *expect* to be protected—even, some might say, overprotected.

If your kid isn't into soccer, there's actually no one left in the neighborhood to play with on Saturdays.

—Jeffrey Smith, father of a 5-year-old boy in his second soccer season

These days, extremes of parents insisting that their children carry the weight of their ambitions are becoming increasingly mainstream: the soccer parents of seven-year-olds frothing on the sidelines; parents holding their five-year-olds from kindergarten so they will have an edge the following year. . . . Perhaps the careerist culture of the Baby Boomers has come unmoored from any greater purpose than self-aggrandizement and, by extension, the aggrandizement of our children.

—Pamela Toutant

Millennials and Confidence

In Canada, Millennials have been dubbed the "Sunshine Generation"—and, on both sides of the border, kids and teens do comprise today's sunniest age bracket. Nearly nine in ten feel positive about themselves, 92 percent say that the statement "I am usually happy" is close (50 percent say "very close") to how they feel, and solid majorities feel "very positive" about their own lives. Eighty-three percent of young teens are either "completely" or "mostly" satisfied with their lives. These shares are much higher than comparable figures for adults. Since the 1980s, "happiness" among teens has been trending higher, while it has stayed flat or declined for older age brackets.

Where polls show adults believing that being a parent is getting harder, they show Millennials believing that being a kid is getting *easier*. Among teens, this is a very recent development. In 1994, 68 percent of (Gen-X) 13- to 15-year-olds and 72 percent of 16- to 17-year-olds said it's "harder" to grow up now than in their parents' times, but by 1999, among Millennials, those percentages had fallen sharply, to 40 percent and 47 percent, respectively.

What's true for kids' feelings about themselves is also true for their feelings about the future. Throughout the '90s, most polls indicated that adults had serious worries about where the country is heading over the long term. But those worries haven't reached Millennials. In our Class of 2000 Survey, 77 percent say they are "very" or "somewhat confident" about the future, while only 19 percent are "worried" and just 4 percent are "pessimistic." They are equally upbeat about prospects for their own generation. By a three-to-one margin, they believe that, compared with today's adults, they are personally more optimistic about the future of today's young people.

"Why are kids so confident?" asked a KidsPeace report. "Significantly, the word 'crisis' seems not to appear in the teen lexicon." The Cold War is over. The Dow only goes up. "Teens have not had an experience where the world kept them back," says Victor Thiessen, sociology professor at Halifax's Dalhousie University, which explains why "they're totally optimistic."

Two decades ago, Gen Xers feared unemployment and war—words that barely show up today in polls of teenagers who, as far back as they can remember, have known neither an economic downturn nor the loss of more than a few American lives in combat. Recent polls confirm that their biggest personal concerns aren't war or depression, nor even, as many adults think, crime, drugs, alcohol, or sex—but rather grades (44 percent), getting into college (32 percent), and fitting in socially (29 percent).

Confident is a good word to describe how Millennials feel about life after graduation. Back in the early '70s, about 33 percent of Boomer teens planned to attend a four-year college, a figure that rose to 54 percent for Gen-X teens in the mid-'80s. For the Millennials, that figure has now reached anywhere from 64 to 71 percent, according to various late-'90s polls. More than half of all teens agree that "people my age should be optimistic about their chances of having a good job." Among those in families earning less than $30,000, 54 percent believe the world holds "many opportunities for me." Among those in families earning over $75,000, that proportion rises to 78 percent. More than four in five teens (including 95 percent of Latinos and 97 percent of African Americans) believe they will be financially more successful than their parents—a percentage that rose sharply during the 1990s. Our Class of 2000 Survey showed only 6 percent expecting to make less money than older Gen Xers and 78 percent expecting to make more.

At the same time, the teen view of success has become better-rounded and less exclusively focused toward one life goal. Over the last decade, "marriage/family" and "career success" have each declined in importance as "the one thing" in life. What's now more important is the concept of "balance"—especially, balance between family and work. More teens than ever seek to have a good lifelong relationship with parents. A rising share of high school seniors say "making a contribution to society" is "extremely" or "quite" important, while a declining share (though still a majority) say the same for "having lots of money." In a turnabout from Gen X, Millennials have faith that the American Dream will work for them, and for their own children. "Being able to give my children better opportunities than I had" has reached an all-time high—which, given the opportunities they believe they already have, indicates a great deal of confidence indeed.

Call it the benign side of peer pressure. Today's high schoolers operate in groups that play the role of nag and nanny—in ways that are both beneficial and isolating. It's part of the evolution of high school hierarchy, which changes year to year and generation to generation.

—**The Christian Science Monitor**

I mean, if Amanda Beck doesn't pay any attention to a unique spirit like Preston . . . maybe it's because she's a little busy ordering around her little conformist flock of sheep. SHEEP! You are all sheep. Baah!

—*earth girl, in* Can't Hardly Wait

Millennials and Team Orientation

In dress and manner, Millennials *appear* more teamlike. The growing efforts by schools to teach citizenship and group skills indicate that adults *want* them to be more teamlike. What's less obvious is the extent to which today's kids *feel* more teamlike. Surrounded by individualistic older people, yet optimistic about their own abilities, Millennials have stepped into a teen world with little cohesion, decided they don't like it that way, and are trying to turn it around.

The Millennials' team ethic shows up in their aversion to disorder within their own social setting—starting within their classrooms. When public school students are asked what most needs fixing in their schools, a majority of them mention teaching "good manners," "maintaining discipline in the classroom," and making kids "treat each other with respect." Forty percent say unruly student behavior interferes with their schoolwork. Back in the Gen-X youth era, educators disliked "peer pressure" because they associated it with breaking the rules. Today, educators are starting to harness peer pressure—through student juries, peer grading, and the like—to enforce the rules better.

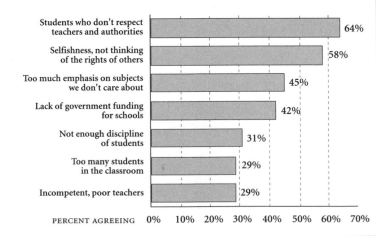

What are the major causes of problems in SCHOOLS today?
Seven top answers from students in grades 7–12 in 1998

Students who don't respect teachers and authorities	64%
Selfishness, not thinking of the rights of others	58%
Too much emphasis on subjects we don't care about	45%
Lack of government funding for schools	42%
Not enough discipline of students	31%
Too many students in the classroom	29%
Incompetent, poor teachers	29%

PERCENT AGREEING   0%   10%   20%   30%   40%   50%   60%   70%

Source: PRIMEDIA/Roper National Youth Opinion Survey (1998)

The Millennial team ethic shows up in their choice of friends. Honesty and hard work are now the highest-valued personal qualities, even though teens admit that those virtues don't necessarily lead to popularity. Ninety-five percent report that "it's important that people trust me." In choosing their leaders, Millennials say they look for maturity, friendliness, and quality of moral character ahead of an imaginative or independent mind.

Their belief in team play has broadened their capacity for friendship with peers. They are drawn to circles and cliques. Only three in ten report that they usually socialize with only one or two friends, while two in three do so with groups of friends. The proportion of eighth and tenth graders who feel lonely or wish they had more friends declined sharply from 1991 to 1998. A rising share want to stay with their buddies after graduation. Their closer peer bonding may be diminishing their need for close friendships with adults. Teachers report that, compared with Gen Xers of a decade ago, today's kids get along less well with teachers but better with one another.

The team ethic even shows up in their political views. When Millennial teens are asked to identify "the major causes" of America's problems, their seven most popular answers all pertain to what they perceive as an excess of adult individualism. Number one (at 56 percent of all teens) is

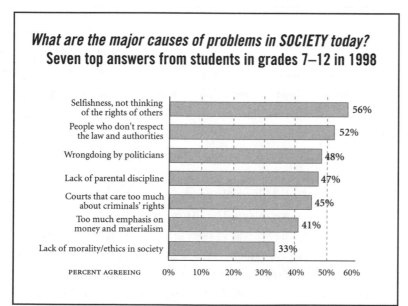

What are the major causes of problems in SOCIETY today?
Seven top answers from students in grades 7–12 in 1998

	PERCENT AGREEING
Selfishness, not thinking of the rights of others	56%
People who don't respect the law and authorities	52%
Wrongdoing by politicians	48%
Lack of parental discipline	47%
Courts that care too much about criminals' rights	45%
Too much emphasis on money and materialism	41%
Lack of morality/ethics in society	33%

Source: PRIMEDIA/Roper National Youth Opinion Survey (1998)

"selfishness, people not thinking of the rights of others"; number two (at 52 percent) is "people who don't respect the law and the authorities." Amazingly, "lack of parental discipline of children and teens" ranks number four. In public life, while Boomers complain of the lack of national leadership, Millennials are more inclined to remark on the lack of *followership*. These attitudes are especially pronounced among girls.

Teens are well aware of a potential contradiction between their dislike of selfishness and their career optimism. A rising number worry that "people are much too concerned with material things." Between 1988 and 1996, the share who felt that "there is too much competition in this society" rose from 43 percent to 56 percent. Meanwhile, the percentage believing that "clothes in the latest style" are "extremely" or "quite important" fell by 17 points among girls, 8 points among boys.

This Millennial cliquishness has elevated peer pressure into a much more important teen issue than before, even as they see more positive potential in it than adults normally do. Only about one-third of teens say they are under "a great deal" or "some" pressure from peers to "break rules," although a larger share report being teased about clothing.

Millennials and Achievement

Back in the heady days of the 1960s, many a Boomer had big plans. So do Millennials. But that's about where the similarity ends. When young Boomers planned their future, they saw themselves plotting their course by an internal compass, asking how a path felt rather than what it tangibly represented. Millennial teens have turned that around. They prefer timetables to compasses. The majority of today's high school students say they have highly detailed five- and ten-year plans for their future. Most have given serious thought to college financing, degrees, salaries, employment trends, and the like.

As for enjoyment, Millennials see their preparations as serious and important, but not exactly fun. The share of kids who "try to do my best in school" keeps going up, but so does the share who "don't like school very much" or "at all," among boys especially. All their lives, many Boomers have been driven to choose specialties and careers that in some way feel like personal vocations. Millennials would rather strike a balance between what they have to do and what they want to do, rather than merge the two (common among Boomers) or compartmentalize the two (common among Gen Xers).

In college, young Boomers made their biggest mark in the arts and humanities. As young professionals, they became precocious leaders in the media, teaching, advertising, religion—anything having to do with the creative rearrangement of values and symbols. Millennial kids show the opposite bent. They like math and science courses best, social studies and arts courses least. Surveys of eighth and tenth graders indicate that Millennials would far rather spend their free time doing active things with friends than doing imaginative, creative tasks on their own.

Their collective ambitions also have a rationalist core. According to our Class of 2000 Survey, teens have a great deal of confidence in their generation's lifelong ability to improve technology (95 percent), race relations (69 percent), and the economy (60 percent)—all objectively benchmarkable "modern" attributes—but far less confidence in their prospects for improving more subjective areas such as the arts (31 percent), family life (28 percent), and religion (22 percent). Other surveys reveal teens as more likely than adults to value friendships, but less likely than adults to value the ability to communicate feelings.

Millennials expect to focus more on outer-world achievement, and less on inner-world spiritualism, than their Boomer parents. By the time

Compared to 10 Years Ago, Are Students' Oral English Skills Better or Worse?

	Better	Worse
Elementary School	33%	21%
Middle School	20%	33%
High School	17%	52%

—asked of teachers in Fairfax County (VA), in Teachers' Survey (1999)

they reach their parents' age, they expect to spend less time on religion, roughly the same amount of time on family matters, and more time on careers, government, and technology. While they don't feel their civics classes are particularly important, they are much more likely than adults

Every year in my journalism class, we've debated whether school-funded newspapers have the right to review and censor a paper that they believe disrupts the learning environment of the school or the safety of its students. Six years ago, my students did not trust authority figures, and typically the class would be split. This year, we could not hold a debate because every student agreed that teachers and administrators are adults whose judgment should be respected. "Why should high school students have full rights?" they ask. "It's not like we're professional journalists."

—Joel Raney, high school English teacher

Just because I'm boring Doesn't mean I'm dumb

—Dana, 9, girlsgamesinc.com

(50 to 26 percent) to trust government. And a large majority expects, later in life, "to keep up with politics and to vote" more than their parents do now.

Millennials and Pressure

Not all generations can be described as pressured. To feel "pressure," youths must perceive that everything they want in life is critically dependent upon their own performance. For some generations, that's how most youths feel. For others, it's not.

Boomer teens felt decreasing pressure, from first cohort to last, as early '60s hopes of a gleaming technocracy ran aground on Vietnam, youth riots, energy crises, and credibility gaps. Each year, their future seemed to grow more chaotic, less linked to work or credentials, and less subject to institutional rules. Gen Xers inherited that trend. While they were in school, the defining symptom of teen alienation was the widespread perception that success was random and "paying your dues," at school or on the job, could often be a waste of time.

But lately, in the 1990s, the alienation is receding, the economy is booming, and the pressure is returning. Today's kids feel a growing sense of urgency about what they have to do to achieve their personal and group goals. They feel stressed in ways that many of their parents never felt at the same age. Pressure is what keeps them constantly in motion—moving, busy, purposeful, without nearly enough hours in the day to get it all done. Things like reputation and credentials matter again. The Gen-X credo—that you can always rebound from failure—no longer seems plausible.

Pressure explains the intensity of today's competition to get good grades, to get into college, and to please employers. Nearly four in five high school students report "some" or "a lot" of parental pressure to get high grades. The grade squeeze is felt hardest by middle schoolers, 84 percent of whom consider it "very important" to get good marks. It makes no difference that grade inflation is continuing its three-decade-long climb since the 1960s. By 1998, one-third of all eighth graders, and one-fourth of all tenth graders, reported receiving an "A" or "A–" average. So many A's merely magnify the penalty of the occasional B or C. This is how the ongoing grade inflation is reinforcing the Millennials' fear of failure, their aversion to risk, and their desire to fit in to the mainstream. A risky and creative project cannot earn a grade above an A—but, if it misfires, could easily result in a lower grade and blight a transcript.

Today's teens are far more focused in their anxieties than adults think. Seventy percent worry a lot about finding a good job when they get out of school—whereas only 37 percent of Boomer adults think they do. Conversely, 83 percent of Boomers think teenagers worry a lot about their appearance, while only 37 percent of teens say they do. Compounding the Millennials' adolescent stress is the nonstop workaholism of so many of their parents, which undermines adult reassurances that the future will take care of itself. To many Millennial teens, it's as though they see a giant generational train ready to leave the station. Each of them knows they'll either get there with their ticket punched and be on that train—or be off it and never have the same chance again.

Millennials and Convention

"Today's teens . . . reject the 'too cool to care' credo of Generation X. They do care, they are optimistic, and they embrace traditional values of home, family life, community, and education." Thus does a major 1998 survey report summarize one of the most important new trends in youth opinion.

Where Boomer children felt overdosed on norms and rules, and came of age famously assaulting them, Millennials show signs of trying to invite them back. Where Boomer teens had trouble talking to their parents—a major cause of the late-'60s G.I.-versus-Boomer "generation gap"—Millennials seldom report any trouble. Where Boomers warred with their parents over values while implicitly acknowledging their parents' competence at managing the world, Millennials are willing to accept their parents' values as stated—but are starting to think they can *apply* them, and someday run the show, a whole lot better.

Millennials generally get along fine with their parents—agreeing with them on matters of right and wrong, consulting with them on buying decisions, and sharing tastes in clothes and music. Nearly half of all kids enjoy the same kinds of music as their parents—clearly, a much larger share than when Boomers were kids. Fully 34 percent say they enjoy

One parent's take on the profanity issue is to educate the kids on all the cusswords, their proper use so you won't sound like an idiot to your peers, and proper times and places to use them.　　　—Lis Libengood

The verb "sucks," used in a pejorative sense, seems to be making its way into the language of what passes for polite society these days. It has, in fact, become so common a term that a lot of the kids who use it, freely and unabashedly, don't even appear to be aware of its unseemly origins and implications.　　　—editorial,
The Washington Post

Nearly every adolescent in our country concedes
I mean, you know, like, are like, you know, I mean, weeds

—*"We Like Like a Lot,"*
StopScandal.Com

"oldie" rock, not much less than the 44 percent who like rap. The share who report having "very different" values from their parents has fallen by roughly half since the 1970s, and the share who say their values are "very or mostly similar" has risen to an all-time high of 76 percent.

Life Goals

Having a well-paying job: **81%**
Having a good relationship with parents: **77%**
Getting married: **57%**
Having children: **38%**
Owning a business: **28%**

—response of students in grades 7–12, in PRIMEDIA/Roper (November 1998) National Youth Survey

---

In a 1997 Gallup survey, nine in ten kids reported being very close to their parents and personally happy—much closer than twenty years ago. The common '90s ad hoc, participatory family style has made it easier for kids to accept their parents' authority, to seek out and rely on their advice, even to look forward to living near them later on—all attitudes that were far less common among Boomers in their own youth.

Young Boomers, many of whom found it easier to be friends with their parents than to "love" them, took that word and nearly wore it out as an all-purpose anthem of peer solidarity during the '60s and '70s (with love-ins, love beads, love bugs, and so on). With young Millennials, "friendship" has again become the vaunted norm among peers—and "love" again the norm between parent and child. In fact, Millennials bask in the sense of being loved by parents. In 1995, 93 percent of 10- to 13-year-olds felt "loved" all or almost all the time.

The relationships between today's moms and daughters are particularly close. In 1998, among families with at least $20,000 annual income, 97 percent of girls reported a "very close" relationship with their mothers, 90 percent of girls and moms reported being "very happy" with their relationship, and 84 percent say they share the same general values. Eighty-eight percent of today's moms claim to be "more open and honest with my daughter than my mother was with me," and 72 percent report a "better relationship" with their teenage girls than what Oprah Winfrey calls the "disease of the need to please" situation they recall with their own moms.

Teens of both sexes remain somewhat more distant from dads, but even here 81 percent report being "very" or "fairly" happy with Dad. Since 1983, while the share of kids who say they have "no respect" for Mom has fallen from 3 to 1 percent, the share who say that about Dad has risen somewhat, from 5 to 8 percent. Over those same years, however, the share of boys and (especially) girls who say they can talk to their dads about personal problems has risen significantly.

Millennials give both mothers and fathers far higher marks on matters of guidance and security than Boomers gave their own parents three and four decades ago. Two-thirds of today's teens say their parents are "in touch" with their lives, and six in ten say it's "easy" to talk with parents about sex, drugs, and alcohol. In a 1998 teen survey, 80 percent say they've had "really important talks" with their parents, and 94 percent mostly or totally agreed that "I can always trust my parents to be there when I need them." Back in 1974, a majority of Boomer teens reported that they "cannot comfortably approach their parents with personal matters of concern," and over 40 percent flatly declared that they "would be better off not living with their parents."

When parents can't help, 87 percent of teens say they have someone other than their parents to whom they can go for help, and 49 percent say they've had one or more teachers who have changed their lives. When asked to name heroes, Millennials mainly name their parents, teachers, or family friends. Beyond their own personal circles, teens find their heroes among workmanlike athletes such as Michael Jordan, Ken Griffey, Jr., Grant Hill, and Derek Jeter. Athletes with self-cultivated "bad" or show-biz images, such as Shaquille O'Neal, Deion Sanders, and Dennis Rodman, score lower. Only 1 percent name a U.S. president or other public figure as a hero—in sharp contrast to the list of heroes rising Boomers would have offered in the early 1960s.

What this is producing, according to teen marketer Kirsty Doig, is a generation of teens who are trying to reverse many of the dominant social and cultural trends of our time. "These kids are fed up with the

Nothing in standard Millennial upbringing stimulates self-reflection. Unfettered success, arranged and realized, doesn't lead to introspection.

—**Neil Murray**

He is very spiritual and loving. . . . While most kids tend to argue with their parents a lot at his age, Zac [Hanson] treats his parents with the ultimate respect at all times.

—**boomerang.nu**

There are wars, death, pain, grief, suffering, famine, plagues, poverty, and world problems every single second of the day, and yet S Club 7 still manage to act like life is some big fun thing which is absolutely great.

—**"Death to S Club 7" web site**

*Feeling well
Life is swell*

—**Kara's Flowers,
"Sleepy Windbreaker"**

superficialities of life," says Doig. "One of the macrotrends we're seeing is neotraditionalism." Millennials overwhelmingly favor the teaching of values in schools—including honesty, caring, moral courage, patriotism, democracy, and the golden rule.

Perhaps the biggest difference between today's teens and their Boomer parents is that Millennials think their generation will do a better job of collectively embodying those values. When asked whether "values and character" will matter more or less to their own generation when they're parents, they answer "more" by a two-to-one margin. On traditional values, Millennials hear their parents talk the good talk, but they themselves aren't satisfied with mere symbol and gesture. They intend to walk the walk.

zero tolerance (conduct)

Now this is not gonna be pretty. We're talking
violence, strong language, adult content.
　　　　　　—BUFFY, in Buffy the Vampire Slayer

In November 1997, Alice Morgan Brown, the principal of Baltimore's Northern High School, announced over the school's public address system that all students should pick up their report cards after school. At the end of the day, after 1,200 students disobeyed her request, she suspended them all—thereby carrying out the largest suspension in the history of American education.

Ms. Brown's message to her students, indeed to the entire generation, could not have been clearer: The rules have changed. Faced with this change, teenage America has been sprucing up its conduct. Nearly everywhere, and especially in urban areas, teenagers have reduced their sexual risk-taking, substance abuse, crime, and violence.

The waning years of the Bush presidency and the opening years of the Clinton presidency—just before first-wave Millennials hit their teens—marked the turning point for teenage misbehavior. Teen sex appears to have peaked around 1990, crime and school violence in 1993, and teen

For 25 years, we asked our teenagers to raise themselves, and they didn't do a very good job of it. That's why youth violence has gone back down—the adults are back. **—Jack Levin, Brudnick Center on Violence, Northeastern University**

If someone asked me to do something wrong, I would ignore them or ask them why. **—Ryan, 7**

Not all experiences are good, Bianca.

**—Kat
to her younger sister,
in 10 Things I Hate About You**

homicides in 1994. Curiously, substance abuse reached a low in the 1991–92 school year, after which it leveled off or (for marijuana and tobacco) began slowly rising again. Blame or praise late-wave Gen Xers for all this: They set the table for Millennials—who, in the years since, have shown clear signs of redirecting most of these trends in a positive direction.

You wouldn't know it from the media. You can barely pick up a newspaper or watch the TV news without seeing some anecdotal story about how badly teenagers behave. From time to time, some real data arrive showing that teens aren't so bad and that their behavior is actually improving. But that's a more complex and less mediagenic story line. It never leads the news. (Which is better TV—a breathless reporter interviewing weeping teenagers behind yellow police tape and flashing sirens, or a sober reporter reading numbers against a backdrop of teenagers behaving nicely?) When positive teen trends are reported at all, credit is often given less to what teens are doing than to what adults are doing—their robust economy, tougher rules, stricter sentences, more aggressive social services, and new "character education" programs.

The roaring economy helps teens pay for cars, clothes, and cell phones, but has little to do with their improving behavior. The last decade of front-to-back economic growth (the 1960s) had soaring rates of youth sex, youth crime, and youth drug use—and the twentieth-century decades with the best-behaved teenagers (the 1930s and '40s) defined an era of economic emergency. So much for that explanation. What about tougher crime laws and stricter sentences? That's led mostly to the warehousing of Gen-X miscreants, with no direct impact on teen crime (aside from the sobering influence of their example). A better case could be made for a conservative-style focus on personal responsibility and a liberal-style focus on public intervention, but these factors only tell part of the story.

At root, what's going on is this: Partly because they have to but also because they want to, Millennials are becoming a *corrective* generation. They've started to reverse the negative youth trends that Boomers initiated in the '50s and fully launched in the '60s, and that Gen Xers propelled in the '80s and pushed to culmination by the early '90s. There's still a long way to go, but Millennials have turned the corner. In part, that's because of what Boomers and Gen Xers are demanding of them in schools, on the streets, and at home. But it's also the result of negative object lessons these older generations are setting for them, in public and private life, and in the culture.

Zero Tolerance

Where Gen-X teens grew up amid mixed adult messages that ranged from "If it feels good, do it" to "Just say no," Millennials have confronted one starkly simple slogan: "Zero Tolerance." Those two words—known in some circles as "ZT"—have dramatically altered the teen landscape of the 1990s.

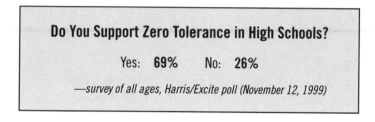

Do You Support Zero Tolerance in High Schools?

Yes: **69%**   No: **26%**

—survey of all ages, Harris/Excite poll (November 12, 1999)

The concept of ZT arose at the end of the '80s, out of national alarm over skyrocketing murder rates, crack cocaine, graffiti, and "wilding," exacerbated by anxiety over the rising nastiness of the pop culture. This

PUBLIC SCHOOLS DETENTION CENTER

THE ZERO-TOLERANCE FOUR

If someone is falsely accused in this atmosphere of zero tolerance, they could find themselves being expelled because someone doesn't like them.

—Kent Willis, Virginia ACLU

In this "zero tolerance" approach in schools, there isn't a whole lot of attention paid to why the kid might have broken the rules or to what happens to the kid afterwards, as long as he gets his punishment and isn't around to bother the "good" kids. What seems to be happening is a trend toward morally separating kids. . . . This ties into Boomers' virtue-obsession and narcissism: "My kids get the best, but I don't care about yours." **—Ben Weiss**

We do not know what produces teenage serial killers and have no proven way to deal with them. But we have seen what unfounded panic gets us: scared children, empty desks, delayed lessons, and ill-considered discipline for students who do little more than lampoon the reigning paranoia. **—Jay Matthews, The Washington Post Magazine**

[W]e're going to protect the rights of everyone before we protect the rights of someone.

—Bill Bosher, school superintendent, Chester County (VA)

was the era of George Bush's "weed and seed," of drawing a line between Gen-X teens and younger children.

The specifics came from two cities, Cincinnati and New York. In 1991, frustrated by lagging achievement linked to discipline problems, Cincinnati schools became the nation's first to impose a "zero tolerance" rule. Henceforth, schoolchildren who committed even small acts of incivility were shamed, punished, often suspended, and sometimes expelled. The results were so good and so quick in coming that Texas imposed ZT rules statewide in 1993. The year after, in the Safe and Drug-Free School Act of 1994, Congress required schools to expel any student found in possession of a weapon or lose their eligibility for federal aid.

Meanwhile, New York's new mayor, Rudy Giuliani, was just beginning to apply a no-nonsense "not one broken window" theory of urban policing. The basic idea is that if you crack down on all the little stuff—the panhandlers, graffiti sprayers, and squeegee people—then the muggings and murders will decrease too. This new ZT approach to police enforcement made an impression on the longtime head of the American Federation of Teachers, Albert Shanker, who had long insisted that teachers couldn't teach, and students couldn't learn, unless bad kids were removed from classrooms. Thus did the major teachers' organizations begin to sign on to ZT. While the main impetus came from culture-war conservatives, their liberal adversaries soon followed, developing what columnist John Leo describes as "a surprising taste for draconian punishment as a way of coping with the mess their no-rules ethic helped to create."

Through the rest of the '90s, under pressure from mostly Boomer parents and media, school systems and police departments began applying ZT to kids across America. This was no Gen-X-style "three strikes you're out" crackdown on repeat offenders. No longer would kids get off with just a warning for their first strike. For any Millennial kid, no matter how perfect the report card, no matter how flawless the past behavior, the message was clear: Utter one threat under your breath, write one darkly worded essay, get caught once with any banned substance, have one brush with the law, and—in the words of Sterling, Virginia, Middle School Principal Charles Haydt—"You're only one day away from it happening."

Under ZT, the "it" is the boot. "The country is witnessing a vast increase in detentions, suspensions, and even expulsions," reports *The*

New York Times. Millennials face severe punishments for infractions that, a decade ago, often went unpunished. Roughly a quarter of all eighth and tenth graders report having been suspended from school at least once, at times for behavior that occurred *away* from school.

Certain behaviors (threats, diaries, essays, kissing, pinching) that were mostly ignored among Gen Xers are now routinely punished among Millennials. And other behaviors that before brought only minor wrist slaps (fighting, threatening a teacher, first-time marijuana possession) can now lead to instant expulsion. In some districts, grade school roughhousing is now looked upon as violence, which teachers can be forbidden to handle with only a lecture. Instead, by school board edict, they must report it, which starts an administrative process with quite specific punishments for which leniency is rarely granted.

Many schools now enforce their rules "24-7," every hour of every day, and troublemakers face a coordinated front among the schools, police, and community leaders. In Chicago, if a kid gets in police trouble on Sunday, he's automatically in school trouble on Monday.

Penalties are often automatic. This lack of discretion, though it draws many complaints from parents, is actually one of ZT's biggest selling points for schools—which would otherwise face endless arguments (and lawsuits) about racial or class bias in who gets shown leniency and who doesn't. In many districts, the principal has no choice but to "write up" the kid, call in the school police, and set in motion a punitive process that's hard to stop. "It is not so much the issue of whether the threat is serious," says Edwin Merritt, school superintendent in Trumbull, Connecticut. "You don't differentiate." This is very unlike the circa-1960s G.I.-teacher, Boomer-child era, when case-by-case discretion was the norm, and arguments were rare. So, too, is it unlike the Silent-teacher, Gen-X-child era, where less classroom order was expected and misbehaving students could easily slide by—until they either reformed or turned criminally violent.

Many districts support ZT with an infrastructure of new punitive rooms and "alternative learning centers" for kids with disciplinary records or criminal convictions. In the Gen-X youth era, alternative schools were created for kids with medically diagnosed "emotional disabilities" (ED) under the special education rubric. In the Millennial era,

Well, you asked for a horror story. You got a horror story, you know? I don't understand the problem.

—mother of a middle-school child who was jailed for writing a Halloween story about the deaths of teachers and students

A 17-year-old junior was expelled from his suburban Chicago high school after the paper clip he shot with a rubber band struck a cafeteria worker, drawing a small amount of blood. —Associated Press

We've got kids getting kicked out of school for saying "bang-bang" to each other. —Vincent Schiraldi, Justice Policy Institute

While she dressed, she glanced at the TV and saw the Columbine tragedy unfolding in front of her, live. One of her first thoughts was that the school on the screen looked just like hers. The kids wore the same Abercrombie & Fitch and Gap clothes. The cars in the parking lot were the same makes and vintage, which is to say largely imported, not cheap, and not old. "It made me think, 'That could happen here.'"

—The Christian Science Monitor

other placements—with more of a punitive and custodial intent—are providing repositories for kids who are not labeled ED but who are either chronic disrupters or have committed a ZT-covered act. In the middle 1980s, the Fairfax County (VA) School Board held roughly forty to fifty expulsion hearings per year. Now it is hearing six hundred cases a year. In the late '90s, Chicago tripled its expulsion rate. Large school systems now have to hire full-time teachers whose daylong job is to preside over in-school suspension or time-out rooms, expulsion hearing examiners, and full-time on-site police officers.

Following a publicized rash of school shootings in 1997–98, and especially after the 1999 Columbine murders, schools have ratcheted up—and criminalized—their ZT enforcement. With the onset of more in-school police with arrest authority, in a setting where Miranda warnings aren't required, kids increasingly face a double dose of public punishment, from schools and courts, for offenses that range from the serious to the petty. In Langley, Virginia, two Class of 2000 seniors who sprayed "00" on nearby street signs were caught, suspended, forced to pay for the cleanup, and prosecuted. In Oneonta, New York, a Halloween prankster who planted a rooftop bomb was not merely expelled, but his name and photos were ordered expunged from the school yearbook. One student was suspended for suggesting "you will die with honor" when asked to compose a fortune-cookie message, and another for saying in a class discussion that she understood how unpopular students could react as they did at Columbine. One student was *arrested* for splashing other kids by stomping in a mud puddle and another for writing a Halloween essay about the bloody deaths of students.

In the wake of such cases, schools are talking about pushing the ZT schema to new frontiers. A growing number of states and cities are fining or even jailing the parents of chronically truant kids. Some are proposing that students be made to wear identity cards bearing bar-coded Social Security numbers. Others are calling for a national registry of school disciplinary incidents, listing the names, dates, and charges down to the smallest kindergarten sandbox incidents. There's talk of applying the "Mosaic 2000" diagnostic test to probe for *potential* violence and mandate counseling for kids who, based purely on this multiple-choice test, reveal supposedly dangerous tendencies. (In some school districts, if you write about "the dark side of life" and are known to have access to guns, you face mandatory counseling.)

The ACLU doesn't like it, school boards have mixed feelings about it, principals feel trapped by it, and students fear the grindings of its machinery, but there's no question that ZT is on a roll. Especially after Columbine, when nearly every district notched up its rules, enforcements, and penalties, American schools are becoming no-nonsense places that—no surprise—are producing no-nonsense kids.

Policing the Little Things

There's still a way to go on discipline. Experienced teachers in our Teachers' Survey consider students of all ages, elementary through high school, to be louder, more profane, worse dressed, less respectful, and generally harder for adults to get along with than students were a decade or more ago. Those same teachers acknowledge that while the rules on the worst behaviors (weapons, drugs, fights, taunts) are tougher than they used to be, the rules on petty behaviors (dress, respect, absenteeism) haven't changed as much.

In response, the ZT attitude is starting to move beyond guns and drugs into a more systematic climate-improvement mode, led by school systems that want to do to less-than-perfect Millennials what Rudy Giuliani did to squeegee workers: crack down hard on petty misbehaviors in the hopes that everything else will improve as a result.

What Boomers are enforcing is much the opposite of what G.I.s enforced on them around 1960. Back then, adults looked upon youthful misbehavior, and their attendant "Gee, Officer Krupke" alibis, with a sympathy and tolerance that increased by the year. (Meanwhile, the teen crime rate was in the early stages of what would become a four-decade rise.) Nowadays, an Officer Krupke would have none of it—a fact brought home to high school kids in Amherst, Massachusetts, who weren't allowed to produce *West Side Story* in part because its celebration of teenage violence couldn't pass muster today.

School systems are cracking down on classroom manners. In its 1998 *Davis v. Monroe County* decision, the U.S. Supreme Court warned that a school can be sued if it shows "deliberate indifference" to a child's sexual-

As sad as it was to see our school turn into a chapter from the book 1984 (in which Big Brother is constantly watching you), every citizen of West Rogers Park is now aware how sorely the new security is needed.

—Beth Pollack,
whose high school was
terrorized by a gunman

To end school violence . . . we as teenagers shouldn't shrug comments off as jokes. We should report [them] to adults. . . . [W]e should make it the popular, right thing to do. —Katie, channelone.com

Fire drills are mere child's play compared with student rehearsals for armed intruders. —Newsweek

North Carolina has quietly launched a program that allows students to call in anonymously or fill out a Web-based form to report on classmates who might appear depressed or angry—or who just scare them.

—Wired News

In the beginning they were sort of chuckling about it. Now they realize we are tracking them through the day. It's much more serious.

—Sam Karlin,
principal of a Philadelphia
high school that uses bar-coded student IDs that
set off a siren if a student
skipped school the day before.

harassment complaint, so many schools no longer allow boy-girl touching or teasing. Some have added new "shaming" penalties for petty acts—such as teachers sporting soccer-style red or yellow cards on which they write offenders' names, or special porches where miscreants must sit in view of student passersby, or the Knowledge-Is-Power Program rule that requires everyone to leave the room and return quietly any time a teacher declares a student out of line.

Vulgarity has recently become an adult target, partly because it's linked to other bad behaviors. "Profanity is the way disrespect is expressed," says Maryland school board member Doyle Niemann. By word count, Millennials are clearly more vulgar than Boomers or Gen Xers were as youths—or at least, more than nine of ten respondents in our Teachers Survey think so. Yet they are, on the whole, less profane than the pop culture adults provide them. And if you inquire into their intentions, their profanity is not as inherently disrespectful. When Boomers said "Up against the wall, ———," they truly meant the next word as a contemptuous insult. When Millennials say the same word, it's more likely to be just a synonym for "guy." Language inevitably evolves from one generation to the next, and while many adults wince at the innuendoes in phrases like "this sucks" or "that bites," kids see absolutely nothing sexual in them. Even some racial epithets have far less meaning to Millennials than to older people. (By contrast, the expression "to shag" a girl, a baffling expression to American adults, can sound obscene to a kid's ears.) In school systems where profane words have been deemed unacceptable, their use has reportedly declined.

The early report card on ZT is very favorable. Often, it produces an immediate, measurable drop in criminal activity. It makes schools demonstrably safer and more orderly, thereby contributing to better environments for learning values, teamwork, and basic skills. It also makes schools less fun and more pressured, which may harm schools' ability to teach self-motivation, creativity, and imagination.

The Millennial-era crackdown stands in marked contrast not only to what Boomers faced in their own youth, but also to today's broad social tolerance of coarse or aberrant adult behavior. The characters portrayed by Mike Myers (*Austin Powers*) or Adam Sandler (*Big Daddy*) talk and behave in aggressive, harassing, vulgar ways that would get a kid suspended. A U.S. president commits clandestine sex acts and deceits that would get a kid removed from his school. WWF wrestlers do something every few seconds that would get a kid arrested for a felony. Jerry Springer's guests engage in stupid and hysterical antics that would land a kid in a time-out room, counselor's office, hospital, or police station.

Do kids know this? You bet. Do they know they're being held to a higher standard? Yes. Does this double standard bother them? Not as much as you might think. Polls show that today's teens want more discipline and order in schools. After gazing up at a chaotic, over-the-edge adult world, Millennials can return and find comfort in their own more structured environment—quite the opposite from what Boomers saw, or felt, as teens.

Sex

Some early signs were already there, before the data began rolling in. A 1993 *Washington Post* article described new teen "virgin clubs" and "vocal virgins." A year later, *Mademoiselle* heralded a "New Chastity" in which teen abstinence had become a badge not of repression, but of strong will and character. In 1994 and '95, *Newsweek, The New York Times,* and *Vogue* weighed in with articles about "virgin cool," "virgin pride," and virgin "smart, sassy, and hip." In some teen circles, sex that had once been tagged "carefree" was now being labeled "careless." Meanwhile, "True Love Waits" signatories were blanketing the Washington Mall and state capitols with hundreds of thousands of virginity pledge cards.

Then, in the mid-1990s, the results of three federally supported surveys on sexual activity appeared—two in 1995, funded by the National Institute of Child Health and Human Development, and another in 1997, funded by the Centers for Disease Control and Prevention. What all three studies had to say surprised most teen-trend watchers. Since the late 1980s, for the first time since sex data had been tracked, teen sex was declining. Between 1988 and 1995, among high school girls and boys alike, the proportion with sexual experience had fallen from 54 to 48 percent. The share having had more than four partners had similarly dropped. Sex rates for men were falling a bit faster than for women, and for blacks and Caucasians faster than for Latinos (leveling the rates some-

I don't fool around. We, like, hug and stuff. But that's it. And none of the guys ever pressured me.

—Elie, 16, Seventeen

Believe it or not, public displays of affection (PDAs) are not considered to be hip by the students of Langley High School.

—The McLean (VA) Connection

I wanna be ready for what you do . . . 'Cuz I don't know when you're gonna make your move

—Fiona Apple, "Shadowboxer"

You ain't gotta get physical, 'cuz I'll still respect you, girl We can just slam and kick it though, on another level, baby, yeah

—Imajin, "No Doubt"

Like all great romantics, Shakespeare realized love was a lot more likely to end with a bunch of dead Danish people than with a kiss.

—Dawson, Dawson's Creek

Deborah White, Miss Teen Clovis County, said that even though she, like everybody else, sometimes feels evil, demon-planted desires deep within her loins, she was keeping herself pure and waiting for marriage . . . She told us that if we were patient and waited until child-conceiving age before learning anything about sex, that would make it so much more special! Isn't that rad? —The Onion

what among those three groups). The only disturbing sign was a rise in the share of girls reporting a first sexual encounter before age 14 (up from 11 to 14 percent).

> ## Can Sexual Urges Be Controlled?
>
> Always: **51%**   Never: **4%**
>
> —*Survey of 10,000 12- to 16-year-olds, "Project Reality" (1999)*

These studies also showed major improvements in teen use of contraceptives. The proportion of teenage girls using birth control at first intercourse rose from 48 percent in 1982 to 65 percent in 1988 to 77 percent in 1995—with black teens showing the biggest jump (from 36 to 72 percent). Teenage boys reported similar increases in condom use. While suburban girls mostly used condoms, pills, or vaginal devices (with an annual failure rate of 6 to 16 percent), urban teens were turning to more

Rates of Pregnancy, Abortion, and Birth for Girls Aged 15–17, 1980 to 1996*

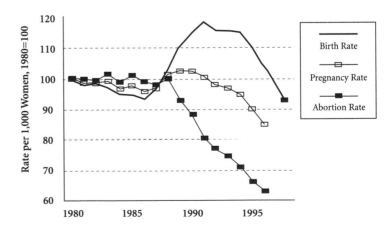

*1998 for Births

Source: Alan Guttmacher Institute (1999)

effective Norplant and Depo-Provera shots (with failure rates of 0.4 and 0.05 percent, respectively). One result of this has been a steep decline in the pregnancy and abortion rates among girls under age 18, down to their lowest levels in nearly three decades.

By the late '90s, the pop culture began taking note. In stark contrast to the Gen-X role model Doogie Howser's much-hyped loss of virginity, a newer crop of teen-drama stars (Donna in *Beverly Hills 90210,* Dawson in *Dawson's Creek,* Cody in *Step by Step,* all three teen leads on *Family Matters*) now celebrate their virginity—as do major characters in recent teen films such as *She's All That* and *10 Things I Hate About You.* Teen celebrities such as tennis star Anna Kournikova have boasted of their sexual chastity the way Gen-X teen stars once did of their sexual athleticism.

Why this Millennial sexual counterrevolution? Call it a sex-ed triangulation—three forces that have together produced a turnaround. On one side of the culture wars, you've had Joycelyn Elders, SIECUS, the Alan Guttmacher Institute, and various other sex-ed and condom advocates, warning that unsafe sex can kill, that promiscuity spreads disease, and that sexual harassment is morally wrong. On the other side, you have MTV's Dr. Drew, Laura Schlessinger, Christian conservatives, and other abstinence and "resistance skills" advocates, warning that premarital sex (safe or not) violates a moral code, can get a girl pregnant and make her either an unwilling mother or a fetus killer, and may leave all parties physically wounded, emotionally scarred, and in mortal sin. Who's ahead in the debate? From the Millennial perspective, *both* sides have made their point. Today's teens are having less sex, and what sex they're having is safer.

The third factor is generational. When Boomers were on the brink of their push for sexual freedom, the midlife G.I. Generation struck teenagers as "hung up," sexually repressed, incapable of letting go. As Millennials look up the age ladder at middle-aged Boomers, they see the reverse. To their eyes, today's 50-year-olds seem far too sexually obsessed and pleasure driven. The Millennial periscope extends from people they know, in their families and hometowns, to people in the news. To them, the Clinton-Lewinsky scandal was a big Comedy Central joke gone bad. In the context of their own world, and what their parents and teachers were telling them, it was irresponsible—and (worse) distasteful. Mean-

If you're in high school and you've never gotten any—whether you don't want to or just can't—you can stop worrying: You are now officially in the statistical norm. —**Rolling Stone**

It's all about finding "the right one"— as opposed to sleeping around.

—*Kirsty Doig, Youth Intelligence*

Teen demonstrators at the 1997 Washington for Jesus march brandished buttons that read "Pet your dog, not your girlfriend" and "Stop your urgin', be a virgin." They prayed for "the strength not to have sex," and so many pledge cards were staked in the Mall in Washington, D.C., that they looked like a layer of snow. —*Wendy Murray Zoba,* **Generation 2K**

I never thought I'd be so happy to be a virgin! *Randy, in* **Scream**

They're old enough to date when you determine they're old enough to date, not before. And that may be sixteen, and that may be twenty.

—*Len Fellez, author,* **Guerrilla Parenting**

What is the proper age to get married? Eighty-four, because at that age you don't have to work anymore, and you can spend all your time loving each other in your bedroom.

—*Judy, 8, creativity.net*

time, the pop culture's Boomer producers and Gen-X scriptwriters have decided that sexual gross-out humor is what teenagers want to see, so they have to deal with that, too.

A Gen-X "don't repeat your older sister's mistake" phenomenon has also come into play. Millennial girls have looked up the age ladder and seen that sex is risky. It doesn't get you far in life—especially if you end up with a baby, no man, and perhaps a disease, too. For boys, there are other new dangers: An unwanted sexual advance can lead to a lot more trouble than in the "boys will be boys" days when their parents were young.

Small wonder that Millennials are starting to put sex a little more on the shelf, crafting a sexual ethic that looks to be based more on responsibility than morality, reflecting, says Youth Intelligence's Kirsty Doig, "a backlash, a return to tradition and ritual. And that includes marriage." Small wonder that rising percentages of teens oppose casual sex, or that (according to a federal survey) 9 percent of boys and 16 percent of girls in middle and high schools say they've taken a virginity pledge. In high school, group dating is popular, and many middle schools are shifting from dances to "fun nights."

And small wonder that physical modesty is returning to fashion. Adults might think that, amid an R-rated culture with sexual innuendo standard sitcom fare, getting naked with each other means nothing to today's teens. Not so. Go to a public gym and see who gets naked in the locker room. It's older people—not teenagers, who in all likelihood are showering in their swimsuits and changing clothes under a towel. In a sharp reversal from the Boomer-youth days, Millennials "don't undress in front of each other," says Illinois teacher John Wrenn. Even after playing a varsity football game, "they just want to go home, all muddy, so they could have their privacy." Kids are agreeing with Wendy Shalit, that "embarrassment is natural." The new modesty is especially apparent among boys, who have to worry more than Boomers ever did whether their chest is "cut" and "buff," and navigate a high school social scene in which sexual preference is a far more open topic of conversation.

This new aversion to nudity suggests that the Boomer-era ranking of sexual intimacy—what constitutes first, second, and third base, and so on—could be changing definition. In *A Tribe Apart*, Patricia Hersch describes a teenage girl who told a boy that she'd have sex with him, but only as long as he didn't see her without her clothes. One kind of sex that could be increasing is oral sex, seen by many teens as a less intimate act than intercourse. Perhaps (as they hear tell) it's not even sex—or, as one Arlington, Virginia, middle schooler explains, it's "a sexual thing that keeps us from having sex."

Lastly, of course, there's the new kind of sex, cybersex. Millennials didn't create it, but they know how to find it—and some do, amid much public outcry. But virtual sex doesn't get anybody sick, pregnant, or sued nearly as often as the real variety, and a person can say "no" at any time with a click of a mouse. Besides, tech-wise teenagers will tell you, kids don't scan porn sites or dip into sex-chat rooms nearly as much as adults might think—and (kids insist) not as much as adults do.

According to polls, younger kids show even more reticence toward sex. More than half of the kids who responded to a recent internet poll declared that premarital sex is "never OK," and a 1999 *Time* poll of 12- to 14-year-olds found that 76 percent believed it was "very" or "somewhat" important to wait until marriage before having sex.

By decade and generation, here's how the bottom line has shifted since World War II: In the 1940s and '50s, when the Silent were coming of sexual age, adults didn't think much was going on, and there wasn't. In the '60s into the '70s, the Boomer era, adults didn't think much was going on, but there was. From the late '70s through the mid '90s, the Gen-X era, adults figured a whole lot was going on, and there was. Now, in the dawning Millennial era, adults still fear that a lot is going on, but that's not necessarily true—and less may be going on with each passing year.

These [middle school] kids were raised knowing about AIDS, so they've seized on oral sex as a compromise. They see it as safe and casual.

—*Margaret Sagarese, author of* **The Roller Coaster Years**

None of the teens I interviewed said they had been encouraged to be more promiscuous by what they learned online. . . . But others say that what they've read online has convinced them that they shouldn't *be having sex. . . . In fact, founders of teen sites like Razzberry and gURL point out that conversations about chastity, virginity, and "How young is too young for sex?" are among the most popular topics in the sexual areas of their communities.*

—*Janelle Brown, salon.com*

Cybering is kind of like phone sex, where you're describing sexual stuff you want to do to each other—only you're typing instead of talking. When this guy asked me to cyber, I felt weird. I thought it would be interesting to see what it was like, but I was totally grossed out at myself for feeling that way. Not knowing what to do, I signed off. —*Jennifer, 14*

Substance Abuse

When considering the Millennial experience with illicit drugs, two facts must be kept in mind. The first fact is that, in recent U.S. history, the worst youth drug abusers by far—whether you're talking about pot, cigarettes, alcohol, or pills—are today's 35- to 45-year-olds. These are last-wave Boomers and first-wave Xers, dubbed "Generation Jones" by pop-culture writer Jonathan Pontell, most of whom reached their late teens in the '70s when the drug culture was at peak postwar potency. The second fact, stemming from the first, is that not since Prohibition has any child generation had to cope with parents who are (or once were) such heavy abusers themselves.

According to data gathered by the federal government and other sponsored agencies, here's what's been going on:

Illegal drug use began rising gradually in the 1960s, steeply in the '70s, and then peaked in the early '80s, after which it declined until the early '90s, whereupon it began rising slightly again—even as, ironically, teen sex and violence began falling. Teen marijuana use has climbed back to its late-'80s levels, but remains well below the peak levels of around 1980.

Alcohol—the drug that imposes the largest social costs (from accidents, crime, domestic violence, and job loss)—was a huge Gen-X success story.

Throughout the 1980s, alcohol consumption plunged sharply among 12- to 17-year-olds, more modestly among high school seniors. Through the '90s, it leveled off among younger teens and rose slightly among high school seniors. In 1979, one of every two teenagers reported having drunk alcohol in the prior month, whereas in 1998, less than one in five did. The share of 12- to 17-year-olds who admit to monthly binge drinking has fallen from over 20 percent in the mid '80s to under 10 percent now. Arrests for drunkenness and drunk driving declined by more than half from the early '80s to a low point in 1993, and have since risen slightly (back to the levels of the early '90s, but far below those of a decade before).

Among 12- to 17-year-olds, cigarette smoking fell through the '80s and into the early '90s, at which time it gained new popularity among girls. It spiked up a little in the mid-'90s and has since leveled off. Among high school seniors, teen smoking remained flat through the '80s, rose slightly (from 28 to 35 percent) in the '90s—remaining below its '70s peak—and is showing signs of declining again.

Teen use of more dangerous drugs—cocaine, crack, heroin, stimulants, and the pharmacopoeia popularized in the '70s—declined through the '80s to near-zero levels in the early '90s and has risen only slightly since then.

In a nutshell: For youth substance abuse, the '70s had a bad record, the '80s a good one, and the '90s a mixed one. But the late 1990s produced some hopeful signs.

>> In 1998–99, most rates of abuse among twelfth graders declined.

>> In 1997–99, most rates of abuse among eighth and tenth graders declined.

>> An annual survey asking students whether "In my school, marijuana users are really popular," found that those who "agree strongly" fell from 20 percent in 1996 to 10 percent in 1999.

>> The share of teens who feel that rap, rock, or pop music stars "make drugs seem like an OK thing to do" dropped from

Girls didn't want to date drug dealers anymore. Girls felt they were unreliable. That had a big effect.

—Richard Curtis, John Jay College of Criminal Justice

I'm not going to risk my life for someone stupid.

—Topaz Thompson, 14, who refuses to date boys who take or deal drugs

See, I don't need no alcohol Your love makes me feel ten feet tall

—Lauryn Hill, "Nothing Even Matters"

Today the culture of sobriety extends down to adolescence, and kids are cleaning up quicker. —Rolling Stone

The best antidote to drinking and drugs is friendship. —Alex Berke, 15

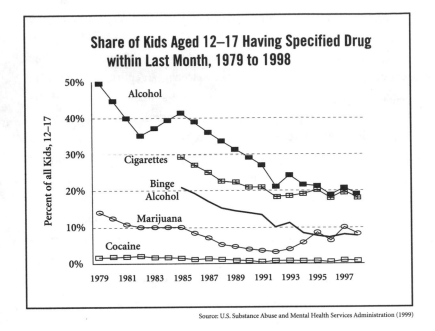

Source: U.S. Substance Abuse and Mental Health Services Administration (1999)

about half in 1995 to about one-third in 1999. (However, the share who feel that way about TV and movie stars remained unchanged.)

>> A 1998 survey that asked teenagers if marijuana should be legal found those under age 16 opposing by nearly two to one, those age 17–18 opposing by a bare majority, and 19-year-olds favoring legalization. (Whether today's 16-year-olds will change their minds as they grow older remains to be seen.)

Exactly what is causing this strange mix of substance abuse trends is the subject of much conjecture among academics and argument among politicians. Conservatives pursue hard drugs, praise tough sentencing and the Reagan-era "Just Say No" campaign for successes, and blame Clinton and Hollywood for backsliding. Liberals pursue the tobacco industry, which they blame for its advertising and other corporate misdeeds, and complain about harsh sentences for nonviolent drug offenders. Both sides of the culture wars agree that teen drinking is bad. Perhaps as a consequence, that's the area that has consistently shown the greatest improvement.

Cigarettes remain a puzzle. Nowadays, the best-behaved, high-achieving teenagers—many of them the offspring of nonsmoking parents—can be spotted with "jacks" in their hands, or even chewing tobacco in their mouths. It's too facile to blame Joe Camel, or Congress, or cigarette machines, or bogus IDs, or retailers who openly sell smokes to teens. Today's kids are under more pressure than kids used to be. They live in an accelerated culture. A greater percentage than ever before are on Ritalin or other prescribed psychotropic drugs. For some of these kids, cigarettes may serve a calming purpose. Once kids are hooked, the heightened pressures at school may make breaking the habit harder than a decade ago. And, among teen smokers, all the constant lecturing from middle-aged Boomers (known by today's teens to have had far worse teen drug problems) may be sparking a mild sense of rebellion.

The successful antismoking campaigns tend to be those that abandon adult moralizing (what some call "The Big Talk") and instead apply positive peer pressure. In Florida, kids themselves designed antitobacco ads that were so effective—cutting middle-school smoking by over 50 percent over two years—that the tobacco lobby leaned on the state legislature to eliminate funding for them.

Whatever today's teens are doing with alcohol, tobacco, and harder drugs, they're not doing it as self-destructively as older generations did as youths and are still doing as adults. In the '90s, as in the '60s, substance-abuse fatalities remain primarily a Boomer problem. In 1979, the drug-overdose death rate nationwide was approximately the same for teenagers and adults in their forties. By 1996, the teen rate was basically unchanged, but the rate for fortysomethings was *ten times higher* than it had been before. Today, in other words, overdoses are mainly a malady of the middle-aged. Social historian Mike Males queried Los Angeles County hospitals to find out the age and number of people who died from heroin, cocaine, crack, or methamphetamine in 1997. The final count: adults, 250 deaths; teens, *zero* deaths.

Throughout U.S. history, dangerous drugs have tended to mean different things to different generations. "Other generations take drugs (like

On Thursday, an officer dressed as the Grim Reaper will remove one student from a classroom every 15 minutes. The students' faces will be painted white, and they'll wear black robes to represent the "walking dead"—or students who die in alcohol or drug-caused crashes. These students will return to their classrooms, but they won't speak or take part in activities the rest of the day [and will] stay out all night with adult chaperones. The parents of two students will be told that their children have been killed by a drunken driver, and share their reactions at Friday's assembly.

—**Gresham Outlook,** *describing the* **Gresham (OR) Police Department's** *antialcohol program for high schools*

We have the power to lead these teens and tell them what brands are hot. We need to leverage that power and make it cool not to smoke—and brand that concept.

—**Linda Platzner,** *publisher,* **Teen** *magazine*

My coworker's 15-year-old is faced with being forced out of a gifted-and-talented high school into a much less desirable one because she was caught smoking. She was told that there are 800+ kids on the waiting list to replace her. —*Mary T*

Kids don't see [drinking] as a big problem. It's a regular thing, not like they're rebeling. There is no pressure to drink. —**Marcus Ruopp,** *high school student*

pot, cocaine, and LSD) so they can be messed up," wrote a Gen Xer on geocities.com. "Kids today take drugs (like Prozac and Ritalin) so they can be normal." For Boomers, marijuana and more potent drugs offered a ticket to another world, a means of reshaping reality, a badge of youthful defiance, a symbol of their desire to escape. For Gen Xers, illicit drugs lost most of their political symbolism, instead becoming highly personal instruments of alienation—or business. For Millennials, drugs (including cigarettes) are just another choice that brings personal results—a high-risk choice, at that—which, like all such choices, must be handled with care.

According to a 1999 report of the Partnership for a Drug-Free America, "The tide appears to be turning.... [T]eenagers are disassociating drugs with critically important badges of teen identity.... In kids' minds, marijuana is less and less associated with popularity.... Attitudes are changing in the right direction, and when attitudes change, behavior changes usually follow, gradually at first and then, if trends continue, steadily."

Crime

The year 1993 was truly a horrible one for youth crime. The nation's biggest cities were setting murder records. Newspaper headlines screamed about carjackings, drive-bys, and gang executions. A brief plateauing of the crime rate during the next year did not deter criminologists from making dire predictions. "This is the lull before the crime storm," said James Alan Fox. Beware "superpredators," said John DiIulio. Here comes a juvenile "time bomb," warned *U.S. News* in a sobering cover story about "an ever greater bloodbath" in the wings.

In the years since, America has enjoyed a plunge in youth crime, the speed and distance of which has no precedent since the birth of modern data. What's more, the most dramatic drops have occurred in the worst crimes (such as murder and serious violent crime) and in the most accurate and comprehensive measures of crime (victimization rates, *not* arrest rates).

From 1993 to 1998, the rate of murders committed by youth aged 12 to 17 fell by 56 percent, and the teen murder victimization rate fell by nearly as much (48 percent). Both those rates are now below where they were before the late-wave Gen-X murder binge, and barely higher than the late-'70s rates for Boomer teens. The teen murder-rate reductions in large urban states has been staggering: down 54 percent in California, down 55 percent in Texas, down 66 percent in Massachusetts, down 78 percent in New York. In a dramatic reversal from the Gen-X youth era, when the murder arrest rate doubled while the rate for older adults fell, the Millennial murder rate is falling considerably faster than the rates for older generations.

From 1993 to 1998, the rate for all serious violent crime (murder, rape, robbery, and aggravated assault) committed by youths aged 12 to 17 fell by 45 percent, and the victimization rate fell nearly as much (38 percent). These rates are the lowest ever registered for these measures, dating back to 1980. In all likelihood, the overall youth victimization rate (and perhaps the offender rate) is lower now than in any year since the 1960s. The violent crime rate (including "simple assault," which roughly doubles the total) shows Millennial teens producing a lesser drop—but a far greater improvement than for older age brackets. Teen arrest rates for most property crimes are hitting their lowest levels ever. Through the

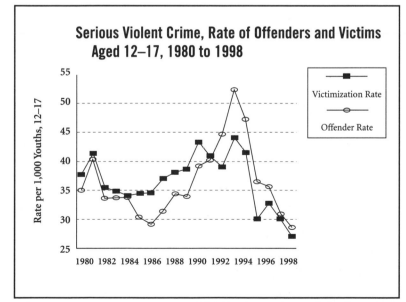

Serious Violent Crime, Rate of Offenders and Victims Aged 12–17, 1980 to 1998

Serious violent crimes are murders, rapes, robberies, and aggravated assaults.
Source: U.S. Bureau of Justice Statistics (2000)

Something's happened in the school, Ma. —Frank Jones, 7, *after an elementary school shooting in Mount Morris, Michigan*

first six months of 1999, there were large further reductions in all these crime and victimization rates.

Over the same period, teen gang activity also declined, especially among blacks. Leaders from the high-crime era have been convicted and incarcerated, new truces have been negotiated, and new youth programs created. Most cities are now much better at mobilizing community institutions, from church groups to fathers' groups, to create more opportunities for kids, after school and at night.

In urban America, when teenage and child Millennials look up the age ladder at Gen Xers in their twenties, they see a quarter of them in prison or dealing with probation officers, many of them absentee fathers who can't help their children or marry the women who bore them, barely literate, with poor work habits and no marketable skills. Who wants to follow in *those* footsteps? Thus arises the "older brother" syndrome, the tendency of a successor sibling (or generation) to heed the negative object lessons of the next-elders in their lives. This is why crime, like so much else, reaches a point where it becomes nonlinear. For two generations in a row—Boomer and Gen X—it had been getting worse. But Millennials are drawing the line.

Yes, there is one major crime indicator that makes Millennials look worse than Gen Xers: Today's teens are being arrested more than those of a decade ago for "status" offenses such as loitering, drunkenness, DWI, and drug possession. But that's the exception that proves the rule—or in this case, all the rules now being enforced by ZT police tactics. More arrests mean more police activity, not more crime. According to a 1999 report from the National Center for Juvenile Justice, "arrest increases . . . can reflect positive policy changes."

School Violence

Forget what you've seen, read, or heard to the contrary. School violence is down, way down. Fifteen people died violently at Columbine, but rebroadcasting the scene a hundred times doesn't make it fifteen hundred—though you might think it does, from all the hearings and commissions and metal detectors.

Here are the facts. According to the official data compiled by the

National School Safety Center, the number of violent student deaths at schools was much lower in the late 1990s than when the NSSC first started compiling these at the beginning of the decade. Violent deaths at schools declined from a high of 55 in the 1992–93 school year to 25 in 1998–99. If you exclude Columbine, there were only 10 violent deaths (including suicides) in that year. Of these 10, only 3 were intentional homicides by other kids—and of these 3, only 2 were committed with guns. Now consider: There are over 20 million teenagers who attend U.S. schools each day. Each of these kids is much more likely to be struck down by lightning or run over by a freight train than to be killed by one of his peers. Even of all teen murders, and these aren't very numerous, only one in a hundred is committed in a school.

And that's not all. From 1991 to 1997, 30 percent fewer high school students reported ever bringing a weapon to school, 20 percent fewer said they got in fights, 25 percent fewer skipped school because they felt unsafe, and 50 percent fewer feared being mugged, raped, or shot. In the fall of 1998, before Columbine, three times as many students in grades 3 through 12 believed that school violence was going down rather than up. In urban schools, the ratio was five to one.

Although Millennial kids, on the whole, are feeling safer these days both in and out of school, they have acquired a special dread of mass gun killings, for much the same reason many people fear airline travel: When it happens, it's horrible, spectacular, the lead on the nightly news, the cover on all the newsmagazines. Why has this crime suddenly become a Millennial trademark? Each side of the culture wars has its own preferred explanation—on one side, guns and hate; on the other, a jaundiced culture and derelict parents. There's some truth to all these explanations, certainly. Yes, many adults today keep a lot of firepower hanging around their homes without much supervision. And yes, the Harris-Klebold goal of being portrayed in a Spielberg-Tarantino movie does have a jarring '90s ring to it. But the question worth asking is why, when other teen crimes are ebbing, these peculiarly horrible incidents—at Jonesboro, Pearl, West Paducah, Fayetteville, Springfield, Littleton, Fort Gibson— keep happening.

Media hype is one answer, but some other patterns are discernible. Unlike the bulk of the more urban, bicoastal school killings of the early

I have a small collection of LPs. I have a nicked Eurythmics record that sounds like the school shootings: Here comes the rain again (bip) Here comes the rain again (bip) Here comes the rain again (bip). . . . My record will "bip" until I lift up the arm and set it down one groove over.

—Chris Loyd, 17

People coming in trench coats Am I going to die?

—Amberly, highwirednet.lycos.com

Just because we have chains and spikes doesn't mean we're going to go shooting people.

—Patrick Connor, 15, on a post-Columbine dress code

The athletes and stuff are really popular. . . . They'd make fun of the Trench Coat Mafia. They'd say, "White trash," and "Why don't you comb your hair?" and "Are you Gothic, man?" and "You need some new clothes."

—Mindy, 15, Columbine High

At Columbine High School, we will have zero tolerance for cruelty, harassment, excessive teasing, discrimination, violence, and intimidation.

—Frank DeAngelis, principal, Columbine High, at its reopening

School shootings are rising because of cliques at school. —Amanda, 13

'90s, these have been committed by Caucasian males in small to middle-sized towns, mostly along a swath from the central South through the southern Great Plains. Rather than one youth gang attacking another, these Millennial-era crimes were instead acts of rage against the well-behaving mass of the student body by loners who despise popular kids and are teased by the "in" cliques. In the Gen-X era, loners like these would have felt less pressure to conform, not so out of place or so motivated (as Harris and Klebold were) to pull off a crime whose horrendous scale would forever keep them in the pantheon of wax-museum evil-doers.

These Columbine-style crimes are thus a symptom of a breaking generational wave, of a better-behaved and higher-achieving generational core confronting the residue of an earlier youth era. However horrible these atrocities, and however justified the security measures needed to prevent their recurrence, adults should not let a few crimes committed by a few kids detract from the Millennials' gathering success in improving youth conduct. America doesn't need more commissions on youth violence that is declining, led by adult generations who, in youth, increased it sharply. In 1970, at the height of the Boomer youth era, there were less than two violent-crime arrests of adults for every one arrest of a kid aged 10 to 17. Now, as Millennials arrive, the ratio is more than three to one. Maybe what America needs is a youth commission on adult crime.

Today's high school students understand what's going on around them. In 1994, 22 percent said violence was the worst problem they faced. By 1998, only 7 percent said that. In a *Time* poll, 93 percent of 6- to 14-year-olds declared their schools "very" or "pretty safe." These days, they're more worried about college, grades, and peer pressure—problems that, considering the alternatives, aren't so bad.

Raising the Bar

Let's put this good news in perspective. Millennials are not nearly as well behaved as Silent Generation youths were back in the "teen canteen" days of World War II. In many ways, they're not as well behaved as their global counterparts in Europe or Asia. Nor are they yet as well behaved as Boomers were in the early 1960s. But their conduct is improving—a claim no other post-World War II youth generation could make.

What's extraordinary about the behavioral bar adults are setting for Millennials is, first, that they're expected to behave better than adults do, and, second, just as with academic achievement, the bar is moving, ever upward.

Case in point: Gambling. It's become a new adult worry, even though Millennials are turning away from it on their own. "These are the first kids to grow up with gambling all around them," says Richard McGowan, professor of economics at Boston College. The 1990s boom in American gambling—from lotteries and casinos to on-line gambling and day-trading—marked a liberating change of pace for older generations. Not for Millennials, who mostly don't like it. A 1999 Gallup poll found that 47 percent of 13- to 17-year-olds oppose gambling, versus only 32 percent of adults—and that 70 percent say it "damages family and community life." "I've seen adults lose property over this," says high school student Erica Sanchez, "and a lot of the time it's their children who end up suffering. . . . If the person is married and has children, they shouldn't do it."

Where Boomer youths were drawn to risk, and in middle age are enamored with wide-open gambling as a once-taboo activity, gambling runs directly counter to the emerging Millennial mindset of planning ahead for an orderly future. "They're quicker to see its harmful effects," reports McGowan.

Teens gamble far less than adults—in part because they're barred from most forms of wagering—yet twice as many teens (20 percent) as adults (11 percent) say they wager "too often." Even so, a recent study by the National Gambling Impact Study Commission focused more on youth than adult gambling. In 1999, when the first Millennials were 17, the Commission proposed raising the legal gambling age from 18 to 21. That may not be necessary. Brad Stuart, 18, dabbled in a state lottery, won a small sum on a scratch-off ticket, and then swore it off. "You should only gamble when you're totally sure you're going to win," he says.

There's always more to be done, more to be fixed, with kids. Cheating and other honor-code violations are now in the crosshairs, as are bullying, disrespectfulness, and vulgarity. These are indeed problems—but not just for Millennials. To teen eyes, it will seem odd indeed to see Boomers and Gen Xers set and enforce harsh new rules in these areas. Imagine how Millennials might regard a national crackdown on cursing, given the language in movies and songs those older generations have

Bullying has become so extreme and so common that many teens just accept it as part of high-school life in the '90s. —Newsweek

Among teens, 72 percent say their high school has tension between athletes and nonathletes, and 57 percent say athletes bully nonathletes.
    —*Chilton survey, espn.com*

Most athletes are not bullies, say teens. Many are true student leaders, who treat other students with respect and, often, serve as bridges between different social cliques. Even the term "jock" is an elusive concept, applied to some athletes, but not others, and used more often to describe those students who are empowered in the school social structure.
    —*Tom Farrey, espn.com*

If you dress like a trenchy and talk like a trenchy, you will be treated like a trenchy. If you dress like an outcast, and are rude and obnoxious, you will bring much disrespect upon yourself.
    —*Father Peter, Boys Town USA*

In five years, will there even be an "outcast" group left in most high schools? Based on the trends I've seen, no. The past three years have witnessed a dramatic decrease in personal expression as conformity and uniforms take over student culture.
    —*Michael McSwain, 18*

Columbine, friend of mine
Peace will come to you in time

—*Jonathan and Steven Cohen,*
"Friend of Mine"

made for teenagers. Sheri Parks, a college dean and mother of a 4-year-old, says it "just delights my daughter to think that grownups also don't have good control over their words."

Invariably, the closer Millennials get to the bar, the higher it gets set. When older generations see their strategies working, they don't ease off. Instead, as with Zero Tolerance, they keep piling more pressure on kids to be and do better. Here, too, as with so much else, this rising generation is growing up accustomed to the task of meeting and beating standards older people couldn't—and often still can't—handle themselves.

CHAPTER TEN

Junior Citizens (community)

Now is the time for us to reunite. . . .
Feel the flow, and here we go
                    —*'N SYNC, "Here We Go"*

In 1998, as part of a promotional campaign for a new museum in Philadelphia, the National Constitution Center gave 13- to 17-year-olds a test explicitly designed to embarrass their generation. The results confirmed that more Millennials can name the Three Stooges than the three branches of government, four times as many know the number of Hansons than know the number of senators, and so on. One editorial described the findings as "humorous if not pathetic."

Set aside the question of how informed the typical *adult* really is. Yes, it may be true that today's teens know less than their elders about the wars, presidents, and causes of the twentieth century. But keep this in mind: To Millennials, "Remember Pearl Harbor" is as distant in time (from their first birth year) as "Remember the *Maine*" was for Boomers. The Eisenhower-era freedom riders are as distant as the Harding-era KKK. Betty Friedan is as distant as Isadora Duncan. Richard Nixon and Watergate are as distant as FDR and the New Deal. Today's kids can't be

> We work together, probably a lot more than adults do.   —*Lauren, 16*

> They are problem-solvers by nature. It may have something to do with the way we are teaching them and parenting them, but just get a group together to discuss any area of concern, and they all have a solution. It's exciting to watch.
>
> —*Johnnie Crawley,*
> *Montessori principal*

expected to think of those events the way their parents and grandparents do. They may at times be unfamiliar with the old causes, but that doesn't mean they're disrespectful of what those causes achieved.

To the contrary, as the true children of postmodern America, Millennials often feel that whatever respect they do have for those old causes they have to acquire on their own. They are growing up in a world that feels *post*-truth, *post*-sacrifice, *post*-heroic, *post*-anything truly ennobling. Much of what they learn about civic matters gets filtered through the lens of cynicism, irony, satire, and parody—that is, through the '90s-era pop culture. The great causes are over, their agendas in place, their foibles grist for Jay Leno, the Capitol Steps, and *Politically Incorrect*. So much is tongue in cheek that not much seems at stake anymore.

From the youth perspective, today's adult generations have done much that is good, much that has enhanced their own lives and prospects for the future. At the same time, Millennials often fault adults for being too self-centered, too smug, too wrapped up in grand causes that have strayed beyond their original purposes—leaving the nation with pointless arguments, endless hypocrisy, and no capacity to make the pieces fit together anymore.

That's where they're finding a role. Already, Millennial teens are hard at work on a grassroots reconstruction of community, teamwork, and civic spirit. They're doing it in the realms of community service, race, gender relations, politics, and faith. In each of these arenas, they've had to start from a different location in history—and face a different life challenge—than today's older generations remember from their own youth.

Community

The town of Soldotna, Alaska, is spread out, without buses, and many of its younger and poorer residents don't have cars. Jason Redmond, a Class of 2000 senior at Soldotna High, decided to fix this as part of the "government lab" in his civics class. Jason came up with a plan to create a public bicycle system, through which Soldotnans could use free yellow bikes to go from one bike rack to another, all across town. Jason didn't just talk about his idea. He put it in motion, with help from the police and local merchants. In the words of his teacher, Jason was "trying to build com-

They have no sense of individualism, thriving, rather, from close interpersonal networks.

—*Don Tapscott,*
Growing Up Digital

Part of what Hanson is, is that there's not just one guy who sings. Having three voices is what makes us Hanson.

—*Taylor Hanson, 13*

I was impressed with their focus, their discipline, the way they played together as a unit. —*Glen Ballard, the Moffatts' producer*

Schools have started programs to make freshmen feel more connected, as opposed to simply bewildered.

—*Abraham McLaughlin*

What's happening now is adults, they all bring their kids over and they have their kids "team" baby-sit a whole mess of kids. —*John Costello, on the growing trend toward "team" baby-sitting*

munity. Everyone can use the bicycles equally, and it will take everyone in the community working to make it happen."

In 1990, when Amber Lynn Coffman was 8, she visited a homeless shelter in Baltimore. Two years later, at age 10, she decided it would be nice to make lunches for the people there, so she started a little home-based program she called "Happy Helpers for the Homeless." Six years later, Happy Helpers boasted fifty volunteers, was serving six hundred lunches a week to Baltimore's homeless (along with clothing giveaways, pizza parties, and special haircutting days), and had chapters in forty-three states.

America has many Jason Redmonds and Amber Lynn Coffmans, Millennials who aren't just taking stands, but building hands-on organizations to get things done. Elementary schoolkids in Waukazoo and Woodside, Michigan, formed a volunteer choir, 230 strong, to make choral music videos to give to sick children. In Tukwila, Washington, elementary schoolkids launched a children's drive to aid Honduran victims of Hurricane Mitch. Students in Denver's Highline Community School raised money to "buy" two Sudanese slaves and return them to their families, and then began organizing dozens of other schools to release over a hundred more slaves. Fourth and fifth graders in Lynnwood, Washington, petitioned the INS and won citizenship for the mother of the school's custodian. In Florida, middle school kids went to Tallahassee to lobby lawmakers on behalf of school funding. "We're the ones in the schools," said one 14-year-old, "and we know what's going on."

Millennials aren't doing this as entrepreneurial loners. Instead—in keeping with their generation's team orientation—they're banding together, in their own clubs and classes, on-line, and (especially) in national uniformed service organizations. In their childhood era, they have propelled a huge increase in Boy Scout members (up 50 percent since 1980) and Girl Scout members (up 20 percent since 1985), reversing long periods of decline for both. Kids in uniform, doing good deeds, in public buildings: That's how today's adults want to see Millennials—many of whom, given the chance, willingly oblige.

Adults give a higher priority to helping kids do good deeds than to doing good deeds themselves. (On average, middle-aged Boomers spend fewer hours doing community service than do Millennial teens.) The Do

There's this real warm feeling you get. I don't know how to explain it. Like we're all in something together, and it's even OK to lose. —Martin, 13

Basketball teams consist of five men. So why do we see three members of the Chicago Bulls off to the side watching Steve Kerr pass the ball to a posted-up Michael Jordan? . . . One of the reasons that fans are starting to turn to college basketball games is because college basketball uses all five players. —Nick, 16

Less-skilled players will get more playing time. . . . Parents will cheer for all the kids at a game. —Dean Conway, reciting rules of the Massachusetts Youth Soccer Association

Team Cheerios is looking for youth sport teams with great teamwork stories. —Cheerios box (1997)

This is a great thrill for all of our skaters. These girls practice many long hours to perfect their performance. They put individual styles aside to compete as one; no superstar can capture a win for you. —Nancy Rossi, coach of the Precision Skaters of Warwick (RI), Team Cheerios 1998 Team of the Year

Something organization sponsors a National Kindness and Justice Challenge, a contest challenging middle school students to win prizes by launching the best civic projects. Burger King's "The Big Help" campaign and McDonald's bulletin boards are promoting and publicizing kid-service programs.

The definition of "community service" has morphed from one generation to the next, dating back to World War II. For the Silent, community deed-doing was channeled by the Selective Service law, which pushed young males toward socially acceptable deferments such as teaching, science, or even marriage. For leading-edge Boomers, the term "community service" often meant cleaning hospital bedpans to avoid Vietnam—or, for the more radically minded, spurring oppressed neighborhoods to vent their grievances against the "establishment." When the draft ended, in 1973, first-wave Boomers had eliminated mandatory civic duty for their later cohorts and the generation to follow. Growing up in the era of the Volunteer Army, Gen Xers developed their own ethic of volunteerism, de-emphasizing great crusades in favor of simple acts of charity to help needy people. For teenagers, "community service" came to mean punishment for drunk drivers and *Breakfast Club* miscreants.

By the Millennial era, the notion of volunteering gave way to a more compulsory "service learning," which is now often required for graduation from middle or high school. Bolstered by Acts of Congress in 1990 and 1993, which created the Learn and Serve America program, the integration of community service with academic study has spread to schools everywhere. From 1984 to 1999, the share of high schools offering any kind of community service program grew from 27 to 83 percent, and the share with "service learning" grew from 9 to 46 percent. Two-thirds of all public schools at all grade levels now have students engaged in community work, often (as in Soldotna) as part of the curriculum.

A new Millennial service ethic is emerging, built around notions of collegial (rather than individual) action, support for (rather than resistance against) civic institutions, and the tangible doing of good deeds. Surveys show that five of every six Millennials believe their generation has the greatest duty to improve the environment—and that, far more than older people, Millennials would impose extra civic duties on themselves, including taxes, to achieve results. Tellingly, the new Boy Scout

Handbook has a distinctly Millennial new ethic, the "Principles of Leave No Trace," requiring Scouts to leave camping areas not the way they found them, but in better shape than when they arrived.

Race

When the TV networks revealed their twenty-six new shows for the fall of 1999, the NAACP's Kweisi Mfume erupted over the fact that not one of them had a black person in a lead role, and few had any blacks whatsoever. By the late '90s, television had no crossover shows like *The Jeffersons* or *Cosby.* Instead, it had what *The Washington Post* called "Them-and-Us TV," with a white list (*Seinfeld, Ally McBeal*) and a black list (*Martin, Roc, Living Single*). The top-rated TV show among blacks, *The Steve Harvey Show,* was 127th among whites, and the top among whites, *Friends,* was 88th among blacks.

Through the '90s, TV executives tried hard to target the splintery Gen-X crowd in all its various niches. Meanwhile, the civil rights leadership tried to keep its old causes alive. As the two sides duked it out with press releases, neither paid much attention to the newest generation of TV-watching teens—many of whom wanted America to transcend these tired debates.

In fact, Millennials are less likely to regard themselves as either "white"

URBAN KIDS

SUBURBAN KIDS
TRYING TO LOOK LIKE URBAN KIDS

At one desk, a child lifts a phone and hears a list of slurs encompassing everything from color to generic insult. Then a voice offers ways to respond. . . . At another station, children play "What's My Stereotype," pressing a buzzer when they hear stereotypes on a video. Nearby, others write words they find hurtful and push them through a shredder.

—**Dallas Morning News**

At one civics class for high-school seniors, the question arises of how many are applying to the University of California. A dozen hands shot up. How many wrote their essays about overcoming challenges? Nine hands. And this is Beverly Hills High.

—**Los Angeles Times,**
describing student response to a new alternative to racial preferences

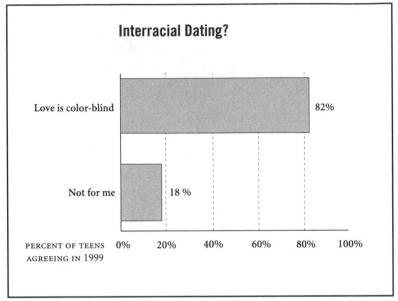

Source: "Youth Poll" on react.com (1999)

or "black" than any prior American generation. So, too, are they, according to *American Demographics,* "the least prejudiced about race" *and* "the most dissatisfied with race relations." What bothers them is decidedly *not* their own behavior, but what they perceive as the odd racial conceptions of the adult world. Of a Boomer such as Mfume, Millennials might ask why he clings to a white-versus-black morality play that worked when he was young but doesn't work so well now. Why, for example, do TV shows and ads depict blacks far more often than Latinos and Asians, even as the latter two substantially outnumber blacks among today's kids? Through the '90s, the share of TV characters who are Latino roughly doubled, but remained below 4 percent, less than one-fourth of their actual share of Millennials.

To Millennials, diversity doesn't mean black or white, it means Korean, Malaysian, Latvian, Guatemalan, Peruvian, Nigerian, Trinidadian, and skins in more hues from more places than seen on any generation in any society in the history of humanity. "Where there were clear lines between Caucasian and Asian American and African American," says Michael Wood of Teenage Research Unlimited, "those lines are becoming very blurred." While Millennials still see ethnic inequalities in America, they're becoming inured to the constant discussion of black-white issues in the media. In their eyes, race has become so fluid, complex, and multifaceted that the old answers seem less persuasive, the old struggles less purposeful, and the old racial equations less relevant. And, to this point, they don't see the new verities reflected in the pop culture. Children Now polled a multiracial group of 10- to 17-year-olds, who said that TV showed whites and blacks in a mostly positive way, but Latinos in a mostly negative way.

Race has meant something unique to each of today's generations, in youth. The Silent were children in a time when multicultural consciousness was weak and official segregation strong. They later became, in their thirties and forties, America's great civil rights generation, the demonstrators who marched with Martin, the adherents of nonviolence, the believers that "we" (all races united) "shall overcome," the ones who crafted affirmative action but were seldom personally affected by it. Boomers were coming of age when the civil rights movement was already in high gear. They were the rioters who rejected nonviolence, the angry radicals for whom bullets and bandoliers were political statements—and, later, the icebreakers on affirmative action. Gen Xers cannot personally recall race as a uniting element or nonviolent movement. As children, they were bused to public schools that (in the late 1980s) reached their apogee of integration. Their childhood era marked the cresting of welfare dependency, along with disintegrating families, crack cocaine, street crime, and harsh prison terms. As college students, they encountered affirmative action as the status quo. While they were growing up, Latino and Asian immigration swelled, and America became more diverse in nonracial ways—in cultures, lifestyles, and economics—as "multiculturalism" became entwined in the culture wars.

By the time Millennials came along, the civil rights wars were over, the positions were established, and the old turns of phrase were more descriptive of what *is* than what *could be*. The leftover agenda does not excite them. What does is a new agenda—*their* agenda—to create opportunities for racial groups to shed their adult-imposed sense of separateness. Born at least twenty years after Selma, Millennials have never personally seen black-white race issues divide America. Affirmative action programs are now nearly two generations old, their original reasons altered by time and complicated by diverse new ethnic arrivals.

The talk of a bilingual society ignores the enormous power of American culture. Spanish has no chance. . . . The average education of a Mexican immigrant is the fourth grade, and they're teaching their children Spanish? No. —*Gregory Rodriguez, New America Foundation*

She'd be the black sheep of her friends if she spoke Spanish around them.

—*Walter Enriquez, a Peruvian immigrant, describing his 12-year-old sister*

In the Millennial world, race is less a cutting-edge issue than a game of political nostalgia. Today's kids are growing up in a world in which the language of oppression has become pop culture play. Their lack of living memory has combined with Gen-X gangsta-rap edginess and Boomer judgment-by-context to produce an oddly disjointed set of adult-imposed rules on youth behavior. Rap now has hard and sweet kinds, both of which have edged closer to pure entertainment. In a time of declining youth violence, all the new talk about extra punishments for "hate crimes" emanates from middle-aged people who seem angry themselves, unwilling to let the old passions ebb, always searching for racial motivations.

Do You Have Friends of a Different Race?

Yes: **90%**

—*Survey of 6- to 14-year-olds,* Time *(July 5, 1999)*

To the eyes of kids unfamiliar with the old causes, charges of racism seem to be flying from all directions, race cards played by people in power just as much as people on the outside. While adults tell kids not to make racial distinctions, adult institutions hire credentialed experts to collect racial data, debate the racial makeup of new hires or new ads, pore over standardized test questions to decipher how members of various racial groups might answer them differently. Meanwhile, busing is going down and schools are resegregating, more by income than race, reinforced by the declining interest of Boomer and Gen Xer parents in raising their kids in multiracial settings. Kids would never guess that overcoming racial consciousness was the main original goal of the civil rights movement.

The Millennials' own ethnicity is far more complex than any in U.S. history. Latinos can be from Bolivia, Cuba, Puerto Rico, Guatemala, Mexico, and blacks from Jamaica, Haiti, Brazil, or Nigeria. What exactly is an "African American"? Why (as some California Latinos have questioned) is black history celebrated for a month (February), and Latino history for only a day (Cinco de Mayo)? How can the old racial arguments explain the vast wealth and prestige of countless black athletes and entertainers?

How do the old racial categories cope with the likes of Tiger Woods, a self-professed "Cablinasian" (a mix of Caucasian, black, Indian, and Asian ancestries)? So many images exist that they become noise, fill every frequency, induce exhaustion—and seem useless. The logical recourse, for a Millennial teen, is to discard race as a criterion for judging people and behavior.

Much the opposite of Boomers at the same age, Millennials feel more of an urge to homogenize, to celebrate ties that bind rather than differences that splinter. Where Boomers were raised on the idea of a racial melting pot—an idea many of them later rejected—Millennials are being raised on culture as a "mosaic" of many hues, a notion many of them show signs of rejecting. Today's teens are confident that they can do this and believe they can handle twenty-first-century racial issues a lot better than other generations. In our Class of 2000 Survey, 69 percent said they'll handle race relations better than adults now do. Only 6 percent said worse. In our Teachers Survey, respondents reported that racial taunting is on the decline. Today's teens date freely across ethnic lines, and they're far less likely than adults to gape at other kids who do. Ninety percent say they have friends of a different race. The whole idea of a color line simply doesn't mean as much to Millennials as it does to older people.

Certainly, racial problems still exist. Black academic achievement, though gaining, is still well below white levels. Black child poverty, teen crime, and teen pregnancy, though all falling sharply, are still far above white levels. Black teenagers aren't as optimistic as their white peers that the racial situation will improve over their lifetimes. But Millennials share a solid optimism about race, and teachers agree that there is less racial discord now than a decade ago.

Boomer youth mentors, such as author Joyce Ladner, worry that today's black youths seem too "fragile" and could be losing the "timeless values" of the civil rights struggle. What Millennials of all races lack are not values, but merely the living memory of valued events. Rather than backsliding, rather than turning their backs on the agonies and triumphs of their ancestors, Millennials are intent on achieving Dr. King's dream of a truly race-blind society. They may not get there themselves, but their children could.

Not like previous generations, we teens have eliminated prejudice.

—Loc Dao, 16

You're seeing more cultural mixing. Where there were clear lines between Caucasian and Asian American and African American, those lines are becoming very blurred.

—Michael Wood,
Teen Research Unlimited

I call myself a Chinese American, because I am exactly that. I am raised with the morals of both cultures. . . . My father quoted Twain and Confucius at one sitting at the dinner table. *—Lydia Chin,*
high school student

Mixed girls! That's the way to go! All the mixed girls I know are fine!

—Gino Jackson,
teenager

Gender

In May 1999, a committee of teachers at Virginia's Langley High School gave out awards for academic achievement and moral conduct. "Once again the women dominated," remarked Youdus Mirza afterward. "Boys are beginning to receive less and less attention, while girls are beginning to receive more"—yet, admitted Mirza, they earned those extra awards. "At almost every meeting designed to organize something or volunteer for a community function," he said, "more young women appear than young men. It seems to me that women are more eager and enthusiastic in taking leadership and being on top."

Mirza's experience is becoming the norm. To this point, leading-edge Millennial girls are the generational pathbreakers, setting the standards for their peers—and leading teen watchers to speak of a new "boy problem" in America. Of the roughly 750,000 teens in the 1997 *Who's Who Among High School Students,* nearly two-thirds were girls—and, among those listed, girls were twice as likely as boys to have "A" grade averages. Another study has shown that, among America's top academic achievers,

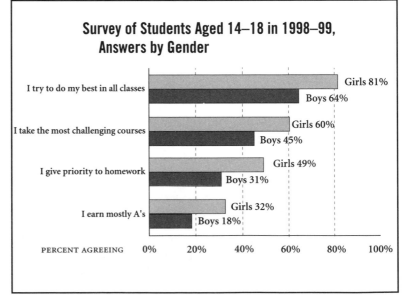

Survey of Students Aged 14–18 in 1998–99, Answers by Gender

Source: Horatio Alger Association (1999)

63 percent are girls. The Horatio Alger Association's "State of Our Nation's Youth" report found that "Females challenged themselves more frequently to take the most difficult courses available . . . (and) worked harder at their course work and received better grades than males."

Girls still have their own special set of problems. They account for nearly all the early-'90s increases in middle school cigarette and pot smoking. From 1991 to 1996, eighth-grade-girl cigarette use rose from 13 percent to 21 percent, marijuana from 5 to 17 percent. Girls are half-again more likely than boys to describe themselves as overweight, and nine times more likely to admit to an eating disorder. Yet these problems are residues of the *Reviving Ophelia* Gen-X "grrrl" era and do not reflect Millennial trends.

What's fresh about today's girl life involves traits that are recognizably Millennial: teamwork, action, civic deed-doing, and robust achievement. The federal government's "Girl Power" antidrug ads, which show teams of cheerful girls in motion, have been far more effective than their male equivalents. Even in sports, girls do a better job embodying the Millennial spirit. Title IX, which mandates gender equality for sports funding, is certainly one reason so many girls are engaged in team sports. But Title IX's impact is deeper than that. Today, the group values stressed by amateur girl athletes are on the upswing, while the one-on-one swagger of adult male pros seems tired. In this post–Michael Jordan era, the cutting-edge role models among Millennial athletes have come from the U.S. Women's World Cup team.

In school, girls are showing more progress than boys in nearly every area. Across all ethnic groups, girls do up to ten hours more homework per week than boys. They take more Advanced Placement tests, have higher enrollments in every level of math and in every science except physics and advanced technology, and receive more honors in everything except sports and science. On the NAEP math and science tests, girls have eliminated half of the advantage that boys once had in the Gen-X era. On the NAEP reading and writing tests, girls enjoy a much larger advantage over boys (15 to 17 points), and that gap is not closing. Boys still do a few points better on the SATs and hold an edge in the top one percentile. But the next tier—the top 10 percent—is mostly female. At the bottom end, boys are everywhere. Boys are half-again more likely to be held back a

This is the first generation to grow up with true images of female empowerment. —**Jancee Dunn, Rolling Stone**

Right now, we're totally in the age of the female. The whole girl-power thing is quite huge. In fact, a lot of teen boys feel quite disenfranchised because they don't have as many role models. —**Todd Cunningham, MTV**

Every 14-year-old girl today really believes she can become president, that she can run Exxon. —**Steve Kahn, CEO, Delia's**

I have big dreams, and they don't revolve around what a man wants. I want to be an astronomer and work for NASA. —**Laura Banuelos, 13**

grade, and outnumber girls two to one at the lowest reaches of reading comprehension, perceptual speed, and word-association memory.

High School Seniors (per 1,000) Who Took AP Examinations		
	1984	1996
Male	50	117
Female	50	144

—U.S. National Center for Education Statistics (1998)

Before the Millennial era, girls were considered disadvantaged in the classroom, winning less teacher attention and suffering in self-esteem. No longer. Most recent measures of self-esteem show girls and boys faring about the same. A 1997 survey found that about 85 percent of both boys and girls consider themselves "a person of worth" with "a number of good qualities." Studies show that teachers compliment girls more often, think girls are smarter, and prefer to be around them. To the extent today's boys get more attention in the classroom, it tends to be pharmaceutical, special-ed, compensatory, or disciplinary attention—all of which boys receive two to ten times as often as girls. In a flip from the Boomer youth era, girls are more ambitious than boys—and, for the first time ever recorded, expect to earn incomes at least equal to those of boys. Three times more girls than boys now say their top career choice is medicine or law.

Between the Boomer and Millennial youth eras, the gender landscape has changed enormously. In the economy, the pay gap between young men and women who are educated and childless is now vanishing, and the number of women-owned businesses has grown more than tenfold since the 1960s. Women passed men in undergraduate attendance in 1982 (at the start of the Gen-X college era) and now earn 55 percent of all bachelor's and master's degrees. In 1998, 70 percent of female high school graduates entered college right after high school, versus 60 percent of boys. Once in college, boys are quicker to drop out during their freshman year. From 1970 to 1995, the share of medical degrees awarded to women rose from 8 to 39 percent; of law degrees, from 5 to 43 percent. Today's children see countless girl role models in the popular culture. Kids can see war heroines such as Mulan, huntresses such as Buffy, Xena, and Nikita, and watch teenage girls become sexual aggressors (*Can't Hardly Wait*).

Just as young Boomers noticed an extreme differentiation of gender roles and were troubled by its cost to the individual, young Millennials notice a new absence of differentiation and are troubled by its cost to the community. Compared to child Boomers, child Millennials see men and women as far more interchangeable and the family as more multifaceted and unstable, with celebrity adults holding marriage in low regard. Where Boomers grew up seeing one kind of family, with two kinds of people, mothers and fathers, each highly dependent on the other, and where Gen Xers landed in the warp of change, Millennials face a new status quo. They know many kinds of families, mothers with no fathers, fathers with no mothers, ex-thises and step-thats, within which anyone can be or do anything.

The rise of Boomer women in the 1980s and '90s, and their empowering effect on Millennial girls, parallels the rise of G.I. men in the 1940s and '50s, and their empowering effect on Boomer boys.

Back in the 1950s, Boomers grew up noticing that the ascendant gender was the male war hero and world shaper. This new "superman" was celebrated not just because he could do all things, but because his male power was always in harness—never complaining and never doing for himself but always for the community. Meanwhile, women's problems were mostly ignored, sparking the beginning of a protest movement. In the 1990s, women were ascendant in nearly every aspect of life outside the home, and the "supermom" became the object of widespread sympathy for having to sustain the family (and community)—and, very often, having to do it all on her own. Meanwhile, men's problems have been more ignored, prompting the growth of grassroots men's groups.

Relative to girls, Boomer boys thrived because the events that took place just before they were born elevated the male role. In a socially disciplined postwar world of parents who sought to cultivate more initiative and creativity in kids, boys may have had a further edge as the gender more easily induced to show aggression and break rules. In the early '60s, rebellious boys dominated the cutting edge of the new youth culture. Now, Millennial girls thrive. The Consciousness Revolution that took

Boys Used to Be Boys, But Do Some Now See Boyhood as a Malady?

—headline,
The Wall Street Journal

After so many years of hearing about silenced, diminished girls, teachers do not take seriously the suggestion that boys are not doing as well as girls even if they see it with their own eyes in their own classroom.

—**Christina Hoff Sommers**

Over the years, girls have steadily improved their performance in math and science. . . . The same cannot be said of boys and reading.

—**William Pollack,**
Real Boys

Many boys . . . rush through their work in an effort to be the first, fastest, and smartest. Remind them that "smart" can be slow and thoughtful, and that the first one in class who finishes an assignment is not necessarily the best.

—*family.go.com*

Who has to wait while the boys get settled? Whose time is not always used as well as it might be? Who can do more in a group where no one's thinking about throwing blocks? The girls. —**Barbara Root,**
Convent of the
Sacred Heart, an all-girls preschool

You're not a little Oompa-Loompa anymore, Dawson. You're a big, bad, manly Oompa-Loompa. —*Pacey,*
in **Dawson's Creek**

place just before they were born elevated the female role. Many of their moms are better educated than their dads, and are excelling in their new roles. In this more chaotic social environment where greater teamwork is sought for kids, girls may have an edge as the gender better able to cooperate—and, hence, to dominate the cutting edge of the new youth culture.

Much as the Boomer boys' advantages fueled a narrowing of gender roles (and a budding feminism), the Millennial girls' edge is fueling a rewidening of those roles. There's plenty of early evidence of a budding masculinism, as boys battle to differentiate themselves from a more uni-sexed elder world. Gender-specific toys are freshly popular among children, and male toy bodies have never had bigger muscles. When boys go on-line, they typically play games, while girls chat with networks of friends. Boys and girls seldom read the same magazines for pleasure. The TV-watching habits of boys (WWF wrestling, BEN, Xtreme sports) and girls (*Dawson's Creek,* WBN, *Friends*) have never been more different. When school sports such as wrestling go co-ed, boys in the audience playfully scream "sexual harassment," prompting some boys to forfeit rather than wrestle a girl. Fairfax County teachers report that sexual taunting is on the rise.

"We have come a long way from the '60s and '70s when everyone said boys and girls are the same, their tastes are the same," says Rich Cronin, president of the Fox Family Channel. "Boys and girls are different." Child development experts have begun noticing that—in an era when kids are raised by parents who challenge the old male-female differences—boys now act like boys, and girls like girls, at earlier ages than before. What experts call "male and female play patterns" used to arise around age 5; now they can be seen in preschool. "Boys start to be fascinated with battle and competition," observes Lisa Bannon in *The Wall Street Journal,* "while girls become more interested in creativity and relationships."

The same adult generations that produced feminism are starting to catch the trend too. Single-sex schooling is again on the rise, and serving a new purpose. In the Boomer era, an all-boys or all-girls school was considered antiquarian. Now, it's cutting edge. In 1972, federal legislation pushed single-sex public schools out of existence. In the '90s, the regulations have been eased—and, in 1997, California established seven pairs of state-subsidized single-sex middle schools.

As they reach dating age, Millennial kids are modernizing new gender-role definitions. Many are going back to courtship, back to fanfare when asking somebody out, back to glamour at the prom, back to sublimated passions, back to modesty, back to romance, and back to monogamy. Their leading edge is just now entering colleges whose student bodies are majority female and whose gender-studies departments are steeped in the conviction that males oppress females.

A major challenge for college administrators—if they want to stop the male flight and incorporate men into the campus community—is helping Millennials turn this new masculinism into something socially constructive. Likewise, a major challenge for the entertainment industry is telling real stories about Millennial teen boys as they actually are, rather than as comic foils or stereotypes. Even when producers try to focus on male teen protagonists, they typically fill the roles with older actors who show an implausible physical maturity and social polish (perhaps, in part, to please largely female film and sitcom audiences). For now, today's teen boy is a tough read—in the pop media as he is in society at large.

Among Millennial boys and girls alike, sexual preference is far more widely discussed than it was in earlier generations at the same age. According to various polls, anywhere from 3 to 10 percent of today's teens believe themselves gay, lesbian, bisexual, or "questioning"—roughly the same percentage as adults. Who is or may be gay has thus become a common topic of conversation. Amid the emergence of a newly masculinized boy culture, many male teenagers are bothered by all the talk about gayness. A 1998 Primedia/Roper national survey revealed that 31 percent of seventh- through twelfth-grade boys identified "gays and lesbians" as one of the groups "most responsible for current problems at my school." On the other hand, a large share of teens are comfortable with gays—and, in true Millennial fashion, are trying to build a sense of community that encompasses gays and straights. In the Boomer era, young gay activists were adversarial. Now, in the era of Gay-Straight Alliance clubs (hundreds of which have sprung up at high schools since the 1998 Matthew Shepard killing), their goal is inclusion.

In sum, Millennials don't interpret gender and sexuality like their parents do or ever did. They look at the Boomer feminist ethos much as Boomers looked at the G.I. cult of macho—that is, as the main part of the gender landscape where some fixing is in order. The young Boomer challenge was to promote sexual independence by trashing social norms. The young Millennial challenge is to create a new sexual *inter*dependence by energizing social norms. "My apologies, Ms. Friedan," says 17-year-old Sarah Abrams, "but the simple fact remains that there are great differences between the male and female sexes, and there is nothing wrong with recognizing them."

Much as boys did for teenage Boomers, girls are thus far leading the way for Millennials, setting the tone for much that adults are demanding in kids. Where cutting-edge Boomer boys pushed for more risk-taking, cutting-edge Millennial girls are pushing for *less*—for studying hard, behaving well, taking fewer risks, learning and playing in teams, constructing a more orderly, better-balanced teen world. But don't forget: Come the 1970s, Boomer girls stepped forward and began setting the generational agenda. The moment for Millennial boys is yet to come.

Once the Boomer boys were joined by the girls, their generation became a major force in American cultural life. The day is coming when the Millennial girls will be joined by the boys and become a major force in American *civic* life. That's when this generation will reveal its true power.

Politics

Bill Clinton was first elected president in November 1992, when the Class of 2000 Millennials were in fifth grade. The following January, at an Inaugural Gala, he nodded with approval while listening to Barbra Streisand sing the Stephen Sondheim lyric "Careful the things you do, children will see. . . . Children will look to you for which way to turn, to learn what to be." Five years later, in 1998, every student in Yoder Elementary School in Mebane, North Carolina, was assigned to write an essay on a hero. Of the 380 essays submitted, not one named the only U.S. president those children have ever seen live on TV. "They're very well informed," said teacher Ann Tangerose, "and President Clinton is not their hero."

Before all the scandals, Millennial kids generally admired Clinton as a

6TH GRADE OFFICERS

CLASS PRESIDENT — PEDRO
INTERN — NATASHA
SPECIAL PROSECUTOR — XIU XIU
HOUSE MANAGERS — ZACH, MAX, CALVIN
TALK SHOW HOST — MADISON
CLASS POLLSTER — LATEESHA
SPINMEISTER — AHMAD

Whenever his name is mentioned, they laugh and show disrespect. But that has more to do with Clinton himself. If I mentioned any other president, or the presidency itself, they don't giggle. —Rhonda Phillips, *sixth-grade teacher*

There's a sense among some kids in my grade that the president is just a player like everyone else. I wouldn't want to be in a room alone with him.
—Rebecca Regan Sachs, 15

He should be ashamed of himself, for teaching kids bad things.
—Keith Lynch, 11

They should give a punishment like not to be president the rest of the year.
—Cory Hinojosa, 7

cool, smart, and energetic leader roughly their parents' age. On the news, they often saw him visiting schools and talking to kids, and he seemed to work hard on their behalf. In 1996, school polls showed kids widely supporting his reelection. Their attitude changed, swiftly and dramatically, with the Lewinsky scandal. Polls in Nickelodeon, *TechnoTeen,* and elsewhere revealed that a majority of Millennials felt Bill Clinton should have left his job. "If the sixth graders of America were to vote, he would be impeached," said Linda Wiley, a middle school teacher in Round Rock, Texas. When *Baltimore Sun* columnist Susan Reimer asked her teenage kids and their friends about Clinton, "their answers whipped my head around. Forget him, they said. Dump him and move on. . . . In the black and white world of children, Bill Clinton has crossed some moral line—a line we arrogant parents thought to paint for them—and these children have cut him bloodlessly out of their hearts."

The Clinton-Lewinsky scandal left a mixed imprint on the Millennial mind-set, tarnishing the presidency a bit but not altering their sunny view of public institutions. Among 12- to 17-year-olds, three in five think they could be elected president someday, but only one in five say they'd want the job. However, more than half of Millennial teens say the federal government can be trusted to do what is right "most" or "all of the time" (versus only a third of adults), and two-thirds believe that public officials usually tell the truth. A CNN youth poll showed overwhelming insistence that behavior like Clinton's is *not* all right for them. Rather than engendering cynicism, the impeachment saga seems to have encouraged today's teenager to enlist in what E. J. Dionne calls "a revolution against cynicism, despair, and selfishness."

Percentage of 12- to 17-Year-Olds:

Who believe they could be elected president someday: **62%**
Who would want the job: **Girls—21%, Boys—13%**

—Survey of 12- to 17-year-olds, ABCNEWS.com (February 15, 1999)

Yet that's not the whole story. Better than any other politician of his era, Bill Clinton understood the special feelings Americans shared toward

Millennials, tirelessly placing them (and their "soccer moms") at the top of the public priority list. He has reminded Americans of the child component of every issue from welfare reform and health care to Iraq and Kosovo. Indeed, much of Clinton's success as a politician is attributable to his skillful reading of America's desire to raise a more public generation. For better *and* worse, Bill Clinton has come to represent what Millennials notice in prominent Boomers. On the plus side, there's the sensitivity, intelligence, cultural cool, and sense of principle—but there's also the narcissism, gabbiness, hypocrisy, and inability to control impulses.

This is very different from how teenage Boomers looked up at John Kennedy and other G.I.s. When Boomers were growing up, kids saw adults who outwardly seemed well disciplined, who suppressed personal emotion, who trusted government, and who believed in progress—so long as everyone pitched in. Voters paid increasing attention to the news, lawmakers controlled how markets worked, institutions (not values) set the nation's direction, and the main complaint was about a single "establishment." Millennials see adults who outwardly seem undisciplined, who freely reveal their emotions, who distrust government, and who regularly vent pessimism about progress—except what can be achieved by everyone doing his or her own thing. Voters pay less attention to the news, values (not institutions) set the direction, dollars control how people vote, and the main complaint is about myriad "special interests."

Boomers follow a generation (the Silent) that had seen electoral politics as important, whereupon they applied their youthful energies to decivilize public life. Millennials are following a generation (Gen Xers) that has seen politics as unimportant, and show signs of wanting to recivilize public life.

The first Millennials have yet to cast their votes, so they're still flying low under the adult radar, presumed to be alienated cynics who don't care about voting, much less organizing. Yet adults who watch them perform civic tasks may sense something different brewing. Today's school kids take the Pledge of Allegiance, and flag saluting, more seriously than Boomers or Gen Xers did. *Growing Up Digital* author Don Tapscott describes their "very strong sense of the common good and of collective social and civic responsibility." Check out Kids Voting USA, Children's Express, or the web world, and you'll see kids discussing issues, participating in polls, and organizing mock elections, at times quite energetically. "If

It [the Pledge of Allegiance] means a lot to me. When you stand up and put your hand over your heart, it's like you're making a promise to the flag, to never wreck or bother it.

—Jon Garr, 7

I have just finished a cursory exploration of many Millennials' web sites, for kids and by kids. I was struck by the large number of sites related to politics, science, and community action. **—Brian Rush**

With this new Web site, teens can find information to help them do their homework, pursue a hobby, or choose a career. **—www.americasteens.gov,** *"a gateway to federal and other publicly supported Web sites for teens"*

www.peacecorps.gov/kids . . . is a virtual tour of the Peace Corps experience (but without the dysentery). **—The New York Times**

Before you explore the rest of this site, I would like to introduce myself. My name is Christian Shelton, and I am a 16-year-old Californian Democrat. I hope I can count on your vote in 2024 and be the first Democratic president elected from California!

—home.earthlink.net

you don't vote," says 13-year-old Julia Dotson of New York City, "you can't complain about what the mayor or the government does, because you didn't contribute your opinion to what was going on."

From Grade School Essays About Politics:

Some of our presidents never did much else and are famous only because they became president.

The nominees are usually called candidates or campaigners, although I have heard them called other things.

Noncommittal is to be able to talk and talk without saying anything.

Political strategy is when you don't let people know you have run out of ideas and keep shouting anyway.

—collected in the 1990s, at San Diego State College

Teen polls show that Millennials share a number of Gen-X issue positions (on the environment, technology, crime, substance abuse, and gay rights)—but have a distinctly un-X view of the political process. A 1999 Close-Up Foundation survey of 500 high school students learned that Millennials share a rather traditional view of political parties—which they consider useful, albeit too argumentative. They're less interested than older people are in third parties. For leaders, they don't want Jesse Ventura–style celebrities, but rather experienced politicians who know how to enact laws and administer governments—or military leaders experienced at command. Unlike Boomers, Millennials show no gender gaps in their political views.

Millennial teens are very interested in voting—though less interested in actually pursuing politics or government as a career. They're deeply distrustful of the media. They get their political information less through the usual adult news sources than through comedy shows (candidate appearances on Jay Leno or David Letterman leave quite an impression), internet web sites and chat rooms, and—especially—conversations with one another. Most of what today's teens learn and do in politics lies beyond the radar of the adult world.

When unleashed, Millennials display a potent ability to get what they want in adult settings. In May 1999, a teenage reporter named Alex somehow made his way into the White House press corps for President Clinton's post-Columbine briefing on youth violence. After Clinton's statement, Alex and Sam Donaldson each shouted queries, but the president ignored them both. A press aide tried but failed to shoo Alex away. When Alex ambushed Clinton by the exit, the surprised president answered his question, after which Alex piped out two follow-ups, which Clinton also answered. "Alex three, Sam zero," a reporter yelled out.

Today's teens are confident, even cocky, about how they can improve things when their turn comes. By a two-to-one margin, in our Class of 2000 Survey, they expect to spend more time on politics and government than Boomers now do. Also by a two-to-one margin, they expect that, when they're in charge, government will work better. By a three-to-one margin, they expect the economy will work better. When the *Philadelphia Inquirer* hosted a 1997 town meeting, Millennial teenagers from nearby Cherry Hill, New Jersey, became among the most vocal people present. "The people there were astonished," recalls Michael Eliason, who was 15 at the time, "not only that we held strong views on subjects like campaign reform, taxes, and political ethics, but that we had *ideas* on how to deal with them, ideas that were often more detailed than those of the older people in the room."

When Millennials focus on a political problem, they can be smart, persevering, and adept at high-tech research skills—as the sophomores at Maryland's Montgomery Blair High School recently proved. Before every congressional election, *The Washington Post* invites prominent pollsters and pundits to join in a Crystal Ball competition to pick the outcome of the 435 races. In 1998, a batch of Montgomery Blair tenth graders was asked to take part. After identifying seventy-one contested districts, they scoured the web for data, analyzed voter trends over the last twenty years, charted the money raised and federal money spent in each district, and made their projections. The pollsters and pundits, meanwhile, relied mostly on back-channel chitchat to make theirs. Who won? The Montgomery Blair Millennials.

Young people like to be where the action is. Just look at the popularity of summer youth mission projects. . . . Teenagers spend a week in the summer building houses in Mexico, working with children in West Virginia or cleaning up flood damage in North Carolina—focusing more on Christian action than on Christian doctrine. . . . I'm seeing a strong distinction . . . that seems to break roughly along generational lines. —Henry Brinton

Wuzup, God? —billboard campaign, www.wuzupgod.com.

Religion

At 7:37 A.M. on December 1, 1997, Ben Strong was leading a prayer circle at Heath High School in West Paducah, Kentucky, when a 14-year-old freshman burst in with a pistol. The freshman belonged to a "skateboarders" clique that revered punk rock and taunted "Christians." The freshman started shooting, killing three and injuring five. The principal came running, and the killer aimed his pistol at him. Ben jumped between them and demanded that the boy stop. The boy did, with one bullet still in his gun. Ben is widely proclaimed as a hero for risking his life to save his principal—a deed he attributed to his faith. And, of course, all America knows the story of Cassie Bernall of Columbine, challenged by her killer to deny her faith, which she refused to do.

In 1990, there were no prayer circles or clubs in U.S. public high schools. Now, there are over 10,000 of them, full of devout kids like Ben Strong and Cassie Bernall. Religion has become the basis of what the *Los Angeles Times* calls "a new teenage social caste" that includes groups such as the Knights of Christ, who square off regularly against students who idolize antireligion rockers such as Marilyn Manson. This tension is a new fact of life in today's middle and high schools.

Millennials think and talk more about faith, and do more with it, than older people realize. It matters to them. In one poll, teens cited religion as the second-strongest influence in their lives, just behind parents, but ahead of teachers, boy/girlfriends, peers, and the media. Four teens in five say they've prayed at least once in the past week. The share of kids who regularly go to church is down a bit from Gen Xers at the same age—but in an era when churchgoing is becoming an increasingly family-oriented activity, it may be rising relative to all other Americans. A recent Gallup poll showed that 55 percent of teens go to church regularly, versus 45 percent of Americans as a whole.

When Millennials do get to church, they are preached at to behave more than to believe—a message they are taking to heart. Religion matters most to them when they can apply it in the usual Millennial manner—by organizing it themselves, by forming clubs, by bearing witness collegially, by focusing on team deed-doing ahead of solitary spirituality.

Their childhood experience with religion has been quite unlike their parents'. Boomers grew up back in a highly secular era, when newsweeklies asked if God was dead, when politicians almost never mentioned religion, and when adults helped kids seek scientific answers to religious questions. The premise was that this would help kids think more for themselves. Religion was not something most kids could comfortably display at a public school. By contrast, Millennials are growing up in a spiritually driven era, when newsweeklies announce that God is back, when politicians chatter incessantly about faith, and when adults help kids seek faith-based answers to secular questions. Today, the premise is that this will encourage kids to think and (especially) behave the way adults want. And now it's quite acceptable for a kid to display religion, *any* religion, at public schools. Overtly Christian themes now appear in mainstream pop music and teen magazines.

When Boomers were young, adults viewed religion as a public ritual that was not intended to provoke argument—at a time when faith was less a destination than a starting point. Now in midlife, Boomers have transformed religion into a personal and often incendiary credo—at a time when faith is supposed to reveal life's true meaning. Having come of age in a spiritual vacuum, they propelled an awakening whose aftermath left them in control of faith-related issues. In her book *Generation 2K*, Wendy Murray Zoba remarks that her fellow Boomers remain convinced "that our narrative is all that matters in the grand scheme of things. We like to think that 'the story' is ours to write, and we attempt to advance the plot according to what we think we deserve." One part of that story is the linking of faith to family. Many Boomers (and Gen Xers) report that their rediscovery of religious feeling—what some call the "born-again moment"—occurred at the birth of their first child.

With Madalyn Murray O'Hair's successful assault on school prayer, Boomers grew up in a time when religion was being removed from school. Millennials are seeing it return. In 1992, the U.S. Supreme Court ruled that privately organized prayer gatherings in schools were constitutional as long as they weren't part of school operations. In 1995, the federal government declared that public school students had the right to pray privately and individually, to meet in religious groups on school grounds, and to use school facilities like any other groups. In 1999, the

The most attractive aspect of church to me is the fellowship that comes with it. Going to church, and other church activities such as youth group, gives me the opportunity to congregate with people who become somewhat of an extended family. . . . We can easily be turned off by an incessant insistence upon a "right way" of doing things.
—*Kwame Boadi, 17*

People in general, and probably especially young people, don't like being told what to think, or what's right and wrong. But then again, I don't think religion should be changed in order to draw people in.
—*Robin Lyon, 17*

When you're in this country, there's a lot of distractions to Ramadan—cars, making money. The majority of my friends and classmates are more into having fun, so it's hard staying focused. —*Azam Junejo, 18*

People think that women in Islam are like slaves [saying] "Yes, master, no, master." But I'm not like that. I love my family, my religion. And I have a future. —*Susannah,* Seventeen

guidelines were expanded to let teachers include certain religious subjects in their classes and to authorize partnerships between schools and faith-based organizations. While the ACLU and some other groups have resisted these changes, public support for more religion in schools has become deep and broadly bipartisan.

There is far more religion in schools today than when Boomers and Gen Xers were students. Kids pray in circles before school, on their own before tests, and in clubs after school. Many wear WWJD ("What Would Jesus Do?") wristbands. On Sundays, many public schools now *are* churches. Not long ago, students who tried to pray were barred from school events. In May 1999, a Maryland student who *opposed* a graduation prayer was blocked from the ceremony by police and later barred from the all-night party. The big issues now range from whether students can write and lead prayers before football games to whether high schools should be allowed to do plays (such as *Jesus Christ Superstar*) that many believe to be sacrilegious.

Like Gen Xers before them, Millennials see church as a way to cut through the clutter of contemporary life, to find relief from the pop culture, to meet like-minded members of the opposite sex, and to do good civic deeds. What's new is the volume, energy, and team instinct. More than 17,000 high schoolers attended the National Catholic Youth conference in 1997, up from 7,000 in 1993. Membership in Kadima, the conservative Jewish organization for middle school kids, stands at the highest level ever.

Boomers wanted religion that challenged them spiritually more and institutionally less, while Millennials seek the reverse. Boomers reached their teens in the era of Vatican II, when the Catholic Church along with many mainline denominations worked to dilute the liturgy and revive the inner experience. Millennial teens are growing up in the era of Pope John Paul II, whose tireless focus on personal and social duties reflects the desire of many denominations to fortify the outer forms and rituals. And Millennials are responding. They're drawn to such complex ancient rituals as the Jewish Kabbalah, the walk of the labyrinth, the meditations of St. Ignatius, or the mantralike recitations of the Taizé, in which kids sit in a candlelit room and sing the same songs, over and over.

At church, today's teens can get bored and turned off when modern services get too casual, too MTV-style. They're pulled in a new direction. "Anything that seems very old-fashioned, that's where they're going," says youth minister Mary Pat Tilghman. "Intimacy, interactivity, tradition, and getting out of the pew" are what attract them, agrees Zoba. The Boomer spiritual seed has taken root with Millennials. But it may not be their parents' religion in how it grows, and in what it does.

The New Millennial Communitarianism

In the 1950s, the vacuum was individual conscience—in race, gender, politics, religion, and so much else. Who stepped up to fill it? Boomers. In the 1990s, the new vacuum was community, in all the same places. Who's now stepping up to fill it? Millennials.

When youth has a negative reputation, there's a strong temptation to splinter. There's nothing to be gained by being associated with other kids, by acknowledging any membership in a generation, or by caring about your age group more than your cultural niche. Now, with Millennials, a new and very un-Xer-like challenge is arising: how millions of diverse kids will manage to crowd together into a newly positive definition of youth.

Free-market incentives, individualism, and the search for inner fulfillment are all the rage for many Boomer adults, but less so for their kids—who are constantly told that what *they* need are selfless values. Rather than resist this message, kids seem to accept it. On the whole, they're not as eager to grow up putting self ahead of community the way their parents did.

When older generations see Millennials busy building community, they go out of their way to help, to do all they can to empower this rising generation to serve adult agendas. From kid-targeted government web sites to all the new teen-targeted newsmagazines, TV shows, and newspaper sections, today's America reflects a broad national hunger for the rebirth of collegialism that Millennials are starting to provide.

The day is approaching when Millennials will be adults themselves. That's when they'll start forging their own institutions, their own media, and their own agenda.

Our class is starting a campaign to help stop violence. . . . We want to send our violent video games like Golden Eye, Duke Nukem, and many others back to the makers. We will pledge not to buy them anymore. . . . We did some estimating with game costs and the number of students in our town and then the number of students in just 10 other cities in our state that are larger than our town. We started to see how this could make a really big difference if we got a lot of kids involved.

—Kirsten Thulien, Noele Ranta, and Betsy Boone, 11

CHAPTER ELEVEN

The Happiness Business *(culture)*

the happiness business *(culture)*
the happiness business *(culture)*

*Oh, I'm going for fearsome here,
but I just don't feel it.*

—*REX, in* Toy Story

In 1996, the recording industry confronted "one of the most perplexing crises it has faced in decades . . . All that is certain," wrote *The New York Times*, "is that a malaise is sweeping every facet of music—its production, distribution, and consumption." On the heels of recent robust growth, sales were plunging for new CDs by famous Gen-X bands such as R.E.M., Nirvana, and Hootie and the Blowfish. Attendance was sinking at rock concerts. From rap to grunge, the familiar Gen-X styles of the early '90s were no longer connecting with new-style kids who seemed less angry and alienated, and more cool with their parents, than the ones who came before.

Caught off guard, music industry executives ran focus groups and "finally woke up to the fact that they had nothing the teenagers wanted, and nothing the parents would allow them to have," noted Tower Records chairman Stan Goman. The music industry was bollixed. According to Neil Strauss of *The New York Times*, "not one, including the presidents

A long-anticipated younger generation has taken control of the stick shift of pop culture . . . with bright pop songs, interchangeable teen-age heartthrob stars and mindless yet ironic movies.

—*Linda Lee,* **The New York Times**

They are rummaging through culture's garage sales in a search of the wonderful combination of innocence, fun and sophistication that they have seen in old movies and heard in old songs. It may be a sign of something big beyond the music scene. . . . The next adults could be the ones who embrace and recast the great traditions of our culture.

—*Bruce Chapman*

and chief operating officers of four record labels, was willing to guess what the next big thing would be, where it would come from, or how soon it would arrive." They simply couldn't believe that what the kids wanted was happy music to a dance beat.

Over the next four years, more surprises hit American youth pop. From Pokémon cards to Harry Potter books, from troubles at Fox to the rise of WB, a Millennial tremor shook through pop-culture boardrooms. Right around the time Gen-X filmmakers, scriptwriters, and stars were rocketing past aging Boomers in industry favor, the teen market was changing into something odd and new, something adults did not understand.

Every twenty years or so, a new generational tremor rips the popular culture, signaling the arrival of new teens, and presaging an even greater pop earthquake to come. Throughout the last century, every time a new generation has reached its teens, the sudden change in adolescent taste causes the engines of pop-culture production to stutter and stall. Then comes a period of trial and error, as the entertainment industry churns uncertainly until a new musical style catches on and thrives.

The music recession of 1996–97 marked the collision of the Millennial early teens (especially girls) with a Gen-X pop regime that had spent nearly two decades going in essentially the same direction and wasn't going to change course on its own. What the music industry needed, and got, was a good smack in the wallet.

The Millennial Tremor

In the heyday of grunge, back when the '80s bled into the '90s, two kid-oriented groups with upbeat sounds (New Kids on the Block and Menudo) enjoyed brief flurries of popularity—less with Gen-X teens, for whom loathing clean-cut music was a badge of cool, than with the Millennial preteens who formed the heart of their fan clubs. These kid groups dissipated, but not before laying the seeds for the youth music that would dominate the pop music scene a half-decade later, once those same kid fans reached their teens—and, in the case of Ricky Martin, once those teen stars reached vocal and physical maturity.

One person who saw this tremor coming was Lou Pearlman, a

"DADDY, I WANT YOU TO MEET MY NEW BOY BAND!"

Boomer impresario whose shrewd mid-'90s instinct for Millennial culture parallelled Bill Clinton's shrewd use of Millennial politics. From his home base in "O' Town" (Orlando), Pearlman had observed how local theme parks had entertained Millennial kids with upbeat, uncomplicated sounds from smile-sing-and-dance machines. Thus was born the "boy band" concept. Recruiting from theme parks, he helped assemble groups such as the Backstreet Boys, 'N Sync, and other less-known singer-dancers, which he marketed into global sensations.

Soon this new mix was joined by other fresh flavors—a classical revival signaled by 13-year-old Charlotte Church ("This kid is so clean," said *The Washington Post*'s Ken Ringle), new country, led by the Dixie Chicks, and swing, popularized by Gap ads. Teens adored the old dance-worthy riff-rooted jump blues, an intensely synchronized old-new style that offered teens what *Swing Time* magazine described as "the return of manners, a backlash against grunge and rap where manners are the least thing they are concerned about." Singer Peaches O'Dell called it, more simply, "the happiness business." By the end of 1997, Millennial middle schoolers—girls especially—were back in music stores.

Since then, pop has bathed in bubblegum, as more people in the business caught the wave. Hanson, Spice Girls, Robyn, Savage Garden, Cleopatra, Mandy Moore, the Moffatts, S Club 7, and assorted others

Rock is exhausted; funk rock is exhausted; folk rock is exhausted; glam rock is exhausted; hippie rock is exhausted; punk rock is exhausted; soft rock is exhausted; hard rock is exhausted; angst rock is exhausted; pop rock is exhausted; country rock is exhausted; alternative rock is exhausted; . . . even Rolling Stones grow moss in time. —**Eric Felten, The National Review**

All you rappers yellin' about who you put in a hearse
Do me a favor, write one verse without a curse
—**Will Smith, "Freak This"**

"New Bubble Gum Flavor"
—**Los Angeles Times,** *headline for story about teen music (1997)*

have propelled a new teen- (and parent-) friendly style the *Times* called "a blend of the 1950s and the millennium," with nary a trace of angst or vulgarity. "There was a cry in America for more positive images," said Johnny Wright, Britney Spears's manager. "We had a gangsta-rap situation, with killings, and a lot of negativity," against which his young star began cultivating what she termed the "just really sweet" style "so supported by parents."

Like their audiences, the hot new performers were generally upbeat people who got along well with their parents and saw themselves, as 'N Sync's Chris Kirkpatrick described his band, as "an American group, with an American attitude, and American songs." "We're role models for a lot of people," said the group's JC Chasez. "We're not going to come out there and be dirty dogs!" The boy bands pulled stage antics as frantic as Marilyn Manson's, but without being offensive to anyone. They borrowed energy from raplike cadences, but without the hardness. When they flirted too closely with the Gen-X edge, they were quickly chastened, as when Disney made the Backstreet Boys swap the line "Am I sexual?" for "Am I sensual?" before releasing their video.

This new made-for-Millennials music reversed the major Boomer and Gen-X pop trends of the prior four decades. The sound came with total synthesizing, unvarying rhythms, predictable melodies, and silky harmonies, with nothing atonal, ear-jarring, or innovative. The lyrics came without nuance, with frequent reference to blue skies, warm hearts, flying eagles, and staying together forever. The songs were about virginal love, sweetly sentimental love, kindling the image of a teenage Barney's "I love you, you love me" with a beat. There was nothing negative or profane, nothing Mom, Dad, or God would mind hearing. Mom, Dad, and God even earned the occasional nod in the lyrics. (In concert, the Backstreet Boys began to invite moms onstage.)

The new style catalyzed a cultural generation gap. To Millennial ears, the new music was ear candy, brighten-my-day pick-me-uppers confirming teens in their self-confident happiness, digitally enhanced by nimble techies, marketed on brisk and bright videos and web sites, downloadable with MP3, fungible on homemade CDs, playable whenever, portable wherever, sharable with whomever. To many kids, the overall effect was, in the words of one 15-year-old fan, "so much fun, you can't even imagine."

Older critics demurred, labeling the new styles "fluff," "pop culture lite," "the sonic equivalent of warm milk," "doesn't smell like teen spirit." "I hate my MTV all of a sudden," complained *The Village Voice*'s Eric Weisbard, feeling musically pastured along with the rest of his "Generation Ex." The new youth culture, wrote Jon Pareles of *The New York Times,* "holds nothing new and difficult, nothing agonizingly sincere or brutally realistic, nothing barbed or underhanded or unruly or obtuse . . . and it's less troublesome than genuine rejuvenation could ever be."

The fading Gen-X music styles aren't letting go without a battle, and they are supported by plenty of teenage boys willing to rally around the old banners. On MTV, the daily boy-band sweet-pop hangout *Total Request Live* is preceded by *The Return of the Rock,* which bills itself as a show for kids sick of that kind of music. "Two opposing forces tangle on today's charts," wrote *Entertainment Weekly* in 1999. "In this corner, you've got hardcore hip-hoppers, like DMX, and metalheads, like Korn. In the other, you've got the boy and girl teen acts, dewy-eyed cuties singing some of the most saccharine and conservative music since the dawn of rock." Though the cuties are easy to spoof, the most popular parodies (such as MTV's 2Gether) have disappointed many Gen-X and Boomer music critics by ending up nearly as upbeat and musically fetching as the original article.

Like shadows of the early '90s, rock'n'rappers such as Limp Bizkit, Kid Rock, and Eminem were stepping in and producing outcast music as nasty as they wanted it to be—or as their promoters would allow. "Hi, kids, do you like violence?" shouted Eminem. "Wanna see me stick nine-inch nails through each one of my eyelids? Wanna copy me and do exactly like I did?" This rough stuff was raw boy music, a middle school male's answer to the sweeter stuff the girls liked. Yet the industry is now making even these performers soften their corners. Eminem's latest album offered Millennial teens artificial angst in two flavors: vulgar (with a parental advisory) and sanitized. Radio versions have started blipping out Tupac's use of the word "crack" and Everlast's use of "drugs."

The Millennial tremor of the late '90s followed a well-worn pattern the pop industry could have anticipated. Throughout the last century, the next new thing in pop music has repeatedly arrived at just the moment when a new generation's leading edge reaches its teens. Roughly every

They want me to have a sexy image. . . . That's not my thing.
—Elan Sara DeFan, 16, Latin pop star

To sum up Taylor [Hanson] in a nutshell, he's one happy young dude.
—boomerang.nu

Kara's Flowers seem positively elated at the very idea of waking up in the morning, and it's so natural and fresh-faced and honest you simply cannot help but hum along.
—Sam Smith, alt.music.alternative

Teens (and 25-year-olds masquerading as teens) have kidnapped pop culture.
—David Plotz, slate.com

Now the Millennials rule the music market, while the Xers cringe, roll their eyes, and cover their ears.
—Jake, 21

two decades, a generational passage thus announces itself—first with a warning rumble and then, a few years later, with a real earthquake. For about a decade following the tremor, a market emerges for a new kind of music made by the latter wave of the next-older generation, performers in their twenties to early thirties (the equivalent of today's Fiona Apple, Alanis Morissette, or Jewel). Increasingly, that music reflects the younger generation's tastes. In the following decade, the rising generation makes music for itself (including its younger cohorts), and its style reaches full flower. Then another new teen generation asserts itself with a tremor, and the rhythm rolls on.

The following chart shows how this has happened since the 1920s. Notice that each generation first launches a new pop style as teenage buyers, then enhances that style as buyers and makers, and later helps launch

DECADE	MAKERS	BUYERS	MUSIC	STAR
1920s	Lost	G.I.s	gin fizz jazz	Louis Armstrong
1930s	G.I.s	G.I.s	big band	Benny Goodman
(TREMOR: teen canteens and sock hops)				
1940s	G.I.s	Silent	crooning	Frank Sinatra
1950s	Silent	Silent	crossover	Elvis Presley
(TREMOR: *American Bandstand* and the twist)				
1960s	Silent	Boomers	protest rock	Bob Dylan
1970s	Boomers	Boomers	disco	Bee Gees
(TREMOR: MTV and new wave)				
1980s	Boomers	Gen Xers	alternative	Madonna
1990s	Gen Xers	Gen Xers	grunge, rap	Nirvana
(TREMOR: MP3 and boy bands)				
2000s	Gen Xers	Millennials	synthetic pop	Backstreet Boys
2010s	Millennials	Millennials	————	

its successor's style as pop makers. Give or take a bit, this process has coincided with decades. The tremors have typically arrived right at the ends of odd-numbered decades, and the full-fledged earthquakes during the even-numbered decades that followed.

By 2010, the Millennial pop culture will be fully locked in. Until then, the pop style will reveal a tension between what Gen Xers want to say and what Millennials want to hear—with the Boomer role confined to writing the checks and (decreasingly) setting the parental limits.

Reflect back on the last three times a new generational wave has broken over pop music. During World War II, a new batch of Silent "teenagers" (then a new word) didn't jive with the big, collective-action culture of the older big bands, many of whose members were off fighting the war. The young Silent found what they wanted in the croonings of the draft-dodging G.I., Frank Sinatra. By 1944, the "bobby-soxers" swooned to the sentimental sounds of "heartthrobs" and their achingly personal lyrics. Not long into the '50s, small-group jazz, rhythm and blues, and crooner sentimentalism fused into new Silent crossover genres (early rock'n'roll), which pushed the old G.I.-style music off the new "Top 40" playlists.

In 1958, when first-wave Boomers were the same age as first-wave Millennials were in 1997, any tune that cut through the prevailing blandness struck a chord with kids—who yearned for something wilder, riskier, and more assertive than what the crooners, do-woppers, or even "the King" were providing. The media responded by retooling around loosening social strictures. While Dick Clark was launching *American Bandstand* and Berry Gordy Motown, rock'n'roll found a new "Good Golly, Miss Molly" manic energy. Wacky songs became hits ("Witch Doctor," "Charlie Brown," "Tequila"), hinting at a new "Yakety Yak, (Don't Talk Back)" teenage agenda. Surprised G.I. adults reacted sharply, with editorialists blasting the "vibrating teens" and "wreck and ruin artists" who kept pushing up the voltage to ecstatic teen approval. This tremor was followed by a few years of girl groups, surf music, hootenanny folk, and new dances (like the twist) that no longer required personal contact. In the middle '60s, the Beatles and Stones arrived, Barry McGuire keynoted "Eve of Destruction" and (the Silent) Bob Dylan and Simon and Garfunkel tuned in to the mood of their juniors, producing what

A long time ago, rock was about rebellion—subverting the conventions and restrictions of repressive mainstream culture. But in an era of ludicrously violent television and video games, sexually explicit films, and an American president whose sexual exploits are the sort we might have expected from a rock star, there's not a whole lot of convention left to subvert. What we're left with is belligerence. —Alona Wartofsky, **The Washington Post**

And while boys can be as decorous or punky as they choose . . . teenage girls are expected to be mannerly again. Recording companies have been scouring the talent contests, kiddie shows and hinterlands for girls who'll seem like sisters or pals to their prospective audience. —Jon Pareles, **The New York Times**

The younger teens seem wild for those cheesy boy-toy "singing" groups like 'N Sync or Backstreet Boys, although for the life of me I cannot figure out why. —Amber Hawkes, 18

This is a good time for you to stay calm and assure your parents in a positive way that you know the difference between some of the lyrics on your CDs and appropriate reality. —Father Peter, Boys Town USA

Boomers today recall as the era of "classic rock." By decade's end, Woodstock's wake produced a total takeover of rock genres by Boomer counterculturists.

The Gen-X tremor came in the late '70s, just as the first Gen Xers were filling high schools and the era of Boomer protest and psychedelia was nearing exhaustion. In the bicentennial year of 1976, the great truths of the universe were being summed up by John Denver and disco mirrors. Neither style spoke to the new teens, and neither lasted long. Around the time of the 1979 "Disco Sucks" rally, when disk jockeys and their young fans fed Boomer-era LPs and 45s into a Cleveland bonfire, pop hit a downturn. As in 1997, the mainline music makers hadn't a clue what would catch on next. What did? New wave and punk rock, the B-52's and the Sex Pistols, plus new jokes from Elvis Costello, new vulgarities from the Pretenders, Prince's *Dirty Mind*, Michael Jackson's turn away from Motown, and (in 1981) MTV. After a few years of Michael Jackson and Madonna, heavy metal and early rap beats began thudding from boom boxes across America. By the end of the '80s, leftover Boomer performers were mostly replaced by Gen Xers, who took full control of grunge and gangsta rap.

Through most of the '90s, the prevailing pop music styles spoke expressively and exclusively to the Gen-X mind-set—until Millennials arrived, in 1997, with their own tremor.

To this point, the pop music industry has felt the Millennial presence more strongly than movies or TV, simply because its core market is younger. Cinema serves more of a college-age bracket, and teens are at the periphery of the 18-to-34-year-old demographic that TV advertisers covet. Even in the video game market, teens are less cutting edge than late-wave Gen Xers, who make most of the products, buy roughly one-third of them, and write most of the reviews. Accordingly, these other media have been slower to hear the new generation's approaching footsteps—even if the incredible popularity of *Titanic* among middle schoolers signaled that something was in the air. The breaking Millennial wave is only just starting a process of trial and error in the studios, whose formula is gradually changing. In today's teen-targeting cinema and TV, well-adjusted characters and virtue-affirming plot lines have become more commonplace. The old Gen-X alienation themes are still around—but as a stylistic veneer, no longer as the core message.

With the onset of a new century, the teen culture is evolving quickly—but a more dramatic Millennial takeover is occurring in the younger kid culture.

The Millennial Child Makeover

In the late '90s, "in a nation distracted by greed and grandeur, by tinsel and technology," wrote *The Washington Post*'s Linton Weeks, "Americans are making a mad dash to buy books about a gifted boy wizard with a good heart, noble intentions, extraordinary powers, and a lightning-bolt scar on his forehead." These Harry Potter books so powerfully pulled upon Millennials (and parents) that Edinburgh's J. K. Rowling became the first author ever to hold the top three spots, in the same week, on *The New York Times* bestseller list.

Harry Potter books are classic boy stories. The hero is a regular kid, popular, courageous, stout-hearted, and full of derring-do. Though an

Back when I was in sixth grade, Nickelodeon suddenly canceled all the Xer stuff like You Can't Do That on Television, Salute Your Shorts, Welcome Freshmen, *and* Fifteen. Fifteen *would never make it today, because it was a sort of proto-*Felicity *for high school, complete with violence, insults, and implied drug use. But that's what was on Nickelodeon when I was a kid.*

—**Chris Loyd, 17**

They're squeaky-clean.

—**Haim Saban, creator of Mighty Morphin Power Rangers, *describing his protagonists***

orphan, he was spared from death himself (at the hand of an evil sorcerer) by the sacrificial love of his dying mother. Blessed with magical powers, wearing his school uniform (including protective dragon-hide gloves), Harry excels at real-world exploits. He overcomes enemies ranging from bullies and monsters to ruthless and spiritually deranged adults, and saves the day time after time. The happy outcomes hinge on well-applied acts of violence. "It's an old story," wrote Danielle Crittenden in *The Wall Street Journal,* "but one that, in its various forms, has taught generations of boys to grow up into brave and even heroic men." The Harry Potter stories only feel old because tales like these were seldom written for Gen-X boys.

Rowling's hero has tricks in common with another surprise import of the late '90s: Pokémon. Cartooned in Japanese *anime,* a style of maximum action and minimum feeling, this classic Asian war game offers a traditional boy-style adventure. Its characters need basic virtues (honor, courage, loyalty, energy) and well-planned strategies to execute big tasks and get out of enormously complicated situations. Ash (the hero) is the ultimate straight-talking regular kid. Team Rocket (the villains) are whiny prep-school mercenaries. Like Harry Potter, *Pokémon* trainers cannot prevail without constant, albeit bloodless, violence. Even the cuddly Pikachu carries an electric charge. In its *anime* cousin, *Dragon Ball Z,* the carnage is more intense. "There's nothing wrong with being angry," says its bubbleheaded, space-suited host. "It's all in how you deal with it. Anger can be a motivational tool."

> "A Friend in Deed"
> "Friend and Foe Alike"
> "Friends to the End"
>
> —*titles of consecutive* Pokémon *shows,*
> TV Guide *(September 30, 1999)*

Thus, with Harry Potter and Pokémon, did the Millennial mainstream announce its cultural arrival. The core Potter and Pokémon fans are 8- to 14-year-old tweens, Millennials born in the late '80s and early '90s who lie near the heart of their generation. As such, they are fated to follow (and energize) trends set by the leading-edge Millennials, whose girls produced the music tremor of 1996–97. By the time the older Millennials are ready to write and sing their own songs, these younger kids will be ready to buy them, dance to them, and sing along with the lyrics.

Before they arrived, U.S. culture makers had no idea that this new wave of kids was going to be any different from the Gen Xers they'd served over the prior two decades. Dating back to the 1970s, booksellers and toy makers had served kids a culture of Judy Bloom realism, full of Bart Simpson bluntness and Dungeons and Dragons danger, and framed by disintegrating social structures that required kids to improvise in order to survive. All of a sudden, this formula no longer worked. Had the culture makers traced these kids since birth, they would have seen what was coming, and why.

The Potter-and-Pokémon kids were the first "Barney Millennials." A 12-year-old in 1999 would have been a preschooler in 1991, the year the purple dinosaur invaded the minds of American tykes. Projecting what its creator, Sheryl Leach, describes as "a magical simplicity" that "parents don't understand," *Barney & Friends* was everything *Sesame Street* was not: pastoral, not urban; lyrical, not kinetic; sweet, not wry; promoting teamwork, not self-esteem; celebrating what makes kids the same, not what sets them apart. There was absolutely no adult subtext, nothing to amuse college students between classes. One *Washington Post* TV writer called the show "so saccharine it can send adults into hypoglycemic shock." Child TV gurus had no clue what was coming. In 1992, when PBS tried to drop the show after politely trying it out for several months, moms and kids mobilized a grassroots protest and forced the network to change its mind. Ever since, *Barney* has outdrawn *Sesame Street* and has been admired (if less-often watched) by parents who like its pace and values.

From the early to mid-1990s, while these Barney Millennials passed through early childhood, all aspects of the little-kid culture—television, books, movies—were changing and growing rapidly. Focus groups revealed what Dale Russakoff called a "seismic shift in how kids feel toward parents." Where TV shows had once nonjudgmentally encouraged Gen-X kidlets to look, listen, and explore, they now provided Millennials with crisp, clear, and constant moral lessons, often wrapped around achievement-oriented story lines. In due course, the old era of *Zoom* and *Teenage Mutant Ninja*

[Barney] has a magical simplicity to it that parents don't understand.
—Time *(1992)*

I hated [Barney] because I thought he was boring, but [my 2-year-old daughter] loves him. And he teaches her values and morals that I want established in my child. He teaches her love, respect, kindness, taking turns, not to mention the seasons and safety. —Bonnie, *rainforest.parentsplace.com*

Perhaps the song parents would rather hear Barney singing would be "I love you / you hate me." —Nino Tolentino, *bunnyhop.com*

alt.barney.purple.dinosaur.die.die.die
—usenet newsgroup

Turtles was supplanted by a new era of *Rugrats* and *Mighty Morphin Power Rangers*. Entering the '90s, Nickelodeon attracted young viewers by brashly billing itself as a "parent-free Kidzone." Exiting the '90s, most of its top-viewed programs were bringing parents back into their story lines—to the apparent delight of the focus-group kids who first watched them.

Meanwhile, these newly visible parents were finding common ground on an issue that hasn't traditionally allowed one—the use of religious messages—thereby closing a cycle that dated back to World War II. When Boomers were small, religion was uncool and nearly nowhere to be seen on children's TV. By the late 1990s, faith-based cartoons and songs were everywhere, from the classy *Prince of Egypt* to the more elementary (though musically innovative) *Veggie Tales*, animated munchables who drill home Old and New Testament lessons with the tag line, "Remember kids, God made you special, and He loves you very much."

As the '90s progressed, the Millennials became the most catered-to kids in the history of the pop culture. Thanks in part to Congress's new educational-TV rules, Nickelodeon became less an island for a few cable-ready Gen Xers than a generational bond for Millennial millions. The Learning Channel, Cartoon Network, and other (mostly) kid-friendly networks joined the mushrooming market. By 1999, according to the *State of Children's Television* report, 1,324 kids' programs appeared weekly on 29 channels. The top-rated kids' TV shows included *Rugrats* (about well-behaving kids, created by two Bart Simpson writers who had children of their own), *Teletubbies* (about a bright, safe-feeling fantasy world described by its producer as "technical but full of warmth") and *The Thornberrys* (about a close family with nice kids and cool parents). Several of these shows spawned a soundtracked, "skip-on-the-set and wave-to-the-kids" live performance trade that pulled in $300 million per year from tickets, T-shirts, and toys.

In these years before the Barney Millennials could assert their own tastes, Boomer parents pushed the new cultural trends along. Far more than their own G.I. parents, Boomers believed that culture mattered—that the right choices could elevate and the wrong ones destroy. Ergo, parents from both sides of the culture wars issued demands for censorship, in rearguard efforts to control their kids' access to allegedly anti-Christian (or evangelical), homoerotic (or homophobic), or "politically correct" (or "undiverse") points of view. Parents complained to schools and libraries about books and web sites, to Congress about TV, movies, and video games. Parental advisories became commonplace.

Near the end of the '90s, Boomer moms and dads noticed that their Millennial kids were entering new and dangerous territory. They were becoming teenagers—and, as teens do, they were starting to make more of their own cultural choices.

The Millennial Teen Makeover

On a spring evening in 1999, a Minneapolis theater company performed a private showing of *A Streetcar Named Desire* for an Illinois high school choir and a gaggle of teacher and parent chaperones. After Act One offered up plenty of profanity, sexuality, and a little nudity, parents told the company that the play was "not appropriate without changes." The cast refused to change the script, so a compromise was reached. Instead of continuing the play, the cast, students, and chaperones engaged in a conversation about artistic issues. Students asked questions ("What's the difference between simply dropping pants on the street and nudity in a play?") which the cast did its best to answer. Then the school choir sang, the cast applauded, and everybody went home friends.

That same year, Fox TV ran into the same Millennial juggernaut. The network planned a new season of prime-time shows full of the familiar Gen-X formula that had catapulted it to prominence through the '90s, but this time the results shocked the entertainment world. Fox's prime-time audience fell 18 percent. *Harsh Realm* was canceled after three episodes, the teen-cop *Ryan Caulfield* after two, *Manchester Prep* before going on the air. In cinema, Millennials were likewise confounding the adult tastemakers. In 1998, MGM studios came out with *The Mod Squad* in an effort to reproduce for Millennials the same formula that had worked for teens of the past two decades, going for grunge just as the market trended toward *She's All That* sweetness. "We misread it," said the studio's Larry Gleason. "Apparently, not everyone is aspiring to be a juvenile delinquent who's given the choice of going to jail or becoming an undercover cop."

Hollywood had captured the new child wave well enough during the

Moviegoers have been reeling at the level of sexuality, vulgarity, obscenity and gross depravity in movies aimed at teenagers.   —Roger Ebert,
     film critic

The movie South Park: Bigger, Longer, & Uncut *has 399 profanities in 80 minutes.*   —The Movie Index,
    Parade

The four-letter words aren't always even intended to shock; they're often just part of the verbal furniture. Most of this behavior comes from teenage characters, in movies aimed at the teenage market.   —Roger Ebert

Between 1989 and 1999, references to genitalia [on prime-time TV] increased seven-fold, five and a half times more foul language was used, references to homosexuality were 24 times more common, and overall sexual content, coarse language, and violence tripled.

     —Parents' Television Council,
     describing prime-time TV

CBS, the "Tiffany Network" regarded as a bastion of good taste on TV, made a bit of history on October 14 when it aired the four-letter word that rhymes with "hit" in an episode of the medical drama Chicago Hope.

     —Reuters

late '80s and early '90s, with unerringly upbeat live-action children's films that replaced the Gen-X bad-child genre of the '70s. In those new story lines, kids helped grownups behave better. After enduring a drought during the Gen-X child era, animators and producers of cartoon movies got busy again in the '80s—and worked overtime in the '90s. No longer a sleepy backwater, kid animation became a huge market in which Disney now had to vie with well-funded competitors such as Warner Brothers, MCA Universal, Fox Video, and spinoffs like DreamWorks SKG.

Until the middle '90s, movies for and about teens had trended toward the dark and nasty. A transition of sorts took place in 1995 with *Clueless* (when the first Millennials were 13), and, a year later, with *Scream.* By 1998–99, multiplexes hummed with the likes of *10 Things I Hate About You, American Pie,* and other boy-girl coming-of-age stories. First-wave Millennials didn't make these movies any more than they made the Cabbage Patch dolls they played with as babies, but they found their goofy grossness entertaining. Their reaction to similarly ribald TV shows was surprisingly negative—as though what might be OK in movie theaters wasn't OK when Mom and Dad were around. In 1995, a Children Now survey discovered "how strongly [kids] wanted better moral values on TV." The gap between fiction and reality was stretching further than Fox and other networks realized. "The portrayal of teens in the pop culture conflicts with what's actually happening in the adolescent populace," remarked Jason Gay of the *Boston Phoenix.* "Surveys of actual (read: not Hollywood) teens show that they're not all a bunch of hardened hedonists."

The Fox and MGM miscalculations were reminiscent of what had happened back in the early '60s, when CBS miscalculated with teenage Boomers. This time, though, the fruits went to a network (WB) that toned things down a little, whereas in the Boomer era, the advantage went to a network (ABC) that pushed the edge.

Teen-targeted TV programming has changed dramatically over the four decades since first-wave Boomers reached adolescence. Back in the early '60s, none of the top twenty children's shows was one designed for them by adults, two of every three adults felt that TV was getting better, and teenagers ached for a more risqué realism. In the Millennial era, by contrast, kids are mainly watching shows that *are* designed for them, TV is widely derided for being too vulgar, two of every three adults feel that

TV is getting worse, and two-thirds of all teens think the shows made for them are "moderately" to "extremely" offensive.

Back in the Boomer teen era, G.I. adults blamed themselves, not kids, for what was then called a "vast wasteland" (meaning, bland pap) of TV programming. Today, adults tar Millennials for the ways in which Boomer and Gen-X producers have solved the old blandness problem. "Sex and pop culture are now the only realities for the teen generation," writes columnist John Leo, leveling a charge that applies more appropriately to Boomers on the eve of the Consciousness Revolution than to Millennials the morning after.

Many adults would be surprised if they actually watched the Millennial-targeted films they criticize. Sure, there's plenty of blunt sex chatter, substance abuse, backbiting, the occasional over-the-top gross-out, and other behaviors that would get a real kid suspended. But, as with today's high school sex-and-drugs scene, there are often better choices being made by the central characters than most older people think.

In the years since *Clueless* mocked the virgin teen, TV-show and movie makers have been moving away from Gen-X-era characters and plots toward what appeals more to Millennials and their parents. Not long ago, most shows were as they appeared in trailers, full of characters older people had trouble liking, unmotivated kids who just rattled around, inhabiting plot lines that started or stopped anywhere, as though teen life were a steady stream of *whatevers*. You can still find this genre, but it's aging right along with Gen X.

In the new Millennial mode, what adults see as nastiness is mainly just a veneer, beneath which lies a palpable sentimentality. "In fact, for all the naughty talk and edgy sound tracks," reports *Maclean's*, "most teen movies offer up archetypes that seem closer to the 50s than the 90s. There is nothing as playfully subversive as *Fast Times at Ridgemont High*, or as seriously sexy as *Risky Business*." Though *American Pie* was hyped for a masturbation scene that repels many adults, *Newsweek* described it as "a surprisingly earnest and cautionary movie, careful to attract female viewers and not freak parents out too badly." The teen TV brew of *Dawson's Creek*, *Popular*, and their imitators depicts characters who have close emotional ties with one another (and with their parents) and who speak an upscale vocabulary that reads like an SAT prep course.

A new concern of mine is the media's corruption of children. . . . I can't turn on any of the major stations without watching a marginally funny sit-com character talk about how many people he or she has "had." . . . Just recently, I saw the sequel to Austin Powers. *After the movie, my friends and I watched a group of six boys no older than nine repeat every vulgar line from the movie. We were shocked and almost sad that these adorable, innocent boys had been exposed to so much profanity and smut.*

—*Emily Barker, 17*

The adult sex these under-age movie characters are having is being presented and styled like adult entertainment. Has sex between teenagers really become this much better since I was one?

—*Rick Marin,* The New York Times

I don't think there needs to be a movie out where a child has sex with an adult . . . I think there's enough exploitation out there that it's not necessary to do more.

—*Natalie Portman, 19, describing why she turned down the lead role in* Lolita

No, it's just what's the point? They're all the same: some stupid killer stalking some big-breasted girl, who can't act, who's always running up the stairs when she should be going out the front door, it's insulting!

—*Sydney, in* Scream

> ### Which Show Do You Think May Be Inappropriate, But You Let Your Child Watch It Anyway?
>
> *The Simpsons:* **57%**
> *South Park:* **4%**
>
> —*"Mom and Pop Culture Survey,"* Child *(April, 1999)*

To attract Millennial viewers, these shows are telling real stories, often quite touching ones, involving kids who are essentially decent, friendly, well-adjusted, and serious about the future. Plot lines have beginnings, middles, and ends—a bit funny, sweet, and sad all at once—that affirm the parental precept that conventional kids with *neo*traditional morals can be rewarded with the love of their dreams. Usually, things turn out OK, sometimes because kids see the light on their own, sometimes because parents come to the rescue, other times because friends help each other out.

Millennials see film sex and film violence from a very different perspective from most of their parents. In general, video violence bothers them less. They stand at a far enough distance from real war to be unphased by brutal depictions of large-scale destruction. Since they are growing up in an era of declining crime, Zero Tolerance schools, and no-U.S.-casualty wars, cinematic violence is like a manufactured nightmare, putting youthful adrenaline through test runs. Teen slasher movies such as *Scream, I Know What You Did Last Summer,* and their sequels flow with rivers of blood, but none of it seems any more serious than a video game. Indeed, cinematic violence can be positive, focusing the viewer's attention on courageous, even heroic deeds. In many a story line, violence is necessary to save innocent lives, achieve justice, repel evil, or restore order out of chaos. To a generation that has never known war, the moral fabric of the story is real, the mechanics of killing mere special effects.

Video sex, on the other hand, bothers many teens more than it does their parents—particularly Boomer parents. Unlike violence, sex is an issue that is close to home for every teen, no matter how active or chaste they may be. In the films they see, sex seldom means marital bonding, nor romantic liaisons between committed partners—nor, as with vio-

"COME ON KIDS! WOULDN'T YOU REALLY RATHER GO BACK TO DISNEYWORLD?"

lence, does it reveal self-denying courage or life-affirming heroism. Instead, it usually showcases weaknesses like jealousy, treachery, or infidelity. In their experience, characters engage in film sex less to affirm commitments than to betray them, less to love than to hurt. The sex acts that are shown, described, or joked about remind kids why parents split up, how girls get pregnant, how people can get AIDS, how kids can get suspended from school—and, especially, why youths are so sternly warned to abstain in a world so full of libidinally supercharged adults. When a Millennial teenager goes with a parent to an R-rated movie with sexual scenes, the teen can be more troubled by knowing that the parent is watching than the other way around.

Another generational warp affects irony and film noir, which Millennials today regard (even in the so-called "gothic" films they flock to) as a formal shell, entirely emptied of any innovation or creative energy. For Boomer teens, the horrifying discoveries of Rod Serling or Alfred Hitchcock felt fresh. To their youthful eye, the cheerful and ordered culture around them was often just a cover for a darker world of repressed pain

Now, nobody, least of all me, actually believes that video games are responsible for pushing these boys over the edge, but seeing the police carry a plastic wrapped copy of Doom out of the boys' bedrooms really hit home for me and a lot of other people in the industry. —Allen Rausch

Realistic gore I have no problem with. It's the "Maximum Gore Incredible Blood and Guts All Over the Place" setting that I don't approve of.

—John, 17

Get in touch with your gun-toting, testosterone-pumping, cold-blooded murdering side.

—Ad for Sony video game

that demanded attention. Come the '60s, irony and pessimism burst forth onto a cultural terrain that was later to be fully explored, along all of its thematic rivulets, by young Gen-X writers and producers.

For Millennials, the irony has flipped. Now, the pain is on the surface, the order within. Today's teens find the adult world outwardly chaotic, full of Oprah's victims, Jerry Springer's accusers, and the WWF's dirty tricksters—yet in their own circles, the irony is that few people actually are that way. Where the Boomer-era ironic teenager was a pleasant-seeming kid who behaved worse than adults thought, his Millennial-era counterpart is a foul-mouthed teen who behaves better than adults think. Where Boomer teens reacted to adults who seemed all too eager to paper over life's dark side, Millennial teens are reacting to adults who seem all too eager to dwell on the dark side. The hallmark of the gothic genre—a pessimistic vision of man as victim, unable to escape his past sins or his own inner demons—reminds them of what they sometimes find irritating about older generations.

Hollywood has mirrored this anti-ironic trend in its casting of Millennial kid characters. Where cinematic Boomer kids behaved worse than adults (charmingly so), and Gen-X kids at times far worse (annoyingly so), Millennials are often shown to be polite, clean-cut, in angel wings or uniforms, kids who tend to have high-quality relationships with the adults in their lives.

Film and TV producers are still in search of a Millennial blueprint, and seem unsure how to write for them—much as older Gen-X actors seem unsure how to portray them (males, especially). Through trial and error, the industry has been buoyed by a hot, parent-funded teen market that, to quote *Entertainment Weekly*, "can be had on the cheap, as long as they're reflected vividly on screen." Teen movies cost less to make than to promote, and can overcome bad reviews because plenty of trusting Millennials will "see them even though we know they're going to be bad," as 15-year-old Alan Anders admits.

The late '90s saw a phase-of-life shift among TV shows and their audiences. Millennials have pushed the Gen-X teenage *90210* crowd up to a young-nester *Felicity* and *Time of Your Life*, and *Buffy the Vampire Slayer* has gone off to college. Meanwhile, the Boomer detached-single sitcoms—*Thirtysomething, Cheers,* and *Seinfeld*—have been pushed aside

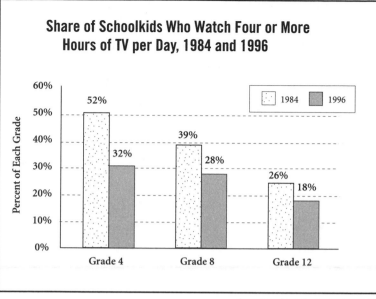

Share of Schoolkids Who Watch Four or More Hours of TV per Day, 1984 and 1996

Percent of Each Grade

Legend: 1984, 1996

- Grade 4: 52% (1984), 32% (1996)
- Grade 8: 39% (1984), 28% (1996)
- Grade 12: 26% (1984), 18% (1996)

Source: National Center for Education Statistics (1998)

by the Gen-X *Friends, Singles,* and *Ally McBeal.* Back in the early 1960s, similar transitions took place among G.I.s, Silent, and Boomers, but to opposite effect on the culture at large.

Millennials have grown up with video games in the same manner that Boomers grew up with board games—but where the slow speed and little action of '50s board games prompted imagination and conversation, the hyperspeed and furious action of '90s video games controlled the one and stifled the other. The games culture is still heavily Gen-X but growing rapidly among teens, who sometimes spend more aggregate dollars on a hot new game than on a hot new movie. The major games (Doom, Quake, Duke Nukem) are producing what *The Washington Post* calls "a quaint adolescent subculture, albeit a very violent one." Yet with the Millennials' arrival, gamers are showing a new sensitivity to language, now calling themselves "athletes" and using bloodless words such as *automatons* to describe killing machines. Among teenage boys, video sports games are starting to supplant pro sports on TV (which networks, by way of response, are dressing up to seem more like video games). "Computer gaming is on the way to becoming a full sport like chess [through which] you can achieve social standing," insists 17-year-old Simon de Montigny.

I've been in the business for 30 years, and I don't remember anything like Teen People.

—**Dan Capell, editor of** Capell Circulation Report

Teen girls really bond with their magazines. They're like a sister and friend rolled into one.

—**Michael Wood,** **Teenage Research Unlimited**

Introducing a kids' breakfast serial fortified to nourish young minds.

—**Washington Post** *ad, announcing the serialization of* "Orphan Journey Home"

In February 1999, the first Kids' Playbill *was distributed to 14,000 youngsters under the age of 18 at* "Kids' Night on Broadway" *in New York City.* —**Kids' Playbill**

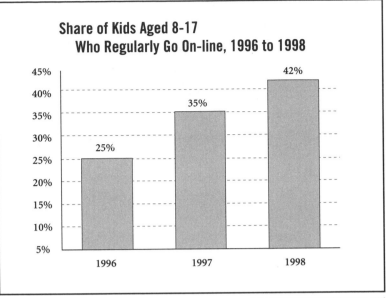

Share of Kids Aged 8-17 Who Regularly Go On-line, 1996 to 1998

Source: Roper Starch Worldwide (August 23, 1999)

Most games still reveal a Gen-X residuum, but gentler, more cooperative games are in the offing, in the wake of the recent school crimes.

The internet has more of a Millennial flavor. When kids log on, one of the first things they do is click on to "IM" (Instant Messaging) to see which of their friends is on-line. Governments, businesses, news bureaus, and servers have teens' and children's web sites offering vast stores of information on every subject imaginable. Thus are adults helping to instill in this generation a new institutional culture, and sense of belonging, beyond what those adults feel themselves.

In the publishing world, Millennials have created a youth market far larger than anything seen before. Back in the early Boomer youth days, mainstream teen magazines and cartoons—what little there was, such as *Mad* or *Peanuts*—had a satirical or precounterculture ring. Apart from action comic books, not much new was offered Gen-X high schoolers. But now, in the Millennial era, the racks rustle with recently launched teen-oriented news, sports, and celebrity magazines, which—in a sharp turnaround from the Boomer-teen era—are more wholesome and less cynical in content and style than adult fare. Where the regular *People* revels in adult misbehavior, *Teen People* celebrates kids whose worst vices are vanity and shopping. Yes, in their ad-laden blandness, today's teen magazines are sometimes hard to distinguish from clothing-store catalogs. "Every other word is *babe*," says 15-year-old Vanessa Silverton Peel. "The headlines are '101 Ways to Tell if He Likes You.' Not very often is there an article on preparing for the SATs or something you would actually need."

Millennials have definitely captured the eye of a print-news business that fears kids are drifting away from old-style reading habits. Where news organs ignored Gen X apart from sports and crime, they're now launching tween-to-teen sections (like *The New York Times Upfront*) that discard all the attitude and dumbing down and opt instead for a more declarative, informative style. The *Washington Post* has started to print read-aloud "breakfast serials" and high school theater reviews written by students themselves. *Teen Newsweek* and other weeklies are heavy on factual background and cover only those celebrities who are good role models.

All across the culture, Millennials are starting to win adult concessions to their emerging mind-set, much as Boomers started to do forty years ago. Early in 1999, no studio dared touch a proposed new *Lolita* project, prompting the film's publicist to say "it's very bizarre that this film is considered too hot to handle today and it wasn't too hot to handle in 1962." Only a few holdouts—like Fox, with its new Boyz and Girlz channels—persist in the assumption that Millennials will buy into the old X formula.

Perhaps those Fox executives would change their minds if they visited Vans Skate Park, a few miles from their studios, to watch Millennials de-Xing the skater culture. The new skateboarders now say "thank you" and "excuse me." Millennials, says Jonathan Last, have "legitimized skateboarding, making it sociable and about as rebellious as soccer."

Toward the Total Millennial Makeover

Thus far, Millennial kids and teens are shaping the culture mainly by picking and choosing from the offerings of others. That will change, and soon. During the Oh-Ohs, American pop culture will experience a Millennial makeover—a reconstruction that will help determine the flavor of the coming decade.

This makeover will happen when young Millennial males—including the Potter-and-Pokémon boys of the Barney wave—match the cultural

Overall, the flicks easiest to sell to teens have been those with—brace yourself for some new marketing buzzwords—aspiration and relevancy. —Jeff Jensen, **Entertainment Weekly**

The movies are playing catchup to comic books. Until recently, the superhero genre was proccupied with mythic deconstruction and pulp fiction. Good guys were fascist vigilantes, motivated by sexual insecurities or obsessive vengeance—and often barely distinguishable from the bad guys. Yet more traditional archetypes have made a comeback. "Kingdom Come" tells the story of an old guard of heroes who quash a revolt of reckless, self-destructive young wannabes. —Jeff Jenson, **Advertising Age**

Millennial movies are usually funny and okay, but the whole popularity thing is such bull. . . . It would be like if the Hitler Youth in Animal House *won instead of the Deltas.* —Jake, 21

impression already made by teenage girls. The outlines of the Gen X-to-Millennial girl transition are clear. From Buffy to Britney, from *Ally McBeal* to *Dawson's Creek,* from *Clueless* to *She's All That,* the girl culture has moved from a risk-taking and go-it-alone survivalism to a more serious and adult-approved sweetness. The outlines of the boy transition cross a larger age divide, but are nonetheless discernible. From Eminem to Pokémon, Duke Nukem to the Legend of Zelda, Bart Simpson to Harry Potter, the boy culture is moving away from cynicism and diffuse, pragmatic violence toward positivism and focused, heroic violence. This X-to-Millennial break is a fissure that has yet to appear in full beyond the younger kids.

When Millennials make their major cultural move—which the experience of the prior generations suggests will occur late in the Oh-Oh decade—this new male element will be decisive. When their new style of high-tech macho combines with the confident action-orientation of young women, fused with all the ethnic currents that lie within this generation, the product will feel quite fresh indeed.

Whatever the coming Millennial mark on the late Oh-Oh culture, it will not be as central to them as the new culture of the 1960s once was to their Boomer parents. Youth generations typically trigger explosive change in those spheres of social life in which older generations are weakest and least active. With today's aging rockers and scriptwriters still winning national awards, and with "style" and "arts" departments the favorite hangout of most middle-aged journalists, Millennials hardly sense any elder vacuum in the culture business. The attributes Millennials are developing—teamwork, friendship, rationalism—are, instead, the formula one associates with the big deeds that culture doesn't directly *do* but rather inspires beforehand and celebrates afterward. Collectively, Millennials share the kind of background and cultural inclination that is ideal for building spaceships to Mars, less so for making original movies about why anyone would want to go there.

The modesty with which Millennials talk about how they will change the culture comes through clearly in our high school Class of 2000 Survey. When asked what their influence will someday be on American arts, nearly as many say they'll make them worse (25 percent) as better (31 percent). When asked if they will take more or less interest in the arts when they reach their parents' age, the response (33 percent more versus 30 percent less) seems surprisingly tepid to anyone who recalls a '60s-era campus dormroom. By contrast, when Millennials are asked if they will take more interest in technology than their parents, the yes vote (73 percent) overwhelms the no vote (8 percent).

Yet, in the end, a generation that doesn't expect to make big waves in the culture could set a lot more in motion than it expects. If Millennials fit the usual pattern of youth rebellion, some decisive cultural break will occur over the next decade. If they correct the perceived excesses of Boomers, while breaking stylistically from Gen Xers, the pop culture of 2010 could be as different from today's as 1970 was from 1960. Where Boomers applied a new spiritualism to burst the culture to pieces, Millennials could apply a new rationalism to bring it back together. Picture not an "Eve of Destruction," but an Eve of Construction. Picture a defining musical that is an anti-*Hair,* stressing communal purpose, staged (like McLean High School's treatment of "Age of Aquarius") as a Busby Berkeley ballet in metallic-blue uniforms. Much as Boomers turned the culture from syrupy to a bit sour, Millennials may switch those flavors around.

The Gen-X veneer remains, but thins by the year. Where Gen Xers used emerging technologies to produce broken fonts and crooked camera angles, throwing everything out of balance in a flagrantly subjective way, Millennials are learning to use settled technologies to spruce up the fonts and straighten the camera angles, putting everything back in balance in a flagrantly objective way. When you peruse high school publications and see high school plays—or, especially, when you surf teen-built web sites—you can see how Millennials are synthesizing, simplifying, and lending order to a world that looks far more fragmented to others. And nearly everything they do in their culture, from dance to theater to the internet, is fully and unabashedly accessible.

In *Bobos in Paradise,* David Brooks limns an unforgettable portrait of midlife Boomers as America's ascendant "bohemian bourgeoisie"—creatively obsessive about the meaning of everything (down to the subtext of their ads for gourmet latte) yet indifferent or uncooperative on the big questions facing society's public life. As such, Boomers have created the perfect foil for a new *anti-Bobo* generation. Millennials are primed to give

Zero is a book that is a waste of a tree. One is a good bathroom read. Two is a good beach or leisure read. Then three is the book you skip your favorite activity for.

—*Adam Balutis, 16, describing his on-line book-rating system*

We'll throw away the TV. We'll perform Shakespeare in front of him.

—*Gil, on how to amuse his son, in* Parenthood

higher priority to the outer world than the inner, to push America toward a blander culture yet also toward a more aggressive and ambitious definition of the nation's collective agenda.

As the generation that has taken the '90s-era "accelerated culture" as its life-cycle pivot point, Millennials are searching for a speed at which it all makes sense—not too fast, not too slow, just the right balance. They have the tech tools to do this. There's no piece of Boomer music, or Gen-X film, that these kids couldn't slap into a computer and fix up, if they're so inclined, in a *Pleasantville* in reverse, extracting what older generations might perceive as color while re-establishing a sense of order.

Change in generational culture never satisfies all eyes and ears. It didn't in the '40s, '60s, or '80s, nor will it in the Oh-Ohs. But whatever the creative regime Millennials have in mind, it's coming. Soon.

CHAPTER TWELVE

rocket cash *(commerce)*

I feel just like Julia Roberts in Pretty Woman,
except for the whole hooker thing.

—LANEY, in She's All that

"Has anyone ever gone broke overestimating the alienation of the American teenager?" asked Alona Wartofsky in *The Washington Post*'s "Style" section. In its context (an article about Limp Bizkit), Wartofsky's question seems to be what circa-2000 teen marketers might call a no-brainer. Says Yankelovich's President, J. Walker Smith, "pushing the extremes" is how to get teens to respond. "Porn chic, *South Park,* the edgier the better."

The late-'90s rise of Abercrombie & Fitch seems, on the surface, to support the "push the extremes" view. A&F's catalogues, pitched to teens, are famous for their mixed-drink recipes, rules for Strip Yahtzee and Naked Twister, and photos of bare-bottomed young men alongside more modestly dressed girls. A&F's shopping bag has a teenage boy in bed with four girls. Its store personnel, many of them teens, don't wait on customers, on purpose. "We don't have salespeople," says company spokesman Lonnie Fogel. "We have brand representatives." In 1999, A&F brand reached a

They're here. They arrive to a backbeat of Britney Spears and the Backstreet Boys, their bodies draped in Abercrombie & Fitch tops and Gap cargo khakis. . . . They worship gods with names like Leonardo, Claire, Cartman, and Jay-Z. . . . They have more money than you did, too.

—Jason Gay, Boston Phoenix

The great virtue of teens from a consumer marketer's point of view is that virtually all of their income is disposable. . . . It's no surprise, then, that seemingly all of corporate America wants to know how to separate teenagers from their money.

—Rolling Stone

We are going to own this generation.

—Stephen Kahn, CEO, Delia's

ranking of number eleven among teens, close to Coca-Cola, thanks to a veneer of nastiness over a product line that 16-year-old Molly Melamed of Farmington Hills, Michigan, calls "very preppy clothing. It's supposed to look nice and conservative. But all this nudity, it's almost tacky." Think of A&F as *American Pie,* naughtier on the outside than on the inside. With teens, that's a marketing straddle that works—for now.

Today's teen marketing business has few antecedents before 1990, few creative minds older than Boomers, and few ideas of any trend line other than a straight path from Boom to Gen X to Gen Y. In a nastier update of the old VALS typology, the Fallon-McElligott consultants have segmented teenage consumers into eight "value systems," seven of which (cult of me, glorification of despair, alternate reality, conquer the streets, extreme, searching, cultural connoisseurs) wrap around the image of kids as *über*-Xers, except more liberated and with lots more money to spend—$140 billion in total, says Teenage Research Unlimited, or $4,500 per teenager per year. Surely, teens are spending all this money on grunge, baggy pants, sports logo jackets, and whatnot, right?

Wrong. Recently, all those styles have begun fading, including A&F. What's returning among teens is a more conventional look—to the consternation of the Gen-Y marketing school. "More often marketers do it wrong than right," explains Jane Rinzler Buckingham, president of Youth Intelligence. "They assume teenagers want loud music and quick cuts and people screaming in their face." Instead, the musical ads that have connected best are the Gap's, with swing dancers—still loud, but bright and happy, with simple fonts and smooth edits.

Return to Wartofsky's question. No, no one has ever gone broke overestimating the alienation of any generation *since Boomers.* Come the late '60s, there was no edge that wouldn't sell; by the 1980s, none that wasn't being commercialized; and by the late '90s, none that wasn't branded, logoed, niche-pitched, focus-grouped, ad-supported, and cross-marketed with tie-ins with a fast food chain or TV series. But if you go further back, you'll find many times in American history when more alienation would have fallen on its face. Woe to the marketer who took the licentious cynicism of the 1920s and then tried to serve it up even wilder to the youth of the '30s or '40s or '50s. The first rule of generational change is this: Trends oscillate. Nothing happens in one direction only.

War-era Silent teens had the quietest teen economy of the century, and their budding "silence," cultural *and* commercial, gave them the name that stuck. In the 1960s, Boomers forged a new youth economy defiantly apart from the adult one, based on instant rather than deferred gratification. From the '70s into the '80s, as older generations paid less attention to the Gen-X teen world, the new cultural edge took commercial root. When adults rediscovered an interest in children in the late '80s, and in teens by the latter '90s, Millennial consumers entered the mainstream economy—and youth marketing skyrocketed.

But as the Millennial hold on the youth economy strengthens, many of today's unthinking assumptions about kids in the marketplace will require wholesale revision—and not just the ever-more-alienation trend. Millennials are beginning to *reverse* the separation of youth and adult markets, to *reverse* the splintering of buying habits within the youth market, to *reverse* the inflow of school-age kids into paying jobs, and to *reverse* the seemingly unstoppable commercialization of the youth world.

The real way Millennials are shifting the economy is not through in-your-face rebellion, but rather through positive peer pressure, cooperative choice-making with parents, and easily accessible new teen media, flavored by Millennial motifs discernible in only one of Fallon-McElligott's eight teen value systems, "integrity focused." Splintery edges, self-focus, weak product loyalties, and hypercommercialism may still be in their heyday, but they've peaked. Mass fads, big brands, group focus, and a lower-profile commercial style are ready for a comeback.

These days, kids have cash and know what to do with it. It's not like your childhood anymore, Bart Simpson. And in many ways it's the opposite of yours, Beaver Cleaver.

Consumerism

Millennials are a consumer behemoth, riding atop a new youth economy of astounding scale and extravagance. Plainly, not all kids have shared in the recent prosperity, but tens of millions have—and the aggregate numbers speak for themselves. Purchases by and for children age 4 to 12 tripled over the 1990s, and teens hit their stride at the decade's end. Nothing reflects this growth more than the sudden plethora of expensive summer camps (for which weekly bills can top $2,000) and the ever-denser crowds at theme parks (at some of which, kids can hire a pricey "tour

Baggy Pants: They're So Yesterday
—headline, USA Today

I used to have that thug look—big and baggy. *—Josh Langsam, 17*

If you need to fit a family of five inside your pants.
—Denise, Can't Hardly Wait

They were always sagging. It was annoying. *—boy, 14*

There's a point to which you just can't go.
—Steven Toyota, 17, on baggy pants

My mom buys all my clothes and my car, but I have to pay for my pager, my phone, and going out on weekends. *—Chais White, 16*

At 7:45 A.M. teenagers descend on Napervile North like an invading horde of the Cargo Pants Liberation Army. They hop from wave after wave of Passats and Explorers and dash inside the front doors, with few goodbyes directed back toward the drivers
—Petre Grier, The Christian Science Monitor

guide" who takes them to the head of the line). You can see crowds of rich Manhattan teens with Prada handbags and designer clothes, yet also kids in poor neighborhoods possessing enough electronic gear to stock a small store. Major companies keep adding new product lines just for Millennials, such as Pert Plus for Kids, Dial for Kids, even Ozarka Spring Water for Kids.

12- to 17-Year-Olds Who Own Stock
1998: 7%
1999: 11%

—*Merrill Lynch survey*

What's behind this explosion? It's come much too fast to be solely the result of the rising number of youths or (even) the growth in youth or adult income. The fact is, everyone is spending more on kids—kids on themselves, parents on their own kids, and nonparents on their young friends and relatives. Many Americans worry that all this spending is spoiling today's youth. But no one can deny that adults are trying to favor this new generation by steering more money toward its wants and less toward their own—or, some might say, by *identifying* its wants with their own.

A closer look at what kids are buying reveals many distinctively Millennial traits. In clothing, brands on the way up include Adidas, Old Navy, and American Eagle; on the way down, Nike, Levi's, Calvin Klein, and Sega. Bright colors are back.

Gender distinctions are widening. "After two decades of adopting a 'gender-neutral' tone and carefully avoiding boy-girl stereotypes," reports *The Wall Street Journal,* "many marketers have decided that it is once again safe to emphasize gender differences in products and pitches aimed at children. And this time, companies are starting with children as young as two." Toys "R" Us recently added a "Boy's World" (with action figures, Tonka trucks, and walkie-talkies) and a "Girl's World" (with dolls, kitchen toys, and makeup)—prompting complaints from parents, but not from kids. Mattel prompted a similar outcry when it made a royal blue Hot Wheels computer for boys and a pink-flowered Barbie computer for girls. Gender marketing "is very out of step with what adult men and women are doing," insists women's issues specialist Pamela Haag. "It really is anachronistic."

Yet the biggest changes go beyond mere product or fashion trends. Look closely at today's youth consumerism, and you'll recognize four major components.

>> Parental influence over kid purchases is growing.

"Though children clearly have a good deal of autonomy, parental influence is also more pronounced than just a year ago," concluded the 1996 Roper Report on kids' spending choices, noting that this ongoing trend is "confirmed" by other evidence of growing parental intrusiveness. Many other teen watchers concur.

Obviously, the parental role varies enormously by age, gender, and product type. The younger the child, the higher the price, and the less technological a product, the more apt the parent is to control (or, at least, intrude on) the purchasing decision. Boys rely more heavily than girls on parents for everything except books, jewelry, food, and personal care. With parental help, girls are more likely to use such financial services as ATMs, checking accounts, and credit cards (of which they have twice as many as boys). Overall, the parental presence is strong. Most teens consider parents to be the biggest influence on their spending decisions, ahead of advertisers and peers.

Moreover, this influence is growing—motivated in large measure by parental worries about safety. Not only are parents demanding that government do more regulating of products sold to kids, they are looking more closely at the products themselves—to see whether they can choke, stab, scrape, explode, crash, burn, zap, suffocate, or do anything else that's harmful. Hazards unheard of twenty years ago (such as carcinogenic phthalates in rubberized bath toys) now make producers jump to respond. Parents also want to keep kids away from nasty cultural messages. Parental advisory labels can be seen on practically every type of "message" product today, from CDs and video games to books and magazines. Even when shopping alone, many kids know just where their parents draw the line.

Jackson Longhofer hustles out of the car and enters the building where he will spend the next several hours. He passes the uniformed guard who holds open the front door, crosses over a bubbling brook stocked with fish, moves through the 32-foot-high vaulted interior with its Victorian-style shop fronts, passes the bibliotheque, the Coconut Theater, the music room, the math room, the computer room, and the TV station with its four clocks displaying times around the world. Jackson is 4 years old. —Jacqueline Salmon, **The Washington Post**

The Toys R Us store is replacing Santa with a toy registry for children. . . . Instead of dropping off "Dear Santa" letters at stores, kids will use hand-held scanners to register—much like brides-to-be —for toys. —**Associated Press**

Look around any high school now, and you rarely see kids dressed in black or punkish clothes anymore, or in faded jeans and tattered flannel shirts. What are they wearing? They almost seem in uniform, with the girls wearing sweet little J. Crew dresses with floral patterns on them, pastel or brightly colored twinsets, headbands and dark blue, new (not fadded or tattered) jeans. The boys wear polos and chinos and colorful sweaters.

—*Susan Brombacher*

The Millennial era has seen a huge growth in educational toys, some
of them extravagantly expensive. These selections are made less by kids
than by parents and other relatives—along with a huge market of childless adults who like playing with toys. (The American town that splurges
the most on toys per child—Arlington, Virginia, at $900 per child—has a
population disproportionately single and retiree.) In the late '90s, adult
concerns about whether a toy is "fun and enjoyable" and "safe for the
child to use without adult supervision" ranked far higher than concern
for the child's imagination, which fell 11 points as a criterion between
1994 and 1998. Parents don't want toys that get kids to express themselves. They want toys that can substitute for their own active parental
voice. "A generation ago most kids played with toys," wrote *The Economist*. "Now toys are expected to play with kids. They talk, grimace, and
generally interact for all they are worth."

>> Kid influence over parental purchases is growing.

In any era, parental purchases, whether it's a house, a car, a vacation,
insurance, a mutual fund—all the way down to Mom's purse and Dad's
necktie—all reveal prevailing adult attitudes toward children. But this
changes by generation. In the Boomer child era, kids influenced parents
collectively rather than personally, by steering parents as a group to relo-
cate to suburbia, to make larger cars the new norm, and to vote for bigger
schools and parks. In the Gen-X child era, adult purchases were more
likely to be made without any special regard for children, personal or collective. In some cases, such as the sporty family hatchback or the swinging Club Med vacations or the huge master bedrooms and baths of that
era, parental spending choices came at the direct *expense* of the kids. (Not
surprisingly, this is when school-age teens sought their own spending
money by surging into the labor force.)

In the Millennial era, parental spending is again coming under the
sway of kids, but this time the influence is more personal than collective.
In the early '80s, coinciding with the first Millennial arrivals, Detroit
introduced the hugely successful minivan, which—along with its later
sport-utility incarnation—was the first time ever that an entire genre of
automobile had been expressly designed to serve the needs of children. By
the mid-'90s, the trend in new designer homes no longer leaned toward

more outward show and ever-larger bedrooms; the new trend was toward more inward security and ever-larger family areas. Even Club Med did an abrupt about-face. The same resort hotels that once teemed with '70s-era singles are now overrun with kids. Cruise ships that once catered entirely to retirees now do so mostly to families with children, in season.

This "kidfluence" or "backseat consumer" market is a Millennial Generation phenomenon. Texas A&M marketing professor James McNeal estimates that the market for kids aged 2 to 14 was $5 billion in the Boomer child era around 1960, $20 to $50 billion in the Gen-X child era around 1980, and $188 billion now. To some extent, this rapid rise reflects new product categories (such as computers and audio-video systems) over which kids hold special sway, but also how Millennial kids simply wield more economic influence over their parents than earlier generations of kids did over theirs. In the Boomer child era, says McNeil, a kid's influence on parental choices usually began around age 12, but in today's "filiarchy" the child influence typically begins around age 2. This Millennial influence is not just over products, but also over income-leisure tradeoffs, hours and telecommuting choices, job locations, school districts, even career paths.

One-tenth of these "kidfluenced" dollars ($18 billion in 1997) involves auto purchases. In families with minivans and SUVs, according to J. D. Power, 76 percent of children age 6 to 8 and 73 percent of children 9 to 11 say they were involved in their parents' most recent car-buying decision—from make and model to music options, colors, and seating arrangements. Kids seldom press for less-costly options, which may explain why many car dealers now keep a Lego pile handy or why General Motors advertises cars to young "backseat consumers" in *Crayola Kids* magazine. Advertisers for parental products have learned that it costs a lot less to reach millions of kids on *Rugrats* than adults on prime-time shows—an opportunity that is helping to boost children's programming more than any act of Congress.

>> Kid marketing is toward a smaller number of bigger brands.

The reigning wisdom among "Gen-Y" marketing gurus is that infinite splintering is the wave of the future. That is the trend they've extrapolated from Gen X. But it won't bear out for Millennials.

Kids in the '90s are just followers of everybody. We don't have our own fashion. —**Shovan Quintana, 15**

It is so pathetic because all of the dependent carbon copy girls at my school went out and bought identical gray tech vests and are now wearing them every day.

—*rosie, magzine.gurl.com*

Last year, when Aly entered sixth grade, the tyranny of clothes conformity hit. . . . When I comment on the fact that they all look alike, Maura points out the different colors of the Gap Body tank tops they are wearing, watercolor distinctions of the faintest hue. She says they did not plan it. "It's easier to trade clothes this way," she adds, and shrugs. Even though it took them a solid hour to get ready, and despite the fact that they police their own conformity, they feel distinctive.

—*Adrian Nicole Leblanc,*
The New York Times

GAP is working on my Millennial mind. Conform. . . . conform . . . conform . . . How different from ten years ago. —*Chris Loyd, 17*

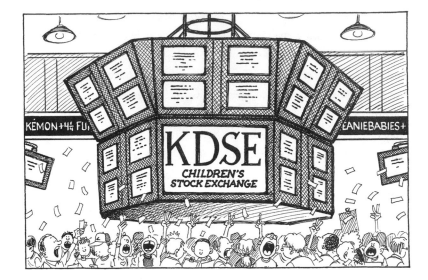

Where Gen Xers occupied a youth marketplace that was getting more fragmented and complicated by the year, Millennials are coming along at a time when the adult world, aided by technology, is simplifying kids' shopping choices. Beneath the appearance of a diverse and chaotic marketplace lies the reality of big brands and new teen loyalties to them. Suppose a girl wants to dress in a way that appeals to her peer group. All she has to do is make one brand-name choice, one core style selection, and she can shop for nearly anything. There's an incredible variety, but it's the *same* variety her friends are wearing, so she can be confident that what she's getting will fit in at school. That's how, even at schools that don't impose uniforms, Millennial kids (particularly girls) are dressing more uniformly by the year.

Pokémon may get more media attention, but outlets such as Delia's and Claire Stores lie at the heart of the new Millennial economy. Famous for its catalogue and mailing list, Delia's grew from $5 million to $170 million in sales between 1995 and 1998—roughly the same era in which Claire Stores accumulated 2,000 boutiquelike outlets, stocked with piles of items (average price tag, $3.50) for accessorizing kids who get clothes at the Gap or Old Navy. Then, thanks to the new teen magazines in which these companies advertise, and thanks to the web sites and chat rooms which they (and so many others) host, teens of all ages, regions, and ethnicities can locate themselves at the cutting edge of pop culture and fashion. This tends to standardize tastes, even as fads come and go.

This new Millennial market reaches all but the poorest kids. Back in the Boomer teen era, well-off kids in Cambridge, Ann Arbor, Madison, New York City, Chicago, San Francisco, and maybe a few other big cities and university towns had access to cutting-edge culture and commerce, but everybody else had to wait. In the Gen-X era, cutting-edge items were becoming broadly available, but kids had to know where to look. Now they're easy to find, and nearly all kids can buy variations of the same stuff. This makes life easier not just for kids, but for marketers too. Once a business figures out what's cool and what's not, it can get on an instant highway to nationwide (or even global) megaprofits.

Stores That Treat Teens the Best:
supermarkets, discount stores

Stores That Treat Teens the Worst:
computer stores, car dealers

Strongest Brand Loyalties:
magazines, music, jeans

Weakest Brand Loyalties:
electronic games, computer products

—*PRIMEDIA/Roper 1998 National Youth Survey*

Understandably, pollsters and consultants are busy like never before. Nickelodeon alone surveys 4,000 children every week, in offices and schools, over the phone, and through online chat. Youth Intelligence seeks out the young and cool and asks them to tape conversations with friends. It then prepares elaborate data digests that businesses can buy for up to $26,000 a pop (the reported price for the Nickelodeon/Yankelovich *Youth Monitor* study). Once so arduously and expensively obtained, Millennial data then goes into product design and marketing strategies for the countless new product lines, designer boutiques, and catalogue shops that cater to particular styles and looks (Hot Topic for Goths, Gadzooks for "nouveau hippies," Wet Seal for glam girls, or Delia's four "closets,"

The old-style advertising that works very well with Boomers, ads that push a slogan and an image and a feeling, the younger consumer is not going to go for. —**James Palczynski, author of YouthQuake**

To rejuvenate its Gen X hit House of Style, *MTV switched the emphasis on the weekly fashion show from celebrity lifestyles to practical information, with segments on decorating your bedroom and buying a prom dress.* —**Newsweek**

[I saw] a Coke ad where a teen sits in class taking a boring test. Then a Coke bottle appears from the sky. He reaches up, grabs it, then turns around and rescues a girl in the same test. The two fly off to a subway and rescue a boy of the same age from the platform. The threesome then fly off to some sort of festival where a girl is getting overwhelmed, and they rescue her too. The foursome then fly right toward you (the viewer) and are all happy. Cute. —*Chris Loyd, 17*

like the one for a "funky" girl who "can dip into the hippy thing but in a glammy non-granola way").

Geography, transportation, ethnicity, even money no longer matter as much, which makes Millennials a more nationally unified and to-the-moment synchronized target market than any previous youth generation. "Once upon a time, it was possible to monitor coolness by tracking teen likes and dislikes in Los Angeles and New York and adjusting products accordingly," observes youth trend watcher Shelly Reese. But now, "thanks to the internet, national media such as MTV and VH1, and a proliferation of teen magazines, any kid anywhere can keep up with the trendsetters. . . . Kids in the Midwest and South and Southwest finally have parity." And, by checking out all the on-line interactive ratings systems, kids anywhere can see what kids everywhere think about a new product—and, by clicking a mouse, they can become part of that tastemaking process themselves.

The fact that so many "Gen Y" marketers keep saying that this generation is so splintery only helps to facilitate this emerging homogeneity. By keeping kids from feeling as though they're selling out to adult tastemakers, kids who buy this idea can retain a sense of individuality, but also the ease, simplicity, and trust that comes with a brand name. This total orchestration of consumer wants is so comprehensive, and so accessible, it's beginning to forge today's teens into an economic force more potent than the size of their wallets would suggest. "Kids fancy themselves free-thinking individuals when it comes to personal style," writes *USA Today,* "but the truth is that teens are pretty much a huge wad of fashion conformists with a teensy population of innovators whose style will set the trends."

>> Kids are redefining the purpose of information technology.

Technological progress—which served as a liberating purpose to Boomers, and a diversifying purpose to Gen Xers—is serving a new unifying purpose for today's teens. Ownership of tech tools and toys has become a badge of generational membership. While the percentage of kids with their own rooms keeps rising (76 percent in 1997), those rooms keep filling up with gadgets. More than half of today's teenage rooms have TVs and cable hookups, 42 percent a phone extension, 36 percent a video game. Boys are more likely to own equipment for watching or playing, while girls are more likely to have technologies for listening to music, making movies, or linking with friends. Roughly three of every five school-age kids now has access to a personal computer, up from two in five in 1997.

Millennials are growing up as familiar with computers as Boomers were with television. In fact, more of today's teens say they can live without a television (28 percent) than without a computer (23 percent). With computer ownership becoming more essential, gender and income gaps are narrowing. Slightly more boys than girls have their own computers, and three of four affluent teens have access to one, versus roughly half of those below the poverty line. Through the late '90s, the percentage of on-line kids continued to grow rapidly. Among those aged 8 to 17, the share rose from 25 percent in 1996 to 35 percent in 1997 to 42 percent in 1998, to somewhere around 50 percent in 2000. Of those who are on-line, 60 percent log on once or more a week.

Top Web Sites (grades 1–12)

1. Nickelodeon
2. Disney
3. Geocities
4. Yahoo
5. National Basketball Association
6. Public Broadcasting System
7. Worm World

—American Library Association

The high-tech industry believes that kids on-line will produce $1.3 billion in revenues from on-line sales by 2002. If so, the internet will be the most heavily policed youth shopping mall in history. New dot-com companies (Flooz, DoughNET, iCanBuy, RocketCash) are setting up systems through which parents can restrict which merchants their kids patronize, the hours they can shop, the amount they can spend, even whether they can spend the money on themselves or only on parent-approved gift recipients. Meanwhile, kids are joining their parents in the eBay craze, trading everything from Beanie Babies to downloadable computer game patches (like a hard-to-earn fortified castle that makes a game easier to win), sometimes for prices over $1,000.

Technology always means something new to each generation. The young Silent regarded computers as necessary adjuncts to American technocracy, with mainframes at the apex of vast institutional pyramids. Young Boomers shattered the telscreen and invented the new personal computer, which allowed each person to be his own creative island. Gen-X hackers and IPO dealmakers have taken this new high-tech individualism and exploited its bottom line. Now Millennial teens are using computers to do group projects and communicate among networks of friends. For this generation, computers are definitely fun—but not necessarily liberating. In software ads, adults are shown solo near the monitor, but the kids are shown in groups. As more of them spend a growing share of the day at on-line computers equipped with Instant Messaging and

"buddy lists," Millennials can stay in almost uninterrupted contact with each other—at home, on vacation, wherever. On-line or off, Millennials usually maneuver in teams and under adult supervision, far beyond anything Boomers or Gen Xers ever encountered with the technologies of their own child or teen years.

Money and Jobs

No one can put an accurate dollar figure on how much money school-age kids actually spend—but a lot of people try.

Journalists often cite $150 billion in 1999 for youths aged 12 to 19—a figure calculated by Teen Research Unlimited—but this sum is surely too large because it includes collegians and full-time young workers. The Rand Youth Poll says $84 billion in 1997 for teens, lower (perhaps) because it excludes purchases teens make on behalf of parents and others. In 1996, the National Association of Secondary School Principals estimated that 13- to 17-year-olds collect only about $13 billion annually ($622 per teen), of which 26 percent is savings, leaving only about $10 billion in actual spending. That number includes only school-age teen use of their own

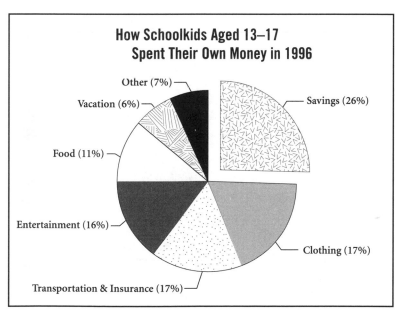

How Schoolkids Aged 13–17 Spent Their Own Money in 1996

Other (7%)
Vacation (6%)
Food (11%)
Entertainment (16%)
Transportation & Insurance (17%)
Savings (26%)
Clothing (17%)

Source: National Association of Secondary School Principals (1996)

Q: What do you predict your future will be?

A: Predict? I'm already working as an internet provider, offering consulting and repair services to my community. As well as designing a few business web pages. . . . I love this kind of work.   —Matt, 16

I am only 13, but people pay me to make web pages for them.—Alana, 13

Working too much too soon only jeopardizes a child's future.

—Alexis Herman,
U.S. Secretary of Labor

There are challenges running a business and being a kid.

—Matt Boch, 15,
web designer

Adults tend to see all things computer-related as work, even when they're play; kids tend to see them as play, even when they're work. It's a profoundly different mindset.

—Elizabeth Weil,
Fast Company

Daddy, when we get home from the pool, can I go on my computer and plan my future business?   —boy, 8,
at a swimming club

money, a definition that vastly understates their direct impact on the economy. Another calculation put the 1996 weekly cash flow for 8- to 12-year-olds at about $7 per week and for 13- to 17-year-olds at about $25.

Whatever the sum of money teens have to spend, it's a lot. The more interesting question is: Where do they get it? The short answer is that Millennial income is rising fastest from sources their parents most control (gifts, joint purchases, and paid household work) and is rising slowest—perhaps even declining—from sources they least control ("allowances" and paid employment). Both trends clearly defy the free-agent "proto-adult" stereotype of the Gen-X youth era.

Over the last decade, the fastest-growing source of kid cash has been direct ad hoc payments from parent to child, often for a specific purchase on which parent and child confer. By their very nature, these consensual transactions resist the adultlike categories favored by many marketing experts, since they're not child spending nor parent spending. One teen in three now says ad-hoc cash from parents is their biggest source of income. Supplementing parental payments are gifts from grandparents, 55 percent of whom say they've given their grandkids one or more gifts in the prior month, Today's kids are getting "play dough," observes Jeff Brazil in American Demographics. "In other words, if they ask, it comes."

Another rapidly growing teen cash source is income earned through household chores—which often mingles with the parental "gift" category. The Millennial childhood is an era in which more parents are working longer hours. Millennials spend substantially more time than Gen Xers did on tasks previously performed by a parent, from food shopping to cooking to laundry to caring for siblings—and they're being paid for it. Between 1991 and 1997, money from teen chores more than doubled.

The Millennials' experience with housebound chores, and their close contact with home-working adults, is influencing their attitudes about work. More than four teens in ten say that, in their future adult careers, working from home will be "extremely important," whereas only 8 percent say it's extremely important to "be a boss" over other people. Less than half as many say they want to gain personal recognition from work as say they want "to help others who need help." Other surveys reveal a rising teen desire to stay close to parents and a greater comfort level for working in groups.

Other income sources are declining in importance. These include "allowances," defined as a regular payment with no particular strings attached, which have shrunk to a smaller share of teen spending than at any time since World War II. The size of the typical 13- to 17-year-old's allowance was $8 per week in the mid-'80s and it's still $8. Adjusted for inflation, that's the equivalent of about $1.50 in the circa-1960 Boomer-teen era. Adjusted for family income, that's less than a dollar. To many Boomer and Gen Xer parents, the shortcoming of the straight allowance is that it limits the parent's opportunity to reward, instruct, pay, punish, cajole, warn, or moralize.

Income from paid employment (outside the home) is also waning in importance. Over the postwar era, the trend in teen employment has shifted by generation. It was low for the Silent, rising for Boomers, high for Gen Xers. But now it's going *down* for Millennials. Although teen employment is highly sensitive, year to year, to adult employment, its decade-by-decade level bears little relation to the rest of the economy. One would think that the stagflating '70s would have been a shakeout time for teen workers, and the roaring '90s a growth time, but very much the opposite occurred. Shifting parental and youth attitudes have played a much larger role in pushing teen employment up or down.

The Silent grew up in probably the most "cash-free" child economy of any generation in the twentieth century. Many passed through their child years in a hunker-down era of the family wage, when students were expected to stay out of the work force unless or until they dropped out of school, graduated, or had to support a family. In the 1940s and '50s, very few teen girls worked. Among Boomer teens, the "right" to work was one of their newly won youth freedoms. Both summer and after-school teen work grew strongly and almost continuously from the mid '60s to the early '80s. As the old '60s causes ebbed, G.I. Archie Bunkers accused Boomer Meatheads of being too impractical and not appreciating the value of a dollar, so older people hardly objected when late-wave Boomers and first-wave Xers, girls especially, pushed teen employment to its post–World War II apogee. The purpose of teen work shifted away from supporting families and toward personal spending money (or career-building or self-fulfillment). With the growing concentration of service-sector jobs in the suburbs, white middle-class youths became more likely to hold jobs than lower-income blacks and Latinos.

Through the 1980s, the gravitation of teens into the workplace became

Call them Generation $. As a group, today's teens aren't just the richest in history—they may also be the sharpest when it comes to earning, spending, and even saving money.
—USA Weekend

Among kids age 8 to 12, just over half get a weekly allowance. Of those who do, one-quarter get more than six dollars, 20 percent between three and six dollars, and twelve percent less than three dollars. —AAHS survey

[We] see a larger-than-normal desire for kids to save, which is interesting because their parents' saving is at an all-time low. —Mark Clausen, allowancenet.com

They're better savers than we thought they'd be. They're saving roughly 15 percent of their money, and we thought it would be 5 percent to 10 percent. —Ginger Thomson, DoughNET.com

a Gen-X trademark and the source of "Would you like fries with that?" jokes. The early Gen-X teen years of the late 1970s marked the postwar high-water mark for 15- to 17-year-old employment. One of every six 15-year-olds had an after-school job, one of every three a paid summer job—and, for the first time ever, girls outnumbered boys in youth employment. Later in the '80s, as adult immigrants began moving into the service sector, teen employment began to ebb slightly. By the late '80s, employment rates for the 16- and 17-year-olds were roughly 5 percent below those of the late '70s. Rates for 15-year-olds were 20 percent lower.

The 1990s saw a major change in adult opinion toward teen work, right around the time the oldest Millennials entered middle school. Parents and educators began to have second thoughts about whether teens should be wrapping tacos when they could be studying math—and, indeed, whether all the cars, CDs, trinkets, and movie tickets were worth all those hours of labor. By 1998, a federal commission issued *Protecting Youth at Work,* which confirmed that high school students who worked over twenty hours per week did worse in their classes, drank and took drugs more, and had more high-risk sex. Student attitudes were changing too. Many Millennial teens feel that the payoff on the skills and credentials they could acquire by studying, training, or interning are worth a lot more than the $8 or $10 an hour that an employer might pay them for the skills and credentials they have now. In 1983, 92 percent of teens felt a high school student should have a job; by 1996, only 69 percent did. Meanwhile, the share who worry about the negative impact of jobs rose from 13 to 37 percent.

The bottom line is that, in the Millennial youth era, employment has fallen among teens (especially younger teens), despite the hot economy. From the late '80s to the late '90s, the employment rate for 16- and 17-year-olds fell by 5 percent, and for 15-year-olds by 30 percent—which put it at barely half its Gen-X-era peak. Only 26 percent of teens now get most of their money from jobs, and the job rate for black teens lingers at only half the rate for whites.

OUT: Bad boy Dennis Rodman
IN: Good guy Kobe Bryant

—Advertising Age *(1999)*

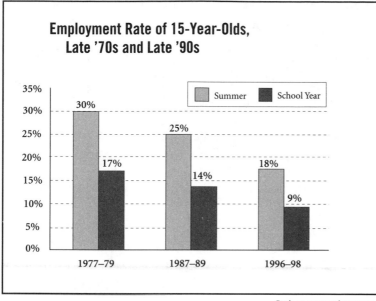

Employment Rate of 15-Year-Olds, Late '70s and Late '90s

Legend: Summer | School Year

1977–79: Summer 30%, School Year 17%
1987–89: Summer 25%, School Year 14%
1996–98: Summer 18%, School Year 9%

Employment rates are three-year averages
Source: U.S. Bureau of Labor Statistics (unpublished, 1999)

To date, reports are positive from employers of summer teen workers—"A Fine Crop of Young Workers," headlined the *Seattle Post-Intelligencer* in 1999. Millennials reportedly show a better on-the-job attitude than Gen Xers did a few years ago. Today's teens "are looking for careers and job stability," reports Sherwood Ross. They're not bracing to be quite as footloose or entrepreneurial as Gen Xers were back in the '80s. According to *American Demographics,* these Millennial attitudes, combined with their on-the-job performance so far, suggests that "the workplace atmosphere of 2010 could be a much calmer and more low-key place than it is today."

The corporate world shouldn't rest too easily, though. According to Ross, "these teens may very well clash with a new breed of employers whose goals are to establish a more flexible work force, including large numbers of temporary employees." When wronged, Millennials show a knack for collective action. In 1998, a 19-year-old fry cook named Bryan Drapp organized twenty teenagers in a strike against a McDonald's in Macedonia, Ohio. Against an adversary known to be hostile to unions, the kids swiftly prevailed with all their pay and benefits demands, failing only to rid themselves of an unwanted supervisor. For that, they became local heroes, and McDonald's became grist for the late-night comedy

Members of this [teenage] generation have been reared to be winners and successful in the activities in which they participate. This group seems to have more respect for advice and procedures than Xers and does not mind institutional input and involvement. . . . [They] are used to working and playing games (e.g., soccer) in well-organized groups. . . . They will want to seek long-term employment within a given industry for stability.

—David Johnson

91 percent envision working in traditional patterns—full-time jobs and a five-day work week.

—Arthur Shostak,
Drexel University

Millennial workers will go to the organizations that provide security and reciprocate with an ongoing loyalty and commitment that most Xers could not even imagine.

—Neil Murray, University of California–San Diego

circuit. This case stands as a warning: Once Millennials hit the labor force in full, they will know how to organize to get what they want.

Do You Worry About Family Finances?

A lot:	**12%**
At times:	**46%**
Not really:	**42%**

—*survey of U.S. teens,* USA Weekend *(August 2, 1999)*

Commercialism

"When I had the idea," said Sheryl Leach, the creator of Barney, "it was almost as if I could see into the future." Since 1991, the purple dinosaur has sold 45 million home videos, peddled 80 million books, and starred in stage shows that have sold out in sixty cities. Eight years after Barney helped them learn to talk, today's elementary schoolers are emptying their Hello Kitty purses even faster for Pokémon. "In the history of the toy industry, there has never been a hit so global, so multimedia, so rapid, so long-lasting as Pokémon," says toy-industry analyst Sean McGowan. "When you look at it from a marketing and a branding perspective, it's brilliant," adds Lynn Rosenblum of Toy Power Consulting. "It covers television, it covers video, it covers things on your computer, there's the cards, there's the toys, there are art contests. It's really one of those products that has done the best job of covering all those bases." Not to be outdone, Nickelodeon recently cut a deal through which *Rugrats* sounds and screen savers will be preinstalled in Gateway computers for kids.

Today's small child enters a consumer culture overflowing with logos, labels, and ads almost from the moment of birth. As an infant, says *Business Week,* she "may wear Sesame Street diapers and miniature pro basketball jerseys. By the time she's 20 months old, she will start to recognize some of the thousands of brands flashed in front of her each day. At age 7, if she's anything like the typical kid, she will see some 20,000 TV commercials a year. By the time she's 12, she will have her own entry in the massive data banks of marketers."

From 1986 to 1996, spending on advertising directed at kids rose from $100 million to $2 billion—and it's still mushrooming. The effects are daunting. According to James McNeal, the average 10-year-old Millennial now knows roughly four hundred brand names and asks for products by brand name 92 percent of the time. More is in the works for infinitely expandable Pokémon-style product lines. On the internet's vast ocean of teen and child web sites, dot-com ads and logos are popping up everywhere, their web "cookies" sometimes transferred onto kids' hard drives, and tastemaker polls are offered everywhere, their participants' email addresses often showing up in marketers' databases. The Digital Entertainment Network plans to run "fun-o-mercials" with teenage actors on window screens the size of wallet photos, in sitcoms that get interrupted every six minutes by those same actors pitching products right at the face of the computer user.

Back in the Boomer-child era, the biggest toymaker, the Louis Marx Toy Company, never signed a single license. Toys, books, movies, food, and clothes were each separate items that seldom got linked to anything else. In the Gen-X era, the concept of the cross-market tie-in was famously launched by a Boomer filmmaker, George Lucas, with his *Star Wars* trilogy. Since then, the tactic has been perfected to the point where his 1999 prequel, *The Phantom Menace,* seemed more market than movie, more commerce than culture. By then, two of every five toy dollars were spent on licensed products, and a child's world had become a blizzard of cross-promotions. Millennials have never known pro sports arenas that weren't named for companies, or happy meals that didn't have movie toys, or schools that didn't have soft-drink logos and candy ads. ("Better than Straight A's," runs the M&M's ad on a high school wall.)

Many Americans take kids' logo clothing for granted, but it's a relatively recent arrival. The Silent semirebel of the '50s wore nothing more than blue jeans and a plain white T-shirt. In the early '60s, many a Boomer teen boasted a tiny Izod alligator on his shirt pocket, but that was it. In the '70s, shirt messages became chichi not so much to indicate a brand as to point to some personal experience—a band seen, an album heard, or a resort visited. Then came the 1980s, when the new Gen-X message billboard, the baseball cap, always had room for a logo. After the financial success of the 1984 Olympics, pro sports franchises aggressively promoted

When I was growing up back in the '80s, the basic plot of the Frosted Flakes commercials was that there'd be some loser outcast who was no good at sports, so Tony the Tiger would pump some Frosted Flakes into him and the kid would turn out to be a world beater, and the other kids would decide that he wasn't so bad after all and let him in on their games. Today I saw one that has Tony giving a pep talk to a bunch of kids in a locker room. No one kid stands out; they're all uniformed and kind of interchangeable. He tells them that they've all worked hard and practiced and eaten lots of Frosted Flakes, and that's why they all get to be on his Team of Tigers. —Matthew Elmslie

logo apparel, much of it darkened and nastied-up to suit the emerging Gen-X proclivities. As the Nike swoosh began appearing everywhere, blue jeans became prefaded, even preripped. By the early '90s, when first-wave Millennials began to look around, logos had emerged as fashion statements, pure and simple. Athletes wore them simply because they liked the contract (not the product), and kids wore them because they liked how they looked (not the teams). In came Tommy Hilfiger, Adidas, Fila, JNCS, Nautica, and acres of others, with logos that stood purely for commerce (for them) and style (for kids).

With the spread of youth logos came a new explosion in kid marketing. When Gen-X teens showed up in the early '80s, business understood their attraction to things commercial ("Hamburger ads pop up in my head on the edge of Aquarius," sang the B-52's), but few yet saw much potential in the teen market. Then came the youth marketing flood tide of the early '90s, when marketers belatedly woke up to Gen X (though it was too late for most of them) and vowed not to wait so long for the next batch of teens. In 1993, at the onset of the late-Gen-X advertising push, *Advertising Age* produced its "Gen Y" taglet for the teens of 1993 (age 20 to 27 in 2000). The new era of Millennial marketing had begun—for teens, tweens, and little kids, too.

Corporations have learned from the accelerated Gen-X push that the stakes of generational marketing can be big. Hit the new kids early enough, and your company can be Volkswagen of America, the top car brand among Gen Xers, with 40 percent of its customers under age 30. Get it wrong, and you can be Levi's, whose market share collapsed from 31 to 14 percent in the '90s.

Yet just as corporate America brings out its biggest marketing cannons for its biggest target yet, the Millennial Generation, there are signs on the horizon that it may be committing an ancient strategic blunder: mobilizing for the last war—or, in this case, for the last generation. Heinz did exactly that when the company switched advertising agencies and began targeting X-ish teenagers just as the last Gen Xers were leaving that age bracket, with attitude-heavy ads and the slogan: "Heinz, the Rude Ketchup." But Millennials may not be the target that Heinz, or their Gen-Y marketers, think they are.

Just as the '90s ended, Millennial teens led the way in breaking America's logo fever. Sports logos stopped selling so briskly. Text on shirts and jackets started to shrink. Logos of any kind became harder to find on girls' clothing. School uniforms and stricter dress codes began to make significant inroads into the demand for fringe teen fashion. What's more, companies saw their traditional ad pipeline starting to narrow. Kids were spending less time (though on more stations) with TVs and radios, less time reading magazines, and less time watching the big three pro sports, once a surefire tie-in opportunity. When businesses began advertising on the web, they encountered kids web-smarter than they were—while the government began carefully scrutinizing how companies go after kids on-line.

That's not all. Many parents, especially of second-wave "Barney" Millennials, are beginning to fire back by taking active steps to shield their kids from an overdose of marketing. "We have deliberately tried to keep Madeline from becoming brand-aware," says Nancy Brophy of Illinois about her daughter. "If something's hot, like Beanie Babies or Power Rangers, I'll avoid it." Many of today's affluent parents are so obsessed with shielding their kids from money, logos, and luxury, and with teaching them "middle-class" values, that what *The Wall Street Journal* calls a "bratlash" is sweeping the country. Some parents are taking extraordinary measures—"denying their wealth . . . deliberately living below their means, living in a smaller house or driving a smaller car than they could afford. Some dish out philosophical lectures before every purchase."

The changing response of this generation (and its parents) to kid marketing could have been predicted. In the early '90s, most advertising that targeted small children had an X-ish quality—and most of it failed. Perhaps the biggest single flop was Pepsi's heralded "Gotta Have It" campaign (a slogan first uttered by a Millennial boy during the 1992 Super Bowl, prompting one mother to retort, "Not if you ask for it that way, you don't!"). From then on, marketers started to learn from experience. Nike gradually phased out its "Just Do It" slogan and replaced it with a more upbeat "Yes, I Can." Several of the late-'90s slogans expressed distinctly post-X sentiments: "Give them a fresh box and see how they grow" (Crayola). "A breakthrough in child development" (Dutch Boy paints). "Taste the rainbow" (Skittles). "Tested by kids, approved by moms" (Kix cereal). "Presenting the next generation of brain power" (Intel). "Where do you want to go today?" (Microsoft). "Mom, Sam won't stop doing his homework" (Dell).

By nine years old, kids are brand-washed. —**Linda Mangnall, Imagination Youth Marketing**

The slew of licensed toys leaves less time for imaginative play.
—**Business Week**

Children now want more warm and fuzzy games—like marbles, where you compete with live players.
—*Stevanne Auerbach ("Dr. Toy")*

One day a student brought a yoyo to school and it wasn't even one week, and fifty of the student body owned a yoyo and were trying to teach each other all of the tricks they just learned. —*H. William, 12*

Recent kid-marketing campaigns show a number of new Millennial twists. More ads are in bright colors, right out of the Fuji Film hue box. Several almost look like public service announcements, with kids getting smarter, doing good deeds, often in teams, sometimes (as in Gap or Nautica ads) having crisply choreographed fun in uniform clothing. Some new ads are simple statements of fact, as if to say: Here's what the product looks like, here's the web site, check it out, you decide. Kids appear in countless adult-targeted ads for cars and tires, real estate, financial services, airlines, and resorts. Much of the Ford Windstar campaign was built around images of kids and soccer moms. ("At Ford, we always listen to the mothers.") Among athletes, good role models now score better than bad ones, but none can match the draw of sassy animals. Among Millennials, the top ads star Budweiser's frogs (which teens rank number one in entertainment value only) and Taco Bell's chihuahua (which they rank number one as a sales message).

Today, a corporation can wrap its entire public image around child-oriented values aimed at kids and their parents. Much of today's Boomer philanthropy is Millennial-targeted. Bill Gates's Millennium scholarships—the first of which will go to the high school Class of 2000—are cementing his personal popularity among today's kids. Burger King is fusing local marketing with community service linkups, to good effect. On the downside, Calvin Klein weathered a public relations disaster when it tried to erect a huge Times Square billboard showing tweens in their underwear.

High-tech and financial services industries are echoing the call from educators, parents, and politicians to wean this next generation from the me-ism and now-ism that marked the youth eras of Boomers (for whom the cult of self felt new) and Gen Xers (for whom it did not). Early signs are promising. Today's children and teens have roughly a 25 percent child savings rate, versus a near-zero savings rate among adults, and they're showing a far greater interest in long-term investing than kids did twenty or forty years ago. The strong Millennial interest in college and professional careers also reflects this broad push from an adult world that, driven by economic self-interest, finds itself far more shoulder-to-shoulder than a decade ago on matters of youth marketing.

One showdown still looming between marketers and parents is over the intrusion of commerce into public schools. A growing number of companies give schools free teaching aids (books, brochures, field trips, videos) in return for a chance to get their logos into classrooms and pass out free samples. Soft-drink companies pay schools in return for "pouring rights" and vending machine placements. In the early '90s, Channel One began offering free but ad-bearing educational TV programming to grade-school classrooms. Channel One now reaches 12,000 schools in 47 states. More recently, Zap Me! began loaning computers and internet access to classrooms—in return for having students go on-line through a "Netspace" that delivers on-screen ad messages and records their web activity.

Marketers say that the practice of paying for information by selling ads is totally ethical (even *The New York Times* does it), and many schools plead that they are desperate for funds. Grassroots opponents, who hail politically from both the right and the left, insist that a "wall of separation" be erected between schools and commerce. The Center for Commercial-Free Public Education sponsors "Unplug," a program to help students oppose commercialism in their classroom, and a "Classroom Integrity Pledge" to mobilize organizational support. In some districts, Millennials themselves have organized to block any further commercialization of their schools.

The Winds of Change

Parents are of two minds about the impact of commerce on today's America. When they reflect only on their own lives—especially on their

Our Millennial teens take this new level of prosperity as a given. . . . Perhaps, as Boomer parents, we should give ourselves credit.

—Jennifer Park, *msnbc.com*

A child-raising paradox: how to raise normal, unspoiled kids embodying America's cherished "middle class" values—hard work, frugality, sacrifice—when you're floating on the froth of la dolce vita.

—Nancy Ann Jeffrey,
The Wall Street Journal

My kids use RocketCash because it's so convenient, and they can shop at their favorite stores, while I know that they are shopping in a safe environment.

—Chris Zamara, *parent of two "RocketCash" teens*

Companies are already sponsoring local school teams, so why not the teachers themselves? "Hello, I'm Jason, your substitute today. Before we start our math lesson, I'd just like to say a word or two about Levi's . . ."

—Jeff Backman, **Literal Latte**

It gets annoying. If you try and print, it prints the ad right in the middle.

—James Ghiloni, 13, *complaining about his school's N2H2 web filter*

own various quests for individuality and fulfillment, most of which happened in an earlier and simpler era—they see the positive side. Commerce gives them all the choices they want when they want them. What can be bad about that? Yet when they reflect on what would be best for their children, most of them see the negative side. The cult of me, the glorification of despair, the conquer-the-streets attitude, the cultural connoisseurship—all these certified X-ish youth attitudes are just what they want kids to avoid. Facing this tension, parents respond in every manner along the continuum. Some figure it's too much trouble and give up, others try hard to simplify their own lives, and still others try to live one way and bring up their kids another.

On the whole, Millennials give Boomers very high marks for managing a prosperous economy and for including kids in their earning and spending priorities. At the same time, Millennials seem willing to heed their parents' message about excessive commercialism. Both attitudes represent a reversal from the trends of the past two generations.

Marketers beware: Those who pursue the edgy path had better find a secure niche soon and brace for the onslaught. The "pushing the extremes" strategy—with its tattered sails of Boomer anger and Gen Xer angst—could find itself tacking against headwinds no less stormy than what white shirts, narrow ties, and accordion music faced in the youth gales of the 1960s.

Someday soon, predicts McNeal, "Advertising that encourages children to defy their parents, make fun of authority, or talk unintelligibly will be replaced with informative ads describing the benefits of products." Millennials could be the generation to inspire this change. "There should be some safe haven from advertising," says Annie Granger, a Canadian 16-year-old, a bit more simply. "You have to sometimes see the sky between the billboards."

CHAPTER THIRTEEN

planet pokémon *(world)*

Colors of the world
Spice up your life

—SPICE GIRLS, *"Spice Up Your Life"*

On January 1, 2000, Nickelodeon broadcast clips of preteen kids from around the world, cheerily talking about the future. From all continents, kids of all cultures and races predicted how science and technology would solve problems large and small. Progress was a given. Scourges like war, poverty, and totalitarianism were seldom on their minds.

This program was distinctly Millennial. Back in the Boomer child years, satellites hadn't yet been launched to allow such conversations. In the Gen-X child years, the satellites were going up, but transoceanic discussions seldom included children, who had yet to become a global priority. The most interesting difference, though, lay in the new child sunniness. Turn-of-the-millennium triumphalism has touched not only American children, but those elsewhere as well.

Reflect on what earlier kids would have said (had such a global conversation been possible) during the Silent, Boomer, and Gen-X child eras. In 1940, world events were ripping apart the lives of children. In 1960,

Separated by distance, yet united by the desire to have a greater impact on the world, young people are coming together. Through friendships and fiber-optic cables, youth are taking positive action to shape their planet.

—*nation1.com, Jan. 1, 2000*

Pokémon, you're my best friend
In a world we must defend

—**Pokémon** *opening*

kids knew that their parents had fought in terrible wars for or against terrible dictators, that science had invented H-bombs, and that computers might well empower Big Brother. In 1980, through a child's eye, the world was full of family and economic turmoil—overshadowed by a Cold War threat from two superpowers who had enough warheads to destroy the world in fifteen minutes. But today, the world's children pay little mind to those old anxieties. They're growing up in a different time.

Much as American millennials share a *national* location in history, kids around the world today share a *global* one, based on both cultural and family trends as well as changes in geopolitics and technology.

Are they a global generation? Indeed, is there ever such a thing as a global generation?

Since World War II, if not earlier, the answer to the second question is yes. Throughout the developed world, the Depression and total-war decades of the 1930s and (especially) 1940s left a life-cycle mark on everyone who participated, according to their age—on midlife parents, on young-adult soldiers, on growing children, and even on the babies born in the immediate aftermath. One could say that global generations began to take shape in the 1940s, even if no one yet spoke of humanity in those terms.

The first self-conscious announcement of a transatlantic youth kinship came with the "generation of 1968," when American and European collegians shared new bonds of music, drugs, blue jeans, and riots against whatever their parents expected them to do. In the years since, as global travel, culture, commerce, and telecommunications have grown, a larger share of the world's youths have come to share common life-cycle markers—the Berlin Wall's collapse, Tiananmen Square, Desert Storm, Princess Di's death, Michael Jordan, *Titanic*—prompting talk of a global Gen X. Every year, satellite news, pop culture, and the internet gain more cementing power over the world's young people.

Since World War II, much of the world has seen six generations, each with its own linkage with events, each with its own persona.

Global Generations

Recall the foot soldiers of World War I who became the generals and home-front managers of World War II—and, afterward, the initial shapers and leaders of a bipolar world. Through the Boomer childhood, they included Harry Truman, Dwight Eisenhower, Dean Acheson, and John Foster Dulles, the creators of a survivalist Cold War defense posture that remained essentially intact through the 1980s. Overseas, this no-nonsense generation encompassed the likes of Konrad Adenauer, Charles de Gaulle, Nikita Khrushchev, and Mao Zedong (and the despised memories of Hitler, Tojo, and Mussolini). In the year 2000, their survivors are over age 100. Throughout the world, this is the group that, for ill or good, most deserves to be called the World War II Generation—but, instead, they're known in the United States as the Lost Generation, in Europe as the "generation of 1914" or (in France) *génération au feu*.

The next generation, now in their late seventies and beyond, is more familiar: Allied and Axis soldiers, revolution and resistance cadre, Rosie-the-Riveters and nuclear scientists. Their impact on world history peaked young, in the 1940s. Their global impact as national leaders peaked much later, around 1970, with several of their larger-than-life members staying

Small families live better.

—Gloria Muñoz Castro, Mexico

The children already are developing much more, with a mentality more advanced than before.

—Juana Cornoa Salazar, Mexico City

at the helm well into the 1980s and '90s. In America, this G.I. Generation held the White House for thirty-two years, from John Kennedy through George Bush. Overseas, they have been known as the generation of the Long March (Chou En-lai, Deng Xiaoping), of the Blitz (Mrs. Miniver, Margaret Thatcher), of the Resistance (François Mitterand, Giulio Andreotti), and of the Great Patriotic War (Leonid Brezhnev, Yuri Andropov). From China to Russia to Europe to the United States, they are still associated with civic deeds and big institutions.

Next comes the grown-up children of World War II, now between their late fifties and early seventies, a generation that has produced the likes of Boris Yeltsin, Jiang Zemin, Helmut Kohl, Jacques Chirac, John Major, Kofi Annan, Romano Prodi, and Buru Utara Barat. Around the world, these war-era children grew up so seared by organized hatred that they have spent a lifetime trying to spare their own children from similar horrors. From one continent to another, they have become global technocrats who tout diplomacy, communication, and compromise—while old alliances meander and old empires splinter. In Europe, the peers of Anne Frank (in England, the "Air Raid" generation) grew up to be the '80s-era Eurocrats who staked their future on multilateralism, the Euro, and increased cross-border trade. In the Soviet Union, the "glasnost generation" presided over the dismantlement of their own empire over the objections of older war heroes. In Canada, today's sixtysomethings furnish the patient conciliators for endless separatist arguments. In America, the Silent Generation could become the first never to occupy the White House.

The familiar generation now rising to the top of the world's power pyramid consists of the middle-aged postwar children who lack personal memory of World War II; who came of age amid sixties youth riots, seventies anti-Americanism, and the Chinese Cultural Revolution; and who now mix varying degrees of moralism, nationalism, ironic detachment, and inward satisfaction. The name Boomers, now heard outside North America, is attachable to the likes of Tony Blair, Gerhard Schroeder, Javier Solana, Vladimir Putin, Joerg Haider, and Benyamin Netanyahu. While this generation has thus far made only a light impact on world affairs, its ethnic hatreds ravaged former Yugoslavia and its moralism transformed NATO into a more aggressive military body. A youth generation that announced itself with ideology and terror (Red

Guard, Baader-Meinhof, the IRA, the Weathermen) has today matured into the global age bracket most inclined to use military force. Already its loud debates over values, standards, and "third way" realignments reflect the inner passions of Vladimir Putin–style nationalists and Falun Gong–style spiritualists, with more waiting in the wings.

Lately, the world generation receiving the most media attention has been the global "Gen X," a name used along with "'90s generation" and (in France) *génération bof*, as in "who cares?" Global Gen Xers are acquiring a reputation as fun-loving and rootless, pragmatic and market-oriented, environmentalist and entrepreneurial, technologically smarter but otherwise dumber than older people, and far less interested in politics than in business. From London to Singapore, young adults are the free-agent nomads at the cutting edge of the new global economy and its culture. The high-tech IPO is their pride, temp work their curse. In fledgling capitalist countries (China, Russia, Eastern Europe), young adults comprise the *byiznyizmyin* who are handling the transition to freer markets—and, typically, they're faring better than older pensioners. In more-settled societies (Japan, Western Europe), they're doing substantially worse. One-third of young-adult Italians not in school are jobless, with more living at home with parents than at any time since the Great Depression.

What about the world's teenagers? Only in the United States and Canada have educators, political leaders, and the media identified a post-X adolescent generation. Outside North America, the term "Generation X" is still used much more widely than any other term to refer to teenagers. The "global teen" focus is far less on politics or ideology than on technology, family success, moneymaking, fun, and other quality-of-life issues. They're rootless, with 38 percent not expecting to live in the country of their birth. They believe in their right to go wherever they want to work or play—or in having that work or play delivered to them in a nanosecond, on their doorstep or at their PC. In 1998, a British study of a so-called English "Millennial Generation" found youths between the ages of 16 and 21 to be cynical (44 percent thinking that "most people can't be believed"), risk takers, and strong Labour and Blair supporters. Nearly half want to own their own business, and only 1 percent list a job in civil service as a career goal. Seven in ten see voting as pointless, and most oppose bans on smoking in public places.

Youngsters are cosseted from any risk of accident and schools are fearful of instigating trips beyond their own gates. . . . [T]he adventurer David Hempleman-Adams said: "We are becoming a society of softies. It is a crazy reflection of our times that we are surrounding our children in cotton wool . . . they will not be able to cope with risk when they encounter it as adults."

—**Electronic Telegraph** *(UK)*

Perhaps what is needed is a real look at what it means to be a boy in the twentieth century. —**Linda Croxford, Edinburgh University**

Bob the Builder, can we fix it?
Bob the Builder, yes we can!

—*song from children's show (UK)*

Some of these traits clearly aren't in sync with the U.S. Millennial Generation. The reason? *Abroad, the leading edge of a new Millennial generation, in most countries, probably has not yet reached its teens.* This misalignment dates back to how different societies experienced World War II. "Most contemporary European and Asian generations are at least five years younger than their American counterparts," explains war historian Davis Kaiser, "because it took at least that long for their societies to become stabilized after the Second World War." Where Americans began to talk and feel "postwar" even before VJ Day, other nations—Japan, Germany, Italy, China, Russia, even (to a lesser degree) Britain—had to deal with far more residual wreckage and suffering. North America produced an earlier (and much larger) postwar "baby boom" than Europe or Asia. Among global Boomers, therefore, the "postwar" mind-set attached to different birth-year boundaries.

Similarly, the conditions that produced global Gen Xers came later to nations outside North America. Europe's youth tumult didn't begin until 1968, when America's was already well under way (explaining why even Parisians could learn from Berkeley "veterans" about what to do with a billowing tear gas cannister). Where America's youth unrest ebbed after 1971, China's persisted for another five years. Today's triumphal individualism reached America ahead of other societies. The Clinton era crescendoed a few years before Blair's "Cool Britannia," while global Boomers elsewhere are just now making their mark.

For Millennials, the difference came with America's prior (early '80s) shift in popular attitudes toward babies and small children—a trend that didn't reach the rest of the world until around 1989, the year the United Nations began taking children's issues seriously. While the first discovery of new-style teens occurred in the United States and Canada in 1997, with the new teen pop music, this trend is just now reaching England and remains weaker elsewhere. And while youth violence is on the wane in the United States, it's still on the rise in Japan and much of Western Europe. Nowhere has there been nearly the same interest in post-X teens and children as in the primarily English-speaking countries.

America's Millennial-child fixation has had a global penumbra. Other nations see the same CNN camera shots Americans do, of global children in distress. Over the past two decades, the unrelenting pro-child crusading of the U.S. cultural elite has spread to the elites of other countries, helping to propel a new activism by multilateral agencies. European hysteria over child abuse (in Belgium) and school shootings (in Scotland) has furthered this momentum. In November 1989, just after the Berlin Wall fell, the United Nations hosted a Convention on the Rights of the Child (which, since then, has been ratified by every nation in the world except Somalia and the United States). In the ten years since, new multinational agreements have been reached on such agendas as discouraging the use of children as soldiers, regularizing cross-national adoptions, prohibiting the worst forms of child labor, and stepping up the prosecution of war crimes against children.

So even if the Millennial child era is arriving later in many countries, it has recently gained real force. In the 1990s, over fifty nations amended their constitutions or legal codes to improve the status of children. Japan, Thailand, and the Philippines, long the locus of "child sex holidays" and child pornography films, have imposed strict new laws against both. Sri Lanka raised the age of sexual consent from 12 to 16. In Indonesia, the World Bank is testing a new plan to pay school costs to keep small kids out of the work force. Sweden banned TV ads aimed at children, and Italy, Poland, Denmark, and Latvia may soon follow. Greece wants to ban ads targeting anybody under age 18. Brazil's national budget now shows how much money is spent on children. Through the spring of 2000, the fate of 6-year-old Elián González dominated the news across the western hemisphere.

The only significant exception appears to be in the Islamic world, where World War II did not create similar generations, and whose cultural defenses are stronger. Islamic nations have joined neither the downward global fertility trend nor the trend toward market-oriented individualism.

In summary, global Millennials seem to be most concentrated in societies that share a fairly similar generational constellation: East Asia, China, all of Europe, Russia, and the more prosperous nations of Latin America. Their birth-year boundaries vary. American and Canadian teens are at the leading edge. In Britain and Australia, the Post-X generation seems to be two or three years younger, and in the non-English-speaking developed world, several years younger still. This means that

There is no doubt in my mind that [the UN Convention on the Rights of the Child] has improved the lives of millions of children. —Carol Bellamy, U.N. Children's Fund

Americans and Canadians born between 1982 and 1985 lie across a generational divide from like-aged teenagers in most other countries, who remain more X-like. But today's global "tweeners" (born in the late '80s) and younger kids (born in the '90s) share tighter links—from their post–Cold War location in history to their more protective parental nurturing style to their elevated status in the national media.

To picture first-wave global Millennials, think of the age bracket corresponding to tens of millions of Pokémon fans, from 12-year-olds on master-trainer sites to 6-year-olds with their Pikachu figures. By the time these youth legions reach their teens and evolve to the next level, Millennials will begin to recognize themselves as a truly worldwide phenomenon.

Global Millennials

What distinguishes global Millennials from global Gen Xers? As in America, look at their location in history.

Look first at the worldwide fertility rate, whose change over the birth eras of the last three global generations reveals a sudden and stunning change. In the early 1950s (early global Boom births) the rate was 5.0 births per woman. In the late 1970s (early global Gen-X births) it was nearly the same, at 4.9 births per woman. But by the late 1980s (early global Millennial births), it had fallen to 3.3 births per woman—and by the year 2000, it has fallen even further to 2.7.

These declines were especially pronounced in Latin America (5.6 to 3.4) and in East Asia (5.5 to 2.4), led in the latter case by the antinatal policies of the Chinese government. In the developed countries, the average fertility rate by the late 1980s (1.8) had sunk well below the "replacement rate" necessary to keep the population from ultimately shrinking. The main global exceptions to rapidly falling fertility during the Gen-X birth era were the Islamic world and sub-Saharan Africa.

Where Boomers were the children of a fertility "boom" or plateau and Gen Xers the children of a fertility "bust," global Millennials are the children of a lower yet newly stable fertility pattern that reflects an emerging family ethic favoring "quality over quantity." Throughout most of the developed (and developing) world—China, Japan, Russia, Mexico, Europe—smaller families are now the norm. Beijing's mandate limiting

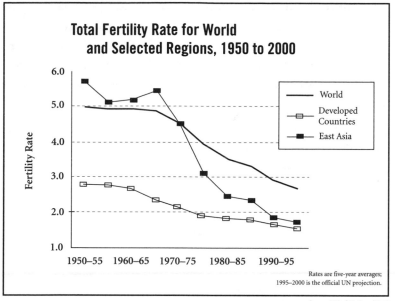

Total Fertility Rate for World and Selected Regions, 1950 to 2000

Legend:
— World
— Developed Countries
— East Asia

Rates are five-year averages;
1995–2000 is the official UN projection.

Source: United Nations (1999)

urban Han Chinese to one child per couple is producing what they call the "Peach" generation, only one seed per fruit. The Japanese have their "Little Emperors," Latin societies their *hijos únicos*.

Look also at the signal event of the late twentieth century—the end of the Cold War—and how that separates today's two youngest generations. Where global Gen Xers grew up with the waning of the Cold War, global Millennials are the first true post–Cold War generation, with no personal recollection of what Ronald Reagan famously called "the Evil Empire." Global Gen Xers arrived in a dangerously armed yet more stable bipolar world, in which America led one of two competing world systems. Global Millennials entered a less immediately endangered yet more disordered unipolar world, in which America rides supreme. To most of the world's 1.5 billion preteens, no ideology competes with the American model— which to them means a world in which ordinary people can do basically what they want and prosper.

During the 1950s, when global Boomers were kids, adults feared that the natural outcome for low-civic-energy societies was totalitarian dictatorship. During the Gen-X child era, that perception gradually changed. Millennials are now arriving in a world replete with democratization and

Not we, but our children will benefit fully [from a democratic Russia].
—Sonya Fetisova, 25, Moscow

Kill Serbs. *—Laurant, 9, Kosovo*

individualism, technology and commercialism—all triumphant, all still expanding, and all apparently requiring not one iota of civic effort to sweep everything else away. As many kids understand it, the tide is unstoppable and will soon wrap around the globe. According to Freedom House, 14 percent of the world's countries (with 31 percent of the world's population) were democracies in 1950, expanding to 62 percent of the countries (and 58 percent of the people) in the year 2000. Again, as with population, the Boomer child era was static, young Gen Xers witnessed the most change, and young Millennials are stepping into the new reality.

U.S. Kids' On-Line Questions to the Third World

"What is it that makes people so poor?"
"Have you ever been teased because you're poor?"
"Have you ever felt left out?"

—from Tapori, a worldwide network of 7- to 13-year-olds

The Vietnam War seems odd, in the hindsight perspective of a middle schooler studying history for the first time: Why would the United States fight for years at such cost when it could have just quit and watched both North and South Vietnam become market-oriented societies within a year or two? Global Millennials have never known a world in which democracy had to pay an enormous price in lives and resources to defend itself against enemies. They only know a world in which high-tech wars can be waged and won with zero casualties to the richer side. They look upon the United States as a rich *and* easy society, running on its own momentum, presided over by leaders who symbolize good times, personal pleasures, and ever-expanding wallets.

For today's preteens, the freedom to move across borders is an established fact. Global Boomers assumed that you stayed put in the country in which you were born—unless (like some U.S. draft resisters) you had a political reason to leave. When global Gen Xers were children, that assumption gave way to a new, more economically driven mobility across borders. Yet even the youngest global Gen Xer can recall a time before the collapse of the Soviet "iron curtain." Today's global Millennials, by contrast, have trouble imagining a world in which any family cannot emigrate if it wants to or needs to badly enough.

The world's youth culture has shown a similar transition, dating back to the first postwar years. Global Boomers were children at a time when indigenous cultures reigned nearly everywhere and "American culture"—then an oxymoron—was perceived as bland and corny by postwar youth nearly everywhere. This global perception changed during the 1960s and '70s. When Gen Xers were children, American TV, movies, and music began to innovate, experiment, and spread through much of the world. By the late '80s and '90s, while U.S. Millennials were children, the entertainment industry learned how to profit from the export of a culture consistently more profane and violent than the domestic culture. Today, to children around the world, "American culture" means the *opposite* of bland and corny. Anyone tired of feature-length cartoons, *Titanic*, and boy bands can easily turn the channel to unprintable song lyrics, sexually charged TV shows, and movies overflowing with casual violence.

Now add technology to this mix. The world's Boomers grew up with domestically produced movies and TV shows. Gen Xers grew up with VCRs and the rise of personal computers. The idea of worldwide high-tech linkages dawned while they were still children. Millennials are growing up *after* this has already happened. For most American children, satellites, cable TV, cell phones, and the internet are a given. For most children elsewhere, those devices remain dreams—but dreams they expect will soon become a shared reality. Even if the kids in some European town or remote Asian village don't yet have cable, the internet, and cell phones, they can assume they probably will by the time they reach adulthood. Where global Gen Xers feel they are pioneering a new high-tech frontier, Millennials are growing up as that frontier is being settled—and, in time, will adapt the new technologies to suit themselves.

Millennials Mobilize

While teens in the rest of the world still look very much like X, or (in Britain) its fading shadow, teens in the United States and Canada are taking the lead in showing the world what comes after X. Others, from

We are making changes to the penal code to prevent offenses against young persons. The laws will prevent use of children for begging, drug trafficking, and sex.

—*Gamini Peris, minister for justice and constitutional affairs, Sri Lanka*

I'm illiterate, and I want my daughters to be smart.

—*Didin Mujahidin, Java, Indonesia*

She is the very embodiment of the Indian youth—ambitious, technology-oriented, and confident.

—*Business Week, describing Neelam Aggarawal, 16, who owns (and rents out) her village's only cellular phone*

Found Generation.

—*Durcharan Das, title of book about South Asian youth*

Tokyo to Berlin, may contribute plenty of new fads in dress and language. And others may later catch up—as Europeans did with Boomers by the late '60s, and as Europeans, Asians, and Russians did with Gen Xers by the early '90s. But for now, U.S. and Canadian youths are the initiators, the pathbreakers, the exemplars of what's new.

Where North American teenagers stand in the year 2000 is similar to where the continent's Boomers stood around 1960 and Gen Xers around 1980—an as-yet-unheralded opening wedge of a global youth movement. To the extent U.S. and Canadian Millennials anticipate this global change—the more they correct for Boomers, turn away from the Gen-X style, and fill the roles vacated by G.I.s—the more leadership they can provide for today's global children when the latter pass through their teens. And to the extent North American teens can fuse bits and pieces of other cultures into a new generational amalgam, the more they can set the trends for the global approach of the Millennial teen.

To date, U.S. and Canadian teens have been doing this. From Boston to Vancouver, L.A. to Halifax, they have been tracking down offerings from all continents—toys and games from here, books and music from there. Whatever they decide they like, they make popular by chatting it up in various media (including the internet), after which younger kids around the world follow their lead.

No other North American child generation ever borrowed so much from so many cultures other than its own. The Boomer childhood was distinctly nativist—and when Boomers came of age, the geographic origin of their youth trends was always clear, whether music from England, clothing from Italy, philosophy from France, or religion from India. In the Gen-X child era, multiculturalism was spreading rapidly, and by the time they reached young adulthood, their global links were subsumed in a vast mishmash of trends. Among Millennial children, this mishmash is all they've ever known, and the multicultural linkages are so pervasive that the national identities of today's youth trends are often hard to pin down. A telling example is the Pokémon game and TV show, known to American kids by its Japanese name but still known to Japanese kids by an earlier English name, Pocket Monsters.

True to the second-generation immigrant pattern, Millennials are today forging a mind-set borrowed from bits and pieces of their countries of origin. The amalgam is part Ricky Martin, part Harry Potter, part

Lego, part Kwanzaa, and part Pokémon. Among those culture groups, kids find unprecedented diversity—and from each, they can extract elements that feel (to them) stylistically fresh and socially corrective. From Latino cultures they find family values, upbeat attitudes, bright colors, and wider gender roles (with men who actually dance with women). From Europeans, they find political history, rules and codes, puzzles and other geometric toys, challenging pedagogy, and structured knowledge. From Africans, they can obtain close community rituals and the courage to assist peers in need. From East Asia, they learn teamwork, honor, deference to tradition, and respect for elders. These cultures offer far broader values than just these, of course—but Millennials are selecting only the aspects of those cultures that comport with their global persona.

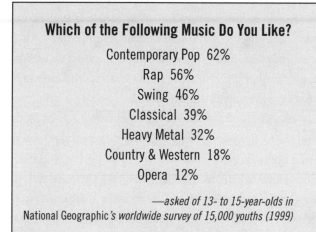

Which of the Following Music Do You Like?

Contemporary Pop 62%

Rap 56%

Swing 46%

Classical 39%

Heavy Metal 32%

Country & Western 18%

Opera 12%

—asked of 13- to 15-year-olds in National Geographic's worldwide survey of 15,000 youths (1999)

The cutting edge of this mind-set is less among today's teens than among "tweens" born in the late '80s and early '90s. By the time today's third through sixth graders fill U.S. high schools—and (unlike first-wave Millennials) feel a bona fide generational kinship with global peers—they could be even busier sifting and sorting from among the world's cultures, coming up with their own distinctly post-X blend and exporting it back to the world.

With the dawning of a new century, American Millennials are on the verge of broadcasting their viewpoint and style throughout the world. By the late '60s, American Boomers had launched their global peers on countless crusades of liberation (from technology, among other things).

We are the future masters of our country, so we have to study hard to build our country stronger.

—Li Jia, 12,
a Beijing Young Pioneer

Today's single children will become the most capable generation in China's history. *—Sun Yuxiao,*
China Youth Research Center

Only children long for communication with others.

—Zhao Ziaoyu, Nankai University,
on Chinese one-child families

Feeling pressure in school . . .
Hope I can leave this place soon

—Flowers (Chinese teenage rock band), "School's Out"

By the late '80s, Gen Xers were setting the global teen standard for a fully liberated consumerism, the commercialism to serve it, and new personal technologies. Millennials are well on the path to setting a global standard for a politics and economics that takes aggressive consumerism and unfettered commercialism as its starting point, and which seeks new community uses for technology.

U.S. and Canadian Millennial teens are already asserting a leadership role among their age mates around the world. One reason is that, in the manner of elder siblings, North Americans are reaching the new generational mind-set ahead of the others. That's what makes overseas kids *ready* to pay attention to them. Another reason is their extraordinary pan-global diversity, through which kids from nearly every corner of the world can find bits and pieces of themselves in what goes on here. That makes kids overseas *willing* to follow their lead. A third reason is the ability of kids from so many countries to communicate with one another—and develop a sense of shared community—through the internet. That's how kids elsewhere are *able* keep up with American and Canadian Millennials.

Teens here are, along with Australians, the world's most aggressive and skillful navigators of the internet. For this, they owe a debt to older generations who provided the necessary tools and training. In 1999, 25 percent of U.S. households had web hookups, versus 13 percent in Japan, 9 percent in Great Britain, 7 percent in Germany, and 4 percent in Italy—and among all global teens on-line, North Americans are the ones most likely to use the web for news, entertainment, purchases, and political action.

Older North American generations are boosting their kids' leadership role by focusing so fervently on children's issues and by constantly repeating the mantra that children are the future. Their own kids naturally focus on these issues, accept this mantra, see their global dimensions, go on-line to learn more about them, link up with kids from other countries, and begin to take action.

Kids around the world are themselves noticing the high Clinton-era priority that Americans place on the welfare of children—not just in their own domestic policies but in their major actions abroad. What causes the United States to intervene in locales such as Somalia, Haiti, Bosnia, or Kosovo? U.S.-produced images of children, broadcast all over the world on satellite TV. Which nationality is most conspicuously willing to adopt orphaned children, no matter how sick? Whose army is most often used for humanitarian reasons? America's movie and CD exports may be violent and profane, its president may constantly preach morals to the world as the world snickers at his, its armies may be forward-positioned in more places than ever—all that may be true and more—but from the standpoint of today's global kids, no people stand readier than Americans to spend their treasure and risk their lives in order to help children anywhere who fall victim to wars, earthquakes, hurricanes, floods, famines, and disease.

These are positive things, duly noted around the planet, which have the effect of enhancing the American Millennials' budding leadership role among their global peers. In a letter to the *Junior Journal*, Taiwan teen Chen Jun-Lin quoted the Backstreet Boys to offer her view from across the Pacific: "I don't care who you are, where you're from, what you did, as long as you love me." Life remains wretched for millions of kids in a world where, each day, 32,000 children under the age of 5 die of preventable causes. Older people sympathize, but assume nothing much can be done. Today's kids are shedding that fatalism and are trying to find a new challenge by taking on soluble global ills every generation before them has come to tolerate.

"Through friendships and fibre-optic cables," says the web site of the global teen activist Nation 1, "youth are taking positive action to shape their planet. The Youth Movement consists of many remarkable projects all over the globe. However, for the true power of youth to be realised, it is imperative that we unite, by using what we know best: technology." Nation 1's organizing motto—"connecting and empowering youth"—speaks to this rising generation's *modus*. Its global-action web sites don't look anything like the noisy, dumbed-down sites older people often design to attract teen visitors. Instead, they are simple, uncluttered, and briskly informative, with trim fonts and clean designs, and proudly state their linkages with the adult institutional world without a trace of Boomer coyness or Gen-X cynicism. They bristle with action plans, lists of prior achievements, and no-nonsense requests for help.

Usually, Millennial internet activists target their own global peers—children on all continents who are abused, hungry, or otherwise hurting. The number-one geographic focus is Africa, whose kids inhabit a bottomless pit of suffering and need. In a vast arc reaching from Sudan across Rwanda and Congo to Angola, an estimated 60,000 children under 15 have

Simon, you up? Simon Bogs, there are children in Mexico who have been up for three hours making shirts for corporate America.

—*Laney, in* She's All That

I saw a boy lose his hand. He had it one minute, and then he didn't have it the next. He was working with the [sisal shredder]. He was crying a lot, and he was bleeding—on his clothes, on the ground. I think it was his left hand. —*Richard Swetenham, European Commission*

been pressed into combat and fight in wars that rage on even after the next-older, soldier-age generation has been largely wasted. Tens of thousands of Sudanese children are enslaved, which has prompted a vast effort by a hundred American middle schools to demand, or buy, their freedom.

The cruelest childhood scourge is AIDS (in Africa, "slim disease"). It has killed so many parents that many villages now contain only the very old and very young. Through this year, nearly ten million African children under 15 have lost their mothers, or both parents, to AIDS. In 1997–98 alone, the number of new orphans was utterly staggering: over one million in Uganda alone, another million in Kenya, Zambia, and Zimbabwe, half a million in Tanzania—even 180,000 in the more prosperous South Africa. "Nobody has an excuse for apathy," writes *Newsweek*. Here lies a great Millennial challenge: Can they rescue their African peers? Can they apply science—or change human behavior—to prevent the next generation from being ravaged even worse? Surely, many will try.

When Millennials get busy, they get results. To date, no one has gotten more results than a 1982-born Canadian, Craig Kielburger. When he was 12, Craig read a *Toronto Star* article about a Pakistani boy his age who had been sold into bondage as a carpet weaver and who one day dared to speak out against child labor—and then was murdered.

Reading that story changed Craig's life. Within five years, Craig (now 17) and his friends had succeeded in establishing Free the Children, a power-packed global youth army with 100,000 volunteers in more than twenty countries. Using the internet and working closely with a variety of public and private organizations, Craig's group has helped build child-worker rehabilitation sites in Asia, set up job cooperatives for mothers of Latin American child workers (enabling the latter to go to school), create rescue homes for Middle Eastern camel jockeys, extract Filipino children from the sex trade, and organize a European boycott of carpets that lack a "rugmark" guaranteeing they are not made by small children. Their volunteers have aided hurricane relief in Nicaragua, sent health kits and baby items to Kosovo, campaigned to get the police to assist Mexico's child beggars, and sought to criminalize "child sex tourism." Free the Children's new goal is to mobilize global teens to get their governments to ban the worst forms of child labor and criminally punish those who are responsible.

"UH, MOM! I HAVE A BAD FEELING ABOUT WHO MADE THESE SHOES!"

When in history has any single group of kids launched so many activities, on so many continents, on behalf of so many less-fortunate members of their own generation? Kudos to Craig Kielburger—and to the internet, without which Free the Children might never have gained traction. Yet for this cause to have gone so far so fast, more was required than energetic kids with high-tech tools. Adults worldwide have been totally supportive in ways they would not have been in earlier eras. Teenage good-deed-doing on a global scale would have seemed incomprehensible in the 1940s, ridiculous in the 1960s, implausible in the 1980s. Today, it makes sense, and it happens.

More, much more, is still to come. As U.S. and Canadian Millennials get older, they will continue to mobilize their global generation. Perhaps, as young adults, they will not deem the plight of their African (and other Third World) peers so far beyond hope as today's older generations seem to think. Who knows what good they can someday do?

Excellencies and officials of Europe. . . . We suffer enormously in Africa. Help us. We have problems in Africa. We lack rights as children. We have war and illness, we lack food. . . . We have schools, but we lack education. . . . We want to study, and we ask you to help us to study so we can be like you, in Africa

—written message found with Guineans Yaguine Koita, 14, and Fode Tounkara, 15, who froze to death in the baggage compartment of an airliner after stowing away on a flight to Brussels

This is a new phenomenon. Children are discovering that they don't have to be helpless, because they can have an impact by getting together.

—Janet Nelson, UNICEF

But the world cannot assume that Millennial deed-doing will always be so benign. What many of today's global Boomers now fear—a perpetuation of global Gen X, with all the splintery cynicism and hardscrabble nomadism that implies—will not be the coming youth problem. Instead, there will be other dangers, coming from unexpected directions. The budding power of this global generation could soon be a source of immense civic energy, for good *or* ill, throughout the world.

The children who have attracted such intense public concern throughout the developed world will reach their teens in the Oh-Ohs and come of age as adults in the Oh-Teens. As they do, their nations may be inclined to mobilize against any obstacle standing in their way. This could pit U.S. Millennials against Millennials abroad (the Chinese "Peach" generation?) or against young Islamics who will not share the same generational kinship. Let's hope that it will do neither—that it will instead pit Millennials *with* Millennials against some of the great unmet challenges facing all of humanity.

Q: "Did you kill?"
A: "No."
Q: "Did you have a gun?"
A: "Yes."
Q: "Did you aim the gun?"
A: "Yes."
Q: "Did you fire it?"
A: "Yes."
Q: "What happened?"
A: "They just fell down."

—*interview of a child soldier in Africa, in* Awake! *(April 3, 1999)*

One prediction can safely be made. By the time today's "tweens" come fully of age as adults, the world will understand that it has not reached the end of history. And by the time today's newborns come fully of age about a quarter century from now, the world will understand that history has *restarted,* powerfully, with a new burst of youthful energy.

PART THREE

where they're going

CHAPTER FOURTEEN

The clock is tickin'

THE CLOCK IS TICKIN'
THE CLOCK IS TICKIN'

Mm-hmm, soda pop bop . . .
The clock is tickin', an' we can't stop
                    —BRITNEY SPEARS, "Soda Pop"

The stroke of the new year on January 1, 2000, marked a major moment of life-cycle reassessment for all of the adult generations who experienced it. Many G.I.s marveled that they had lived long enough to be there. Many Silent reoriented themselves to a high-tech, high-touch future that they presumed would henceforth be more leisure than labor. Many Boomers, with the sci-fi sound of *Zarathustra* still in their ears, counted their remaining mortgage payments and wondered if they still had time to discover the truth. To many Gen Xers, Y2K signaled the final closing of their youth era and the beginning of life's real challenges.

None of this taking stock mattered to the first Millennials, the Class of 2000—those whom young Lindsay Dance calls "the beginning of the future," a future that truly belongs to Lindsay's peers more than to older people. As they speak out about the future, they are beginning to reveal a can-do attitude utterly unlike that of Boomers back in the 1960s. "We're going to get some things accomplished," says 17-year-old Brent Bice.

As I look upon the happy faces in front of me, I see the cure for cancer, the space station completed, and the world changed in unimaginable, profound ways—it seems as if the young are becoming more enthusiastic and more intelligent—I do not doubt that the 2000 graduating class from Village Green will be anything less than superior. —Joshua Shapiro, 17, in a graduation address to preschoolers

Graduation caused me to look at all the kids I went to preschool with in a new light for the first time. Suddenly, it's different. I'm sort of looking at them as adults.

—Ben Snell-Callinan, 18

I'll never turn around, anymore . . .
—The Moffatts, "We Are Young"

This is my generation and my life, and I'm going to do something with it.   —Tyler Hudgens, 15

We are the generation that is finally going to take charge and get some things accomplished. We're not going to be sitting in therapist's chairs or turning into couch potatoes watching low-budget TV movies. We will be the ones who make business big and bring the computer age to its peak. We know what we're talking about, we know where we're going, and we're going to settle for nothing less.   —Brent, 16

Our new young masters will achieve greatness; they're too secure not to, knowing what a winning hand they've been dealt.   —Eric Weisbard,
The Village Voice

I'm at the point now where I need to take some steps forward. People will just have to be ready for it.
—Jonathan Taylor Thomas, 17

Setting goals is easy, but it is not so easy to obtain them.
—Bouavanh Phommachanh, 17

I don't think there will ever be a utopian country, but if we try, we can get pretty close!   —Sarah Trent, 12

"We're not going to be the whiners or complainers or the ones sitting in therapists' chairs or turning into couch potatoes watching low-budget TV movies. We know what we're talking about, we know where we're going."

Where exactly *is* it that the Lindsay Dances and Brent Brices are going? The Millennial Generation is primed and poised to power its way through American society. But when? And how?

The *when* questions are easier to answer, since there are fairly predictable phase-of-life events associated with each age bracket. For example, one can say with some certainty when most Millennials will marry, have children, be of military age, buy their first homes, or fully occupy the youth culture. Even their political timetable is predictable. Over the last two centuries, there has been a fairly regular age schedule by which American generations have risen and fallen in their dominance of different political institutions. A generation attains a plurality in state legislatures, for example, when its first cohort attains its late forties, in the U.S. Congress when it reaches its early fifties, and in the U.S. Supreme Court when it reaches its mid-sixties.

The *how* questions are more interesting, albeit less easy to answer. What will Millennials someday do to families, the culture, the economy, or government? This requires an understanding of how (and why) they will differ from Boomers and Gen Xers, at each phase of life—in other words, how their unique generational persona will shape the behavior and attitudes they bring to young adulthood, midlife, and old age.

History does, of course, always mete out surprises, good and bad. When those surprises and public actions are big enough—as the Great Depression and World War II were for young-adult G.I.s—they can fix a generation's reputation and agenda for the rest of its life. Let's defer those issues until the next two chapters.

For the remainder of this chapter, let's look at what Millennials are likely to do, decade by decade. Barring cataclysmic events, one can at least sketch out a timetable with a fair degree of confidence. Further out, these forecasts all hinge on how history might intrude on the Millennial life cycle. Intrude, it will. No one seriously believes that the next seventy-five years will unfold as smoothly as they do in the official Census projections or Social Security's actuarial tables. This is especially so for a generation

that is likely to have such a great impact on the future shape of political and economic institutions.

The twenty-first century belongs to Millennials far more than to Boomers or Gen Xers, and the Oh-Ohs will be the decade of their breakout. Over time, how history has already shaped them will have much to say about how they will shape history.

The Millennial Life Cycle

The past is record: The first Millennial babies were born in 1982, walked in 1983, talked in 1984, reached kindergarten in 1987, and entered middle school in 1994 and high school in 1996. They started having soccer moms in the late '80s, hit puberty in the early '90s, and stole their first kisses and smokes in the middle '90s. They received drivers' licenses, took their SATs, found part-time jobs, went to proms, and made their first serious sexual

We live in the generation where all that matters is the future.
—Kirsten Johnson, 16

The future is going to look brighter because our expectations of youth have been low for such a long time.
—Dallas Morning News

Our generation has more pressure to be the greatest, which is good as a goal, but is also detrimental [and] can lead to bad decisions in life.
—Lorie Thompson, 17

It's time to see our kids for who they truly are. . . . [M]ost of them could one day make this country an immensely better place.
—David Gergen,
U.S. News & World Report

You have to use us. America needs people, they need young people to keep their communities going.
—Atkinson, 15

We shouldn't be the generation of complainers. We should be the generation of doers.
—Kimberly Huston, 16

I just hope that my kids aren't as rebellious as you Boomers were.
—Michael Eliason, 17

choices in the late '90s. The year 2000 brings their first high school graduations, college admissions, military enlistments, union-hall signups, and lasting separations from Mom and Dad. It's also when they will start voting.

Then what? The timetables are predictable, the meanings more speculative. However, what is already known about Millennials, combined with the historical record of other generations, enables one to draw an outline with a fair degree of confidence.

THE OH-OHS

Here's the Millennial timetable. The first Millennials will start dropping out of college (many to join the dot-coms) in 2001. They will reach age 20 (and graduate from junior college) in 2002. They will reach legal drinking age (and start quitting college for pro sports) in 2003, graduate from college in 2004, fully occupy the lower military ranks in 2005, comprise the pop culture's entire target market in 2006, qualify for lower car insurance rates, be eligible to be elected to the U.S. Congress, reach the current median female marriage and childbirth age, and begin graduating from law schools in 2007, earn medical diplomas in 2008, and reach the current median male marriage age in 2009. Early in the Oh-Ohs, a recognizable generation of Millennial teens will gain attention in Britain and Australia; by mid-decade, in much of Europe; by the end of the Oh-Ohs, in Asia and Latin America.

The public discovery of their existence (which began in 1997) will extend through about the year 2002, by which point most Americans will accept that Millennials are a bona fide new generation. They will fully possess the youth culture roughly between the years 2002 and 2007. Sometime between 2007 and 2012, they will break out as a major national phenomenon.

Here's what this timetable will mean for America. Keep an eye on the Class of 2000. Since birth, they've been something of a public property, a trait that will follow them into their twenties. Through the Oh-Ohs, whatever institutions they newly occupy—from college to pop culture, from armed forces to union halls and voting booths—will receive the same media glare, parental obsession, and political intrusion that high schools felt in the late 1990s. By mid-decade, the nation will have a fascination for 18- to 22-year-old youths, who will be newly protected, pressured, and praised. By decade's end, the public fascination will extend into the middle twenties age bracket.

Through the Oh-Ohs, Millennials will rise swiftly and smartly in pop-culture influence. The gap will narrow between their own tastes and what older culture providers market to them. Much like in the '60s, during which Silent songsters such as Bob Dylan and Paul Simon developed a keen ear for the younger Boomer attitude, the Oh-Oh youth culture will showcase a new round of Gen Xers who move beyond X-ish angst and speak more clearly to the Millennial mind-set.

In music, film, and sports, Millennial stars will begin to emerge, and the male half of this generation will begin to assert itself. Some of this will still reflect a Gen-X shadow, but most will reveal a more recognizably Millennial attitude, exemplified by a new type of team-oriented athlete in pro sports and clean-cut (macho or girlish) star in entertainment. Pop music will become more melodic and singable. Gen-X genres such as new wave, alt-rock, and rap will still be around, but, by degrees, these styles will be tamed and domesticated to suit the new youth taste. Sitcoms will become more melodramatic and wholesome, casting away much of the residual Gen-X veneer (that will now be considered "very '90s"). Film and theater will blend the high-tech with the traditional. Many older people will applaud these trends, but some critics will complain that "bland" is in, and that nothing profound or provocative is being expressed.

Colleges and universities will buzz with activity, change, new pressures, and new arguments. As more college-bound students from the United States and around the world compete for a fixed number of desirable slots, elite schools will become even more selective, second-tier schools (and top-caliber state schools) will rise in prestige, and single-gender and sectarian schools will grow in popularity. Most colleges' average SAT scores will rise. Rejected students and their parents will complain about perceived unfairnesses in admissions. Affirmative-action criteria will be retooled to pay less attention to race and more to socioeconomic background. The stakes will seem very high. More than ever, college and entry-level jobs will act as societal sorting mechanisms, through which young adults will learn where they stand in relation to their peers.

School spirit and the quality of college life (dorms, food, library reading rooms) will enjoy an upswing, fueled by fussy Boomer parents who will have more than the usual trouble "letting go." The college decision

It seems that the people who run the dorms on [the Cal Poly] campus have decided that it is a right for incoming freshpeople to have a spot in the dorms, as space permits. Note that this means that the Xers currently populating the dorms will get thrown out. . . . I guess they want to provide the college experience. Weird. Cal Poly has been very student-unfriendly in all of my experience. —Justin Smith

There has been a lot of talk around [Marietta College] here as to how "bad" the students are and how they don't have respect for each other or their living space, so with the incoming freshmen they really wanted to emphasize being community-oriented . . . making a conscious effort to civilize younger people.

—The Marcolian

Boston University is now building a superdorm at a cost of $100,000 per student, double the national average. The glass-and-steel tower looks less like a rooming house than a sleek yuppie condo, with sweeping views of the Charles River and the Boston skyline. All bedrooms are private, shared carpeted suites and genuine kitchens—adult-size fridges, built-in microwaves, garbage disposals, the works.

—The New York Times Magazine

will become more of a joint parent-student issue. Colleges will be expected to provide the complete traditional collegiate experience, from ivy-covered halls to pep rallies to classic subjects. Prodded by parents and the media, administrators will toughen on-campus security and rules of student conduct. By the end of the decade, colleges will scale back or eliminate their remedial freshman classes. Except at elite schools, the academic standards movement will reach college in some form, perhaps through pregraduation competency testing. Grades, honor codes, internet behavior, and cheating on exams will all become major issues.

The old Boomer-era campus causes will recede, to the chagrin of aging faculty, and be replaced by others of more urgency to the Millennial life experience. Women will win rising shares of leadership positions, academic honors, and graduate admissions. At the same time, men will feel less at home on campus, male dropout rates will rise, and gender-studies programs will come under student attack. How to bring young men back into higher education will become recognized as a national problem. A more multiethnic student body will seek common ground rather than bastions of separatism. Students will prefer the melding of ethnic-studies programs into more traditional academic fields. Class (and money) will rise above gender or race as a flashpoint for student political argument. Dating across racial and ethnic lines will be more common, while dating across class lines will become less so.

The younger Millennial cohorts, meanwhile, will show a marked improvement in achievement and behavior. That, in turn, will make scholastic competition more intense and professionalized (with more private tutors and precollege counselors). The academic side of school will be more rigorous and less fun. Educators, political leaders, and the media will edge away from their '90s-era criticisms of teenagers and will more often declare the quality of school-age children to be a badge of national progress.

By the time Millennials entirely fill the ranks of college and graduate schools, they will resolve longstanding debates about substance abuse. Most rates of what is now defined as "abuse" will go down, but tobacco and marijuana could go either way. Their use may become ritualized into this generation's peer-driven sociability and be perceived as a salve to rising academic and social pressures. What Millennials decide is acceptable will be transformed, cleaned up, domesticated, given a lasting stamp of social approval, and no longer considered dangerous. In any case, they will decide by behavior what culture-warring Boomers could never decide with rhetoric: which substances constitute "use," and which "abuse." If Millennials decide that tobacco smoking is OK, the current antitobacco siege will lift. If they decide it's wrong, the U.S. industry's domestic markets will collapse—and perhaps, with the help of global Millennials around the world, its export markets as well. Whatever Millennials decide will settle these debates for decades.

Millennials will redomesticate the dating-and-mating process. Teenage balls and proms will become more formal and fully supervised. Postadolescents will strip the singles scene of much of its current edginess and danger by placing a new emphasis on manners, modesty, and old-fashioned gender courtesies. They will introduce courtship rituals that stress reciprocal duties and deference to parents—modern variants of the young prince delivering a dragon's head to the father of his beloved. Compared to Gen Xers, though, these young couples will have much clearer plans for where they want to go in life—plans which parents will find hard to obstruct. To reduce the risk of disease and infertility, and to conform to new peer social standards, Millennials will begin to reverse the trend toward later marriage and childbirth.

Young workers will demand that employers adjust to the needs of workers who wish to build careers and families at the same time and to lead lower-stress lives than their parents did. "Fair play" on pay and benefits will be at issue, and new labor problems will arise, especially among male workers. The American workplace will become less nomadic and X-ish, and—following the next recession—more cooperative, standard, and loyal. Entry-level youths will be attracted to solid companies with career ladders and standardized pay and benefits (including, for men, continuing education programs). They will be less attracted to consulting, contracting, temping, freelancing, or new business startups. Older employees will admire their skills, confidence, and team spirit, but will question their creativity and toughness. Millennial women will dominate entry-level medical, legal, and media positions, while Millennial men will dominate business and technology. These and other gender separations will protect and enhance a new sense of role identity and esteem for females and males alike. In a reversal of young-adult Boomer trends, men will specialize more on construction and institution building, women (with their growing lead in arts and humanities degrees) on values and culture.

Young-adult Millennials will start constructing a new definition of "middle class." As their cliquishness ages with them, a clearer generational center of gravity will emerge than ever existed for Gen X, within which social prestige (and pecking order) will become important. Millennials will define certain ways in which it will be more (or less) acceptable to make a living, with social status accorded to those who fit those definitions and denied those who do not. Within a more tightly defined order of higher and lower class, Millennials will be less inclined than Gen Xers were at like age to take big career risks or turn their personal lives inside out to make more money.

When You Reach Your Parents' Age, Do You Think You Will Be:

Better off than they are now: **52%**

Worse off: **4%**

—survey of teens, in USA Weekend *(May 2, 1999)*

Big brands will return to the youth shopping cart, as Millennials simplify their choices. They will take the pieces of the splintery Gen-X commercial culture and gather them all under the umbrella of a few huge happy-looking logos, each of which will subsume all individuality and diversity within a choice of product lines. This will enable Millennials to enjoy a vast diversity of personal choice—while at the same time building trust with a small number of commercial providers and creating a single overarching generational style. They will begin buying big-ticket items such as cars and appliances, after consulting with (and often receiving major financial help from) their parents. Durability and "class" in the eyes of peers will be big new concerns. Young adults will be drawn most to products that combine their focus on family formation and community approval with breakthrough technologies.

Leading-edge Millennials will render the internet and other new technologies less chaotic, more reliable, and less dangerous for the younger members of their own generation. They will embrace and help develop groupware, community networks, cooperative games, and web devices that credential, simplify, segment, and screen the infosphere. A new breed of internet activists will marshal global peers on political, economic, military, and environmental issues of common concern.

In politics, young voters will emerge as a new powerhouse, surprising most older people with their activism and determination. Youth voting rates will rise. Collegians and high school students will use the internet to build a whole new style of grassroots politics and erect electronic national arenas in which youths won't just talk and run surveys, but organize, agree on action plans, and delegate authority. The armed forces will increase in prestige by becoming, to the public eye, less an outpost for solo gladiators and more a camp for public-works teams. Some form of national service will emerge as a natural outgrowth of the school-uniform movement, trampling libertarians under an emerging consensus from both sides of the culture wars. In 2009, the fortieth anniversary of Woodstock will bear little resemblance to the original, as Millennials clean it up and lend it a distinctly can-do political bent.

By decade's end, the Oh-Ohs will feel much more different from the '90s than the '90s did from the '80s. Millennials will set the tone for the Oh-Ohs just as Boomers did for the 1960s, though not at all in the same

As we enter the twenty-first century, teenagers face greater opportunities for personal growth and economic success than ever before.

—*Council of Economic Advisers*

Yes, we have a bright future, and we see that you need money to survive on this planet, period.

—*Courtney Snowden, 17*

You will not make forty thousand dollars a year right out of high school. You won't be a vice-president with a car phone until you earn both.

—*Charles Sykes, author of* **Dumbing Down Our Kids**

The more the market climbs now, the less room there will be in later years for younger investors to gain.

—*Peter Coy,* **Business Week**

The outcome might be a very large upper-middle class if everyone's goals are fulfilled. —*Rima Tatevossian, 17*

You see the jobs people have, the high cost of living . . . and you feel a lot of pressure to support this lifestyle.

—*Chris Powell, 17*

HIGH SCHOOL SWEETHEARTS IN "THE BIG STEP"

LET'S GET MARRIED FIRST — 1950

LET'S GET STONED FIRST — 1970

LET'S GET TESTED FIRST — 1990

LET'S DO NATIONAL SERVICE FIRST — 2010

way. Where the Boomer upheaval focused on issues of self, culture, and morals, the Millennial upheaval will focus on issues of community, politics, and deeds. They will rebel against the culture by cleaning it up, rebel against political cynicism by touting trust, rebel against individualism by stressing teamwork, rebel against adult pessimism by going positive, and rebel against societal ennui by actually getting a few things done.

For the rest of their lives, Millennials will look back on the songs, films, and events of the Oh-Ohs with the *when-we-were-young* nostalgia a generation always attaches to the time it broke out as a new phenomenon.

THE OH-TEENS

Here's the Millennial timetable. The first Millennials will reach age 30 in 2012 (and become eligible for the U.S. Senate). They will produce their first national leaders (governors, senators, and members of Congress) early in the decade, emerge as the largest generation of eligible voters and become eligible for the presidency in 2017, and attain roughly 5 percent of national leaders in 2019. This will be their peak decade for marriage and for the birth of first children. Millennials will be the leading writers, performers, and consumers of the pop culture, and will be reaching their peak of cultural influence. By now, a truly global generation of Millennials will be emerging in many parts of the world.

Here's what this timetable will mean for America. Millennials will begin the decade at the peak of their breakout, and will end it with their generation being a tired subject (much like Gen X became by the mid-'90s). Their breakout will seem utterly uncreative in the cultural sense, but enormously powerful politically. Millennial youths will go for tangible results, not gestures or feelings. They will coalesce and mobilize around any challenge that admits to a measurable, quantitative solution. Their hugely powerful political influence will start being embedded in national institutions, with which they will be bonding and identifying—much as Boomers bonded and identified with the culture during the 1970s.

On campus, as in other youth environs, the Oh-Teens will be more a decade of consolidation than change. Millennials will still dominate university life, but their influence will no longer be new. In the pop culture, they will overwhelm the residue of Gen-X influence. Mature Millennial stars will emerge, many of them Latin and Asian, who will reflect a more mature and domesticated concept of masculinity and femininity than did the first batch of (Oh-Oh-era) Millennial stars.

The Oh-Teens will be the first of the Millennials' two main family-forming decades. While they have babies, they will begin to make their mark on schools and community life. As always, their priorities will land right atop the public agenda. They will expect government to be *pro-parent*, not merely pro-child. They will evaluate institutions on the basis of how well they enhance their ability to fulfill their roles as parents, to raise children, and to provide for their households. Institutions seen as favorable to family life will be reinvigorated; those seen as harmful, challenged. The very definition of marriage may be reinforced with new forms of certification. Family-making will become more popular and better facilitated by public policy. Men and women will together create a more conformist peer culture, with new and diverging standards and

You're the past, I'm the future, the future
Get away it's my time to shine
— Brandy, "The Boy Is Mine"

We're told we will produce a generation . . . who will expect the world to be as delighted with them as we are. And even as we laugh at the knock-knock jokes and exclaim over the refrigerator drawings, we secretly fear the same thing. —Joan Ryan,
San Francisco Chronicle

Things changed so fast between my mother's generation and mine, and you wonder, will things change that fast again? —Gen Xer mom

We all have that dream to make it to the top
When we do we know we're never gonna stop —Cleopatra,
"Cleopatra's Theme"

Whatever the Millennials touch, whether good or bad, it all turns to gold. . . . Once any band of Millennials conforms with each other, they end up with that power to make everything work. From gangs to sports to politics, Millennials are going to strengthen almost every different element in American society.
—Josh Braxon

Happiness is just around the corner.
—Vengaboys, "We Like To Party!"

expectations for each sex. As this happens, feminist ideas of the 1970s (or even 1990s) will feel outmoded—displeasing many aging Boomers and Silent.

Racial and ethnic divisions will be supplanted by a new sense of societal cohesion. Transracial marriages and multiracial children will be more common, with less attention paid to the cultural differences once associated with various races and ethnic groups. As the browning of America reaches critical mass, diverse Latin, Asian, African, and Arab elements will mix into an increasingly pureed "melting pot."

In the workplace, new gender walls will begin rising. Health care, in particular, may become a bastion for Millennial females, much as teaching did for women in the G.I. Generation—with surgeons providing a male outpost much as math and science teachers once did for male G.I.s. To the emerging generational ethos, such a new arrangement could make total sense. Similar bastions may arise within law, journalism, the ministry, and the arts. Politics could become a gender battleground, as young women who were the circa-2000 high school student-body presidents confront male peers who are increasingly ambitious in that sphere of life.

By the Time You're 30, What Do You Expect to Earn?

Median answer: $75,000
Actual median earnings of 30-year-olds in 1999: $27,000

—survey of teens, in USA Today Weekend *(May 2, 1999)*

A new middle class will emerge. With thirtyish Millennials filling the lesser-paid ranks, a distinctly modern form of unionism could resurrect class-consciousness, culminating in political class warfare and demands for higher taxes on rich Gen-X tycoons and reduced benefits for affluent old Boomers, whose old-age entitlements might be resented by Gen Xers and Millennials alike. With the disappearance of the generations to whom the original Social Security and Medicare "promises" were made, Millennials may feel free to press for a "new new deal" that would reduce payouts to Boomers and Gen Xers in return for better long-term treatment of Millennials, who by then will embody America's hopes for its national future.

THE OH-TWENTIES

Here's the Millennial timetable. The first Millennials will reach age 40 in 2022. Their officers will begin retiring from the military. They will dominate the teaching profession early in the decade and school boards and juries by late in the decade. They will comprise roughly 20 percent of national leaders by 2025. Still giving birth in large numbers, Millennials will begin to control the child's world for a new generation of babies that start arriving in the Oh-Twenties. Millennials will be at their peak of cultural influence, as producers, writers, and performers of the pop culture for their successors in youth.

Here's what this timetable will mean for America. On the brink of midlife, first-wave Millennials will combine confidence, energy, and conformism to fashion a new era of political vigor and family-friendly "normalcy." Little social argument will be tolerated. By now, the browning of America will be accepted as fact—accompanied, perhaps, by new restrictions on further immigration. When people want to attack a group, they'll put their criticism in terms of politics and economics, quite unlike the moral and cultural wedge issues of the late twentieth century. Income and class disparities will narrow, as Millennial unionism and corporatism rise in power.

Millennials will aggressively apply their stamp to every aspect of American life. In the culture, they will clean up the elder "mistakes" of their youth era, in ways that might today seem authoritarian and intensely anti-individual. In the workplace, they will add stress-reducing structures to settle expectations, even at the cost of innovation. In technology, they will launch big projects to improve people's daily lives.

Late in the decade, Millennials will start shaping a new child generation—as voters and educators, not just as parents. Here they will be inclined to encourage personal qualities not seen, and widely missed, in the orderly social and cultural environment they have created. They will correct what they will consider the Boomers' stress-inducing parenting "mistakes" by imposing less structure and allowing more freedom. Long

How we are is gonna change
We'll make this world a better place
—*Cleopatra, "Life Ain't Easy"*

I'm going to law school to become a judge. Somebody has to clean up the streets. —*Christen Sutton, 11*

We are the new age, the age of electronics, of better technology and medicine. —*Loc Dao, 16*

In the next twenty years, I hope to develop a way to regenerate the part of the brain that is dead after a stroke.
—*Curry Cheek, 14*

Why did they make [the universe], if we can't go any farther than that?

Lorenzo Hernandez, 10,
on why human exploration
should not stop at the moon

skeptical of the heavily protective and behavioral Gen-X parenting style, Millennial parents and voters will now be in the position to correct it. In schools, they will ease up on the pressure throttle, in an effort to make learning more fun and children more creative.

By decade's end, Millennials will be more robustly involved with American political and economic institutions than Boomers were in the late '80s or Gen Xers in the late Oh-Ohs. Asserting itself with great fanfare, a fresh-faced "power elite" will begin to challenge the aging Gen Xer entrepreneurial elite, who might be willing to praise their juniors as a group while questioning their mettle as individuals. Millennials will herald a modern technocratic vision of progress, whose lofty goals will require long-term civic action and a costly new infrastructure.

The Oh-Twenties will be the decade during which a large number of Boomers begin to pass away, leaving behind nettlesome wills and artifacts of "wisdom" that will be ineffably precious to them but of little use to Millennials, who by now will have their own robust agenda.

THE OH-THIRTIES

Here's the Millennial timetable. The eldest Millennials will reach age 50 in 2032. Their generation will come to include a majority of state governors and members of Congress, and will produce its first serious presidential candidate. This will be the Millennials' peak decade for buying houses, acquiring debt, and raising children. Their leading wave will pour into business leadership positions. They will provide the leading producers, but no longer the writers or performers, of the pop culture for the younger generation.

Here's what this timetable will mean for America. The Oh-Thirties will be the Millennials' decade of civic belonging—when "normalcy" moves beyond schools and families into all elements of daily life. By now, they will be taking the cutting-edge basic research of the late twentieth century and applying it to large-scale public-private projects. The Oh-Thirties will become an orderly decade of capital broadening, much as the '90s will then be remembered as a chaotic decade of capital deepening. Millennials will lay costly new infrastructures, build big things, and develop other grand plans to make life still better. New public devices that provide collective security against risks—economic, social, global—will be a major goal for midlife Millennials.

Issues involving children and schools will remain high on the agenda, but with the focus shifting to how strong public institutions can make up for weak parental convictions, rather than the other way around. Millennial voters will approve gleaming new schools and community facilities, embodying new materials and technologies. Millennial politicians will chafe at any resistance they encounter from what remains of the Gen-X political leadership, and will look forward to the time when they are fully in charge.

The Oh-Thirties will mark the apex of Millennial influence on community and cultural life. The family-oriented, peer-approved gender-role divisions that felt fresh to Millennials in the Oh-Teens, back when the largest number of them were getting married, will now feel routinized, on autopilot, seeding as-yet unexpressed misgivings in younger people. To the snickers of youth, Millennials may work hard to disavow, conceal, or even electronically delete whatever they perceive was excessively vulgar or violent in the cultural artifacts of their youth. And as Boomers pass on, the fulsome encomia offered to honored Aquarians by their middle-aged Millennial children may prompt guffaws from some sixtyish Gen Xers.

THE OH-FORTIES

Here's the Millennial timetable. The first Millennials will reach age 60 in 2042. Their leading edge will have a firm grip on the White House, corporate America, and lower-court judgeships, and will be making inroads into the Supreme Court. This will be the Millennials' peak decade for income and college-tuition payments. They will start becoming grandparents. They will contribute little to the pop culture, and their tastes will be largely ignored by others. In 2047, the eldest Millennials will reach 65, what in the late twentieth century was considered the "normal" retirement age.

Here's what this timetable will mean for America. With Gen Xers no longer in the way, the Millennial elite will feel the hubris of their previous achievements—and consider themselves ready at last to give America the grand overhaul they've always dreamed about. Public action will become a vehicle for every kind of new social aspiration, and public facilities will

This is a revolution in waiting. This generation will redefine society in the twenty-first century just as baby boomers shaped social, political and economic changes in the last half of the twentieth century.

—Gerald Celente,
Trends Research Institute

[Today's teens] give me the greatest hope for newspapers because they have the attributes of a 60-year-old, and 60-year-olds are our greatest newspaper readers.   —Mark Smith,
Northwestern University

Since we are leading the world into a new millennium, society is giving us a chance and a good rep. I think we will prove them right and take the world politically, economically, and socially to new levels.   —Sarah Boone, 17

acquire unprecedented mass and grandeur. But by now, Millennials will be pushing some of their projects a bit too far to suit younger generations. On the elder side of the first real generation gap they will ever have experienced, Millennials will hear themselves judged and denounced by their own coming-of-age children. They will remember having gotten along much better with their own parents, way back when.

THE OH-FIFTIES

Here's the Millennial timetable. The first Millennials will reach age 70 in 2052. This generation will hold presidential power through the decade, and reach its peak of CEOs early in the decade, but will gradually lose its majority of national leaders and corporate board members. This will be the Millennials' decade of highest net worth, though their incomes will be declining. They will attain a majority on the U.S. Supreme Court. The later-born ('90s baby) Millennials will start to eclipse the earlier-born. By now, this generation will be largely irrelevant to the culture.

Here's what this timetable will mean for America. Now on the far side of a values divide from younger people, Millennials will find their optimism tested more sorely than ever before. They will be upset by a decline in community spirit. Their political and economic acumen will be taken for granted by younger people with more cultural and spiritual interests. Aging Millennials will look upon the quantitative improvements wrought in their lifetime as benchmarks toward national progress—and will not be pleased when their children refuse to follow their lead.

THE OH-SIXTIES AND BEYOND

Here's the Millennial timetable. The first Millennials will reach age 80 in 2062, 90 in 2072, and 100 in 2082. The last Millennial president will be ousted. While still holding a firm grip on the judiciary, Millennials will see their share of national leaders falling from 20 percent in the middle Oh-Sixties to around 5 percent by the late Oh-Seventies. They will lose their Supreme Court primacy sometime in the 2070s, but their last justice may stick around until the Oh-Nineties. The last prominent Millennial leader could make it to the turn of the next century. Unless major advances are made against human senescence, Millennials will require long-term elder care from the Oh-Seventies through the Oh-Nineties. Barring an unforeseen lengthening of the human life cycle—which this generation of scientists may work mightily to extend—the last Millennials will die sometime around 2120.

Here's what this timetable will mean for America. In old age, as always, the needs of Millennials will remain a public priority. They will make major demands from younger generations, and will not be denied by their middle-aged children, who will feel inferior to their parents in lifelong civic contributions. Around the Oh-Seventies, old Millennials will receive rewards and honors. As they depart, their lifelong virtues (optimism, community spirit, teamwork) will be newly missed, creating a void that a new generation of children, born around the Oh-Sixties, can start to fill.

Part of a Larger Story

One should stop here and ask: What will Millennials have done to deserve these rewards and honors? Why will younger people consider them so worthy? Has something larger than this narrative been going on in the world?

You can easily read all the above in the context of an end-of-history society—a place in which all that Millennials will do is grow up, get married, have children, make a few movies, sing a few songs, earn some money, hold high office uneventfully, retire, and die. This assumes seven more decades like the 1990s, without the kinds of critical events that shake societies from time to time and cause major turns in the course of events.

But history never runs so smoothly, certainly not for a generation loaded with as much potential economic and political power as this one. If, by contrast, you assume that the interaction of history and generations will someday produce great discontinuities—that is, extraordinary challenges, dangers, urgencies, and triumphs—you can read the decade narratives as simply one aspect of a far more meaningful story. On top of this chronology, let's lay one of history's great rites of passage, within America's borders or even around the world. Suppose there is a major war or economic disaster. Picture how such a crisis might lend dimensionality, motivation, adrenaline, and drama to all aforementioned trends, giving them shape and texture, motivation and character, adding guideposts and touchstones not just for Millennials, but for all generations alive at the time.

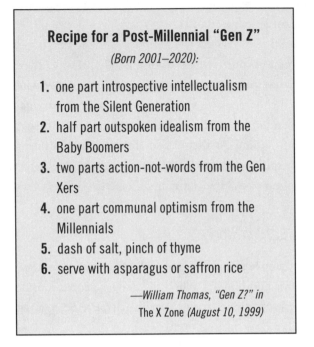

Recipe for a Post-Millennial "Gen Z"
(Born 2001–2020):

1. one part introspective intellectualism from the Silent Generation
2. half part outspoken idealism from the Baby Boomers
3. two parts action-not-words from the Gen Xers
4. one part communal optimism from the Millennials
5. dash of salt, pinch of thyme
6. serve with asparagus or saffron rice

—William Thomas, "Gen Z?" in
The X Zone *(August 10, 1999)*

Here is where history reveals a very important lesson for Millennials. Go back through time, and once every long human life—roughly every eighty to one hundred years—you can find another American generation that started life much as today's teens and children have. Each of these ancestral generations encountered a crisis, an enormous bend-point in history, while coming of age as adults. The timing hasn't been exact, but has varied by less than a decade.

Were these mere coincidences? Historical accidents? *No.* These crises arose because the persona of the rising generation, and the personae of the generations that preceded them, provoked the society to respond in a more determined fashion to the sparks of history.

Before turning to this question about a Millennial crisis, let's take a step back in time, to learn about four ancestral generations whose early life-cycle stories resembled that of the Millennials to date.

CHAPTER FIFTEEN

Hero Generations in History

Hero Generations in History
Hero Generations in History

His battery is dead. But his memory lives on.
—*CHIP HAZARD, in* Small Soldiers

"**We** were a special generation, and we *were* America," historian William Manchester reminisced of his World War II–fighting agemates. "You get used to that." And they did. "Ours was the best generation," Gene Shuford recalled of his college generation of the late 1920s. "Underneath we really thought we were all right. . . ." And, as their lifetimes demonstrated, they were.

The G.I. Generation (alias the "World War II Generation" or, to Manchester, the "Swing Generation") cut trails and built dams during the Great Depression, landed on beachheads in Normandy and Iwo Jima, built Levittowns, conquered polio, built gleaming suburbs and interstate highways, landed astronauts on the moon, and held the White House for a record thirty-two years.

That's what they *did,* but equally important is how they were *perceived:* as "All-American" youths even back in the 1920s (then known among older people as a "Decade of Bad Manners"); as George Marshall's

Newspapers shout, "A new style is brewing!" . . .

It's all just a little bit of history repeating —*Propellerheads, "History Repeating"*

"best damn kids in the world" who conquered more lands and seas than any generation dating back to Alexander the Great; as the "Best and Brightest" who believed in an "Establishment" and founded a "Great Society"; as America's first self-proclaimed "senior citizens"; and, in their decade of farewell, as the peer group Tom Brokaw admiringly calls "The Greatest Generation." Birth to death, the G.I.s have been the most praised and rewarded generation of their century.

Collectively, the G.I.s comprise a "Hero" archetype, the kind of generation that does great deeds, constructs nations and empires, and is afterward honored in memory and storied in myth.

What did America do to create such a generation? How did the members of such a generation begin life? What was their childhood era like, and how were they perceived as children? Who were the older generations, and what were they like as parents?

When you strip away the modern trappings of the present day, you can see how the G.I.s, through the early 1920s, bore much in common with Millennials up to now. From birth, they were seen as a special generation—protected from harm, pressured to behave, prodded to achieve. They were born after a raucous era that historians liken to the 1960s, and grew up in times historians liken to now. They followed a (Lost) generation that resembled Gen Xers, and were shaped by a middle-aged (Missionary) generation of Boomer-like culture warriors.

Nor is it just the G.I.s who resemble Millennials, as shown in the list of American generations on page 327.

Dating back at least as far as the seventeenth century, you can find a hero generation once every long human lifetime: the Glorious, Republican, Progressive, and G.I. Generations. With one exception, these occur once every four generations. All but one can be classified as following the hero archetype from birth through old age. The Progressives, stunted by the trauma of Civil War before they could fully come of age, had a hero-type childhood but never acquired the same young-adult mantle, midlife hubris, or late-in-life honor.

Within each of these generations' childhood eras, you can see a pattern resembling the Millennial experience:

>> *A hero generation arrives just after an era of societywide upheaval in values and culture that many historians call a "spir-*

GENERATION*	BIRTH YEARS	FAMOUS MAN	FAMOUS WOMAN
Puritan	1588–1617	John Winthrop	Anne Hutchinson
Cavalier	1618–1647	Nathaniel Bacon	Mary Dyer
Glorious	1648–1673	Cotton Mather	Hannah Dustin
Enlightenment	1674–1700	Peter Zenger	Mary Musgrove
Awakening	1701–1723	Benjamin Franklin	Eliza Pinckney
Liberty	1724–1741	George Washington	Mercy Warren
Republican	1742–1766	Thomas Jefferson	Abigail Adams
Compromise	1767–1791	Andrew Jackson	Dolley Madison
Transcendental	1792–1821	Abraham Lincoln	Susan B. Anthony
Gilded	1822–1842	Ulysses S. Grant	Louisa May Alcott
Progressive	1843–1859	Woodrow Wilson	Mary Cassatt
Missionary	1860–1882	Franklin Roosevelt	Emma Goldman
Lost	1883–1900	Dwight Eisenhower	Dorothy Parker
G.I.	1901–1924	John Kennedy	Clare Boothe Luce
Silent	1925–1942	Colin Powell	Gloria Steinem
Boom	1943–1960	Steven Spielberg	Oprah Winfrey
X	1961–1981	Michael Dell	Jodie Foster
Millennial	1982–	Frankie Muniz	Mandy Moore

*hero generations shaded

itual awakening" and passes through childhood during a time of decaying civic habits, ebbing institutional trust, and resurgent individualism.

>> *A hero generation directly follows a youth generation widely deemed to be disappointing, reacts against the older "postwar" generation that fomented the spiritual awakening as young adults—and fills a void left by the passing of an elder generation known for civic purpose and teamwork.*

RUSSELL: *I'll promise you one thing. I'll never take any unnecessary measures. I won't try to be a hero.*

CLAIRE: *Too late. You already are a hero.* —**Promised Land**

>> *A hero generation, early in life, becomes the target of passionate adult efforts to encircle and protect the childhood world, to promote child achievement, and to attach a new sense of destiny to youth—to which it responds by meeting and beating adult expectations.*

Let's see how these four generations fit this pattern.

The Rise of the G.I. Generation

The first children of the twentieth century came along right after a "mauve decade" (the 1890s) that has been widely likened to the 1960s and its aftermath. Often termed the "Third Great Awakening," the end of the nineteenth century was a time of labor radicalism, prairie populism, budding feminism, and Bible Belt fundamentalism. Cities were immigrant cauldrons. Kids wandered the streets, crime and drug abuse were skyrocketing, and family life felt unsettled, even as exciting new vaudeville and "tin pan alley" cultural currents and "social gospel" value systems (the origin of the New Deal) swept through clubs, campuses, and chautauquas.

The Progressive-Era presidencies of Theodore Roosevelt and Howard Taft, during which the social passions peaked and began to calm, was an opportune time for children to be born. Several scholars have suggested that the turn of the last century marked what historian Leonard Cain calls a "generational watershed" and that the children born just after 1900 were far more "favored" than those born before—in families, schools, and the economy.

Who were the less-favored ones? The kids of the Lost Generation (born 1883–1900), who had grown up fast and hard amid gangs, a streetcorner "newsie" culture, and adult-approved narcotics. Lost kids were unusually suicide- and crime-prone, prompting a tenfold increase in the number of magazine articles on "juvenile delinquency." John Carter wrote of that era's "unregenerate youth." Thomas Wolfe described his child peers as having grown up "without innocence, born old and stale and dull and empty, . . . suckled on darkness, and weaned on violence and noise." "At 17, we were disillusioned and weary," wrote Malcolm Cowley, pointing

"WHAT'S *THIS* THING FOR ?..."

out the contrast between his Lost peers and the "brilliant college graduates" who came along in their wake.

Further up the age ladder, the G.I.'s child world was dominated by middle-aged Missionaries, the post–Civil War generation that had come of age with campus rebellions, labor riots, and waves of immigration. While the first G.I. children were born, Missionaries were still deep into their "muckraking" phase. By the time the last G.I.s were born, that older generation had transformed the temperance movement into the more zealous Prohibition. As the 1920s wore on, against the backdrop of a famous bull market, they deported radical aliens, pursued an antisex Code of Decency, launched "vice squads" against bootleggers, and more. The younger Lost satirized them as "Babbitts" or "Tired Radicals," while the Missionary Cornelia Comer lashed back at the "culte de moi" of young adults who were "painfully commercialized even in their school days." In a "Letter to the Rising Generation" in the *Atlantic,* Comer asked,

Baseball hats, beware. A new hat has been tossed into the ring, one that captures the flavor of the 1920's flapper's cloche. . . . These inexpensive, crushable, machine-washable fabric hats are major accessories for young New Yorkers this summer. —**The New York Times**

"What excuse have you, anyhow, for turning out flimsy, shallow, amusement-seeking creatures?" Meanwhile, the old "bloody shirt" veterans of the Civil War were dying off, and Lost doughboys and barnstormers and rumrunners had not the slightest prospect of taking their place in the pantheon of civic heroes.

Amid this carnivalia, Missionary parents were determined to shape the new child generation into something special and good. In 1904, muckraker John Spargo's *The Bitter Cry of the Children* augured the determination of parents and other adults to join forces and seal off the child's world from urban danger and adult vice. Adults were adamant that their offspring grow up as "clean-cut" as the new child image being created for them. From *Pollyanna* to *Little Orphan Annie,* popular literature idealized children who were modest, cheerful, helpful, and deferential to adults. The new role of a child was to be "seen and not heard." G.I.s became the first boys and girls whose pin money came from "allowances" for good behavior (then a new concept), not from marketplace earnings.

As the *Literary Digest* summoned "a reassertion of parental authority," the dominant child-nurturing style was likened to the manner of training dogs: firm repetition, clear rewards, selective use of affection. The family of the 1920s, according to a contemporary source, "maintain[ed] higher standards that test character more severely." Families were small, by the standards of the day, and newly stable. This became the first generation in U.S. history in which a majority reached age 15 without suffering the loss of a parent or sibling.

Applying a resolute grip of adult authority that grew tighter with each advancing decade, Missionary parents injected what one historian described as "a new, explicit insistence on conformity into child life." The first Boy Scouts, Girl Scouts, Camp Fire Girls, and 4-H Clubs redirected the "gang instinct" to useful purpose. Missionaries liked to see their G.I. kids in military-style uniforms. They invented the summer camp tradition of sending kids on woodsy escapes from a city life thought to be immoral and unhealthy for children. They put kids to work building trails, collecting firewood, and doing other tasks that developed group pride, helped others, and demonstrated respect for adults.

Government programs for kids expanded, even in the libertarian 1920s—an era when public programs for adults atrophied. State pensions for widows with kids were instituted in nearly every state between 1911 and 1919. A much-heralded White House Conference on Children in 1909 led to the creation of the U.S. Children's Bureau in 1912, which paved the way for the enactment in 1921 of the first federal health program in America—targeting only kids.

A new child-nutrition movement demanded more "antiseptic" child environments, vitamin-rich diets, and antihookworm campaigns. The milk station movement culminated in widespread pasteurization, while Little Mothers' Leagues advised parents, "Don't give the baby beer to drink." Thanks to the "protective food" movement, capital investment in food processing grew faster than that of any other industry between 1914 and 1929—and infant and child mortality fell by 50 percent. (Still today, G.I. senior citizens are likely to think that packaged foods are better.) The Harrison Act targeted hard drugs, and Prohibition succeeded both in suppressing parental alcoholism and in pushing alcohol away from the child's world. As a consequence, these new children grew up as the brawny, world-moving youths shown in WPA murals, averaging a full inch taller than the prior generation. Later, this better childhood health would translate into an extraordinary 20 percent increase in life expectancy between the Lost and the G.I.s.

From the start, the new kids were treated as a form of public property, off limits to private exploitation. Businesses that had once hired children with impunity now found themselves facing public outcry, even legal punishment. In the 1920s, cash registers replaced cash boys, and pneumatic tubes and telephones replaced child messengers. With news delivery, what children had once done as streetcorner entrepreneurs they now did on bicycles under strict adult supervision. The child labor rate fell by half for boys, by one-fourth for girls, marking the largest single-generation decline ever.

Public education instilled skills of productive citizenship, with a new emphasis on "vocational" education (home economics for girls, industrial education for boys). For the first time ever in America, more teens were in class than out, making school an important socializing force. Thus arose the golden era of the high school, well captured in the later teen movie musicals starring Mickey Rooney and Judy Garland. The ethos: Work hard, play by the rules, and everybody shares in the reward.

Yeah see you once again
Yeah everybody swing

—Backstreet Boys,
"I Wanna Be With You"

Through all American history, G.I.s were the child beneficiaries of by far the largest one-generation jump in educational achievement. Over the span of this one generation, the average length of schooling rose from the ninth-grade level to the twelfth, the share of 20-year-olds attending college tripled, and math and science aptitudes rose sharply. It wasn't long before they would be helping to design those gleaming Oz-like towers featured in the 1939 World's Fair, and not long after that before they would be building them.

In an early twentieth century world in which one adult in four was a first-generation immigrant, this new child generation was overwhelmingly native born—and was prevented from acquiring as many foreign-born peers by the federal enactment of strict immigration controls in the early 1920s. The Lost Generation ended up 18 percent immigrant, the G.I. Generation only 11 percent. Commonly, children lived in relatively homogeneous ethnic neighborhoods, often the second address of an immigrant family. Where their parents had been distinctly Italian (or Slavic, or Jewish), these second-generation kids added the suffix and became Italian or Slavic or Jewish Americans, blending in with a society now more melting pot than polyglot.

Upon reaching adolescence, the new youths began policing themselves. In an increasingly standardized youth culture, teens watched the same movies and listened to the same radio songs. As historian Paula Fass explains, young G.I.s constructed the first modern "peer society"—a harmonious community of group-enforced virtue. Having "fine friends" and engaging in "fair play" was essential to popularity. Youths began taking pride in their ability to "make the best better," to use the words of the 4-H Club motto. By the mid-1920s, the very word *kid* shifted in meaning from a word of elder criticism to one of praise.

When the first G.I.s reached college, they began packing the Rose Bowl and other huge new stadia in cheerful youth masses unlike anything ever before seen. They set to work imposing new social mores that pressured collegians to stay within the bounds of the normal. Their fraternities and sororities administered a ritual of "rating and dating" (understood lists of "dos and don'ts") to control the libido. Couples were expected to dance close, but student organizations policed "extreme dancing." Violators got a card, and repeat offenders could be asked to leave. Holding hands on the first date, kissing on the second, petting later. Being too forward or too shy brought embarrassment from peers.

College drinking stayed within new rules established and enforced by collegians themselves, with drunkenness and "teetotaling" both frowned upon. Smoking, previously considered a questionable habit, was cleaned up and linked to sociability, progress, and good work habits. The term *jazz*, stripped of its sexual connotation, came to include a jaunty, sanitized, mainstream G.I. sound that blasted new "big bands" to fame.

The New York Times described these new youths as "gorgeously emancipated" from Lost Generation badness, and "entirely subservient to conservative public opinion." The president of Williams College summed them up as "nice boys." The Lost writer and critic Joseph Wood Krutch chided them as "not rebellious, or cynical, or even melancholy. They do what they are told, believe what they are told, and hope for the best." College kids increasingly became what a midwestern college newspaper labeled "a political generation" guided by "facts, rather than romantic fallacies." Malcolm Cowley remarked how they "pictured a future to which everyone would be made secure by collective planning and social discipline"—what football coach Knute Rockne popularly described as "causes bigger than ourselves."

The generation that produced the first Miss America also produced the first "All-American hero." Dutifully modest, young Charles Lindbergh startled the adult world in 1927 by turning down the lucrative movie offers that followed his ticker-tape homecoming. Along with the young cartoonist Walt Disney, Lindbergh was definitely setting a trend. From this first wave (the early Oh-Oh babies) to a later last wave (the early Oh-Twenties babies, such as George Bush and Bob Dole), G.I. youth produced, cohort by cohort, progressively lower rates of suicide and crime, higher academic aptitudes, and enormous jumps in educational achievement.

By the time Franklin Roosevelt became president, he summarized common knowledge when he remarked that "the very objectives of young people have changed," away from "the dream of the golden ladder—each individual for himself" and toward the dream of "a broad highway on which thousands of your fellow men and women are advancing with you."

One of my husband's former coworkers has a 13-year-old son who refuses to watch TV or go out and play until he has all of his homework done. His mother couldn't afford to buy him a computer, so he has collected aluminum cans over the last two years and now has enough to buy one himself. Get the job done. Duty before pleasure. Hard work has rewards. All the same kind of tenets the old World War II–winning G.I.s had. —**Lis Libengood**

War stories are interesting to me. I find myself studying my history textbooks reading up on wars, and reading about patriotism. —**Robert Reed, 17**

Upon coming fully of age as adults, during the Great Depression and World War II, the G.I. Generation:

>> *repudiated the cynicism and "culte de moi" recently displayed by their next-elders, and offered a fresh-faced optimism and civic spirit to a nation hit by back-to-back crises,*

>> *mobilized muscular CCC workers and union organizers to attain a "social gospel" and a "higher" civilization that an aging generation of moralists could envision but could not bring about themselves, and*

>> *as conquerors of seas and continents, and masters of the power of the atom, stepped into the hero's role vacated by the last Civil War veterans.*

One frequently hears parallels drawn between America today and the America of the "Roaring Twenties"—the booming stock market and widening gap between rich and poor, the rampant commercialism and breakthrough innovation, the frenetic pace of personal life and the shrinking role of government, the showbiz glitz and celebrity trials and culture wars, the cynical "you don't say?" and "yeah, whatever" attitudes. Yet the most striking similarity is in the collective personae of the people in each age bracket then and now—especially youth. Beneath all the "wonderful nonsense" of the '20s, all the wacky dances and out-of-control adults, it's easy to overlook the collegial, dedicated, hopeful generation of young people poised to make a great mark on future events. They just don't seem part of that decade. But they were. That's when America was just starting to notice them.

Thanks to modern medicine, G.I. elders have remained alive and active longer, in the eyes of children born sixty or more years after them, than any prior generation of heroes. And Millennials afford them a special place of honor—admiring them, according to many polls (including our Class of 2000 Survey), more than any other generation they know. Today's teens respect the G.I. capacity for embarking on big projects, for building big things, for making the family-friendly culture of Nick at

Night, for shouldering big family responsibilities without complaint. "I am proud of my grandfathers, because they fought in World War II and kept the U.S. safe," wrote a 13-year-old Nashville middle schooler in an on-line school project, "and I am proud of my grandmothers, because they kept the economy running." As Millennials open their eyes at today's adult world, they miss what the G.I.s had to offer. "Pullin' together in times of need, that'd always been Big Mama's job," said Shorty, the Millennial child of the extended family in the film *Soul Food*. "But who was gonna do it now that she was gone?"

Shorty's question is all too real. This Millennial affinity for G.I.s isn't just a matter of grandchild's affection, though surely there is some of that, too, but also of a realization that today's seniors are vacating a role that's *available* to be filled, that *needs* to be filled, and that isn't about to be filled by anyone else.

Now let's look at other ancestral generations upon whom these same "special child" dynamics were at work.

The Rise of Earlier Hero Generations

THE PROGRESSIVE GENERATION (BORN 1843–1859)

In 1859, in an article entitled "The Murder of the Innocents," the *Atlantic* magazine reported children going insane or, in one case, dying "from sheer overwork and raving of algebra." These kids arrived just after the great causes of the 1830s and early '40s—communes, religious fads, transcendentalism, feminism—had passed, leaving behind them a generation of young adults (the Gilded Generation) notorious for their wildness, truancy, and contempt for manners. Now adults were cracking down on the younger kids in an effort to make up for lost time.

Looking up the age ladder, these children saw adventuresome if uncultured young adults who were either fast becoming rich or wasting their lives trying. Further up, they could see and hear opinionated midlifers waging passionate arguments that would soon break the nation apart. Among themselves, kids hunkered down and did their best to fit in.

In the 1850s, Americans tightened the strings around these new children. At the time, the adult world was gripped with gold fever,

A parent called me and said, "Help me, my son loves history. What good will that do him? Try to get him into math or sciences." —Tom Rowland, sociology teacher

Whitmanesque self-worship, expanding Catholic (Irish and German) immigrant influence, "bleeding Kansas" sectionalism and "almighty dollar" commercialism. The *Atlantic* author bemoaned how "little ones begin, in their very infancy, the race of desperate ambition which has, we admit, exhausted prematurely the lives of their parents." Families were being dislocated by rapid industrial change, and many of the new jobs were in frontier regions accessible only by dangerous journey. Kids were becoming more class-conscious in their social groupings, more aware than before of the diverging occupational and income situations of parents.

Much like the nightly circle of prairie schooners on the Oregon Trail, families and community institutions established new barriers to separate the young from these threats, reflecting what historian Joseph Kett called "the desire of middle-class Americans to seal their lives off from the howling storm outside." Parental-advice books stressed nurture over nature, family togetherness over the growing adult trends toward social

"SAY ULYSSES, MAYBE WE OUGHT TO GET BACK IN THE TIME MACHINE AND DO IT THE OLD WAY!"

atomism. In his influential 1842 parenting guide, *Christian Nurture,* Horace Bushnell described children as "formless lumps," equally capable of good or evil, always in need of careful guidance within the "organic unity of the family."

Schools imposed the first compulsory attendance laws and expanded the use of report cards. Teachers valued punctuality, orderliness, and duty over creativity. Having earlier complained about the precocity and ill manners of America's (Gilded Generation) kids, foreign observers now began noticing how the new batch was more compliant and group-oriented. A French visitor remarked how "the most absolute obedience and the most rigid discipline prevail in all American schools." *McGuffey*-style recitations and choral singing became popular in schools. "A hundred wills move at once simultaneously," with "an accuracy that was really amazing," remarked a visitor who watched "hundreds of quite young children going through the same evolutions."

A man who worked with kids remarked how, on the eve of the Civil War, they were expected "to carry from the cradle to the grave an unblemished name, with unblemished morals." Historian Kett noted how "the old idea that youth was a time for sowing wild oats, that an excess of prohibitions in youth merely produced an erratic adult, had no place in the thought of mid-century moralists." "I don't regret a single 'excess' of my responsive youth," Henry James later wrote, his only "regret" resting in "certain occasions and possibilities I didn't embrace."

Among the "occasions and possibilities" these kids would not embrace was the chance to become a full-fledged hero generation. The Civil War intruded too early and too harshly for that. Some young Progressives fought and died alongside a mostly older soldier population, but their more typical memory was being cloistered at home by fearful mothers in schools that, to one foreigner, became "centres of the most intense patriotism."

Upon coming of age, during the Civil War and Reconstruction, this generation:

>> *helped tame the instincts of their more freewheeling next-elders, with whom they constructed a postwar "Victorian High" of industrial progress and stable families,*

SIMBA: *That's not my father, that's just my reflection.*

RAFIKI: *No, look harder. You see? He lives in you!* —**The Lion King**

>> *eased America away from the principled passions of the genera-
tion that had fomented the Civil War, and*

>> *systematized the civic achievements of the now-deceased genera-
tion that had founded the Republic.*

Though stunted as heroes—and afterward overshadowed, in the
world of politics, by the "bloody shirts" of the next-elder Gilded Generation—the Progressive Generation did retain a powerful civic instinct.
Through the rest of the nineteenth century, they emerged as America's
first Ph.D.s, civil servants, and professional politicians. They entered the
twentieth century as potent institution builders, bureaucratizers, and
time-and-motion analysts. Late in life, they orchestrated the emergence
of a modern, urbanizing, civilizing nation—now known as "Progressive
Era" America.

THE REPUBLICAN GENERATION (BORN 1742–1766)

For the greatest heroes in U.S. history, one must reach further back in
time to the generation whose last members (Albert Gallatin, John Jacob
Astor, "Uncle Sam" Wilson) were dying just as the Progressives were
being born. The Republican Generation of Jefferson, Hamilton, and
Madison is revered to this day for winning the Revolution as foot soldiers, crafting the Declaration and Constitution as young adults, and
expanding the new nation's reach and securing its institutions as leaders.

They were born and raised in the aftermath of the Great Awakening,
the spiritual revival that spread through the colonies in the 1730s and
early '40s, pitting young believers in faith against elder defenders of
works and leaving social unrest, broken communities, and slave revolts in
its wake. That awakening set the stage for their own youth era, in which a
restless individualism gripped the colonies. Immigration and geographic
mobility quickened. The economy boomed. A newly vigorous British
empire undertook elaborate campaigns against the French. With "liberty" the new catchword, American provincials began to worry that the
advance of their civilization came at the cost of financial debt, political
corruption, and social decadence.

Looking up the age ladder, the young Republicans noticed just above them wild and cynical young adults (the Liberty Generation), whose penchant for risk, adventure, spending, and indigence shocked older people. They had grown up, declared prominent clerics, as replete with "luxury, idleness, debauchery," as children "out of Christ . . . infinitely more hateful than vipers." Now young adults, these (heavily immigrant) privateers and dandies stood accused by elders of being an "evil and adulterous generation," known for drinking, rioting, and mayhem. Further up the ladder, Republican children could discern aging spiritualists and ripening ideologues who inveighed frequently against the tenor of the age. When they reached midlife, the former youth leaders of the Great Awakening demanded that a new and better child generation be raised. By now, the last colonial generation known for civic deed-doing, elders shaped by the Glorious Revolution of 1689, were nearly all gone—and missed.

From the very beginning, historian Charles Royster remarks, "the revolutionary generation knew that they would stand above all their descendants." From adolescence forward, Republican youths did indeed feel like a founding generation. "'Tis but the morning of the world for us," declared Hugh Henry Brackenridge as a Princeton student in the early 1770s. Only one in six was born outside the colonies—by far the smallest proportion to that point in history—and only a relative handful were educated beyond colonial shores.

Historians of colonial childhood have noticed a profound change in the tone of child-rearing beginning around midcentury. The earlier crop of kids had been raised with Hogarthian neglect. The new crop of kids, every clergyman or novelist or diarist insisted, must be spared from harm and vice, taught the difference between right and wrong, and raised to be smart and confident, the dutiful servants to a dawning republic of virtue. In 1753, eager to prevent "horrid profaneness" and to encourage "a spirit of loyalty in the youth of the town," the Massachusetts colonial assembly cracked down on Boston's Pope's Day by passing a stricter Riot Act. A dozen years later, Pope's Day had given way to an orderly demonstration during which, instead of rioting, the two rival youth gangs met, arranged a truce, and organized a public donation for resistance to British tyranny.

Whereas in 1750 routine brutality among teenagers hardly aroused comment, by 1770 the Boston Massacre demonstrated that the violent death of even a single youth could spark outrage throughout the

This continual cycle of learning in each successive generation is why the American Revolution is unfinished and always will be. —*Ralph Mosher*

colonies. Over the course of those twenty years, colonial attitudes toward children had gone from neglect to protection, from blame to sympathy. In the years after 1750, notes historian Daniel Blake Smith, Virginia and Maryland witnessed "a more openly affectionate, intimate family environment in which . . . infants and small children became the centerpiece of family attention and affection." The visiting French essayist Crèvecoeur, traveling through the colonies in the 1750s and '60s, described how colonial children "are gently held by a uniform silk cord, which unites softness and strength. . . . They are corrected with tenderness, nursed with the most affectionate care, clad with that decent plainness." Advances in child nutrition caused the average height of adult Americans to increase by more than half an inch—the biggest one-generation gain until the G.I.s 160 years later.

Eager to push the new children away from the rowdiness of recent decades, towns warned kids to stay off the streets and away from gambling and theaters. Popular child-rearing books reinforced the seriousness of the parents' role. "By 1750," observes historian Jay Fliegelman, "irresponsible parents became the nation's scapegoat." By the 1760s, popular novels such as *Clarissa,* which lauded the "good" (civic-minded) parent and excoriated the "bad" (selfish) parent, became a national obsession. They vastly outsold books on politics in this last decade before the Revolution. Parents accepted Rousseau's warning that "Public manners can only be reformed by beginning with private vices, which naturally arise from parents."

Dismayed by how prior colonial schoolchildren had returned from England (in John Page's words) "inconceivably illiterate, . . . corrupted and vicious," parents now wanted to educate their kids in colonial schools. The ratio of teachers to children jumped by about 50 percent, and many new colleges such as Princeton and Dartmouth were founded (according to historian John Roche) "to raise up a new generation imbued with personal virtue, a common fund of knowledge, . . . and zeal for service to the community." The curriculum shifted away from theology and ancient languages and toward history and modern languages. Moral philosophy shifted away from the spiritual and toward the pursuit of "happiness" or "utility" as the end of good government.

As colleges stressed teamwork and duty, pranks declined, interest in Masonic "brotherhoods" rose, and the share of graduates entering nonclerical callings climbed from one-fifth to one-half. In time, these changes proved consequential. Many eventual leaders of the Republican Generation were educated in these new institutions—and later would take pride in how their colleges had been described as a "nursery of sedition, of faction and republicanism." Harvard's Andrew Eliot boasted how "the young gentlemen are already taken up with politics, . . . (and) their tutors are fearful of giving too great a check to a disposition which may hereafter fill the country with patriots."

The adult fever of "civic revival" and "republican virtue" that gripped America during and after the Stamp Act riots of 1765 was, above all, an expression of outrage at the violation of youthful innocence. No metaphor for the contrast between British tyranny and American virtue was clearer than the image of parents abusing children. Cartoons depicted "the Child, Revolution" as a young maiden accosted by ogling British ministers, while newspapers decried Britain's "whipping" of her "dearest colonial child." John Adams wrote resentfully about how Britain "rocks the cradle, and sings lullaby, and the innocent children go to sleep, . . . while he prepares the birch to whip the poor babes," and John Dickinson described the Stamp Act riots as "the resentment of dutiful children, who have received unmerited blows from a beloved parent."

Those who were in fact emerging from childhood would soon become highly regarded young men and women, praised not just for noble deeds and selfless courage, but also for intelligence and good cheer. "All gaming, tricking, swearing, lying / Is grown quite out of fashion" intoned a popular ballad in 1779, "For modern youth's so self-denying, / It flies all lawless passion." One such modern self-denier was 21-year-old Nathan Hale, who calmly declared before his hanging, to the stunned admiration of witnesses, "I only regret that I have but one life to lose for my country."

Upon coming of age, during the years spanning the Revolution and the founding of a constitutional republic, this generation:

>> *lent civic focus and discipline to the untamed "liberty" instincts of their next-elders,*

>> *gave political substance to the moral vision of elders, the aging generation of that had earlier helped to trigger the Great Awakening, and*

Our conception of the "best" will change. The "best" will no longer be a cultural concern, but a civic one.

—Michael Eliason, 17

>> *stepped into the civic role vacated by the generation that had won the Glorious Revolution of 1689 and built the colonial institutions that had endured for decades thereafter.*

In so doing, this Republican Generation fulfilled what they regarded as an obligation of material service to posterity. Even in their youth, they radiated confidence. "The rising world shall sing of us a thousand years to come / And tell our children's children the wonders we have done." Thus sang New York's patriot recruits in 1776—before it was clear to anyone that the fruits of their courage would outlive the year, much less the millennium.

THE GLORIOUS GENERATION (BORN 1648–1673)

Go back nearly another century, and you can find a similar childhood for the Glorious Generation, born 1648 to 1673, the peers of "King" Carter and Cotton Mather. In time, this "hopeful bud" generation would be stamped by a moment of triumph—the (colonial) Glorious Revolution of 1689—after which they would remain public heroes, institution founders, and commerce builders. Over their lifetime, their generation would transform America's English-speaking colonies from a scattering of rude and violent outposts to a flourishing and stable provincial civilization. It would also codify slavery as a legal and social institution.

Glorious children were born in the aftermath of the Puritan Awakening, an era of religious upheaval and reform originating in Europe that ultimately spawned the isolated enthusiasm of New England's settlements and, a bit later, the expansion of a planter society on the Chesapeake. Their childhood was an era of reaction, drift, and fierce controversy over the ideals of the original settlers. The colonies' leadership was uncertain how to deal with the native Americans living among and around them, or with the French colonists to the north, or with a newly vigorous (and restored) monarchy in England.

Just up the age ladder, this mostly native-born generation of children saw two older generations that could not have been more unalike—midlife believers and young-adult skeptics, youthful sinners in the wake of aging saints. Where the founding generation can accurately be described as "Puritan," the "second generation," wrote historian Oscar Handlin, "seemed a ruder, less cultivated, and wilder people." This Cavalier Generation was variously described by the ruling orthodoxy as a "corrupt and degenerate rising generation," a "wild beast multitude," and a "hardhearted" generation with "a sad face." Above them stood, well into midlife, the generation who had originally envisioned and founded what John Winthrop called a "City upon a Hill," whereupon "posterity may be the better preserved from the common corruptions of this evil world."

Around the time the first Glorious were born, colonists revised their views about how children should be raised, committing themselves to what Thomas Shepard, Jr., called the "more thorough, conscientious, religious, effectual care for the rising generation." Lamenting the "great neglect of many parents and masters in training up their children in learning and labor," the Massachusetts assembly ordered towns to provide primary schooling for their children. "Do we not grievously neglect them?" asked Urian Oakes of his pupils, "to cherish and promote any good in them?" Meanwhile, Virginia mobilized authorities against the growing problem of orphaned children by ordering counties to "take up and educate" them.

During the 1650s and '60s, adults increased the protection of colonial children, while the clergy used a new, more positive vocabulary to speak of the young. "They are a generation of your betrustments," Eleazar Mather commanded parents, "a generation committed to your care." New England churches began teaching good works and civic duty ("preparation of salvation") rather than passive conversion. "Duties cannot work the saving change," preached Samuel Willard, "but it is certain" that they bring young people closer "to the blessing." While telling New England youths that they were "walled about with the love of God," Oakes reminded them that "every true believer is a soldier, engaged in a warfare." For the care of his 6-year-old son Robert, John Carter instructed his guardians to "preserve him from harm" and educate him to be "useful for his estate." The double message worked. By the mid-1670s, a new and more modern colonial generation began graduating from Harvard and taking over Virginia plantations: confident rationalists with a steady eye on the future, pleased to be part of a worldwide effort to build a great English-speaking empire.

Mankind. That word should have new meaning for all of us today. We can't be consumed by our petty differences anymore. We will be united in our common interest.

*—President Whitmore,
in* Independence Day

Between 1689 and 1692, after a stormy era of wars and rebellions, these youths completed their crisis-ridden rite of passage to full adulthood by mobilizing the colonies to rise up, at roughly the same time as London, against the reviled Stuart "usurper" (James II) on the throne of England. "It was a happy revolution," declared Cotton Mather, the tireless peer leader in Boston. According to historian T. H. Breen, it "released long-suppressed generational tensions" and produced a seismic shift in political authority from old to young. "Be up and doing. Activity. Activity," preached the young Benjamin Colman. "This will most likely be followed and rewarded, with triumphant satisfaction."

Upon coming of age, during what came to be known in the colonies and England as the Glorious Revolution, this generation:

>> *began turning away from the nomadic adventurism of their next-elders in favor of establishing, for the first time, an affluent and durable society in the New World,*

>> *translated the original Puritans' "law of love" into a love of law, and*

>> *filled the civic role vacated by the departed Elizabethan generation that had prevailed over Spain in 1588 and transformed England into a seafaring imperial nation.*

In time, the peers of Cotton Mather provided the greatest civic deed-doers of the six colonial generations who came of age before the American Revolution. Today's Americans can see a measure of what they accomplished by visiting Colonial Williamsburg.

The political issues and deadly struggles of their era are now often forgotten. (Who today recalls that King Philip's War in Massachusetts, in 1675–76, killed more inhabitants per capita than any other war America has fought, before or since?) And, from today's vantage point, this generation's "beehive" concept of social order seems utterly dehumanizing. It encouraged the Glorious elite to chisel slavery into law and to import, during their peak leadership years, tens of thousands of Africans in chains—an injustice that would cost future generations far more in hatred and blood than it could ever benefit them in wealth.

Yet for good or ill, this generation—like the more legendary Republicans and G.I.s—embodies the hero archetype. From childhood on, the Glorious lent the colonies order, stability, and durability, pending some distant day when an entirely new set of national political institutions could be forged by others.

Hero Generations Later in Life

After their special and protected childhoods, these generations (apart from the war-damaged Progressives) had life cycles that reveal a parallel pattern. When children of a hero generation come of age as young adults, a special momentum develops:

>> *The special treatment and protections follow them into young adulthood and blossom into a sense of collective confidence and power.*

>> *They and their elders declare a new determination to rid society of dangers that had ravaged the prior youth generation, but which only now are deemed intolerable.*

>> *Entering young adulthood, they undergo a heroic trial, a climactic moment in history in which their courage and fortitude are tested.*

>> *In midlife, as an honored generation of civic heroes, they create powerful and enduring institutions, build big new infrastructures, craft a new modern world, and dominate politics and economics deep into their old age.*

>> *Entering elderhood, they reveal a hubris that sparks angry quarrels with their own children, who help foment a spiritual awakening to challenge their parents' social discipline and secularism.*

So far, Millennials fit this hero-generation pattern. Will they continue to do so? If so, which of these four ancestral generations will they most resemble? The nation-founding Republicans? The globe-conquering

Students should learn to look up to the heroic—in thought and action, in politics and literature, in science and faith. After all, the few men and women who become heroes do so by looking up, and being pulled up by a vision of nobility. —*George Will*

G.I.s? The empire-building Glorious? Or the Progressives, stunted as heroes but grand Victorian modernizers and systemizers nonetheless?

Suppose the future holds nothing but a linear extension of the trends of the 1990s—with its ever-rising portfolios, humanitarian wars, safe streets, benign technologies, civic ennui, and celebrity talk shows. In such a future, the Millennials would face no trial of history and no chance to be a hero generation. They would emerge from their "special child" chrysalis as nothing more than ultra-compliant consumers and workers, husbands and wives, fathers and mothers, voters and politicians, in an unchanging world.

Or, alternatively, suppose history deals them a hero trial.

In *Election,* a smart satire on Millennial student government, Tracy Flick, a hyperambitious candidate, declares that "This country was built by people like me." Miss Flick's guiding light could well have been young David Humphreys of the Republican Generation, who was just as keen on praising his peers for civic skills other generations lacked. "All human greatness shall in us be found," he exuded, Flick-like, "for grandeur, wealth, and reason far renowned." And, of course, to this day Americans honor the generation of Jefferson (and Humphreys) for soldiering the Revolution, drafting the Declaration of Independence, framing the Constitution, acquiring vast territories, building roads and canals, and making the United States a continental republic.

Millennials are America's latest generation with hero potential. In the Oh-Ohs, as they come of age as young adults, they will test the rhythms of history. They and others will learn whether theirs is in fact America's next great generation.

Time will tell, but the groundwork has already been laid. "You can't interfere with destiny," warns Flick. "That's why it's destiny."

CHAPTER SIXTEEN

A capacity for greatness

a capacity for greatness
a capacity for greatness

My little baby's all grown up and saving China!
—*MUSHU, in* Mulan

"The men who landed on Omaha Beach never dreamed that they had been born to do that," reminisced the G.I. economist and essayist Herbert Stein shortly before he passed away in 1999. "We cannot tell just what challenges will occasion greatness in the generations of 2020 and 2050. Yet there does seem to be a capacity for greatness in America. It lies dormant at times, and this may be one of those times. But it will spring to life when the need or opportunity arises."

The next quarter century will reveal whether a "need or opportunity" will in fact arise for Millennials, a hero trial that could reveal a "capacity for greatness" commensurate with what Americans revere in hero generations of the past. "I know we are the future," says 17-year-old Janet Chang, "but sometimes that concerns me."

Chang has a point. Starting in the middle Oh-Ohs, and extending into the 2020s, Millennials could find themselves at the vortex of history. By then, they may well have matured into the same kind of results-oriented

I need you to do somethin' for me. Only you can do it.

—**Big Mama to Shorty, in** Soul Food

The United States government just asked us to save the world. Anyone wanna say no?

—**Harry, in** Armageddon

Sometimes, for the greater good, sacrifices must be made. —*Seti,*
in **Prince of Egypt**

Look on the bright side. We'll all get high schools named after us.

—*Andrea,*
in **Deep Impact**

We're not toys, we're action figures!

—*Chip Hazard,*
in **Small Soldiers**

We must meet this threat with our courage, our valor, indeed with our very lives to ensure that human civilization, not insect, dominates this galaxy now and always! —*Diennes,*
in **Starship Troopers**

young adults those four ancestral generations produced on the eve of the gravest tests of this nation's history. They will be empowered by their specialness, familiar with uniforms, used to meeting and beating high standards, respectful of adults, responsive to command—in short, Millennials will be exactly what older leaders may seize upon as a powerful tool in time of crisis.

These new attributes of American youth may embolden the nation and tempt it to undertake greater global risks than at any time since Boomers started coming of age back in the 1960s. Middle-aged Boomers sometimes say that their generation could have rallied against a Hitler as compliantly as their parents did, but most Americans who have lived through both the '40s and the '60s would probably doubt it. In Desert Storm, Gen-X soldiers were acknowledged as capable and did the job swiftly and well, but heard few accolades about glorious American youth nor of the need to rid the world of future dangers on their behalf.

All this could change, as Millennials replace Gen Xers in the ranks of youth. The higher their confidence, the more inclined they could be to

embrace a world-saving role. The more they uplift the national pride and the more adamant the public feels about securing a better future for them, the more aggressive the nation's leadership could become. As 17-year-old Tim Jones observes, "The optimism our generation feels for the future may be our downfall."

The sagas of hero generations past suggest that Millennials could indeed go in this direction. But that's not the only clue.

Other generations play equally important roles. Youth alone cannot alter the national mood. The social and cultural changes of the '60s required not just riotous Boomer youth, but also middle-aged Silent mentors and aging G.I. foils. The anticivic, market-oriented individualism of the '80s required not just nomadic Gen Xers, but also middle-aged Boomers and aging Silent who derived other kinds of life-cycle satisfactions from the same mood.

Around the middle to late Oh-Ohs, the current generational lineup (Millennial kids, Gen-X young adults, Boomers in midlife, Silent seniors, G.I.s fading) will start moving up a notch. The first Millennials will reach their mid-twenties, receive graduate degrees, and enter the professional world. The eldest Gen Xers will move deep into their forties and enter key managerial roles. The eldest Boomers will reach their middle sixties and find themselves at the apex of their public power. The eldest Silent will be in their eighties and losing influence. Meanwhile, the surviving G.I.s will be so old that their absence will be felt more deeply than their presence—and a new generation will start filling the nation's cribs.

As Millennials, Gen Xers, and Boomers set to work attaching their unique personae to these new life-cycle phases, the pulse of public life will quicken. America will acquire an entire generational lineup more power-packed than any since World War II. The natural order-givers will be old, the natural order-takers young. A just-do-it officer and managerial corps will be in midlife, and the generation most inclined to put on the brakes (the Silent, the only ones who will personally remember World War II) will no longer exert much public influence. Put all that together, and it's not hard to imagine what could happen next.

It's time to apply the lessons of history, superimposed on what is known about each of these generations, to determine how their coincident aging could produce a new era of crisis and, with it, a Millennial hero trial.

Millennials believe in positive change, but that's less the belief that things are getting better than the belief that things can get better. They seek some new form of order and stability—not a return to the 1950s, but the forging of a new national consensus.

—*Tobias Burmeister*

Master Yoda says I should be mindful of the future. —*Obi-Wan Kenobi, in* **The Phantom Menace**

The Generational Lineup of Maximum Power

When you look at today's adults, you can see the modern equivalent of the generational constellation that was present when ancestral hero generations were in childhood. This helps explain not only why Millennials are turning out as they are, but also why America is heading in a new direction—and how its public mood is about to turn.

Let's look at this shifting constellation, from oldest to youngest.

The *G.I.s* will be dependents in deep old age, and few will be available to teach the lessons of past heroism. America's '90s-era thirst for formative heroic *virtues* will deepen into a thirst for heroic *deeds*.

With each passing year, the *Silent* will grow more frustrated. Recalling their crisis-era youth, in which brutal forces of history steamrollered over the rights and lives of ordinary people, they will see the lessons of their own lifetime ignored by younger generations. The Silent will champion civil rights and due process in terms that will be familiar only to themselves, and will be opposed by far more powerful, youth-led forces championing civil duties and public action. This most nuanced, expert, and humane of recent generations could be boxed out by their juniors—who, for their own life-cycle reasons, will want simpler, less exquisite, even (when required) less humane solutions.

The Silent might try to temper the new youth resolve through their last remaining bulwark, the U.S. Supreme Court. If so, any entanglement with the action of youth could rekindle memories of the obstructionist "nine old men" of the Depression years—and, at most, would be temporary. In time, Silent objections will be swept aside, even as society begins to miss their lifelong virtues of compassion and sensitivity to others—qualities no other generation will then display to an equal degree, qualities small children will then be learning from mostly Gen-X parents.

Without a moderating older hand to tame their arguments, *Boomers* will reach their peak of political power and global influence. Old Boomers will "reinvent" old age, much as they have every other life phase, and will lend it a spiritual, inner-driven flavor. Accordingly, Boomer leaders will be even less inclined to compromise over questions of principle than at any earlier time in their lives. They will look to the future with a new sense of urgency, realizing that they are soon fated to relinquish this power and influence to generations that, they will believe, lack their wisdom. Boomers will feel deeply responsible to their grown Millennial children, to American history, indeed to all human civilization, to "fix" unresolved national or global problems. With Millennials now expressing their own opinions, the Boomers' long internecine culture wars will give way—replaced by larger and possibly global crusades. Surveys on U.S. actions in Desert Storm and Kosovo already indicate that Boomers entering midlife have become the most martial of America's living generations, the one most inclined to send troops, bomb cities, and fight to win on behalf of a cause they perceive as just.

Again and again in history, it is the Boomer kind of "postwar" generation, born in the aftermath of a great crisis, that comes of age during a spiritual awakening, enters midlife during eras of aggressive individualism (like the '90s), and in time ages into priest-warriors willing to guide society into its *next* crisis. In the years following World War II, English historian Arnold Toynbee hypothesized that this "Cycle of Generations" underlay the "long war cycle" that had recurred five times in a row in modern Europe, dating back to the Renaissance. The same generation that came of age proclaiming "peace" and "love" could fall prey to what Toynbee described as a "generational forgetting" of the last total war, which it knows only through tales told by its parents. The Boomer-spawned (now Gen-X-led) violent culture of recent decades lends credence to the Toynbeean forecast that, as elders, postwar generations inure themselves to the real-world damage that can result from civic risk-taking.

Whatever public choices old Boomers make, whatever orders they issue, midlife *Gen Xers* will provide the on-site managers (and generals) who will have to get the job done. As the Oh-Ohs reach the Oh-Teens, this forty- to fiftyish generation will tire of rootlessness and seek a more hands-on role in public life, a more enduring link with history than the pop culture now offers them. To date, Gen Xers are a loose political cannon, one that has seldom fired, one for which the flamboyant ex-wrestler Jesse Ventura has thus far generated the most inspiration and voter turnout. Were a great public need to arise in an era of crisis, Gen-X managers would not feel constrained by existing national institutions to which they will have seldom looked for help or guidance. Suddenly, a

All the wisdom is in the very young and the very old. Everybody in between is messed up.

—**Linda Schaffer,**
Nickelodeon

If Boomers and Gen Xers ever lead Millennials down a path they don't want, a path that doesn't seem right, a path that gives leaders new powers without checks and balances, I hope they say no. —**Bob Cooperman**

I know you think my dad's harmless, but you're wrong. —**Jane,**
in **American Beauty**

This world's no fun.
You noticed that, too? —*Two Willows,*
in Buffy the Vampire Slayer

*I'll be back when y'all find a subject
more "Saved by the Bell"-ish!*
—*Joel, in* Scream 2

generation that had appeared invisible in public life could turn into a giant wrecking ball while also providing the cranes and blueprints for building something new. The commercial slogans of their youth—*Why Ask Why, Just Do It, No Excuses*—could become the political catchphrases for a new ethos of public action. When action is required, Gen Xers will not take the tiny incrementalist steps familiar to the '90s. Instead, given the tasks at hand, they will draw a straight line between two points and care little about the rules (or feelings) that might stand in the way.

With old Boomer priest-warriors issuing orders without anyone older around to argue with them, and with action-minded Gen-X executives ready to translate their elders' priorities into effective game plans, the stage could be set for the taking of huge public risks—to span what could be perceived, by Boomers and Gen Xers alike, as a great discontinuity between a corrupt and imperiled old world and a hopeful and modern new one.

The stage would be *almost* set for some unforeseen event to spark a new national resolve, to foment a new mood of crisis. But one other ingredient is required: a young-adult generation of loyal, group-oriented, achievement-minded order-takers.

Enter the *Millennials.*

When today's teens and kids come fully of age, assuming they follow history's usual generational rhythms, they will solve problems Gen Xers couldn't, by fashioning a new sense of community out of '90s-style individualism. They will correct what they will perceive to be the mistakes (and compensate for the flaws) of Boomers, by placing positivism over negativism, trust over cynicism, science over spiritualism, team over self, duties over rights, honor over feeling, action over words. In so doing, they will fill the role vacated by the G.I.s.

Beyond these generational forces, is there something about history itself that could lead Millennials to a hero trial? Yes, there is.

The Next Rendezvous with Destiny

"To some generations, much is given," said Franklin Roosevelt in his second inaugural address. "Of other generations, much is expected. This generation has a rendezvous with destiny." He spoke those words at a time when rising G.I.s faced an economic depression at home and the rising risk of war abroad. Over the next quarter century, if America keeps another "rendezvous with destiny," the Millennials could discover that they are in fact the next generation from whom much is expected.

At the core of modern history lies an important pattern that beats to the rhythm of a long human life. Many historians have remarked on it. Over the past four centuries, colonial America and the United States have entered a crisis era—an era of total social effort and institutional rebirth—roughly once every eighty to one hundred years, akin to Lincoln's "four score and seven years" between the Declaration of Independence and Gettysburg. Start with the Great Depression and World War II, go back through the Civil War, the American Revolution, and the Glorious Revolution (of 1689), to England's triumph over Spain, and you'll see this cycle—alias Arnold Toynbee's "long war cycle"—at work.

Add in the spiritual awakenings (such as the Consciousness Revolution) that occur about halfway in between, and you'll notice their alignment with other patterns that have been examined by historians and social scientists. These include the cycles of political change and realignment noticed by Arthur Schlesinger, Jr., Walter Dean Burnham, and Samuel Huntington; cycles of foreign policy and global power, by Frank Klingberg and George Modelski; cycles of religious revitalization, by Robert Wurthnow and William McLaughlin; cycles of substance abuse, by David Musto; and cycles of commercial flux, by legions of economic theorists from Nikolai Kondratieff to Harry Dent.

Neither accident nor coincidence, this cycle of American history derives from the intersections of the seasons of life with the seasons of time. Put simply, this is *a generational cycle*. Its movement is driven by the same forces that cause each new batch of rising youths to correct for the excesses of midlife parents and leaders and to fill the role vacated by recently departed elders. The concept is as old as Exodus, the "tempers" of ancient Greece, the Celtic wreath, and the circularity of Navajo sand paintings. The antecedents are as profound as they are many and varied. A triumphal modern nation like the United States, feeling like it has conquered the business cycle and stands unrivaled in the world, may deem itself exempt from these larger rhythms—but does so at its peril.

Here's what this cycle teaches, and what it foretells: Roughly once every twenty years or so, around the time all living generations start

Haven't you ever wanted to be part of something special? —*Connie,* in Independence Day

My son, born in 1989, is already accessing his favorite sites on the web. . . . He is already drawing very good renderings of airplanes, rockets and other mechanical devices.
—*Robert Hoffman*

It seems as if half of my graduating class (the Class of 2000) is in the Air Force Junior ROTC program. Maybe that means something. The shocking thing is that most of these teens are not even what you would call political conservatives. —*Robert Reed, 17*

I want to be in the U.S. Navy when I grow up, and, right now, am Life rank in the Boy Scouts of America. It doesn't offend me one bit to be called a Hero. —*Philip, 14*

entering new phases of life, the social mood changes direction. In the last century, this occurred in the mid-1900s, the late '20s, the mid '40s, the mid '60s, and most recently in the mid '80s (when the oldest Silents reached retirement age, the oldest Boomers reached midlife, the oldest Gen Xers came of age as adults, and the first Millennials were being born). If this rhythm continues, sometime around the middle Oh-Ohs—maybe a few years before or after, but in any case when first-wave Millennials are somewhere in their twenties—a spark of history will ignite a public response quite unlike what it would have touched off in most earlier decades, such as the 1990s. History always produces sparks. But some sparks flare and then vanish, while others touch off firestorms out of proportion to the sparks themselves. (Recall how the sinking of the *Lusitania* produced such a mild response, and the attack on Pearl Harbor such a decisive one.) These next sparks could prompt enough of a reaction, and such a powerful mood shift, that America would embark on an era of crisis that could last into the 2020s.

Now add young-adult Millennials to this mix. Think about how such a generation could be energized, organized, and mobilized far beyond what could ever have been achieved with young Boomers or Gen Xers. Realize that the same generational dynamics at work in the United States will apply among the global Boomers, Gen Xers, and Millennials in Russia, China, India, Indonesia, Israel, Europe, and elsewhere. Stir that up, heat it with the blaze of terrorism, nationalism, religious zealotry, and unbridled technology, and you can appreciate why all the late-twentieth-century talk about an "end of history" may have been premature.

Thus could Millennials, and America, confront the next "rendezvous with destiny," giving the rising generation a hero trial, whether its members wish it or not.

A constellation of old Boomers, midlife Gen Xers and young-adult Millennials is a lineup of maximum power and civic risk. It tends to usher in an era when public events move the fastest and furthest, when nations and empires rise and fall, when the likelihood of political or economic calamity (and war) is high, when societies can either self-destruct or ratchet up to a higher level of civilization. This constellation thus represents both a danger and an opportunity that literally comes along but once in a long human lifetime, every eighty to one hundred years.

No one can foresee exactly what the crisis will be, or exactly what role Millennials would play in it. One can reasonably assume that the crisis era will be touched off by festering national and global problems that are familiar to most of today's Americans. How the crisis era climaxes and resolves, however, may be entirely beyond today's imagination—much as no one attending the Scopes "Monkey" trial in 1925 could ever have envisioned what America (and the world) would become just twenty years later upon the end of World War II. History never repeats in its particulars. The crisis could be national or global, economic or environmental, high-tech or low-tech, planned or chaotic. No one can say what combination of causes and events it would include.

Given the Boomers' own collision with Vietnam, one might wonder how likely it is that they would actually put their own Millennial children in uniform and march them into harm's way. Yet twenty years ago one might also have asked how likely it was that the first Boomer president, a man with clear origins in the '60s youth movement, would urge America to put children in school uniforms—which, of course, Bill Clinton did. In due course, some future Boomer president could summon Millennials for a new national uniformed service corps, a tool that yet another president could use as the first step toward the complete mobilization of this generation.

In any crisis era, whatever sacrifices older generations may ask of youth will be asked in part *because* their elders would have such high regard for them. Everyone would understand—much as elder leaders have proclaimed in all of America's past crises—that the very purpose of the societywide effort is to secure a better future for a rising generation that deserves a better future. And if that generation's achievements are great, so too will be their collective rewards. Upon the Millennial homecoming, Boomer and Gen-Xer leaders will retool public institutions in their favor—as was done for G.I.s and for every earlier generation of hero veterans—even to the disadvantage of their own peers. Cutting old-age benefits for Boomers or Gen Xers would be an easy call if Millennials are anywhere in the line of fire.

Should a crisis arise, with Millennial lives at stake, history could mete out good, middling, bad, or truly horrible outcomes. While no one can predict how a crisis would climax, and what a new postcrisis era would be

I don't like wars, but sometimes they just happen. Things have to be solved.

—*small boy,
nickellennium.com*

I feel badly for Millennials. The Young Boomer hatred of the draft kept us Xers out of wars with drafts. I don't think that the Millennials will be afforded any such luxury. If the right crusader (president) comes at the right time with the right message and the right political backing, Millennials may well be put on the march.

—*Pat Nieli*

Universal Military Training would help save our youth. . . . There would be no Oxford University deferments for the Bill Clintons, no plush National Guard hideaways for the George W. Bushes, no cozy tours in safe headquarters for the Al Gores. In boot camp they'd learn the basics— drill, discipline, teamwork, leadership, responsibility, and citizenship—while getting physically hard and mentally together. —*David Hackworth*

like, it would probably include a redefinition of government's relationship to the economy and society, a redefinition of man's relationship to technology, and a redefinition of America's relationship to the world. Millennials could play an epic role, crafting new myths of lore, doing deeds only dimly imaginable today. The consequences, for good or ill, would be enormous—not just for America, but indeed for the entire world.

Thereafter, for the rest of their lives, Millennials would collectively embody the transition into the new modern order, much as the Glorious, Republican, Progressive, and G.I. Generations did in prior centuries.

Alternative Futures

These rhythms of history are quite powerful, with many examples throughout human history, in all epochs and cultures. Given the generational forces at work, in America and around the world, an era of crisis seems unavoidable. It could come early or late, be severe or mild, and end tragically or triumphantly—but come it will.

Can anyone be certain of this? Of course not. Societies are complex human systems, and a full account of all the possible circumstances that might perturb or suppress history's seasonal rhythm is unknown and perhaps unknowable.

If you doubt the rhythm will continue, if you believe that the generational pattern of the twenty-first century will break the patterns of the past, then perhaps you are expecting Millennials to live out a relatively uneventful life cycle that roughly matches the decade-by-decade descriptions in Chapter 14. They'll write a few books, make a few movies, have a few presidents, eat a few pizzas, invent a few gizmos, buy and sell a few stocks, wage a few peace-keeping missions—and say a gentle if prosaic good-bye. That fits the American recipe for "life, liberty, and pursuit of happiness," but not a lot more.

Otherwise, suppose the rhythm continues. Suppose there *is* a crisis, and a Millennial hero trial, followed by a new modern era. How might the forecast be different?

Millennials would still live out the life cycle described earlier, except in much fuller force. The ethnic melding and gender-role separation would be swifter and more enduring. The anti-Boomer flavor of the new Millennial culture would be more far-reaching. The reconstruction of political and economic institutions would be more complete. Everything this generation thereafter does would be more muscular, hubristic, determinative of social change.

Afterwards, the generational cycle would proceed. The children of the crisis would become a "New Silent" generation. The children born after the crisis—the generation shaped by Millennials—would become "New Boomers" who would, in time, launch a spiritual awakening against the secular order that their aging Millennial parents will by then personify. The children born during that spiritual awakening would become "New Xers" who would grow up with a dimming appreciation of what Millennials once did. And the children born after the awakening would become "New Millennials," filling the void left by their honored but fading elders.

All this assumes that the crisis goes well, and that Millennials succeed

It is said our generation will aim to fix the problems that we (collectively) see in our society, and that we will do so by using governments to control unnecessary speech and eliminating dangerous or "subversive" ideas. . . . There is already a feature in new computer systems that will allow individuals to be tracked on the internet. The fact that the trend has already started would lead one to believe that our generation will react to it, [but] I personally doubt it.

—Tim Jones, 17

Sooner or later, you're going to have a national identity card, and it will start in the high schools, conditioning a generations of Americans to say that a national identity card is not only useful and convenient but necessary.

—Lisa Dean, Free Congress Foundation

Children are taught to inform on their friends and teachers—and most of all on their parents. In Hungary, I lived under two regimes that based their existences on that practice. Are we certain we want America to go that way?   —Balint Vazsonyi

The solution to a spiritual problem is not to turn America into a nation of Soviet-style paid informants.

—Steve Dasbach, on a new Oregon plan to pay high school students to inform on classmates' drug abuse

at their hero trial. However, history reminds that many paths are possible. The legacy of the nation-founding Republicans and globe-conquering G.I.s suggests that heroic stature is achievable for a generation with a start like that which Millennials have enjoyed. The experience of the Glorious, whose legacy of slavery took nearly two centuries to undo, warns that the grand constructions of "good child" generations can end up haunting and oppressing their heirs. The damage the Civil War did to the Progressives just coming of age reveals how a crisis that is too harsh and too early can stunt a generation's future potential. As for very bad outcomes, one need not reflect long on the growing variety of weapons of mass destruction, or on the misuse of new technological breakthroughs, to appreciate the full range of possible cataclysms.

Today's children and teens have never known a war requiring any significant American sacrifice—in life, liberty, taxation, consumerism, or even access to foreign travel and imported goods. For many, their only real exposure to violence is on movie screens, TV news, and video games. They have hardly known even a mild economic downturn. For many, their only real exposure to financial sacrifice has been when their parents refuse to buy them what they want.

For such a generation, a collision with economic hard times or a major war poses a gigantic question mark. When a crisis comes, its harshness could explode across young lives like a video game that is no longer virtual. And if, in its early stages, the crisis is not handled well, or if America's leaders are mired in personal scandals or vendettas that undermine their ability to command sacrifice from others, or if fate takes a harsh turn, or if millions of young people find themselves suddenly out of work, then the familiar Millennial sunniness could turn sour.

What then?

Millennials would still rebel against the perceived adult "mistakes" of their youth, but their list of mistakes would grow—and the tone of their rebellion would darken. They might rebel against today's pop culture not just by cleansing it, but by demanding a repressive censorship. They might rebel against today's spreading gap between rich and poor not just by urging new public policies, but by enlisting themselves in an ugly class warfare. They might rebel against today's unfocused multilateralism not just by asking for more focus on action and results, but by prodding an aggressive militarism. They might rebel against today's civic ennui not just by voting and politicking, but by boosting populist demagogues. And, perhaps more frighteningly, they might rebel against today's high-tech individualism not just by enabling high-tech teamwork, but by constructing a new high-tech authoritarianism many of today's older people now consider impossible.

After a crisis era, Millennials could inherit the G.I.s' tendency to apply the cutting-edge technologies invented by their parents with such mastery and exuberance that they could prove unable to check their own excesses—without a corrective rebellion by their children. Two leading technologies of the G.I. childhood and youth eras—the airplane and nuclear power—were mainly the creations of their parents' Missionary Generation (the Wright Brothers and Albert Einstein, respectively). After World War II, whose victory was secured by those two technologies, the G.I.s kept developing airplanes, missiles, and nuclear bombs in an arms race that lasted from their first president (John Kennedy) through their last (George Bush). This arms race—including the scientific rationalism that underlay it and the "domino theory" foreign policy that enforced it—became a key issue in the late-1960s "generation gap" between G.I.s and their Boomer children.

Two leading high-tech fields that Boomers have pioneered—computers and biogenetics—could play a similar key role in the Millennial life cycle. This is especially likely if these technologies are central to the cause, conduct, or climax of any crisis era. Afterwards, one can envision midlife Millennials propelling these technologies in directions as unimaginable today as MIRVed nuclear missiles would have been in the days of dirigible balloons. If the Millennials' heroic trial is twisted by adversity, if their postcrisis hubris turns pathological, if their muscularity turns brutal, this is the kind of generation that could produce an Orwellian era, much like the "Big Brother" people feared back in the postwar years of conformism, bland culture, and midlife G.I.s.

Americans should hope not. They should hope instead that, like the children of the 1750s and '60s, Millennials will emerge from their young-adult collision with history in a way that will make their parents, ancestors, and heirs all extremely proud of them. Or, if postcrisis Millennials *do* push computers, biogenetics, and the rest of modern science in unwise

Soon people will be able to know about anyone or anything. Everyone will be educated and without privacy.

—*Lacey Roddick*

There will be pencils that pick up brainwaves and write or draw whatever you are thinking.

We will have thought transmitters. You step inside, think of something, and voila! *It appears!*

We will be able to tell what other people are thinking.

We won't have to punish criminals anymore because we can make them better people by erasing their brains and putting something better in them.

—*9- to 11-year-old children, nickellennium.com*

You see, Fred, it isn't the size of a guy's IQ that matters. It's how he uses it.

—*Damon, in* Little Man Tate

[I]f the worst should occur, some blame should be placed on the thus far greatly overrated Boomers.

—*Luis Poza, 17*

directions, Americans should hope that their "New Boomer" children will put a stop to it, sometime around the 2040s, with a cultural eruption and spiritual recrudescence that would bring smiles of recognition to a smattering of centenarian Boomers. Succeed or fail, Millennials could follow down the path of Jefferson's and Reagan's generations, both of which got along better with their parents than later on with their own children.

All of today's generations, especially Millennials, are hoping for the best possible outcome. "Whatever the Millennials touch, whether good or bad, it all turns to gold," insists Josh Braxon, a late Gen Xer in his early twenties who senses that his juniors possess "that power to make everything work." "Our new young masters will achieve greatness," agrees Gen Xer Eric Weisbard in *The Village Voice*. "They're too secure not to, knowing what a winning hand they've been dealt."

When history does in fact summon "the power to make everything work" from young-adult Millennials, today's parents—then deep in old age—can look on with pride to see how their grown children did indeed benefit from the values they were taught in their youth.

Millennials as a Hero Generation

The experience of earlier hero generations suggests that, to fulfill their potential, they must be raised as children to think of themselves as special, powerful, capable of great collective deeds. So far, Millennials are on track.

For nearly two decades, this nation has enjoyed large helpings of peace and prosperity, atop civic decline and worries about the long-term sustainability of its present course. The intensity with which Americans riveted first on babies, next on children, and more recently on teens—holding them to higher standards than U.S. presidents and CEOs—has unmasked the older generations' abiding anxieties about the new century.

Anxiety about the future can be a good thing, when directed to useful purpose, and surely one of history's best purposes is the raising of good and capable children. Visions of trouble can valuably remind a society about how crucial its rising generation could someday become in time of need. Whether or not Millennials must ever respond to an epic crisis, his-

tory will propel them to be and do what Boomers and Gen Xers were not and did not do. That much is certain.

Will Millennials become America's next great generation? In the prism of history, greatness is a matter of perspective. The German historian Leopold von Ranke once wrote, "Before God, all the generations of humanity appear equally justified." In "any generation," he wrote, "real moral greatness is the same as in any other." Like G.I.s, Millennials will have strengths that other Americans will celebrate, but like all generations, they will have countervailing weaknesses whose consequences will become more apparent as they reach middle age. That's when they will start creating problems that their children will want to correct. Every generation provides something new, something important, something *necessary* in the context of its own time. So too does every generation, no matter how "great," leave plenty for its successors to do.

Because history may be counting on Millennials to serve a special pur-

We're superheroes. That's what we're supposed to do—save cities, fight monsters. —**Powerpuff Girls**

He's better at this than I've ever been at anything in my life. He's better at this than you'll ever be, at anything.

—*Fred,*
in **Searching for Bobby Fischer**

We saved the world. I say we have to party. —*Buffy,*
in **Buffy the Vampire Slayer**

pose, Americans should hope that today's kids keep their strong game going. The first batch, now in their teens, is loud, proud, and confident, and is likely to become more so as they pass through college and into adult life. The next batch could be tremendous achievers.

No one can foresee exactly what surprises, perils, delights, disappointments, and triumphs lie in store for Millennials. Yet Boomers and Gen Xers can take some satisfaction in how they are raising a generation fully prepared to accept challenges, live up to their elders' trust, and triumph over whatever history has in store for them. "We are comfortable with change," reassures 17-year-old Laura Bennett. "Be it good or bad, we can handle it."

millennials Rising

millennials rising
millennials rising

Stories will be told until we're old
Stories will be told until the end of time
—*HANSON, "Stories"*

Generations are a great key for unlocking the history of any society that believes in progress. In recent decades, America has witnessed tremendous changes in its social mood—from the Great Crash to D-Day, from the Summer of Love to Morning in America—driven in large measure by life-cycle aging. Each time adult generations reach new phases of life, and each time a rising generation comes of age, they separately acquire new perspectives on where their society is heading. The result is a regular and predictable change in that society's mood and direction.

That's what happened in America in the middle 1940s, middle '60s, and middle '80s. It's due to happen again in the middle Oh-Ohs, right around the time the first Millennials reach adulthood.

Those who pay no attention to generational transitions, or who think generations matter only to the producers and consumers of pop culture, leave themselves with precious little to assess where they, and America, stand in the sweep of history. When such people look to the past or

This is a good land. We are good people. The children we raise are overwhelmingly decent. . . . For us to mistakenly assert otherwise is to deny them and their virtue.

—**Bob Lonsberry**

We will accomplish a lot. We're going to surprise a lot of people.

—**Mina Sisouvong, 18**

I like to think that our children might actually turn out as we hope.

—**Joan Ryan,**
San Francisco Chronicle

Reach for the sky
Hold your head up high—
you're a superstar —*Love Inc.,*
"You're a Superstar"

future, they notice only a multitude of discrete events. They see a hurricane here, a bombing there, a bull market, a bear market, an election every four years. They assume that America will remain what it is and where it is, like a rudderless ship, unless some out-of-the-blue event (a scientific discovery, a terrorist attack) knocks it someplace else.

Trying to understand the direction of America by looking at the breaking headlines while ignoring generations is like trying to understand the movement of the ocean by looking at the breaking waves while ignoring the tides. Those who disregard generational change have been surprised by the last several turns in the American mood. Those who continue to disregard it will be just as surprised the next time a new decade and a new generation alter the nation's course.

The decade is the Oh-Ohs. The generation is the Millennials. When the two come together, the young people of America will dazzle the nation much as Boomers did in the '60s, though to very different effect.

This intersection of life and time cannot be stopped. When it occurs, it will please some older people and displease others. On the brink of old age, many Boomers will be delighted to see such civic-spirited young adults, but will despair at their disregard for the inner life. On the brink of midlife, many Gen Xers will welcome the good example young adults will be setting for the next child generation, but will complain about the blandness of their groupthink.

Few Americans have ever seen so many young people with such an appetite for achievement. Indeed, older generations are so accustomed to worrying about kids who accomplish too little that they might not know what to do with kids who may want to accomplish too much. The new youth danger lies less in the direction of entropy than in the direction of order, and few of today's older Americans have any personal memory of what dangers or opportunities that might pose. As Boomers and Gen Xers watch Millennials go to work, they may feel disoriented, uncertain about what to do or how to help.

When America has, at long last, a young generation ready to accept elder leadership, the quality of that leadership will matter far more than before. Millennials can heed moral exemplars, and respond to principled leaders, far better than most of today's adults could when young. That's the opportunity side. Yet these new youths might decisively oppose nominal leaders who fail to provide real direction, and they might be inclined to support misguided leaders if better alternatives aren't available. That's the danger side.

To this point, Boomers and Gen Xers have steered Millennials away from the attitudes and behaviors of their own youth eras. They have done so through new family-life and workplace accommodations, parental protections, cultural screens, educational standards, and disciplinary rules that, on balance, have served this young generation well, while providing guideposts to measure future progress. Adult America has done a decent job with these kids—so far.

But Millennials are growing up. The oldest of them will soon be adults, moving beyond the chrysalis of child-safety devices, Zero Tolerance rules, and standardized tests. With their leading edge entering college, these young people are on the brink of becoming a highly effective social force, given the right leadership and moment.

Today's teens look forward to this. What they may not know—yet what history teaches—is that every generation has a shadow side. For Millennials, the shadow they confront could include excessive collectivism and rationalism, a capacity to push technology too far or follow leaders too unquestioningly. As they age, Millennials would do well to guard against their shadow, while retaining the collegial energy that makes them so remarkable as a generation.

For the sake of Millennials—and, through them, the future of America—the most urgent adult task is to elevate their expectations. Rather than dwell on all the negatives, on problems such as youth violence or substance abuse that are clearly ebbing, America should set goals big enough to engage the imagination of this generation of achievers. Rather than dwell on trying to shelter a generation that needs room to grow, America should require adult leaders to possess the integrity to deserve the trust of youth. And rather than persist in the tired mantra of "if it feels good, do it," older people should heed the fresher advice of 9-year-old Kylie from the GreatKids web site: "Whoever you are and wherever you are," she writes, "keep up doing your best, practice, be nice, and most of all do what's right and what you should be doing!"

During the Great Depression, older people felt increasingly powerless about what they personally could do about the many problems of the

[The teenager,] right now, is the ultimate personification of the American dream, the ultimate personification of the American ideals. —Rider Strong

When I first heard what she had done, I wondered, "Would I have done that?" I might have begged for my life. Cassie didn't. She may have been 17, but she's a far stronger woman than I'll ever be.
—mother of Cassie Bernall, who affirmed her faith to her killer, Columbine High

*We can reach our destiny
We will feast in harmony as one*
—'N Sync, "Forever Young"

Aaron Hall, 16, who saved a 6-year-old boy from a mountain lion, was awarded the Heroism Award with Crossed Palms, an honor bestowed upon Boy Scouts "who put their lives at extreme risk in an effort to help another." —Boy Scouts of America

We are not going to let the world down. —Chaz Schmitz, 16

You have to trust me.
—teenager, in Small Soldiers

nation and the world, but increasingly hopeful about what younger people might someday do. America "cannot always build a future for our youth," declared Franklin Roosevelt at the time, "but we can build our youth for the future."

In today's America, one hears much praise for what the G.I. Generation built, but no one ever asks: Who built the G.I. Generation? The answer is, the generations of Roosevelt and Truman—elders who provided young people with principled leadership, challenges to character, ambitious national goals, and solid foundations for long-term achievement. In due course, that young generation congealed into what Henry Malcolm called "a generation of Prometheus and Adam," capable of turning the corner on economic despair, conquering fascism, outlasting communism, building massive infrastructures, and landing men on the moon.

Boomers and Gen Xers realize that neither of their generations is likely to be remembered as a generation of heroes. Perhaps, however, both can someday be remembered as the leaders, educators, and parents who *shaped* a generation of heroes. To this point, they have made a solid start at this great and good task. But if they wish to do for Millennials what FDR's and Truman's peers did for G.I.s, they must learn from those shining examples, and must accept the fact that America's next generation will not resemble their own.

The Millennial future is what America is destined to become—and soon. John Stuart Mill once defined a generation as "a new set of human beings that have been educated, have grown up from childhood, and have taken possession of society." When you think of today's young people this way, you cannot help but rivet on their potential for *power*—organized power, legal power, official power. As the oldest Millennials reach their twenties, they will fill colleges, move beyond parental control, and begin making up their own minds about their nation and the world. What they will say, *and especially what they will do,* could shock and disturb many of today's adults who have spent most of their lives cultivating individualism and an instinctive distrust for power. But power, when harnessed, can be a force for good. "Change the world" was a fine youth slogan back in the 1960s, but Boomers may need the power of their grown children to get it done.

Hope abounds. Older people should thrill at what today's kids already are, and what they may become. At the 1999 Women's World Cup, four cheerful, red-white-and-blue-bedecked tween-age girls held up a sign that spoke of soccer but could as easily speak to the Millennial agenda for the crafting of a bright new modern era. "This is my game," those four girls signaled to the world. "This is my future. Watch me play."

With Millennials rising, America needs to start thinking bigger. Test them. Challenge them. Put difficult tasks before them, and have faith that they can do themselves, and their nation, proud. Lead them. Love them. And above all listen to 17-year-old Sarah Fulton when she says, "Celebrate the good! Celebrate the youth in America!"

The sun will set on my time here and will rise with you as the new king.
—*Mufasa, in* **The Lion King**

I don't know what my future holds, but I'm sure it's something great.
—*Whitley Lassen, 17*

Every generation has a chance at greatness. Let this one take its shot.
—Newsweek

Fathers have a bias. Go to any school musical, science fair, moot court, or soccer game, and you'll see. Dads root hard, at times too hard, for their own kids and their teams. (Moms have also been charged with this.)

We're both fathers, and we freely admit that we share a prokid bias. We root for our kids, their teams, and their generations. Between our two families, we have six children—two Gen Xers and four Millennials. The four Strausses are Melanie (age 23) the Harvard China expert, Vicky (19) the JMU prepsychologist, Eric (17) the snake and iguana charmer, and Becky (16) the soccer star; the two Howes are Giorgia (8) the Harry Potter maven and Nathaniel (6) the Pokémon master.

For the record, we should say that the Strauss cadre (who have been interviewed many, many times for this book) remain perplexed about how *their* father could possibly know anything about what's hot and what's not in teen music, film, and fashion. The Howe duo are likewise amazed at their dad's cluelessness about Hogwarts and Charizard. We know our limits. That's why, in our daily lives, we turn to the true experts on Millennial matters, our wives, Janie Strauss and Simona Howe.

Beyond our families, we have indeed immersed ourselves in the world of today's kids. We've spoken with history, English, creative writing, and theater classes at several local high schools, and surveyed hundreds of members of the Class of 2000. On a separate track, Strauss has created the Cappies Theater Awards program, has worked with theater programs in two dozen northern Virginia high schools, and has written two musicals on Millennial themes: *MaKiddo* (a full parody of *The Mikado*), about a high school for "practically perfect" kids, and *StopScandal.Com,* about a civic-spirited teenager who tangles with his corrupt congressman. Howe has been an active dad at his kids' schools, while battling as a policy spokesman to save their fiscal future on Social Security, Medicare, and other budget issues.

That's not the whole of it. As the saying goes, Millennials and us, we go way back.

We first came to this topic more as historians than as parents or school activists. The two of us have been collaborating on generational histories for a decade and a half. The idea for our first book together, *Generations,* arose in 1984, when today's 18-year-olds were still in strollers, Jessica McClure was stuck in a Texas well, and most yuppies were hearing the term "baby boomlet" for the first time. We coined the name Millennials in 1987, around the time '82-born children were entering kindergarten and the media were first identifying their prospective link to the millennial year 2000. That was five years before the first American use of the term "Generation X."

We published *Generations* in the winter of 1990–91, when the oldest Millennials were in third grade and only 33 million had yet been born. That's when we publicly named, defined, and described them—and placed them among the pantheon of American generations. In 1991, the very idea of a new child generation, following a young-adult generation that *still* didn't have a name, struck even our supportive readers as somewhat hypothetical.

But we went ahead anyway. In *Generations,* we predicted that the Millennials, when they first reached their teens, would be the target of a raging obsession in America over how best to protect and structure and improve the lives of young Americans. We also suggested that by the late '90s they would become the new epicenter of the culture wars, the new trump card of national politics, and the new focus for reconstructing bedrock social institutions, from fatherhood to schools. Today, in the year 2000, these predictions seem unremarkable. That's because they've mostly come to pass.

Early in 1993, we published *13th Gen*, a sociobiography of Generation X, where we alerted teens and twentysomethings that a very different batch of 10-year-olds was growing up right behind them. In 1997, we published *The Fourth Turning*, a book about the cycles of history, where we described the oldest (15-year-old) Millennials as riding a crest of adult concern that was just about to break over the nation's high schools. If anything, we underestimated the American absorption with teenagers that was about to strike. From polls to TV stories to newsmagazine cover articles, the media has canvassed the minds and showcased the lives of teenagers (and younger kids) far more than has been true for any earlier youth generation in living memory. The internet has meanwhile given young people an independent voice, and global reach, unimaginable just a decade ago.

We decided to write *Millennials Rising* in 1998, a year before Columbine, as our own answer to the "Generation Y" negativity that was seeping into the media and marketing worlds. After Columbine, that task felt all the more urgent. Gen Xers had been conditioned since childhood to weather the caustic reception that they experienced in the early '90s and that they have since largely shaken off. Raised in a more protective and positive fashion, Millennials have not been so conditioned. Another public torrent of bleakness about the next rising generation, we felt, could be damaging for these young people—and dangerous for America's future.

Hence this book. Those familiar with the format of *13th Gen* will notice many similarities, such as R. J. Matson's wonderful cartoons and the sidebar charts and quotes. They will also notice differences. There, we had "Crasher" (Ian Williams) offering a persistent Gen-X perspective. Here, we use quotes from a chorus of more than a hundred 8- to 18-year-olds. More than anything we have written before, this is a true internet-age book, with a broad two-way connection both to our sources and to our readers.

Some of the voices in the sidebars come from a web discussion we've hosted, over the past three and a half years, at www.fourthturning.com.

When we launched that site, we started a single forum with four topics. Since then, the site has blossomed into a massive, intergenerational town meeting, with over two hundred discussion topics and innumerable visitors, many of them teenagers. Our regular visitors have held two readers' conventions, in Washington, D.C., and Nashville. For the success of this web site, we thank our Gen-X webmaster, Nabeel Hyatt (who has gone on to further dot-com triumphs), our current Millennial webmaster, Hayfield Secondary School student Kevin James, and our many contributors.

This book is immensely richer for the vast harvest of other internet elements (search engines, news archives, chat rooms, and book, film, and song lexicons) that make an author's work quicker and more comprehensive. For much of this we thank Sean Carey, who "hangs ten" with the best of them when surfing the net, and Frank Gregorsky, whose contributions, especially on technology and the pop culture, have been immense. Frank's superb "Love Those Millennials" newsletter on this generation reveals a passionate and positive commitment to today's teens. We also acknowledge Lis Libengood for her input on small-child nurture, Scott Beale on education, and David Kaiser on a variety of topics. And we thank Rick Delano, a dedicated advocate of Millennial causes, for his experience, good sense, and consummate ability to make things happen—and for helping us organize our consulting arm, LifeCourse Associates.

We are grateful to our first-draft manuscript readers, especially Third Millennium's Rich Thau and Richmond teacher Rob Peck, and the two dozen students at McLean and Langley High Schools, along with the teachers (Denise Katz, Cathy Colglazier, Josh Hertel, and Mary Jane Regan) who helped arrange these and other student discussions. We thank Fairfax County School Superintendent Dan Domenech for his continuing interest in our work. We appreciate the assistance we received from school officials Tom White and Doug Rice, who helped us fine-tune and launch our Teachers and Class of 2000 Surveys; from the twelve principals and two hundred teachers of the high, middle, and elementary schools who took part in our Teachers Survey; and from Vicky and Becky Strauss, Emily Tavoulareas, and Sarah Abrams, who tabulated these surveys.

Howe wishes to thank many acquaintances for helping out in ways large and small, including Mike Males of the University of California for his principled views and stunning insights; George Carey of Just Kids, Inc., and Lou Eigen of Social and Health Services Limited for the benefit of their long experience; Jenna Marston at the Partnership for a Drug-Free America for her obvious mastery of that subject; Charles Rodin and Christine Nord for helping him thread through data and sources on kids; Adam Burke, at the Institute for Social Research, University of Michigan, for preparing up-to-date results from the Monitoring the Future surveys; Paul Beavers and William Bornschein, dedicated teachers in Tennessee and Kentucky, for their vital perspectives on middle schoolers. He thanks Peter G. Peterson, an unwavering champion of today's kids, for giving him the opportunity to look closely at this generation's economic future. He thanks Richard Jackson at the Concord Coalition and Phil Longman at *U.S. News and World Report,* whose views he often solicits and always values—along with so many others he's "talked Millennials" with, including Susan Baker, Bob Filipczak, John Fraim, Lewis Jaffe, Nat Irvin, John Peterson, Lee Pressler, Bill Roesing, Scott Sanders, Mike Vlahos, Bill Wolfe, and too many in the media to name.

Strauss gives a nod to colleagues in his teen-targeted theater projects, including Bill Lane, Bo Ayars, Steve Rosenhaus, Eric Krebs, Chuck Noell, Trena Weiss-Null, Maria Rendine, Melanie Strauss, and the hundreds of students on the various casts and crews of his two musicals; to Judy Bowns, Gael Reilly, Marylou Tousignant, Kathie West, Rebecca Wilburn, and the many school theater directors and critics who have helped the Cappies bring new excitement and public acclaim to high school theater; to Elaina Newport, Mark Eaton, and his many other colleagues in the Capitol Steps; to the Close-Up Foundation, Presidential Classroom, and National Young Leaders Conference, who have helped the Capitol Steps tailor political satire for teenage audiences; and to Mort Kavalier, Sandy Irani, John Cameron, and Johns Hopkins University for their gift of immeasurable value.

As with all our books, we are grateful to our agent, Rafe Sagalyn, for helping us hone our message, restrain our love for the written word (in quantity), and thereby reach an audience. We applaud our cartoonist, R. J. Matson, whose work is also featured on Capitol Steps record albums and off-Broadway stage sets, along with the occasional *New Yorker* magazine cover. We thank our editor and publisher, Edward Kastenmeier and Marty Asher, Katy Barrett, and the staff at Vintage Books for bringing us on for another collaboration. It's not often that the same authors and the same publishing team get to work together on two books seven years apart. In many ways, *Millennials Rising* has been the most focused and rewarding of the books we've done. For making this happen, Edward deserves much of the credit.

Most of all, we wish to thank our readers for taking the time. We invite those of all generations—especially Millennials—to join a far-ranging discussion on our web site, www.millennialsrising.com.

When the G.I. Generation was in its youth, the historian James Truslow Adams coined a new concept, "the American Dream," which he defined as the promise of giving every young person "the chance to grow into something bigger and finer, as bigger and finer appeared to him." By "bigger and finer," Adams spoke not merely of houses, cars, and other material things, but also of compassion, honor, community, and principle. For Millennials, the American Dream carries a whole new dimension of drama and purpose.

This dream can be every parent's hope. Let it come true for your children, and ours, and for the children you teach or serve, and all other children you know. They are our blessing, all of them to each of us.

Neil Howe and William Strauss

notes

These notes are organized in four sections. The "Author Surveys" section describes the student and teacher surveys that we undertook expressly to assist us in writing the book and to which we refer frequently in boxes and in the text. The "Sidebar Voices" section covers the sidebar quotes—where they come from and how we got them. "Text References," organized by chapter and subhead, provide sources for factual items mentioned in the text. In general, we try to provide sources for all direct quotes or written citations (from people, articles, book titles, and so on) and for all major factual claims applying to all or most Millennials or Americans, especially claims about quantitative levels or trends. Each reference is listed in the order in which the quotation or claim appears in the text; the notation *op. cit.* refers only to another reference in the same chapter subhead. The final section, "Data Sources," explains (by topic group) major quantitative indicators often used in the text. "Text References" frequently refers the reader to this final section.

Given the vast range of topics covered in this book—and the numberless scholarly, journalistic, and pop culture sources that bear a connection to them—there is no way we could reference everything of interest. For readers who wish to dig deeper into sources, we invite them to do their own web searches, starting with newspaper and magazine archives or on search engines run by research institutes or government agencies. As for readers who want to find out more about our generational perspective on American history, or about our earlier treatments of the Millennial Generation, we invite them to read our three previous coauthored books: *Generations: The History of America's Future, 1584–2069* (1991), *13th Gen; Abort, Retry, Ignore, Fail?* (1993), and *The Fourth Turning: An American Prophecy* (1997).

Above all, we invite readers to join other readers and ourselves in discussing any and all aspects of this book, and Millennial issues in general, at www.millennialsrising.com.

Author Surveys

To supplement other youth polls, we designed and conducted two generational surveys for this book: a Teachers Survey of 200 elementary, middle, and high school teachers in twelve public schools in Fairfax County, Virginia; and a Class of 2000 Survey of roughly 660 students (all in the June 2000 graduating class) at four Fairfax County public high schools. Both surveys were authorized by school officials.

In the Teachers Survey, we asked teachers with ten or more years of experience to compare today's students with those of ten or more years ago, on a number of academic, extracurricular, attitudinal, and behavioral measures.

In the Class of 2000 Survey, we asked students to answer a variety of generational questions about themselves, and about their parents, teachers, and siblings.

Comprising the western suburbs of Washington, D.C., Fairfax County has one of the largest and most renowned school systems in the nation. Its student population is ethnically diverse, with 13 percent Asian, 10 percent Latino, 8 percent African American, and 3 percent other. Nonwhites and Latinos thus make up one-third of the high school student body— the same as the national share for this age group. Three of every ten students live in homes where a language other than English is spoken. Though Fairfax County is relatively well-to-do, with a median household income nearly twice the national average, 18 percent of all students are eligible for free or reduced-price school lunches, 9 percent live in households with annual incomes under $25,000, and 5 percent live beneath the official poverty line. The twelve surveyed schools span the full range of this population's ethnic and socioeconomic diversity.

Further information about both surveys is available on-line at www. millennialsrising.com.

Sidebar Voices

We draw our sidebar voices from nearly two hundred sources—including fifty-five newspapers, fifty-four magazines, sixty internet sites, sixteen other media sources, eight books, and three high school classes.

Many of the voices come from familiar periodicals (*The Washington Post, The New York Times, The Wall Street Journal, USA Today, Time, Newsweek,* and *U.S. News & World Report*), all of which have boosted their coverage of youth issues in recent years. Thanks to the internet, we were able to track down Millennial news items and features in dozens of regional papers spanning every part of the country (e.g., Boston, Norfolk, Augusta, St. Petersburg, Amarillo, St. Louis, Chicago, Minneapolis, Missoula, Seattle, Portland, Sacramento), plus Canada, Europe, and Asia. Other sidebar sources include business, religious, educational, political, research, and associational publications—among which *American Demographics, The American Enterprise, Child, Phi Delta Kappan,* and *Teen People* stand out. Frank Gregorsky's "Love Those Millennials" newsletter and Don Tapscott's *Growing Up Digital* book are also excellent sources of youth quotes.

The world wide web provides a variety of candid and colorful personal comments from kids, teens, parents, and others. The most useful sites include standard news outlets such as ABCnews.go.com, channel one.com, and msnbc.com; on-line magazines such as slate.com and salon.com; electronic communities such as discovery.org, geocities.com, and zdnet.com; youth-oriented gatherings such as boomerang.nu, free zone.com, headbone.go.com, kidscom.com, and nickellennium.com; commercial and cultural sites such as americangirl.com, flickfilosopher.

com, girlsgamesinc.com, kidbiz.com, and myfamily.com; and generational links such as generation-y.com and millennials.com.

By far the most important internet contribution comes from our own web site, fourthturning.com, from which we quote over two dozen discussants from across the United States and in all walks of life. Every Millennial voice is identified either by age or student status. A number of the teen quotes are excerpted from essays submitted to us by students at Langley, Marshall, and McLean high schools in Fairfax County, Virginia.

Text References

ABBREVIATIONS

AGI   Alan Guttmacher Institute

AmChild   Donald J. Hernandez, *America's Children: Resources from Family, Government, and the Economy* (Russell Sage Foundation, 1993)

AmDem   *American Demographics*

BLS   Bureau of Labor Statistics, U.S. Department of Labor

CDC   Centers for Disease Control and Prevention, U.S. Department of Health and Human Services

Census   U.S. Bureau of the Census

ChBur   Children's Bureau, of the Administration on Children, Youth and Families, of the Administration for Children and Families, U.S. Department of Health and Human Services

ChildTime   Sandra L. Hofferth and Jack Sandberg, *Changes in American Children's Time, 1981–1997* (Nov. 9, 1998), Institute for Social Research and Population Studies Center, University of Michigan.

CondEd   National Center for Education Statistics, *The Condition of Education* (U.S. Department of Education), published annually.

CPR   U.S. Bureau of the Census, *Current Population Report*, enumerated by series, e.g., P20 or P60, and date.

DrexelPoll   Drexel University, *Drexel University Futures Poll: Teenagers, Technology and Tomorrow* (1977).

FamGr   National Center for Health Statistics, *Fertility, Family Planning, and Women's Health: New Data from the 1995 National Survey of Family Growth* (Vital and Health Statistics, U.S. Department of Health and Human Services; May 1997).

Freshman L. J. Sax, A. W. Astin, W. S. Korn, and K. M. Mahoney, *The American Freshman* (Higher Education Research Institute, University of California at Los Angeles), published annually, yearly surveys since 1966.

Gallup Gallup News Service, The Gallup Organization (see www.gallup.com).

Gen2001 Northwestern Mutual Life, *Generation 2001 Survey* (1999)

GettingBy Public Agenda, *Getting By: What American Teenagers Really Think About Their Schools* (1997).

HHS U.S. Department of Health and Human Services

HighAch Who's Who Among American High School Students, *Annual Survey of High Achievers* (see www.eci-whoswho.com/highschool/annualsurveys). "High-achieving" high school student interviewed annually since 1967.

HSt U.S. Bureau of the Census, *Historical Statistics of the United States: Colonial Times to 1970* (1975).

JAMA *Journal of the American Medical Association*

Kids Public Agenda, *Kids These Days '99* (1999)

LAT *Los Angeles Times*

Mood National Association of Secondary School Principals, *The Mood of American Youth* (1974, 1983, and 1996); students aged 13–17 interviewed early in each year.

Mothers The Pew Research Center for the People and the Press, *Motherhood Today—A Tougher Job, Less Ably Done* (May 9, 1997).

MTF Lloyd D. Johnston, Jerald G. Bachman, and Patrick M. O'Malley (project directors), *Monitoring the Future Study*, Institute for Social Research, University of Michigan; annual questions to students in grades 12 (since the class of 1975) and in grades 10 and 8 (since the class of 1991); reports issued in various years.

NCCAN National Center on Child Abuse and Neglect, of the Administration on Children, Youth and Families, of the Administration for Children and Families, U.S. Department of Health and Human Services

NCHS National Center for Health Statistics, U.S. Department of Health and Human Services

NVSR National Center for Health Statistics, *National Vital Statistics Reports* (U.S. Department of Health and Human Services); released irregularly.

NYT *The New York Times*

RoperYth Roper Starch Worldwide, *Roper Youth Report;* published annually; results reported irregularly (see www.roper.com).

SAMHSA Substance Abuse and Mental Health Services Administration, U.S. Department of Health and Human Services

ShellPoll Shell Oil Company, *The Shell Poll* (1999)

StatAbs U.S. Bureau of the Census, *Statistical Abstract of the United States,* published annually.

StateYth Horatio Alger Association, *The State of Our Nation's Youth, 1999–2000* (1999)

Trends U.S. Department of Health and Human Services, *Trends in the Well-Being of America's Children & Youth: 1998* (1999).

TRU Teenage Research Unlimited.

U.S.News *U.S. News & World Report*

WP *The Washington Post*

WSJ *The Wall Street Journal*

YATS Defense Manpower Data Center, *Youth Attitude Tracking Survey* (U.S. Department of Defense); survey of potential high school-aged recruits; published annually.

YouthOp PRIMEDIA, Inc., and Roper Starch Worldwide, Inc., *The PRIMEDIA/Roper National Youth Opinion Survey* (1998); students in grades 7–12 interviewed in Nov., 1998.

CHAPTER ONE

THE NEXT GREAT GENERATION

On opinions about kids making the world a better place, see *Kids.* **Tyler Hudgens,** 15, at McLean High School, VA, in essay shared with authors. **"The Buzz,"** *Newsweek* 8/9/99.

NOT X, NOT Y—CALL THEM MILLENNIALS. On lost generation, see ch. 4. **On pessimists,** see chs. 4, 8. **On self-absorbed,** see chs. 7, 8, 10. **On distrustful,** see chs. 8, 10. **On rule breakers,** see ch. 9. **On neglected,** see chs. 6, 8. **On stupid,** see ch. 7; and, **for "cool to be smart,"** see "Kids Think Smart Is Cool and School Is In, *RoperYth* 4/16/98. **On progress,** see chs. 7, 8, 12. **Shansel Nagia,** 17, at McLean High School, VA, in essay shared with authors. **Lesley Milner,** 18, at Marshall High School, VA, in essay shared with authors. **David,** 14, on @webtv.net, 2/28/99. **Nagia,** op. cit.

A FRESH LOOK. Three newsweekly covers: "Pokémon!" cover of *Time* 11/22/99; "Dyslexia," cover of *Newsweek* 11/22/99; "Cheating, Writing, and Arithmetic," cover of *U.S.News* 11/22/99. **On money being spent on kids,** see ch. 12. **On number of Millennials and their minority and immigrant shares,** see ch. 4 and Data Sources, "Immigration" and "Population by Generation." **On nonwhite trends:** For uniforms, see ch. 7; see also school surveys reported in periodic "backgrounders" from the National Association of Elementary School Principals (www.naesp.org); for standardized curricula, see ch. 7; for social pathologies, see ch. 9 and Data Sources, "Crime," "Sexual Activity," and "Substance Abuse"; for family structure, see ch. 6 and Data Sources, "Family Structure."

REVERSING HISTORY'S DELTA. Josh Lee, 17, of IL, quoted in "Parents Don't Make Grade, Teens Say," www.suntimes.com 6/20/99. **For share of teens who think that TV shows for them are offensive,** see *HighAch*. **Bill Bradley,** quoted in "Family Angst Driving Politicians," www.news day.com 6/18/99.

OVERCOMING PESSIMISM. David Sarasohn, "Adult Scaredy-Cats of Our Own Kids," *San Francisco Examiner* 6/26/99. **People for the American Way,** *Democracy's Next Generation II* (1992). **William J. Bennett,** in Bennett, John J. DiIulio, and John P. Walters, *Body Count: Moral Poverty . . . and How to Win America's War Against Crime and Drugs* (1996). **For "edgy, in-your-face, Generation Y 'tude,"** see Michael O'Sullivan, " 'Go'? Go!," *WP* 4/9/99. **For share of all households having children,** see *StatAbs.* **On parents grading themselves and others as parents,** see survey summarized in "Parents Tell of Decisions, Struggles in Child-Rearing," *LAT* 6/13/99. **David Whitman,** *The Optimism Gap* (1998). **For *Kids These Days '99,*** see *Kids.* **Josephson Institute of Ethics,** *1998 Report Card on the Ethics of American Youth* (1999). **Donna Shalala,** quoted in "Teen Sex Down, New Study Shows," *HHS News* (HHS press release, May 1, 1997). **Ortega y Gasset,** cited in *The Modern Theme* (*El tema de nuestro tiempo,* 1923), trans. in Julián Marías, *Generations: A Historical Method,* 1970 (*El metodo histórico de las generaciones,* 1967), 94.

CHAPTER TWO

FROM BABIES ON BOARD TO POWER TEENS

Time **cover story,** "The New Baby Bloom," *Time* 2/22/82. Neil Postman, **The Disappearance of Childhood,** (1982). Marie Winn, **Children Without Childhood,** (1983). Vance Packard, **Our Endangered Children: Growing Up in a Changing World,** (1983). **For "rising tide of mediocrity,"** see U.S. Department of Education, *A Nation at Risk: The Imperative for Educational Reform* (National Commission on Excellence in Education, 1983). **For divorce rates,** see Data Sources, "Vital Statistics." **For abortion rates,** see Data Sources, "Abortions." **For violent crime rates,** see Data Sources, "Crime." **For rates of substance abuse,** see Data Sources, "Substance Abuse."

FOLLOW THE BREAKING WAVE. On rise of celebrity pregnancies, see "Moms-to-Be: In Vogue from the Workplace to the Runway," *St. Louis Post-Dispatch* 5/5/94; and "Fertile Images," *WP* 12/26/97. **For ranking of news stories,** see Pew Research Center for the People and the Press, "Public Attentiveness to Major News Stories (1986–1999)," at www.people-press.org/database.htm. **For *Time* reviewer,** see Richard Corliss, "Hollywood's Summer: Just Kidding," *Time* 6/28/93. **For rise in number of periodicals offered to young children,** see Samir Husni, quoted in "The Right Place to Find Children," *AmDem* Feb. 1992. **For rise in sale of children's music,** see "Musicians of '60s Sing New Songs for Tots of '90s," *WSJ* 8/7/95. **On Walt Disney and cartoonists,** see *Fairfax Journal* 11/17/88 B6. **For infertility-related doctor visits,** see "Birth Control That Really Works," *U.S.News* 3/16/87. **For rise in popularity of staying home with family,** see summary of surveys in "Balancing Act, Scale Tips Toward Family," *USA Today* 1/25/95. **"The 60s Generation, Once High on Drugs, Warns Its Children,"** *WSJ* 1/29/90. **"Boomers: The 'Not As I Did' Parents,"** *NYT* 11/30/95. **Vincent Femia,** quoted in "P.G. Youths in Drug Cases Increasingly Tried as Adults," *WP* 11/9/89. **George Voinovich,** quoted in "New Drive to Aid Children Often Cuts Adult Programs," *WP* 3/27/91. **On rise in sales of Gesell Test materials,** see "Debate Intensifying on Screening Tests Before Kindergarten," *NYT* 5/11/89. **Chester Finn,** "A Seismic Shock for Education," *NYT* 9/3/89. **For**

trend in teachers' pay, see *CondEd*. **Ellen Goodman,** "Out of School and Into Trouble," *WP* 7/13/96. **Judy McGrath,** quoted in "A More Tolerant Generation," *Forbes* 9/8/97.

HOW HISTORY SHAPES GENERATIONS. For a discussion of America's ancestral generations, including their birthdates, see Strauss and Howe, *Generations* (1991). **"Millennial Generation"** first appeared in the above, which went to press in October 1990. **"Generation Y"** (editorial), *Advertising Age* 8/30/93. **For 1998 college poll,** see *Gen2001*. **For significant early (pre-1998) media stories on post-X generation,** see "Generation Y," *op. cit.;* "Generation Y," *New York* 5/23/94; Neil Howe and Bill Strauss, "The Millennial Generation," *USA Today* 9/7/94; Kristina Sauerwein, "A Name They Can Claim . . . ," *St. Louis Post-Dispatch* 3/20/96; John Omicinski, "Are 'Millennial Generation' Kids the Next Group of National Heroes?" Gannett News Service 12/24/96; Melinda Beck, "The Next Population Bulge: Generation Y Shows Its Might," *WSJ* 2/3/97, and "Maybe Rock 'N Roll Really Is Here to Stay," *WSJ* 2/5/97; Lauren Rublin, "Goodbye Grunge," *Barron's* 2/3/97; Frank Gregorsky, " 'Millennial Generation' Spurns Grunge and Gloom" (op-ed), *Seattle Times* 4/4/97; "Here Comes the Sunshine Generation," *Toronto Globe and Mail* 5/10/97; Neil Murray, "Welcome to the Future: The Millennial Generation," *Journal of Career Planning and Employment* Spring 1997; Joan Verdon, "Marketing Teen Spirit," Bergen County *Record* 6/13/97; Dyan Machan, "A More Tolerant Generation," *Forbes* 9/8/97; Nina Munk, "Girl Power," *Fortune* 12/8/97; Maya Blackmun, "Governor's Baby Part of a New Golden Generation," *Oregonian* 10/29/97. **Douglas Coupland,** *Generation X* (1991). **On Boomers as a generation of negative behavioral trends** (from first to last cohort), see Strauss and Howe, *Generations,* chs. 2, 11.

HOW GENERATIONS SHAPE HISTORY. Robert Putnam, "Bowling Alone: America's Declining Social Capital," *Journal of Democracy* Jan. 1995. **"Lonely crowd,"** coined in David Reisman, *The Lonely Crowd* (1950). **Michael J. Sandel,** "Easy Virtue," *The New Republic* 9/2/96. **"Cultural elite,"** coined in cover story, *Newsweek* 10/4/92. **"Gen Nester,"** coined in "The Young and the Nested," *Time* 11/10/97. **"Power elite,"** coined in C. Wright Mills, *The Power Elite* (1956). **For "idealistic children,"** see

Benjamin Spock, *The Common Sense Book of Baby and Child Care* (1946), ch. 1.

CHAPTER THREE

THE COMING MILLENNIAL REVOLUTION

ALWAYS A SURPRISE. George Marshall, quoted by Ronald Reagan, speech to Republican National Convention (Sept. 15, 1988). *Fortune* **cover story,** "The Class of '49" (June 1949). **On "trend away from material aspirations,"** see *AmDem* (marketing materials, 1986) on the high school "class of 1986."

HOW ALL GENERATIONS REBEL. Alexis de Tocqueville, *Democracy in America* (1835; Random House, 1945), 62. Otto Butz, ed., *The Unsilent Generation,* 1958.

THE COMING MILLENNIAL REVOLUTION. Bob Dole, quoted in "In Contrasting Himself to Clinton, Dole Finds Voice," *WP* 3/9/96.

CHAPTER FOUR

THE BABY BOOMLET

On number of births, see Data Sources, "Vital Statistics." **On total population of Millennials,** see Data Sources, "Population by Generation." According to a search of all publications archived by the Dow Jones Newswires, **the first of use of "baby boomlet"** was in *NYT* 7/14/81; **of "echo boom,"** in *WSJ* 3/4/82.

BEHIND THE RISING NUMBERS. On fertility rates and numbers of births, see Data Sources, "Fertility" and "Vital Statistics." **On the rising lifetime birth expectations of Gen Xers,** see NCHS, "Birth Expectations of Women in the United States, 1973–88," *Vital and Health Statistics* (series 23, no. 17; Feb. 1995). See also *FamGr.* **On raising a family as a life goal,** see *UCLA.*

AMERICA'S NEW LOVE AFFAIR WITH BABIES. On sterilization rates, see NCHS, "Surgical Sterilization in the United States: Prevalence and Characteristics, 1965–95," *Vital and Health Statistics* (series 23, no. 20; June 1998). **On abortion rates,** see Data Sources, "Abortions." **On wanted births,** see *FamGr.* **On fertility rates,** see Data Sources, "Fertility." **On multiple births,** see NCHS, "Trends in Twin and Triplet Births: 1980–97," *NVSR* (vol. 47, no. 24; 10/14/99). **On childlessness,** see Amara Bachu, "Is Childlessness Among American Women On the Rise?" Populations Division Working Paper No. 37 (Census, May 1999). **On older parents,** see Data Sources, "Age of Mothers." **On singleton children and sibship size of family,** see Data Sources, "Sibship Size." **On the influence of birth order,** see recent summary of research in Frank J. Sulloway, *Born to Rebel: Birth Order, Family Dynamics, and Creative Lives* (1996). **On parental education,** see Data Sources, "Educational Attainment."

WHAT'S IN A MILLENNIAL NAME? On U.S. given names, by year of birth, see summaries and tables in Office of the Chief Actuary, Social Security Administration, "Name Distributions in the Social Security Area, August 1997," Actuarial Note No. 139 (June 1998), available at www.ssa. gov/OACT/pubs.html.

SECOND-GENERATION IMMIGRANTS. On immigration and foreign-born numbers, see Data Sources, "Immigration." **For numbers on second-generation immigrant children, their health, their use of English, and indicators of their well-being,** see *Trends,* Part II; Alejandro Portes (ed.), *The New Second Generation* (Russell Sage Foundation, 1996); and Donald J. Hernandez (ed.), *Children of Immigrants* (National Academy Press, 1999). **On benefits to immigrant families,** see Kristin F. Butcher and Luojia Hu, "Use of Means-Tested Transfer Programs by Immigrants, Their Children, and Their Children's Children," Working Paper No. 71 (Joint Center for Poverty Research, Jan. 1999). **On mixed citizenship families,** see Michael Fix and Wendy Zimmermann, *All Under One Roof: Mixed-Status Families in an Era of Reform* (Urban Institute, June 1999). **For births by state,** see Data Sources, "Vital Statistics" and Jerome N. McKibben and Kimberly A. Faust, "The Baby Boomlet Goes to College," *AmDem,* June 1999. **For race and ethnicity by age and state,** see "State

Population Estimates, 1990–98," Census (downloadable at www.census. gov/population/www/estimates/statepop.html). **Christy Haubegger,** quoted in "Latino America," *Newsweek* 7/12/99.

THE RISING WELL-BEING OF BABIES. On Lamaze, see Nicole Bokat, "Natural Childbirth: From Option to Orthodoxy," *On the Issues* 12/1/95, and "Lamaze—Fruitful and Multiplying," *WSJ* 8/27/99. **On smoking and drinking,** see NCHS, "Smoking During Pregnancy, 1990–96," *NVSR* (vol. 47, no. 10; 11/19/98); and CDC, *PRAMS: 1996 Surveillance Report* (1999). **On prenatal care,** see Michael D. Kogan, et al., "The Changing Pattern of Prenatal Care Utilization in the United States, 1981–1995, Using Different Prenatal Care Indices," *JAMA* 5/27/98. **On Southeast Asian mothers,** see "Born in the USA: Infant Health Paradox," *JAMA* 12/21/94. **On infant mortality,** see Data Sources, "Vital Statistics"; and discussion in *Trends,* HC 1.1. **On SIDS,** see "On SIDS, Parents Ahead of Caregivers," *WP* 12/15/98. **On "low" and "very low" birthweight and Apgar scores,** see *Trends,* HC 2.1–2.3.

THE RISING WELL-BEING OF KIDS AND TEENS. On child mortality by age bracket, see Data Sources, "Vital Statistics." **For statistical overview on most health conditions mentioned here,** see *Trends,* HC 2.4–2.14. **On health insurance coverage,** see "Health Insurance Coverage," *CPR,* P60. **On sick days lost,** see eighth- and tenth-grade student responses in *MTF.* **On youth suicide,** see Data Sources, "Vital Statistics." **On rise of chronic conditions,** see "Trouble Plagues Preemies Who Are Saved," *WSJ* 9/22/94. **On asthma,** see CDC, "Surveillance for Asthma—United States, 1960–95," *MMWR Surveillance Summaries,* 4/24/98, and "Asthma Rates Hit Epidemic Numbers; Experts Wonder Why," *American Medical News* 5/11/98. **On obesity,** see "Overweight children and adolescents 6–17 years of age," chart published by CDC, updated 11/6/98; various CDC news releases; and Colleen Keller and Kathleen R. Stevens, "Childhood Obesity: Measurement and Risk Assessment," *Pediatric Nursing* 11/21/96. **On ADD,** see, for example, Lawrence H. Diller, *Running on Ritalin* (1999); Richard DeGrandpre, *Ritalin Nation* (1999); and "Doing Ritalin Right," *U.S.News* 11/23/98. **Mark A. Stein,** quoted in "Behavioral Drug Use in Toddlers Up Sharply," *WP* 2/23/00.

CHAPTER FIVE

KINDERPOLITICS

Sylvia Ann Hewlett, *When the Bough Breaks: The Cost of Neglecting Our Children* (1991). **"Kinderpolitics,"** first use in headline: "Kinderpolitics '96," *U.S.News* 9/16/96.

MILLENNIALS AND THE LONG BOOM. For dates of economic recessions, see the calendars maintained by the National Bureau of Economic Research (at www.nber.org/cycles.html). **On working mothers and women's education,** see Data Sources, "Educational Attainment" and "Employment." **On the share of dual-earner couples in which wives outearn husbands** (16 percent in 1981, 23 percent in 1996), see Anne E. Winkler, "Earnings of Husbands and Wives in Dual-Earner Families," *Monthly Labor Review* (BLS, Apr. 1998). **On kids with parents in the labor force,** see *Trends,* ES 3.3; *Key Indicators of the Labor Market* (International Labor Organization, 1999). **On family income and poverty,** see Data Sources, "Income and Poverty."

MILLENNIALS AND SOCIAL FRAGMENTATION. C. Wright Mills, *The Power Elite* (1956). **Joel Garreau,** *Edge City* (1992). **Jackson's speech** excerpted in "We Must Forgive Each Other," *WP* 7/18/84. **For findings of the Harvard Civil Rights Project,** see Gary Orfield and John T. Yun, *Resegregation in American Schools* (The Civil Rights Project, Harvard University, June 1999). **Mario Cuomo,** at the Democratic National Convention in 1984. **Charles Murray,** *Losing Ground: American Social Policy 1950–1980* (1984). **On income inequality,** see Census family income data as tabulated in 1999 by the Economic Policy Institute (epinet.org). **Jonathan Kozol,** *Savage Inequalities: Children in America's Schools* (1992). **Mary Gail Snyder and Edward J. Blakely,** *Fortress America: Gated Communities in the United States* (1997). **On family income by race, presence of fathers, and employment of mothers,** see Data Sources, "Income and Poverty."

MILLENNIALS AND KINDERPOLITICS. On spending growth on federal programs for children versus the elderly, we used the unpublished data underlying Neil Howe and Richard Jackson, *1998 Chartbook: Entitlements and the Aging of America* (National Taxpayers Union Foundation, 1998), Chart 3-10. **On share of pregnancies and child births covered by Medicaid,** see testimony of HHS Secretary Donna Shalala to the U.S. Senate Labor Committee (Apr. 18, 1997). **Survey on curfews by U.S. Conference of Mayors,** cited in "Watching the Curfew," *WP* 10/2/99. **On number of states with "graduated licenses" for teens,** see "New Rules for New D.C. Drivers," *WP* 10/5/99. **On decline in bicycling,** see *Chicago Sun Times* (July 1999), in summary provided on www.fourthturning.com, 7/13/99. **On number of kids traveling alone by air,** see "Stranded? But you're only 5," *U.S.News* 7/20/98. **"It's 4:00 P.M. Do You Know Where Your Children Are?"** headline and excerpt from article in *Newsweek* 4/27/98. **On surveys of parents about kids and the internet,** see Joseph Turow, *The Internet and the Family* (Annenberg Public Policy Center, May 1999).

CHAPTER SIX

GROUND ZERO OF THE CULTURE WARS

THE MILLENNIAL-ERA FAMILY. For academic in *The Washington Post,* see E. J. Dionne, "A Parents' Manifesto," *WP* 6/9/98. **"Kids Are Us,"** article by Anthony Giardini, *GQ* (June 1998). **Elinor Burkett,** *The Baby Boon: How Family-Friendly America Cheats the Childless* (2000). **Hillary Rodham Clinton,** *It Takes a Village and Other Lessons Children Teach Us* (1996). **William J. Bennett** (ed.), *The Book of Virtues* (1993). **Cornel West and Sylvia Ann Hewlett,** *The War Against Parents: What We Can Do for America's Beleaguered Moms and Dads* (1998). **William and Martha Sears,** *The Baby Book: Everything You Need to Know About Your Baby from Birth to Age Two* (1993). **Louis Harris,** *Inside America* (1987). **Daniel Yankelovich,** *New Rules: Searching for Self-Fulfillment in a World Turned Upside Down* (1981). **On changes in Census perceptions,** see "Social Trends Show Signs of Slowing," *WP* 11/27/96. **On share of kids not living with two parents,** see Data Sources, "Family Structure." **On employed share of moms,** see Data Sources, "Employment."

SINGLE PARENTS, THEN AND NOW. On family structure, see Data Sources, "Family Structure"—and for long-term trends, see *AmChild,* p. 65. **On**

fathers never married to their children's mothers, see "Coalition Pushes Initiatives for Black Fathers," *WP* 6/17/99. **Ed O.G. and Da Bulldogs,** "Be A Father To Your Child" (song, 1991). **On rise in mediated divorces,** see "In Some Divorces, the Parents Do the Shuttling," *WP* 12/14/98. **Barbara Defoe Whitehead,** *The Divorce Culture* (1966).

FILLING IN THE FAMILY GAPS. On business trips with kids, see Travel Industry Association of America, *Travel Market Report 1998* (1999). **On trends in at-home work,** see Census, "Increases in At-Home Workers Reverses Earlier Trend," *Census Brief* (Mar. 1998); related tables available at www.census.gov/population/www/socdemo/workathome.html; and BLS, "Work at Home in 1997" (press release, 3/11/98). **On nontraditional employment,** see Laura Rich, "Stay-At-Home Workers," *Industry Standard News* 8/23/99. **AARP survey,** reported in "Grandparents Play a Big Part in Grandchildren's Lives, Survey Finds," *NYT* 1/6/00. **On kids living with a grandparent,** see Census, "Coresident Grandparents and Grandchildren," *CPR* P23–198 (May 1999). **On attitudes toward intergenerational living,** see survey by the National Opinion Research Center, cited in "Opinion Pulse," *American Enterprise* (May/June 1995). **On out-of-school time programs,** see fact sheets at the National Institute of Out-of-School Time (www.wellesley.edu/WCW/ CRW/SAC/factsht.html). **For figures on day-care use,** see Census, "Who's Minding Our Preschoolers?" *CPR* P70–62 (Nov. 1997) and related reports; the so-called "gold standard" in longitudinal studies of day care is the *Study of Early Child Care,* funded and published by the National Institute of Child Health and Human Development (see www.nichd.nih.gov/publications/pubs/early_child_care.htm). **The 9 percent figure,** from a Princeton Survey Research Associates survey, is cited in Maggie Gallagher, "Day Careless," *National Review* 1/26/98. **Karl Zinsmeister,** "Brave New World: How Day-Care Harms Children," *Policy Review* Spring 1988.

PARENTAL CARE IN THE MILLENNIAL ERA. On the Michigan finding on children's use of time, see *ChildTime.* **For statistics on self-care,** see Sandra L. Hofferth, Zita Jankuniene, and Peter D. Brandon, *Self-Care Among School-Age Children,* Institute for Social Research, University of Michigan, 2/28/00. **On the results of the University of Maryland's Use of Time Project,** see John P. Robinson and Geoffrey Godbey, *Time for Life:*

The Surprising Way Americans Use Their Time (second ed. 1999). On Michigan research, see John F. Sandberg and Sandra L. Hofferth, *Changes in Parental Time with Children, U.S. 1981–1997* (forthcoming), Institute for Social Research and Population Studies Center, University of Michigan. **For the report by the Families and Work Institute,** see James T. Bond, Ellen Galinsky, and Jennifer E. Swanberg, *The 1997 National Study of the Changing Workforce* (Families and Work Institute, 1998). **Ellen Galinsky,** *Ask the Children: What America's Children Really Think About Working Parents* (1999). **For survey on traditional activities,** see *Mothers.* **On 1976–82 jump in public worries about child abuse,** see Murray A. Straus and Richard J. Gelles, "Societal Change and Change in Family Violence from 1975 to 1985 as Revealed by Two National Surveys," *Journal of Marriage and the Family* (Aug. 1986). **For federal reports on child abuse,** see NCCAN, "Executive Summary of the Third National Incidence Study of Child Abuse and Neglect" (Sept. 1996), available at www.calib.com/nccanch/pubs/stat info/nis3.htm; and ChBur, *Child Maltreatment 1997: Reports From the States to the National Child Abuse and Neglect Data System* (1999). **On Straus's research,** see Straus and Gelles, *op. cit.;* Straus, "Trends in Cultural Norms and Rates of Partner Violence: An Update to 1992," in Sandra M. Stith and Murray A. Straus (eds.), *Understanding Partner Violence: Prevalence, Causes, Consequences, and Solutions* (1995); and chapter by Straus and Sherry L. Hamby in Glenda Kaufman Kantor and Jana L. Jasinski (eds.), *Out of Darkness: Contemporary Perspectives on Family Violence* (1997). **On trend in reported infant homicides,** see David Finkelhor, "The Homicides of Children and Youth," in Kantor and Jasinski, *op. cit.* **For survey on discipline,** see "Discipline: The New Rules," *Parents* Feb. 1998. **John Rosemond,** quoted in "Because I Said So!" *U.S.News* 11/10/97. **On strictness of Boomer versus Silent parents,** see *Mood* (1996 versus 1983). **On Boomer parents comparing how they discipline with how they were disciplined as kids,** see "Discipline: The New Rules," *op. cit.* **On Gary and Anne Marie Ezzo,** see "A Tough Plan for Raising Children Draws Fire," *WP* 2/27/99. **On trends in potty training,** see "Potty Training," *WP* (health section) 10/3/99. **Brazelton,** quoted in *ibid.* **For survey of women asked about today's mothers,** see *Mothers.* **For survey about fathers,** see 1997 Gallup poll, sited in "Opinion Pulse," *American Enterprise* Sept.–Oct. 1999. **On** whether parenting is harder on parents who sacrifice for their children, see *Kids.* **For kids grading parents,** see Ellen Galinsky, *Ask the Children, op. cit.* **On teen attitudes toward marriage, starting families, and having children,** see *MTF,* twelfth graders since 1975. **On whether high school students would raise their own kids as they were raised,** see *HighAch.*

CHAPTER SEVEN

RAISING STANDARDS FOR REGULAR KIDS

For TIMSS results, see Data Sources, "Educational Achievement." **John Leo,** "Hey, we're No. 19!" *U.S.News* 3/9/98. **John Jennings,** quoted in "When Public Equals Elite," *WP* 4/5/98.

THE WAKE-UP CALL. U.S. Department of Education, **A Nation at Risk: The Imperative for Educational Reform** (National Commission on Excellence in Education, 1983). **John Goodlad,** *Roanoke Times and World News* 7/20/83. **"Age of Lament,"** in "Outstanding American Schools," *U.S.News* 1/18/99. **For teachers who wish they'd be teachers again,** see periodic surveys by the National Educational Association (NEA) at www.nea.org. **For teachers' pay,** see *CondEd.* **For teachers with masters degrees,** see *CondEd* and periodic surveys by the NEA. **For parents on homework, teacher meetings, etc.,** see 1995 survey by the Hand In Hand Foundation (www.handinhand.org).

SCHOOL "CHOICE." Jay Mathews, "Take Out Your No. 2 Pencils," *WP* 11/9/98. **For parochial school enrollment,** see *StatAbs;* and the National Catholic Educational Association (www.ncea.org). **For "Christian" school enrollment,** see "Popularity Grows for Alternatives to Public Schools," *WP* 10/1/97. **Matthew Miller,** "A Bold Experiment to Fix City Schools," *Atlantic Monthly* July 1999. **On public support for vouchers,** see 1997 Gallup poll cited in Geneva Overholser, "Coming Around on Vouchers," *WP* 9/20/99. **For charter-school enrollment,** see David Osborne, "Healthy Competition," *The New Republic* 10/4/99; and Center for Education Reform, at www.edreform.com. **For home schooling,** see data and surveys by the Home Schooling Legal Defense Association, at www.hslda.org. **Adam Urbanski,** quoted in "School Boards' Roles Shift," *WSJ* 6/7/99. **On PTA membership,** see "What's Next for the PTA?" *U.S.News* 3/31/99.

VALUES. **Michael Josephson,** quoted in Lisa Miller, "Character-Building Program Linked to Religion," *WSJ* 10/25/99. **On Character Counts!,** see www.charactercounts.org. **Lisa Miller,** *op. cit.* **On Character First!,** see www.characterfirst.org.

TEAMWORK. **Lois Spotilla,** quoted in "A Push for More Focus on the Average Student," *WP* 3/9/98. **On special-ed budgets,** see Jay Mathews, "Averaged Out," *The New Republic* 12/28/98. **James Bryant Conant,** *The American High School Today* (1959). **"Forget Einstein, Think Team!"** *WP* 8/20/97. **On trends in school uniforms,** see school surveys reported in periodic "backgrounders" from the National Association of Elementary School Principals (www.naesp.org). **David Levin,** quoted in David Grann, "Back to Basics in the Bronx," *The New Republic* 10/4/99. **Ann Harmon,** quoted in "Uniforms Level the Playing Field at Public School," *Richmond Times-Dispatch* 9/17/98.

STANDARDS. **Esme Raji Codell,** quoted in "Teachers Eternal," *WP* 4/11/99. **Jay Mathews,** "Take Out Your No. 2 Pencils," *WP* 11/8/98. **On Praxis tests,** "Georgia's Teachers," *Atlanta Journal and Constitution* 1/31/99. **Jenny Hung,** "My Turn," *Newsweek* 9/20/99. **For student attitudes toward school,** see *MTF.* **Public Agenda,** *GettingBy.* **Patrick Welsh,** "Never Good Enough," *WP* 11/28/99.

RESULTS. **For NAEP results,** see Data Sources, "Educational Achievement." **Paul Beavers,** on www.fourthturning.com 1/29/99. **Linda Perlstein,** review of Alfie Kohn, *The Schools Our Children Deserve,* in *WP* 10/17/99. **Gerald Bracey,** "U.S. Students: Better Than Ever," *WP* 12/22/95. **Elizabeth Clement,** quoted in "Who Wants to Be a . . . Fifth Grader," *Sacramento Bee* 12/12/99.

Colin Powell, quoted by Eric L. Wee, "JROTC on the March at Area Schools, Raising Questions of Cost, Philosphy," *WP* 12/18/95. **Janice Cromer,** an author of *StateYth,* in Congressional testimony (Aug. 12, 1997). **Reporter from London *Times,*** cited in "The New Purity," Fox News 6/23/99.

THE MILLENNIAL TIME MACHINE. Stephanie Mazzamaro, of Ridgefield, CN, in "The Crazy Culture of Kids' Sports," *Time* 7/12/99. **For customary teen activities,** see *MTF.* **For listening to or watching sports games,** see *Mood.* **On trend in teen TV watching,** see *Mood* and *MTF.* For other media, see *Mood; RoperYth;* and Kaiser Family Foundation, *Kids & Media @ the New Millennium* (1999). **On computer and internet use,** see *Roper Yth;* and "Teens and Technology," CBS News/*New York Times* poll (Oct. 10, 1999). **For beepers and cell phones,** see "Fear and Violence Have Declined Among Teenagers," CBS News/*New York Times* poll (Oct. 10, 1999) summarized in *NYT* 10/20/99. **For the Michigan finding on children's use of time,** see *ChildTime.*

MILLENNIALS AND SPECIALNESS. Tracy Flick (played by Reese Witherspoon), in *Election* (1999). **Britney Spears,** quoted in "New Kids on the Clock," www.boston.com 3/7/99. **Coalition for America's Children,** *Great Expectations: How American Voters View Children's Issues* (1997). **For high priority adults place on kids,** see Ad Council survey, cited in "What Can We Do About Kids Today," in *Advertising Age* 4/27/98; see also "Most Turn to Family Member, More than State, for Answers," *WSJ* 6/24/99. **Lin Jia,** 18, at Marshall High School, VA, in essay shared with authors. **Tamara El-Khoury,** 17, at Langley High School, VA, in essay shared with authors. **For kids' perception of school and national problems,** see *YouthOp.* **For fault-finding for school violence,** see "Teenagers and Adults Differ on Causes, Cures for Columbine-Type Situations," Gallup 5/21/99. **For helping America to a better future,** see *YouthOp.* **For the greatest impact on the global environment,** see National 4-H Council, *EarthView Survey* 4/20/98.

MILLENNIALS AND SHELTERING. On being treated "like a child," see *Mood.* **Deborah Wadsworth,** in *GettingBy.* **For on-line teen poll,** see USA Weekend, "Teens and Freedom" (annual survey, 1997) at www.usaweek end.com.

MILLENNIALS AND CONFIDENCE "Sunshine Generation," headline in *Toronto Globe and Mail* 5/10/97. **For "I am usually happy,"** see *Kids.* **For "completely" or "mostly" satisfied,** see "Why Young Teens Whistle," *Healing Magazine,* Spring/Summer 1999, KidsPeace National Centers for Kids in Crisis (www.kidspeace.org). **On "happiness" trend among adults,** see responses (1976–96) to "happiness" questions to the General Social Survey. **For "harder" versus "easier" to grow up,** see "Fear and Violence Have Declined Among Teenagers," CBS News/*New York Times* poll (Oct. 10, 1999), summarized in *NYT* 10/20/99. **For KidsPeace report,** see "Why Young Teens Whistle," *op. cit.,* **Victor Thiessen,** quoted in "How Teens Got the Power," *Maclean's* 3/22/99. **On biggest personal concerns,** see *Mood* and *YouthOp.* **For historical trend in kids intending to go to college,** see *MTF* and *YATS.* **On college intentions in late '90s,** see *YouthOp; Mood; RoperYth; ShellPoll; StateYth; DrexelPoll;* and *Gen2001.* **For optimism and belief in economic opportunities,** see *ShellPoll; DrexelPoll;* and *Gen2001.* **For decline in "marriage/family" and "career success" and rise of "balance,"** see *Mood; MTF; Drexel;* and Sue Shellenbarger, "Job Candidates Really Want to Know: Will I Have a Life?" *WSJ* 11/17/99. **For making a contribution and giving children more opportunities,** see *MTF.*

MILLENNIALS AND TEAM ORIENTATION. For what needs fixing in schools, see *Mood; ShellPoll;* and *YouthOp.* **For unruly behavior,** see *GettingBy.* **On trust and other important personal qualities,** see *YouthOp; ShellPoll;* and Josephson Institute, *1998 Report Card on Ethics* (Oct. 1998). **For socializing and feeling lonely,** see *MTF.* **For staying with buddies,** see *YATS.* **For major causes of America's problems,** see *YouthOp.* **For "material things," "competition," and clothes,** see *MTF.* **For pressure to break rules,** "Teens Often Live in a Climate of Fear, Uncertainty and Danger," Gallup 4/28/99.

MILLENNIALS AND ACHIEVEMENT. **For students who have plans,** see *StateYth* and *Gen2001*. **For attitudes toward school,** see *MTF*. **For attitudes toward math and science,** see *Mood; MTF;* and CNN/*USA Today*/Gallup poll, cited in "Teenagers Attracted to Science, Math," cnn.com 4/22/97. **For desired use of free time,** see *MTF*.

MILLENNIALS AND PRESSURE. **On trend in average grades,** *MTF*. **On parental pressure to get good grades,** "Fear and Violence Have Declined Among Teenagers," CBS News/*New York Times* poll (Oct. 10, 1999); and *ShellPoll*. **For worries about finding a good job,** see National 4-H Council, *EarthView Survey* 4/20/98.

MILLENNIALS AND CONVENTION. **"Today's teens . . . too cool to care,"** from *YouthOp*. **For taste in music,** see *Mood*. **For "different values,"** see *MTF*. **1997 Gallup survey,** cited in "The Youth 'Crisis,'" *U.S.News* 5/5/97. **For share of kids aged 10–13 feeling "loved,"** see KidsPeace National Centers for Kids in Crisis, *1995 National Survey of Preteens* (1995). **On girls' relationships with moms,** see *Mood;* and Yankelovich Partners survey, cited in "Teen Girls Say Mom's Become a Pal," *USA Today* 12/13/98. **Oprah Winfrey,** cited in "Boomers Break Tradition of Distant Maternal Ties," *USA Today* 12/14/98. **On relationships with dads,** see *Mood* and *StateYth*. **For parents who are "in touch" and "easy to talk to,"** see CBS News/*New York Times* poll (Apr. 1999), cited in "Teen-Age Poll Finds a Turn to the Traditional," *NYT* 4/30/98; and 1997 CBS Poll of High School Class of 2000, cited in "Looking Forward to the Millennium," *WP* 1/20/97. **For "really important talks,"** see Nathan Cobb, "Meet Tomorrow's Teens," *The Boston Globe*, 4/28/98. **For Boomer responses in 1974,** see *Mood*. **For teens who are close to other adults,** see *Kids*. **For teachers that have changed their lives,** see *ShellPoll*. **For lists of heroes,** see TRU, *Marketing and Lifestyle Update* (Spring 1998). **For favoring teaching of values in schools,** see *ShellPoll* and "Teens Often Live in a Climate of Fear, Uncertainty and Danger," Gallup 4/28/99. **For "values and character,"** see authors' Class of 2000 Survey.

ZERO TOLERANCE. John Leo, "Cracking Down on Kids," *U.S.News* 12/13/99. **Charles Haydt,** quoted in "Schools Crack Down on Threats of Violence," *WP* 6/8/98. **For "The country is witnessing ...,"** see "Schools' New Watchword: Zero Tolerance," *NYT* 12/1/99. **For eighth- and tenth-grade suspensions,** see *MTF.* **For expulsions and exclusions in Fairfax County, VA,** see Fairfax County Public Schools, *Proposed Budget for FY 2001* (2000). **Edwin Merritt,** quoted in "A Superintendent Who Has Learned Unwanted Lessons," *NYT* 6/6/99. **For expulsion hearings by Fairfax County, VA, School Board,** see Fairfax County Public Schools, *op. cit.*

POLICING THE LITTE THINGS. Doyle Niemann, quoted in "Trashy Talk Makes Educators Cry Foul," *WP* 5/12/98.

SEX. **For the rise in the "new chastity" movement among youth in the mid-'90s,** see Gracie S. Hsu, "Revolt of the Virgins," *The World & I* 12/1/96. **On changes in rates of sexual activity and in contraception,** see Data Sources, "Sexual Activity." **Kirsty Doig,** cited by Helene Stapinsky, "Y Not Love?" *AmDem* Feb. 1999. **On shares of college freshmen opposed to casual sex,** see *Freshman.* **For the share of middle- and high-school students who have taken a virginity pledge,** see Demographic and Behavioral Sciences Branch of the National Institute of Child Health and Human Development, *Report to the NACHHD Council* (HHS, June 1999). **John Wrenn,** quoted in "Gym Students Still Sweat, They Just Don't Shower," *NYT* 4/22/96. **Wendy Shalit,** *A Return to Modesty* (1999). **Patricia Hersch,** *A Tribe Apart* (1998). **Arlington, VA, middle schooler,** quoted in "Parents Are Alarmed by an Unsettling New Fad in Middle Schools: Oral Sex," *WP* 7/8/99. **For poll on attitudes toward premarital sex,** see Nickelodeon/*Time* Poll in "The Kids Are Alright," *Time* 7/5/99.

SUBSTANCE ABUSE. On "Generation Jones," see "Keeping up with the Jones Generation," Scripps Howard News Service 1/6/00. **On rates of drug abuse,** see Data Sources, "Substance Abuse." **For arrests (age**

10–17) for drunkenness and drunk driving, see data tabulated by the Office of Juvenile Justice and Delinquency Prevention, at ojjdp.ncjrs.org. **For recent rates of abuse among students in grades 12, 10, and 8,** see *MTF.* **For popularity of marijuana users at school and impact of stars on popularity of drugs,** see Partnership for a Drug-Free America, *Partnership Attitude Tracking Study* (Nov. 22, 1999). **For survey on legalizing marijuana,** see Lewis D. Eigen and Joan Quinlan, *A Profile of Generation Y: The Millennial Generation* (Social and Health Services, Ltd., and Center for Substance Abuse Prevention 5/15/99). **For drug-overdose fatalities,** in 1979 and 1996, see Data Sources, "Vital Statistics." **Mike Males,** "Generation Gap," *LAT* 11/21/99. **Gen Xer,** in "Voices of a New Generation," www.geocities.com 4/21/99. **Partnership for a Drug-Free America,** *Partnership Attitude Tracking Study* (Nov. 22, 1999).

CRIME. **James Alan Fox and *U.S.News*,** cited in "Much-Feared Crime Wave Never Arrived," *Minneapolis Star Tribune* 12/13/99. **John J. DiIulio, Jr.,** "The Coming of the SuperPredators," *Weekly Standard* 11/27/95. **For crime, victimization, and arrest rates,** see Data Sources, "Crime." **National Center for Juvenile Justice,** *Juvenile Offenders and Victims: 1999 National Report* (Office of Juvenile Justice and Delinquency Prevention, Sept. 1999).

SCHOOL VIOLENCE. **For official yearly tally of all reported violent deaths at grade schools since 1992–93,** see National School Safety Center, *Report on School Associated Violent Deaths* (from 1991–92, updated every few months); see www.nsscl.org/home.htm. **For trends in school violence from 1991 to 1997,** see publication for CDC report: Nancy D. Brener, Thomas R. Simon, Etienne G. Krug, and Richard Lowry, "Recent Trends in Violence-Related Behaviors Among High School Students in the United States," *JAMA* 8/4/99. **For student perceptions about violence in the fall of 1998,** see Metropolitan Life Insurance Company, *The Metropolitan Life Survey of the American Teacher, 1999: Violence in America's Public Schools—Five Years Later* (May 1999). **For comparison of violent arrests by age, 1970 and 1996,** see Data Sources, "Crime." **For changing share of students saying violence is the worst problem they face,** see "Fear and Violence Have Declined Among Teenagers," CBS

News/*New York Times* poll (Oct. 10, 1999), summarized in *NYT* 10/20/99. **For poll of 6- to 14-year-olds,** see Nickelodeon/*Time* poll in "The Kids Are Alright," *Time* 7/5/99.

RAISING THE BAR. On 1999 Gallup Poll on gambling, see "How Gambling Affects Skeptical Generation Y," *Christian Science Monitor* 6/18/99. **Richard McGowan, Eric Sanchez, and Brad Stuart,** quoted in *ibid.* **Sheri Parks,** quoted in "Proliferating Profanity," *Washington Times* 8/10/99.

CHAPTER TEN

JUNIOR CITIZENS

On history survey, see the "Need" statement at the National Constitution Center web site, www.constitutioncenter.org/sections/museum/the_need.html.

COMMUNITY. Jason Redmond, described in "16-Year-Old Soldotna High School Student Designing Bicycle Transit System," *Anchorage Daily News* 10/27/99. **Amber Lynn Coffman,** described in "Daring to Care," *Seventeen* (June 1998). **Tallahassee 14-year-old** ("Sara"), quoted in "Students to Sound Off on Vouchers," *St. Petersburg Times* 3/19/99. **For change in Boy Scout membership,** see *StatAbs;* and most recent year in the *Annual Report of the Boy Scouts of America,* at www.bsa.scouting.org. **For change in Girl Scout membership,** see *StatAbs.* **On rise in community-service and service-learning programs in public schools,** see National Center for Education Statistics, "Service-Learning and Community Service in K–12 Public Schools," *Statistics in Brief* (U.S. Department of Education, Sept. 1999). **On duty of kids' generation to improve the environment,** see National 4-H Council, *EarthView Survey* 4/20/98.

RACE. For "least prejudiced . . . ," see "Teens and Race," *AmDem* June 1999, citing a recent Gallup Youth Survey. **On change in Latino share of TV characters,** see "In Networks' New Programs, A Startling Lack of Diversity," *WP* 7/13/99. **Michael Wood,** quoted in "Teens Are, Like, So

Next Week," *WP* 6/17/99. **Children Now,** *A Different World: Children's Perceptions of Race and Class in the Media* (1998). **On optimism of black teens on race,** see "Teens and Race," *op. cit.* **On optimism of generation and teachers on race,** see Class of 2000 Survey and Teachers Survey. **Joyce A. Ladner,** quoted in "Author Provides Parenting Advice," *WP* 3/4/99.

GENDER. Youdus Mirza, 17, at Langley High School, VA, in essay shared with authors. **For membership in Who's Who Among American High School Students,** see *HighAch.* **On 63 percent of top academic achievers,** see *StateYth.* **On increases among girls in cigarette smoking, substance abuse, weight problems, and eating disorders,** see Data Sources, "Substance Abuse"; and "Girls Close Gender Gap in Ways Welcome and Worrying," *WP* 6/17/98. **On boy-girl differences in homework, enrollments by subject, AP tests, grades, honors, and graduation rates,** see *CondEd;* "Where the Boys Aren't," *U.S.News* 2/8/99; Judith Kleinfeld, *The Myth That Schools Shortchange Girls* (Women's Freedom Network, 1998); and National Center for Education Statistics, "The 1994 High School Transcript Study Technical Report," *Special Report* (U.S. Department of Education, Aug. 1997). **On boy-girl differences in poor achievement, emotional disability, and self-esteem,** see Judith Kleinfeld, *op. cit.* **On pay gap,** see BLS, *Highlights of Women's Earnings in 1998* (U.S. Department of Labor, Apr. 1999). **On women-owned businesses,** see "Women-Owned Businesses Top 9 Million in 1999" (National Foundation of Women Business Owners, May 11, 1999). **For college graduates,** see National Center for Education Statistics, *Digest of Education Statistics* (U.S. Department of Education, annual). **For other comparisons,** see Diane Ravitch, "Girls Are Beneficiaries of Gender Gap," *WSJ* 12/17/98. **Rich Cronin,** quoted in Lisa Bannon, "More Kids' Marketers Pitch Number of Single-Sex Products," *WSJ* 2/14/00. **For statistics on sexual orientation of teens,** see Joyce Hunter's data, cited in "Out, Proud and Very Young," *Time* 12/8/97. **For gays as a group "most responsible for current problems,"** see *YouthOp.* **On single-sex middle schools in California,** see "Single-Sex Classes a First for State's Schools," *LAT,* 8/29/97. **Sarah Abrams,** 17, at Langley High School, VA, in essay shown to authors.

POLITICS. **Ann Tangerose,** quoted in "Political Leaders Aren't Heroes to Youngsters Anymore," *WSJ* 4/21/98. **Linda Wiley,** teacher in Round Rock, Texas, quoted in "Class Debate Sparks Congressional Visit," *Austin American-Statesman* 12/4/98. **Susan Reimer,** in "Out of the Mouths of Babes," Baltimore *Sun* 8/23/98. **On kids who think they could be elected president,** see Gary Langer, "Grow Up to Be President: Teens Say No Thanks," abcnews.com 2/15/99. **On trusting the federal government and public officials,** see *YouthOp;* and CNN poll, cited in "Clinton Scandal Has Not Taught Young Americans It's OK to Lie," cnn.com 2/17/99. **E. J. Dionne,** "Once a War Zone, Now a Park," *WP* 6/1/99. **Don Tapscott,** *Growing Up Digital,* **Julia Dotson,** quoted in "Ask Us, Use Us, Include Us!" *Children's Express* (New York Bureau, 1999). **Close Up Foundation,** *High School Students' Attitudes Toward Government and Politics* (2000). **On teenage reporter named Alex,** see Dana Milbank, "White House Watch: Map Flap," *The New Republic* 5/13/99. **Michael Eliason,** on www.fourthturning. com.

RELIGION. **For growth in prayer circles and clubs in public high schools,** see Stephen Braun, "Student-Led Prayer Groups Are Flourishing," *LAT* 5/9/98. **On influence of religion on teen lives,** see "Valuing God Is Cool," from the Eleventh Annual Special Teen Report, *USA Weekend* 5/1–3/98; and George H. Gallup International Institute, *The Spiritual Life of Young Americans: Approaching the Year 2000* (1999). **Share of teens who say they pray,** see survey by Barna Research Group, cited in "Rebels With a Cause," *WSJ* 12/18/98. **On trend in teen rate of church attendance,** see *MTF;* and George H. Gallup International Institute, *op. cit.* **Wendy Murray Zoba,** *Generation 2K: What Parents & Others Need to Know About the Millennials* (1999). **Mary Pat Tilghman,** quoted in "Rebels With a Cause," *op. cit.* **Zoba,** *op. cit.*

CHAPTER ELEVEN

THE HAPPINESS BUSINESS

For "one of the most perplexing crises," see Neil Strauss, "For Record Industry, All Signs Are Gloomy," *NYT* 12/4/96. **Stan Goman,** quoted in "Britney Rules the Airwaves," *USA Today* 2/23/99. **Neil Strauss,** *op. cit.*

THE MILLENNIAL TREMOR. Ken Ringle, "Young Blue Eyes," *WP* 5/23/99. **Michael Moss** of *Swing Time* magazine, quoted in "Back in the Swing," *WP* 10/26/98. **Peaches O'Dell,** quote in "Back in the Swing," *op. cit.* **For "a blend of the 50s,"** see Linda Lee, "Attack of the 90-Foot Teen-Agers," *NYT* 11/9/97. **Johnny Wright,** quoted in "New Kids on the Clock," www.boston.com, 3/7/99. **J. C. Chasez,** quoted in "Score One For The Boys," *WP* 3/19/99. **The 15-year-old fan is Irina,** quoted on www.channelone.com (May 1999). **Eric Weisbard,** "Generation Ex," *The Village Voice* 7/13/99. **Jon Pareles,** "When Pop Becomes the Toy of Teenyboppers," *NYT* 7/11/99. **For "two opposing forces,"** see Jim Farber, "Where the Boys Are," *Entertainment Weekly* 5/21/99. **"Eminem"** (rapper Marshall Mathers), quoted in "The Secret Life of Teens," *Newsweek* 5/10/99.

THE MILLENNIAL CHILD MAKEOVER. Linton Weeks, "Sheer Sorcery," *WP* 9/9/99. **Danielle Crittenden,** "Boy Meets Book" (review of Harry Potter books), *WSJ* 11/26/99. **For "There's nothing wrong with being angry,"** see "Kids Are Glued to a Violent Japanese Cartoon Show," *WSJ* 12/3/99. **Sheryl Leach,** quoted in "Stuuuupendous!" *Time* 12/21/92. **For "so saccharine,"** see John F. Kelly, "The Dark Side of that Smarmy Stuffed Purple Beast," *WP* 2/14/93. **Dale Russakoff,** "On Children's TV, An Unusual New Character: Cool Parent; Shows Tap Into a Longing for Adult Company," *WP* 12/13/98. *The 1999 State of Children's Television Report,* Annenberg Public Policy Center of the University of Pennsylvania; see appcpenn.org/kidstv99/rep28.htm. **Teletubbies creator,** Anne Wood, quoted in "Sesame Street It's Not," *U.S.News* 10/13/97. **On skip-on-the-set and wave-to-the-kids,** see "Attack of the Skip 'n' Waves," *WSJ* 10/23/98.

THE MILLENNIAL TEEN MAKEOVER. On the drop in Fox's prime-time audience, see "Fox Sees its Young Audience Shrink as Rivals Bask in Their Ratings Gains," *WSJ* 10/27/99. **Larry Gleason,** quoted in "Teen Players," *Entertainment Weekly* 5/7/99. **Children Now President James Steyer,** summarizing results of Children Now survey of 10- to 14-year-olds, as quoted by Laura Sessions Stepp, "Youth Say TV Shapes Values," *WP* 2/27/95. **Jason Gay,** "Rebels with a Cause," *Boston Phoenix* 4/22/99. **On top twenty children's shows in early '60s,** see Gerry Roe, "What Kids Really Like," *TV Guide* 11/17/62. **For share of adults who think TV is**

getting worse, see Gallup polls cited in Karl Zinsmeister, "Taking Out the TV Trash," *American Enterprise* Mar.–Apr. 1999. **For share of teens who think that TV shows for them are offensive,** see *HighAch*. **For origin of "vast wasteland,"** a term coined by FCC Chairman Newman Minnow in 1961, see Minnow and C. Lamay, *Abandoned in the Wasteland* (1995). **John Leo,** "Raging Hormones on TV," *U.S.News* 2/2/98. **For comment in *Maclean's,*** see "How Teens Got the Power," *Maclean's* 3/22/99. **For remarks on *American Pie,*** see "Fear and Lusting," *Newsweek* 7/12/99. **For "on the cheap . . . ,"** see Josh Young, "They're All That," *Entertainment Weekly* 3/6/99. **On videogame "subculture,"** see "King of the Gamers," *WP* 12/23/99. **Simon de Montigny,** quoted in *ibid.* **Vanessa Silverton Peel,** 15, of Los Angeles, CA, quoted in "Attack of the 90-Foot Teen-Agers," *NYT* 11/9/97. ***Lolita* publicist,** Ronni Chasen, quoted in "Orphan 'Lolita' Goes to Europe," *Newsweek* 9/1/97. **On skateboarders in Vans Skate Park,** see Jonathan Last, "Doesn't Smell Like Teen Spirit," *Weekly Standard* 2/15/99.

TOWARD THE TOTAL MILLENNIAL MAKEOVER. David Brooks, *Bobos in Paradise* (2000).

CHAPTER TWELVE

ROCKET CASH

Alona Wartofsky, "Rock's Hostile Takeover," *WP* 10/3/99. **J. Walker Smith,** quoted in "Teens Are, Like, So Next Week," *WP* 6/17/99. **Lonnie Fogel,** quoted in "Listening to the Echo Boom," *WP* 3/6/99. **Molly Melamed,** 16, of Farmington Hills, Michigan, quoted in "Adults-Only Catalog Excites Teen Interest," *USA Today* 12/2/99. **For Fallon-McElligott's segmentation of youth market,** see "Competing for Cool," *Newsday* 1/24/99. **Jane Rinzler,** quoted in "Competing for Cool," *op. cit.*

CONSUMERISM. For '90s growth in purchases by and for children aged 4 to 12, see James McNeal, "Tapping the Three Kids' Markets," *AmDem* Apr. 1998. **On widening gender-role differences in toys,** see Lisa Bannon, "More Kids' Marketers Pitch Number of Single-Sex Products," *WSJ* 2/14/00. **Pamela Haag,** quoted in *ibid.* **"Kids Make Many Purchase Deci-**

sions, But Parents' Input Still Counts," *RoperYth* 4/16/98. **On public concerns about toys,** see "Fun and Safety Are Top Draws for Adult Toy Choices for Kids," *RoperYth* 2/1/99. **For comment in *Economist*,** see "Where the Furbies Come From," *Economist* 12/19/98. **On trend in kid influence over parental spending,** see James McNeal, *op. cit.* **On declining age of initial kid influence,** see McNeal, quoted in "Marketers Following Youth Trends to the Bank," *WP* 4/19/99. **On share of kid-influenced money going to car purchases,** see James McNeal, *op. cit.* **J. D. Power,** APEAL study of 28,000 new-vehicle buyers (1995). **On Nickelodeon surveys,** see "Hey Kid, Buy This!" *Business Week* 6/30/97. **Shelly Reese,** "The Quality of Cool," *Marketing Tools* 7/1/97. **For comment in *USA Today*,** see "Baggy Pants: They're So Yesterday," *USA Today* 3/23/99. **On share of kids with their own room, and on the gadgets within them,** see "Sending Kids to Their Rooms Isn't What It Used to Be," highlights from Nickelodeon/Yankelovich Youth Monitor 6/26/97; and "Poll: Teens and Technology," cbs.com 10/19/99. See also "Kids' Computer Use Stabilizes," *RoperYth* (1998) and "Today's Kids—Especially Teens—Are Wired to the Hilt," *RoperYth* (1998). **On teens who say they could live without a computer or TV,** see CNN/*USA Today* poll, cited in "The Keyboard Kids," *Newsweek* 6/8/98. **On share of kids going on-line,** see "Kids Favor Internet for Homework, Chatting and Surfing," *RoperYth* (1998) and "America Is Fastest-Growing Internet Market, as Teens Lead the Way," *RoperYth* (1998). **On 2002 projection of on-line sales to kids,** by Jupiter Communications, see "The Selling of the Clickerati," *WP* 10/24/99.

MONEY AND JOBS. For estimate by Teen Research Unlimited, see "Teens Spend $153 Billion in 1999," Teenage Research Unlimited (press release; see www.teenresearch.com/news/indexnews.html); highly publicized TRU figure for 1998 was $141 billion. **Estimate by Rand Youth Poll,** cited in Equifax, "Equifax Taking Initiative to Educate Students on Financial Responsibility" (press release 12/14/98). **For $13 billion estimate,** see *Mood.* **For second 1996 estimate,** see "Weekly Spending Money for Children 8–17 Spikes Up Sharply," *RoperYth* 3/7/97. **For share of kids saying parental payments are biggest source of income,** see *Mood.* **On gifts from grandparents,** see "The Grandparent Niche," Roper Starch Worldwide; see www.roper.com. **Jeff Brazil,** "Play Dough," *AmDem* Dec. 1999. **On growth in money from chores,** see *MTF;* James McNeal, quoted in

"Tweens," *Newsweek* 10/18/99; and, for preteens, see *ChildTime*. **On attitude toward working at home in their future careers,** see *DrexelPoll*. **For "helping others who need help" and wanting others to report to them,** see *DrexelPoll*. **For teen desire to stay near parents,** see *YATS*. **On teen desire to work in groups,** see *DrexelPoll*. **On trend in allowances over time,** see *Mood* and *MTF*. **On measured trends in youth employment outside the home,** see Data Sources, "Employment"; on history, see *MTF;* and Committee on the Health and Safety Implications of Child Labor, *Protecting Youth at Work* (1998). **On trend in adult opinion toward teen work,** *Mood*. **Committee on the Health and Safety Implications of Child Labor,** *op. cit.* **On trend in teen attitudes toward teen work,** *Mood*. **"Survey: A Fine Crop of Young Workers,"** *Seattle Post-Intelligencer* 11/17/97. **Sherwood Ross,** quoted in "Survey . . . ," *op. cit.* **For *American Demographics* on "workplace atmosphere,"** see Marcia Mongelonsky, "Teens' Working Dreams," *AmDem* June 1998. **Sherwood Ross,** quoted in "Survey . . . ," *op. cit.*

COMMERCIALISM. Sheryl Leach, quoted in "Barney Creator Sheryl Leach," *Investor's Business Daily* 7/29/99. **Sean McGowan,** quoted in "Is Pokémon Evil?" *Time* 11/15/99. **Lynn Rosenblum,** "The Pokémon Craze: A Little Luck, a Lot of Marketing," *NYT* 11/13/99. **For comment in *Business Week,*** see "Hey Kid, Buy This!" *Business Week* 6/30/97. **For spending on ads directed at kids,** see David Siegel, general manager of Small Talk, quoted in Shelly Reese, "Kidmoney: Children As Big Business," *Technos Quarterly* Winter 1996. **James McNeal,** quoted in "Blessed Be Our Little Buyers," *The Boston Globe* 12/14/99. **"Generation Y"** (editorial), *Advertising Age* 8/30/93. **Nancy Brophy,** of Arlington Heights, IL, quoted in "Hey Kid, Buy This!" *op. cit.* **On "bratlash,"** see "The Race Is On in America to Raise Unspoiled Kids Amid Much Money," *WSJ* 1/14/00. **On teen opinion of TV ads,** see "Competing for Cool," *Newsday* 1/24/99. **On child and teen savings rates,** see *Mood;* see also "Virtual Piggy Banks Teach Real Lessons," *Newsweek* 10/4/99; and "Play Dough," *AmDem* Dec. 1999.

THE WINDS OF CHANGE. James McNeal, quoted in "Tapping the Three Kids' Markets," *AmDem* Apr. 1998. **Annie Granger,** 16, quoted in "How Teens Got the Power," *Maclean's* 3/22/99

GLOBAL GENERATIONS. On share of teens aged 15 to 18 not expecting to live in the country of their birth, see results of the "New World Teen Study" by D'Arcy Masius Benton & Bowles, summarized in Stuart Elliott, "Advertising," *WP* 12/23/94. **For study of English "Millennial Generation,"** see Madsen Pirie and Robert M. Worcester, *The Millennial Generation* (Adam Smith Institute, 1999). **David Kaiser,** professor of history at the U.S. Naval War College in Newport, RI, in correspondence with the authors. **On nations that have made prochild changes to their constitutions or legal codes,** see Carol Bellamy, executive director of the U.N. Children's Fund, quoted in "US Asked to OK Child Rights Treaty," *NYT* 11/12/99.

GLOBAL MILLENNIALS. For total fertility rates worldwide, see Data Sources, "Fertility." **For trends monitored by Freedom House,** see Adrian Karatnycky, *The 1999–2000 Freedom House Survey: Freedom, A Century of Progress* (Freedom House, 1999).

MILLENNIALS MOBILIZE. On households worldwide with web access, see "America is Fastest-Growing Internet Market, As Teens Lead the Way," Roper Reports Worldwide 4/26/99. **For statement by Nation 1,** see www.nation1.org. **On the AIDS scourge in Africa,** see "The Plague Years," *Newsweek* 1/17/00; and Kwame Anthony Appiah and Henry Louis Gates, Jr., "Africa Can Regain Its Glory," *WSJ* 1/28/00. **On Craig Kielburger,** see "A Crusade of Children," *NYT* 4/17/99.

CHAPTER FOURTEEN

THE CLOCK IS TICKIN'

Lindsay Dance, 17, at Langley High School, quoted in *The McLean Connection* 1/5/00. **Brent Bice,** 16, at McLean High School, in essay shared with authors. **For tabulations (by election year) of each historical generation's share of U.S. Congress and governorships,** see William Strauss and Neil Howe, *Generations* (1991), Appendix B. **For dates and duration of each generation's plurality on the Supreme Court,** see Strauss and Howe, *op. cit.,* fold-out chart.

CHAPTER FIFTEEN

HERO GENERATIONS IN HISTORY

William Manchester, "In America," *NYT* 3/11/96. **Gene Shuford,** quoted in Calvin B. T. Lee, *The Campus Scene: 1900–1970* (1970). **George Marshall,** quoted by Ronald Reagan, speech to Republican National Convention (Sept. 15, 1998). **Tom Brokaw,** *The Greatest Generation* (1998).

THE RISE OF THE G.I. GENERATION. **Leonard Cain,** "Age Status and Generational Phenomena," *Gerontologist* Sept. 6, 1987. **For tenfold increase in articles on "juvenile delinquency,"** see David Nasaw, *Schooled to Order* (1979), 90. **John Carter,** quoted in Malcolm Cowley and Robert Cowley (eds.), *Fitzgerald and the Jazz Age* (1966), 48–49. **Thomas Wolfe,** *You Can't Go Home Again* (1940). **Malcolm Cowley,** *Exile's Return* (1934), 18; and 1951 ed., 294. **Cornelia Comer,** "A Letter to the Rising Generation" and Randolph Bourne, "The Two Generations," *Atlantic* (July–Dec. 1932). **John Spargo,** *The Bitter Cry of the Children* (1904). **Pollyanna,** by Eleanor Porter, 1913. *Little Orphan Annie,* cartoon strip by Harold Gray, from 1924. *Literary Digest,* cited in Paula Fass, *The Damned and the Beautiful: American Youth in the 1920s* (1977), 37. **For description of the family of the 1920s and share of cohorts reaching age 15 without loss of parent or sibling,** see Fass, *op. cit.* **For "explicit insistence on conformity,"** see historian Daniel Rodgers, cited in Joseph Hawes and Ray Hiner, *Growing Up in America: Children in Historical Perspective* (1985). **For Little Mother's League,** see Joseph Hawes and Ray Hiner, *op. cit.* **On rage over child nutrition,** see Harvey Levenstein, *Revolution at the Table: The Transformation of the American Diet* (1988), chs. 8–10. **On rising adult stature by cohort,** see Robert W. Fogel, Stanley L. Engerman, and James Trussel, "Exploring the Uses of Data on Height," *Social Science History* Fall 1982. **On rising life expectancy,** see *HSt,* B-182 to B-189; and on rising life expectancy at age 65, see Social Security Administration, *Social*

Security Area Population Projections, 1989 (Actuarial Study No. 105, 1989), table 10. **On fall in child labor,** see Carl Degler, *At Odds, Women and the Family in America from the Revolution to the Present* (1980), 70; Leonard Cain, *op. cit.;* and *HSt,* series D-31, D-80. **On rise in schooling,** see Cain, *op. cit.,* 85; Fass, *op cit.,* 123–26; Christian Gauss, "Education" in Harold Stearns (ed.), *America Now* (1938); *HSt,* H-433, H-707, H-755; and John Folger and Charles Nam, *Education of the American Population* (Census Monograph, 1960). **On declining immigrant share,** see Data Sources, "Population by Generation"; and William Strauss and Neil Howe, *Generations* (1991), fold-out chart. **Paula Fass,** *op. cit.,* ch. 3. *New York Times* **and president of Williams College,** cited in Paula Fass, *op. cit.* **Joseph Wood Krutch,** quoted in Calvin B. T. Lee, *The Campus Scene: 1900–1970* (1970), 70. **Malcolm Cowley,** *Exile's Return* (1951 ed.), 294. **President Franklin Roosevelt,** radio message to the Young Democratic Clubs of America (1935), in E. Taylor Parks and Lois F. Parks (eds.), *Memorable Quotations of Franklin D. Roosevelt* (1965), 41. **Nashville middle schooler,** Catherine, 13, on www.fourthturning.com 10/4/97. **Shorty** (played by Brandon Hammond) in *Soul Food* (1997).

THE RISE OF THE PROGRESSIVE GENERATION. "The Murder of the Innocents," *Atlantic Monthly* (1859). **Joseph Kett,** *Rites of Passage: Adolescence in America, 1790 to the Present* (1977), 116; for a similar conclusion, see Mary P. Ryan, *Cradle of the Middle Class: The Family in Oneida, New York, 1790–1865* (1981), 145–85. **Horace Bushnell,** cited in Joseph Kett, *op. cit.,* 114. **French visitor,** Georges Fisch, cited in George Winston Smith and Charles Judah, *Life in the North During the Civil War* (1966), 309–11. **For "cradle to grave,"** see YMCA official cited in Joseph Kett, *op. cit.,* 119. **Joseph Kett,** *op. cit.* **Henry James,** in letter to Hugh Walpole (1913).

THE RISE OF THE REPUBLICAN GENERATION. For "more hateful than vipers," see Jonathan Edwards, *Conversions and Revival in New England* (1740). *An Evil and Adulterous Generation,* by Andrew Eliot, 1753. **Charles Royster,** *A Revolutionary People at War* (1979), 8. **Hugh Henry Brackenridge,** in Brackenridge and Philip Freneau, *The Rising Glory of America* (1771). **Daniel Blake Smith,** *Inside the Great House: Planter Life in Eighteenth-Century Chesapeake Society* (1980). **Saint-Jean de Crève-**

coeur, cited in James Axtell, *The School upon a Hill: Education and Society in Colonial New England* (1974). **On nutrition and rising adult stature by cohort,** see Robert W. Fogel, Stanley L. Engerman, and James Trussel, "Exploring the Uses of Data on Height"; and Kenneth L. Sokoloff and Georgia C. Villaflor, "The Early Achievement of Modern Stature in America," *Social Science History,* Fall 1982. **Jay Fliegelman,** *Prodigals and Pilgrims: The American Revolution Against Patriarchal Authority, 1750–1800* (1982), 22. ***Clarissa,*** by Samuel Richardson, originally published 1747–48. **Jean-Jacques Rousseau,** *Julie, ou la Nouvelle Héloïse* (originally published in 1761; popular in America by 1762). **John Page** of Virginia in 1756, cited in Daniel Blake Smith, *op. cit.* **On jump in ratio of tutors to children, in New York City and Philadelphia,** see Lawrence A. Cremin, *American Education: The Colonial Experience, 1607–1783* (1970), 539. **John F. Roche,** *The Colonial Colleges in the War for American Independence* (1986). **For "nursery of sedition,"** a Tory charge, see Lawrence A. Cremin, *op. cit.* **Andrew Elliot,** quoted in Lawrence A. Cremin, *op. cit.* **John Adams, John Dickinson, et al.,** cited in Edwin G. Burroughs and Michael Wallace, "The American Revolution: the Ideology and Psychology of National Liberation," *Perspectives in American History* (1972). **For "youth's so self-denying,"** from popular ballad in 1779, cited in Catherine Albanese, *Sons of the Fathers* (1976), 56. **Nathan Hale,** quoted in Charles Scribner's Sons, *Dictionary of American Biography* (1930). **For "the rising world shall sing of us,"** see song of the New York recruits, in Charles Royster, *A Revolutionary People at War* (1979), 8.

THE RISE OF THE GLORIOUS GENERATION. Oscar Handlin, "The Significance of the Seventeenth Century" in Paul Goodman (ed.), *Essays in American Colonial History* (1967). **For "the sad face of the rising generation,"** see Richard Mather, cited in Perry Miller, *The New England Mind: From Colony to Province* (1953), 28. **For a sampling of "the bitter charges of the aging first-generation settlers against their sons,"** see Emory Elliott, *Power and the Pulpit in Puritan New England* (1975). **For "wild beast multitude,"** see William Berkeley, as cited in Clifford Dowdey, *The Virginia Dynasties: The Emergence of "King" Carter and the Golden Age* (1969), ch. 2. **John Winthrop,** "A Model of Christian Charity" (1630), cited in Edmund Morgan, *Puritan Political Ideas* (1965), doc. 5. **Thomas**

Shepard, Jr., *Eye Salve* (1673). **Both the Massachusetts and Virginia statutes** are cited in Bernard Bailyn, *Education in the Forming of American Society* (1960), 26. **Urian Oakes,** *New England Pleaded With* (1673). **Eleazar Mather and Samuel Willard,** cited in Emory Elliott, *op. cit.,* 18 and elsewhere. **Urian Oakes,** *The Unconquerable . . . Soldier* (1674). **John Carter,** cited in Clifford Dowdey, *op. cit.,* 101. **Cotton Mather,** cited in Perry Miller, *op, cit.* (1953), 159. **T. H. Breen,** "War, Taxes, and Political Brokers" in Breen, *Puritans and Adventurers* (1980). **Benjamin Colman,** cited in Perry Miller, *op. cit.* (1953), 414. **On casualties in King Philip's War,** see Richard Slotkin and James K. Folsom, *So Dreadful a Judgment* (1978); and Douglas Leach, *Flintlock and Tomahawk: New England in King Philip's War* (1958). **Tracy Flick** (played by Reese Witherspoon), in *Election* (1999). **David Humphreys,** *The Glory of America* (1783). **Flick,** *op. cit.*

CHAPTER SIXTEEN

A CAPACITY FOR GREATNESS

Herbert Stein, "What Makes a Generation Great," *WSJ* 4/29/99. **Janet Chang,** 17, and **Tim Jones,** 17, at Langley High School, VA, in essays shared with authors.

THE GENERATIONAL LINEUP OF MAXIMUM POWER. For support for Desert Storm by age, see "Opponents to U.S. Move Have Poverty in Common," *NYT* 9/8/90; and "An About Face?" *LAT* 2/21/91. **For support for risking loss of U.S. lives in Kosovo by age,** see 1999 surveys available at "Poll Vault," www.washingtonpost.com. **For Toynbee's "Cycle of Generations,"** see Arnold Toynbee, *A Study of History,* vol. IX (1954), 220–347.

RENDEZVOUS WITH DESTINY. President Franklin Roosevelt, speech accepting renomination (June 27, 1936). **Arthur Schlesinger, Jr.,** *The Cycles of American History* (1986), ch. 2. **Walter Dean Burnham,** "Party Systems and the Political Process," in Burnham and William Nisbet Chambers (eds.), *The American Party Systems: Stages of Political Development* (1967); Burnham, *Critical Elections and the Mainsprings of American Politics* (1970); and Burnham, "Revitalization and Decay: Looking Toward the Third Century of American Electoral Politics," *Journal of Politics,* Aug. 1976; Burnham, "The Fourth American Republic," *WSJ* 10/16/95. **Samuel P. Huntington,** *American Politics: The Promise of Disharmony* (1981). **Frank L. Klingberg,** *Cyclical Trends in American Foreign Policy Moods* (1983). **George Modelski,** *Long Cycles in World Politics* (1987). **Robert Wurthnow,** "World Order and Religious Movements," in Albert Bergesen (ed.), *Studies of the Modern World-System* (1980). **William McLaughlin,** *Revivals, Awakenings, and Reform* (1978). **David Musto,** "Drug Use? America Can't Seem to Remember When," *WP* 8/27/90; and "The Futile Crackdown," *Forbes,* 10/18/99. **On legacy of Nikolai Kontratieff,** see Brian Joe Lobley Berry, *Long-Wave Rhythms in Economic Development and Political Behavior* (1991). **Harry S. Dent, Jr.,** *The Great Boom Ahead* (1994).

ALTERNATIVE FUTURES. Josh Braxon, on www.fourthturning.com 2/12/99. **Eric Weisbard,** "Generation Ex," *The Village Voice,* 7/13/99.

MILLENNIALS AS A HERO GENERATION. Leopold von Ranke, *Über die Epochen der neueren Geschichte* (1910), 529–31. **Laura Bennett** (born 1982), quoted in "Love Those Millennials" newsletter, June 1998.

CHAPTER SEVENTEEN

MILLENNIALS RISING

Kylie, 9, of CA, on greatkids.com 6/14/99. **President Franklin Roosevelt,** speech at the University of Pennsylvania in Philadelphia, PA (Sept. 20, 1940). **Henry Malcolm,** *Generation of Narcissus* (1971), 43. **John Stuart Mill,** *A System of Logic* (1843). **Four girls in the stands,** at the 1999 Women's World Cup, in Foxboro, MA (July 4, 1999). **Sarah Fulton,** 17, at Langley High School, in essay shared with authors.

Data Sources

ABORTIONS. The CDC and AGI are the only sources of national figures on abortions. The numbers cited here follow the method of the *StatAbs* in using AGI national totals, which are considered more accurate, and then using annual CDC data to interpolate in years for which AGI did not compute national totals. The **abortion rate** is usually defined as total abortions per 1,000 women aged 15 to 44.

AGE OF MOTHERS. Though no agency tabulates it, the average age of mothers at birth can be derived by taking the NCHS annual birth data and calculating an average age of mothers weighted by the share of mothers in each age bracket. This is what we did at decade intervals from 1900 to 1970, and then yearly from 1970 to 1997.

CRIME. Two major statistical programs measure the nature, level, and rate of U.S. criminal activity. The Uniform Crime Reports (UCR), directed by the Federal Bureau of Investigation, tracks crimes reported to local police and federal authorities. The National Crime Victimization Survey (NCVS), directed by the Bureau of Justice Statistics, uses Census personnel to ask households whether and how they have been victimized by any crime, reported or not. To find out about police activity (such as arrests) or crimes with no surviving witnesses (property crimes and many homicides), the UCR must be used. Otherwise, the NCVS is widely regarded as a superior measure of the societywide impact of most violent crimes. See the Bureau of Justice Statistics, at www.ojp.usdoj.gov/bjs; and the Office of Juvenile Justice and Delinquency Prevention, at ojjdp.ncjrs.org.

EDUCATIONAL ACHIEVEMENT. For overall trends and summary, see *Trends* and *CondEd*. For results and publications on the TIMSS (Third International Mathematics and Science Study), see timss.bc.edu/. For results and publication on the NAEP (National Assessment of Educational Progress), see nces.ed.gov/nationsreportcard/site/home.asp.

EDUCATIONAL ATTAINMENT. For educational attainment by age or birth year (highest grade completed or college degree received), see "Educational Attainment in the United States," *CPR*, P20, various dates.

EMPLOYMENT. Data on employment (by sex, age, race, region, marital status, presence of children, etc.) are collected by the Census Current Population Survey and tabulated by the BLS. For **mothers and fathers with children,** see "Employment Characteristics of Families," annual news release, BLS (available at stats.bls.gov/news. release/famee.toc. htm). The **employment rate** refers to the population share of persons who work at all for pay (even just one hour) during the current week; the **labor-force participation rate** refers to those who either are working or are actively seeking a job. **Full-time** means at least 35 hours per week. The conventional BLS measure of **teen employment** is poor (a single year-round yes-or-no age bracket from age 16 to 19). But for this book we were able to access unpublished BLS tabulations for each race and age (15, 16, and 17) that distinguish between school and summer months. For the purpose of historical comparison, the BLS has aggregated these figures into three time periods (1977–79, 1987–89, and 1996–98), which were all at or near the full-employment peak of the business cycle.

FAMILY STRUCTURE. Census tabulates and annually publishes descriptive figures on family structure in "Marital Status and Living Arrangements" and "Household and Family Characteristics," *CPR,* P20, various dates. Living conditions (including **presence and status of mother, father, siblings, and other relatives**) are tabulated by family and by child. See also the Census historical tables available at www.census.gov/population/www/socdemo/hh-fam.html. Parents include both **natural and stepparents;** reliable cross-sectional data on natural versus stepparents are unavailable—though see efforts in *StatAbs* (1993), table 77; and *AmChild,* 65.

FERTILITY. A **fertility rate** usually refers to the birth rate of a single age bracket of women. The **total fertility rate** equals the number of children that a woman would bear if, over her lifetime, she bore them at every age at the same fertility rate as all women currently do at every age. Demographers often prefer it to the crude birth rate because it reflects only behavioral choice and cannot be pushed up or down by the age distribution of women. In time, absent immigration, a total fertility rate of less than 2.1 (slightly more than two births per woman) must result in population decline. For the United States, the total fertility rate is computed annually by the NCHS in its *NVSR* (see "Vital Statistics"). For every nation worldwide, it is computed and tabulated by the United Nations (Department of Economic and Social Affairs, Population Division) as five-year averages. See *World Population Prospects: The 1998 Revision* (United Nations, 1998), which includes historical fertility for every country since 1950 and projections well into the next century.

IMMIGRATION. The principal source for annual immigration data is the *Statistical Yearbook of the Immigration and Naturalization Service*, U.S. Immigration and Naturalization Service (annual). Another source, which does a better job picking up undocumented immigrants, is "the Foreign-Born Population in the United States," *CPR*, P23, various dates.

INCOME AND POVERTY. All figures on **income** and **poverty** (family, household, or personal) are taken from the Census "Historical Income and Poverty Tables," available through the current year at www.census. gov/hhes/income/histinc/index.html. See also Census, *CPR*, P70. Unless otherwise noted, income refers to **real income** (in 1998 dollars deflated with the CPI-U). The **official "poverty"** designation is applied by the U.S. government to households, and all adults and children living in such households, whose total annual cash income does not meet a fixed dollar standard (that was somewhat arbitrarily chosen in 1963 and is adjusted yearly for inflation). In recent years, the Census has developed and now publishes an alternative **experimental poverty** measure which takes taxes and in-kind benefits into account.

POPULATION BY GENERATION. The population of a generation is the sum of two parts: native births between the birth-year boundaries and total immigrants who belong to the same cohort group. Calculating total native births is easy. To calculate total immigrants, we created a model that used a fixed distribution of immigrants by age to allocate each year's total immigration into birth years. Future native births, future immigration totals, and the fixed distribution of immigrants by age are all taken from the "middle" Census projection (see "Population Projections of the United States by Age, Sex, Race, and Hispanic Origin: 1995 to 2050," *CPR*, P25-1130, Feb 1996).

The following table shows the population totals. All the native birth figures are final except for the last few years for the Millennials. The immigration count, on the other hand, includes millions of immigrants yet to arrive—and for the Millennials, this count is largely speculative since most of it has yet to happen. The Census projection simply assumes a continuation of current immigration levels.

Generation	Birthyears	Total Ever Lived (in millions)	Native Births (in millions)	Immigrants Ever Lived (in millions)	Immigrants (% of Total)	Total Alive as of 1999 (in millions)	Immigrants (% in 1999)
Lost	1883-1900	48.5	39.7	8.8	18.1%	0.1	18.1%
G.I.	1901-1924	74.4	66.3	8.1	10.9%	16.3	8.8%
Silent	1925-1942	54.9	46.4	5.5	10.6%	36.0	10.2%
Boom	1943-1960	78.7	68.2	10.5	13.4%	68.8	11.5%
Gen-X	1961-1981	93.0	75.1	17.9	19.3%	81.8	12.3%
Millennial	1982-2002	100.2	82.0	18.2	18.2%	70.2	3.4%

Generational totals make comparisons difficult since they don't account for the different birth-year lengths of different generations. The following table recomputes the numbers on a per-birth-year basis.

Generation	Birthyears	Total Ever Lived per birthyear (in thousands)	Native Births Only per birthyear (in thousands)	Total Alive as of 1999 per birthyear (in thousands)
Lost	1883-1900	2,694	2,206	5
G.I.	1901-1924	3,100	2,763	679
Silent	1925-1942	2,884	2,580	2,000
Boom	1943-1960	4,374	3,790	3,821
Gen-X	1961-1981	4,429	3,576	3,893
Millennial	1982-2002	4,773	3,900	3,994

SEXUAL ACTIVITY. Three ongoing federally funded research projects are widely cited to describe the trend, level, and type of youth sex and contraception: First, the Youth Risk Behavior Survey, prepared by the CDC, with results for 1991 to 1997; see www.cdc.gov. Second, the National Survey of Adolescent Males, funded by HHS, which focuses on the sex activity of male youths in 1988 and 1995; see www.urban.org/family/teenmale.htm. And third, the 1995 National Survey of Family Growth, prepared by NCHS, which focuses on reproductive activity for women aged 15 to 44; see www.cdc.gov.

SIBLINGS. The average or median number of siblings related to each child can be derived from Census data on families by number of children (see "Household and Family Characteristics," *CPR*, P20, various dates). See also *StatAbs,* and earlier years in earlier editions; *We the American Children,* Census (1993), 6; and *AmChild.*

SUBSTANCE ABUSE. Two major national survey sources are used to track trends and levels in youth substance abuse. The first is *MTF,* whose annual questions to students in grade 12 (since the class of 1975) and in grades 10 and 8 (since the class of 1991) focus heavily on drug use and attitudes toward drug use; see www.health.org/mtf. The second is the *National Household Survey on Drug Abuse,* prepared by SAMHSA, whose populationwide rates of substance use date back to 1979 (annually since 1991); see www.samhsa.gov/gov/oas/nhsda.

VITAL STATISTICS. The NCHS compiles national data on vital events from state and local sources and publishes them in a series of reports (in hard copy as the *NVSR* and on the web at www.cdc.gov/nchs/nvss.htm). The series covers **births** (most recently, "Births: Final Data for 1997," *NVSR,* vol. 47, no. 18), including births by age bracket of parent, by race and ethnicity, by birthweight, by region, and by total fertility rates. It covers **teenage births** (most recently, "Declines in Teenage Birth Rates, 1991–98, Update of National and State Trends, *NVSR,* vol. 47, no. 26), with greater detail on age of mother, marital status, and pregnancy rates. It covers **deaths** (most recently, "Deaths: Final Data for 1997," *NVSR,* vol. 47, no. 19), including **mortality rates** (per 100,000 people) by cause of death and by age bracket and race of the deceased; the NCHS web site includes detailed cross-tabulations by all three variables since 1979. It covers **infant deaths** (defined as death before age 1), including neonatal deaths (defined as death within thirty days of birth) and **infant death rates** (per 1,000 live births). It covers marriages and divorces, including **average age of first marriage** for males and females, **marriage rates** (per 1,000 people age 15 and older) and **divorce rates** (normally, per 1,000 married women age 15 and older).